T0320313

FOUNDATIONS of
MACROECONOMICS

FOUNDATIONS of MACROECONOMICS

Its Theory and Policy

Frederick S. Brooman

Henry D. Jacoby

Routledge
Taylor & Francis Group

LONDON AND NEW YORK

First published 1970 by Transaction Publishers

Published 2017 by Routledge
2 Park Square, Milton Park, Abingdon, Oxon OX14 4RN
711 Third Avenue, New York, NY 10017, USA

Routledge is an imprint of the Taylor & Francis Group, an informa business

Library of Congress Catalog Number: 2008027336

Library of Congress Cataloging-in-Publication Data
Brooman, Frederick Spencer.
    [Macroeconomics]
    Foundations of macroeconomics : its theory and policy / Frederick S.
    Brooman and Henry D. Jacoby.
        p. cm.
    Originially published: Macroeconomics. Chicago, Aldine Pub. Co., [1970]
    Includes bibliographical references and index.
    ISBN 978-0-202-36290-8 (alk. paper)
        1. Macroeconomics. I. Jacoby, Henry D. II. Title.

HB171.5.B6965 2008
339--dc22

                                                        2008027336

ISBN 13: 978-0-202-36290-8 (pbk)

PREFACE

This book is intended primarily for students who have already received a general introduction to economics and who are ready for a more detailed treatment of the theory of income and employment. We have aimed at a verbal rather than a mathematical exposition of the subject; even though a good many equations and symbols appear in the following pages, they are merely a space-saving shorthand that can easily be translated into ordinary speech. None but the simplest algebra is used, so that readers with only an elementary knowledge of mathematics will, we hope, find no difficulty in following the argument.

While the book is an American text in its own right, it is based on an earlier one written by Brooman and published in England in 1962. Since then it has gone into three further British editions as well as being translated into a number of foreign languages. In the present American version, a number of chapters have been added, bringing in a new discussion of prices, wages, and the aggregate supply of goods and services, and expanding the earlier treatment of the monetary sector and the theory of inflation. The principal responsibility for preparing these new chapters has been carried by Brooman. In addition, all the chapters have been revised, some rather extensively, to cast the discussion in the context of American public and private institutions, to adjust to the United States' system of national accounts, and to incorporate the results of recent empirical studies of the American economy. In the process, much of the mathematical and graphical presentation has been revised as well. Primary responsibility for this latter set of changes has been assumed by Jacoby.

We must acknowledge the debt owed to our colleagues on both sides of the Atlantic for their invaluable suggestions and criticism at various stages of the preparation of the text. Special thanks are due to Professors Miles Fleming of the University of Bristol, Roberto Zaneletti of the University of Genoa, and Marc Roberts of Harvard University. We should also like to express our gratitude to Nancy Reynolds for her able supervision of the preparation of the manuscript. Their generous advice and assistance contributed numerous improvements and allowed us to avoid many errors. They are not, of course, responsible for any that remain.

F.S.B.
H.D.J.

CONTENTS

CHAPTER 1

The Economics
of Aggregates

One of the chief objectives of economic theory is to explain the working of the economy as a whole, by identifying and if possible measuring the forces that cause the nation's total output and level of employment to be what they are. The analysis of an entire economy is an extremely complex matter: total output includes a vast number of different goods and services, about whose production and utilization millions of individual decisions are made every day; if it were necessary to examine each one before attempting conclusions about the whole, the economic analyst would be faced with an impossible task. To reduce the problem to manageable proportions, it is necessary to simplify it by aggregation — that is, by arranging the myriad products and decision makers into a reasonably small number of categories or "aggregates." Individual differences between one consumer and another, or between one business firm and another, are ignored; it is assumed that if the categories are well chosen, their members will behave in a sufficiently uniform way to make generalization legitimate.

The kind of analysis that proceeds in this way is called *macroeconomics,* "macro" being the Greek for "large." Though the word itself is a relatively recent coinage,[1] the method of approach is by no means new — the eighteenth-century Physiocrats, for example, adopted it when they divided society into three "classes" to show the "circulation of wealth." Nevertheless, the most important developments in macroeconomic analysis have occurred only within the past few decades, the point of departure being the appearance of Keynes' *General Theory of Employment, Interest and Money* in 1936.[2] The influence of the *General Theory* has been such that the modern theory of output and employment still bears the label of "Keynesian economics." From the title of the book, the term "Employment Theory" has also been adopted as an alternative name for this branch of economics. But macroeconomic analysis seeks to explain a good deal more than the level of employment, important though that is as an indicator of the state of the economy; also, the "Keynesian" label is becoming less appropriate in the light of developments since Keynes' death in 1946.

The obverse of macroeconomics is *microeconomics,* which is the analysis of the economy's constituent elements — "micro," of course, being the

---

[1] It was originated by Ragnar Frisch in 1933.

[2] J. M. Keynes, *The General Theory of Employment, Interest and Money* (New York: Harcourt, Brace & World, 1936).

Greek for "small." As the name suggests, it is not aggregative but selective: it seeks to explain the working of markets for individual commodities and the behavior of the individual buyer and seller. Where macroeconomics is concerned with the level of output as a whole, and for most purposes ignores the numbers of kitchen tables, pairs of shoes, and barrels of beer that go into that output, the objective of microeconomics is to discover why precisely x million tables and y million shoes are produced, why the price of one is greater than the other, why shoemakers' wages differ from tablemakers', and to answer a host of other questions relating to the composition, rather than the magnitude, of the economy's output. In "microanalysis" it is reasonable to take for granted the level of total output when examining the conditions in which the price of a particular commodity is determined, or when studying the behavior of the individual business firm. Where macroanalysis simplifies by aggregation, microanalysis does so by assuming "other things equal."

Though the aims of macroanalysis and microanalysis are different, both make use of the concepts of supply and demand and the equilibrium that may be established between them. In microanalysis the typical market is that for a single commodity: buyers demand a certain quantity at each possible price; sellers decide, in view of the price obtaining, how much to offer. When the amounts demanded and offered are the same, so that no one has any incentive to upset the position, equilibrium can be said to exist. If the price paid by buyers for a certain quantity of the good is so high that even those suppliers whose production costs are highest can still make abnormally high profits, competition will attract new firms to the market, and the amount offered will increase. To tempt buyers to purchase the increased supply, the price of the commodity has to be reduced; by changes in price and in the quantities demanded and offered, a balance of forces is eventually attained.

In the same way, macroanalysis conceives of equilibrium between demand and supply in the economy as a whole: supply consists of all goods and services available in the country, and demand is the aggregate of demands for all commodities. In this case it becomes impossible to work in terms of physical quantities, since there is no way in which numbers of, say, eggs, hats, and piston rings can be added together. So demand and supply have to be expressed in money terms, by saying that buyers wish to spend such-and-such a number of dollars, while sellers are prepared, in the circumstances, to offer so many dollars' worth of goods and services. If the amount of money that buyers wish to spend is not the same as the value of the commodities that sellers are offering, there is no equilibrium; the lack of it will bring about changes in production and prices and perhaps in the level of employment as well, since less labor may be required if, for example, a lower level of production is brought about. What is not so clear, however, is whether these changes will necessarily lead the economy toward a balance of aggregate supply and demand; in this respect, the analogy between the single-commodity market and the economy as a whole tends to break down.

The discrepancy occurs because there are underlying relationships between demand and supply that can be neglected in microanalysis but are very important in the working of the economy as a whole. In any single market, it is reasonable to suppose that buyers and sellers are for the most part different people; for example, few of the housewives who buy breakfast cereals are likely to be engaged in producing and selling them in any capacity. So buyers and sellers can be imagined to act independently of one another, and the two sides of the market influence each other's decisions only through the market itself. If the firms producing some commodity take on more workers, the fact that they are now paying out more wages means that the recipients will be in a position to spend more than before; but the consequential effect on the firms' sales will hardly be noticeable unless the industry employs most of the community's workers, and unless those workers spend most of their income on the commodity concerned. Since this situation is very unlikely, microanalysis can legitimately ignore this kind of behind-the-scenes "feedback" of purchasing power from the supply side to the demand side. When, however, supply and demand are aggregated for the economy as a whole, the feedback can no longer be ignored. Buyers and sellers are seen to be generally the same people. The money received in exchange for goods and services on the supply side of the economy passes into the hands of spenders who appear on the demand side. The spenders may be individuals or business firms or the government of the country; but for the most part they get the wherewithal to spend by selling something to someone else — the major exception, of course, being the government, though even it can be thought of as selling its services in return for the payment of taxes.

Aggregate supply and demand are thus linked through the intermediary of *income*. If buyers should decide to spend more money than before, and if the effect is to increase the value of goods and services supplied, then the suppliers will receive higher incomes out of which they can spend yet more on the demand side. If, in another case, demand should fall, the effect will be to reduce the value of commodities supplied, cut the incomes of those engaged in producing and selling, and so cause a further fall in spending. Whereas the market for a single commodity may be thought to work in terms of the confrontation of the two forces of demand and supply, the operation of the entire economy is to be viewed in terms of a triangular relationship — the three corners of the triangle being aggregate supply, aggregate income, and ' aggregate demand. Consequently, the nature of equilibrium is different in each case. For the individual market, the price of the product is the crucial magnitude. For the economy as a whole, the general price level has nothing like the same significance: an increase in prices will not necessarily choke off demand, since by enhancing the value of supplies it increases the money incomes of those concerned in production; with higher incomes, buyers can afford to go on taking up exactly the same quantities of goods and services as before, in spite of the general price increase. Here the vital consideration is whether or not they will go on buying the same quantities; only if they do *not* do so will the balance of aggregate supply and demand be changed. The question that needs to be asked, then, is not how the economy reacts to a change in the level of prices, but how it reacts to a change in the level of aggregate income. In place of the demand schedule, which in the market for a single commodity shows what quantities buyers will wish to have at each possible *price*, macroanalysis requires a schedule showing the level of aggregate demand at each possible level of *income*.

But aggregate *demand* is made up of many widely differing elements — it must include, for example, the demand of individual consumers for meat, automobiles, and bedroom furniture; that of business firms for machine tools and factory buildings; and that of city governments for the services of firemen. There is no obvious reason to think that all buyers will behave in the same way when their incomes change; some may respond to a fall in income by reducing their expenditures considerably, while others may not reduce them at all. It is necessary to split buyers into groups within which a reasonable similarity of behavior can be supposed to exist; if the number of groups is not unmanageably large, a fairly, clear pattern of response to income changes can be obtained. The usual classification (which will have to be justified later on) divides buyers into four such groups: consumers, business firms, government bodies, and overseas customers who buy the country's exports. There may be times when it is desirable to have different or more detailed groupings; for example, it might be convenient to subdivide consumers into rich and poor, or into wage earners and others, if there are marked differences in the behavior of these subgroups in the face of a change in their incomes. Whatever the nature of the classification, however, it must be such as to elucidate the connection between income and aggregate demand.

On the side of aggregate *supply*, the relationship with income normally requires only one important distinction to be made: that between those goods and services produced within the country and those imported from overseas. The money paid in exchange for domestically produced supplies provides the incomes of the country's inhabitants; payments for imports, however, accrue to the foreigners who supplied them. It is true that payment for imports puts foreigners in a position to contribute to aggregate demand by buying the country's exports, but the connection is more tenuous than that among production, income, and demand at home, since import payments may provide only a small part of foreigners' incomes, and those who buy exported commodities may in fact be a different set of buyers from those who supply imports. While a rise in the value of domestic production will certainly increase the incomes of residents of the country and thus increase their demand, a rise in the value of a country's imports, though it will increase foreigners' incomes, will not necessarily cause any change at all in their demand for the country's exports. Another consideration is that the level of *employment* within the country depends not on the total volume of aggregate supply but only on that part of it produced within the country; so when the purpose of analysis is to explain the existence of a particular level of employment, it again becomes important to distinguish between domestically produced and imported supplies.

When aggregate demand and supply are split up into the component parts described above, the conditions of equilibrium for the economy can be restated accordingly. The money that consumers, business firms, government bodies, and export customers together wish to spend at any time must be equal to the value of the country's output plus its imports of goods and services. The purchase of domestic output provides those who produce it with incomes, from which the spending of consumers, firms, and the government is done. So in addition to the balance of demand and supply, there must also be a balance between incomes and demand such that spenders are satisfied that their outlays are neither too high nor too low in relation to their incomes. On the supply side, income must be distributed in such a way that producers are willing to provide precisely the amount of output needed to satisfy aggregate demand; the part going to profits must be enough to induce business firms to undertake that level of production, while the part going to wages must be such as to induce workers to provide the necessary labor. Similarly, the part of output that is sent abroad as exports must be enough, given the prevailing terms of exchange, to induce other countries to supply whatever imports are demanded at the current level of income.

When all these conditions are satisfied, the flow of goods and services will be exactly sufficient, in total, to meet the current demand for them. But — as was pointed out earlier — the output of the whole economy includes a vast range of different commodities that can be aggregated only in terms of their money values; and those values arise from the fact that, instead of being bartered directly, goods and services are exchanged indirectly through the "circulating medium" of money. In any economy but the most primitive, the multitude of products is so great that direct barter would create intolerable inconvenience. To avoid it, sellers offer their wares for money in the first instance, and with the proceeds they make purchases of their own. The use of money as an intermediary makes it customary to express the exchange values of commodities in terms of dollars and cents. Given the prices at which things are bought and sold, a certain amount of money will be needed to finance the turnover of goods and services in the economy at a given time, as well as to provide for other activities — for example, borrowing and lending — that involve the exchange of money without a corresponding exchange of commodities. If the economy is to be in full equilibrium, the supply of money must be sufficient to meet all these demands for its services. If the existing stock of money is either inadequate or excessive, the imbalance may lead to changes in the aggregate demand and supply of goods and services and in the general price level. The conditions for a complete equilibrium are therefore somewhat complex: not only must the demand and supply of commodities be balanced against one another, but also the demand and supply of money.

Even when equilibrium is attained, however, it is unlikely to be of long duration. One of the elements of aggregate demand is the expenditure of business firms on new plant and machinery; some of this merely replaces worn-out equipment, but the remainder represents a net addition to their productive capacity. With a given number of workers, firms become capable of higher output when the additional equipment is installed; alternatively, they are able to produce the same output as before, but with less labor. Either the level of aggregate output must rise, or the level of employment must fall, or some mixture of both effects must occur; whatever the outcome, the original equilibrium situation will have passed away. No doubt a new balance of aggregate demand and supply will be possible in the changed circumstances, but it will be different from the original one; and it, too, will pass away as yet more additions are made to productive capacity. The greater the lapse of time, the greater the possible increase in the amount of capital equipment; the greater, also, the possible changes in other factors, such as the size of the population and the state of technology, which are important in determining the levels of output and employment in the long run.

This suggests two lines of approach in studying the working of the economy. The first is to examine its state at a given moment, assessing the balance of forces as they stand at that point in time. This is the method of *static* analysis; it is like the scrutiny of a still photograph in which all motion is arrested; its object is to discover whether equilibrium exists or not. A somewhat less strict procedure is to consider a short period rather than a single moment; during the period, certain movements are possible — in the quantity of the output and aggregate demand, for example — but more slowly changing magnitudes, such as the stock of capital, can still be assumed frozen into immobility. The immediate consequences of a disequilibrium of demand and supply can then be examined without the complications arising from longer-run changes. To deal with the latter, the method of *comparative·statics* may be used: the state of the economy at one moment is compared with its state at another, to show the effects of some change (*e.g.*, in the technique of production) that has occurred between the two moments.

The second approach is that of *dynamic* analysis, which investigates the process by which the economy moves from one state to another over time; its aim is to show how the situation at one moment influences the situation at another. For example, if firms adjust output to changes in demand only after a four-week time lag, this month's production depends on the state of the market last month; if consumers decide their expenditures in the light of last week's income, this week's income determines next week's consumption. A knowledge of all the relationships of this sort (including, of course, the length of the time lags involved) would make it possible to predict the levels of output and employment in the future — provided the relationships and their lags do not themselves change, and no "outside" forces act to disturb the sequence. It should be noted that the words *static* and *dynamic* refer to the method of analysis, not to the economy itself: the latter may be "stationary" in the sense that output and employment are the same at all times, or it may be "progressive" in that output and employment are rising, but the two methods of analysis may be applied to both conditions.[3]

Whether static or dynamic, macroanalysis necessarily runs in terms of the "aggregates" mentioned at the beginning of the chapter. Each of its quantities is made up of many smaller ones; consumers' expenditure, for example, is the sum of millions of individual acts of spending; and it has already been seen that the output of the whole economy cannot be stated in simple physical measures, but must be added up in terms of money values. Before proceeding further, it is necessary to define the various aggregates, and this is the subject of the following chapter.

---

[3] See W. J. Baumol, *Economic Dynamics*, 2d. ed. (New York: Macmillan, 1959), Chap. 1.

CHAPTER 2

National Product, Income, and Expenditure

1. Introduction

To compile the aggregates for macroanalysis, it is necessary to have some way to classify and organize both the many producers and spenders who take part in economic activity and the great variety of transactions that take place among them. Masses of data must be reduced to a form in which they can be used in testing hypotheses about how the economy works; within the limits of existing knowledge of these matters, this information must be presented so as to be a useful guide to personal, business, and government policy decisions in the economic sphere. National economic accounts are designed to serve these needs; among other things, they attempt to measure the overall level and character of economic activity.

The flows of production and spending described in the previous chapter are represented in diagrammatic form in Figure 2.1. The economic system is shown divided into two sectors, "individuals" and "producing units." Individuals possess not only their own labor power and management skills, but also all other factors of production such as capital, land, and other natural resources. They make these factor services available to producing units in return for the payment of wages, profits, interest, and rent. As shown in the upper half of Figure 2.1, they receive a flow of in-

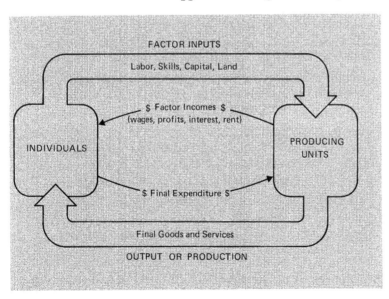

FACTOR INPUTS

Labor, Skills, Capital, Land

$ Factor Incomes $
(wages, profits, interest, rent)

INDIVIDUALS

PRODUCING UNITS

$ Final Expenditure $

Final Goods and Services

OUTPUT OR PRODUCTION

Fig. 2.1

Transactions in a Simplified Economy

comes in payment for a flow of inputs to production. Individuals, in turn, use their incomes to purchase the goods and services made available by the producing units in the economy; they give up a flow of money in exchange for a flow of physical goods and services: for food, clothing, shelter, and whatever other commodities they desire and can afford. Or, to begin with the producing units, they initiate a flow of money to individuals in payment for needed factors of production, and then convert these inputs into output goods that may be traded for a flow of sales revenue.

For simplicity's sake, this example omits the influence of government, foreign trade, and even the demand by producing units for new investment or changes in inventories. It also ignores the fact that some productive activity may be considered to take place within the individuals' households. But, following the approach adopted in Chapter 1, even this diagram of a simplified economy shows the three flows that must be measured numerically. First, an account can be designed to measure *production, i.e.,* the net output and sale of final goods and services by the different producing units. A second account can focus on *expenditure, i.e.,* the money flow initiated by individuals as they buy the output of the producing units. Since, by definition, everything purchased must be produced and sold by someone, the sum of all expenditures on final goods and services is identical to the value of all production, although each of these aggregates has distinct internal subdivisions.

Finally, accounting efforts are directed to the measurement of *income*: the distribution of returns from the sale of final goods and services back to the owners of the factors used in the productive process. Since in this simplified economy individuals can spend only the amount they earn from the sale of factors of production, total expenditure over any period will be identical to total income. Thus the three aggregates – production, income, and expenditure – are just different approaches to quantifying the same phenomenon, *i.e.,* the overall level of activity in the economy. Of course, the full set of accounts for a modern economy is more complicated than this simple example indicates, but the concepts are the same.

In the United States, the basic source of information about the performance of the economy as a whole is the National Income and Product Accounts prepared by the Office of Business Economics of the U.S. Department of Commerce,[1] and this discussion follows the U.S. statis-

---

[1] Current national economic statistics are published by the Office of Business Economics in its monthly *Survey of Current Business*. The conceptual framework of these

tical procedure. In place of the "producing units" and "individuals" in the simplified economy introduced above, the Department of Commerce defines four sectors: business, households (the personal sector), government, and the rest-of-the-world (foreign sector). Estimates of the economic activity occurring in each of these sectors are combined or "aggregated" to produce the income and product accounts for the economy as a whole.

In the pages to follow, the concept of production and the different methods for measuring aggregate output are taken up first. Next, the estimation of expenditure is considered. As noted below, the term "aggregate expenditure" is not used in the U.S. national account summaries, but the concept is central to macroeconomics and thus is emphasized below. Finally, the estimation of national income is discussed along with other income concepts that are important in macroeconomic analysis.

2. What Is "Production"?

The first concept to be defined is that of *aggregate output*. Up to this point, this has been taken to be the whole mass of commodities produced in the economy over a given period of time, added together in terms of their money values. But what exactly *are* "commodities," and what is production? This seems a trivial question as long as one thinks only in terms of steel plates, loaves of bread, and other tangible objects that can be easily recognized and counted. But there are many parts of the economy whose activity is not so easy to classify. For example, can banks really be said to "produce"? If so, what are they producing? What about railroad systems, hospitals, colleges, TV stations, and barbershops? These are cases where it is obviously difficult to identify and measure the amount of "production," yet where useful though intangible services are being rendered; that they are useful is indicated by the fact that someone is willing to pay for them to be carried on. Such payment would not be made if the various services were not wanted; accordingly, it seems rea-

national economic indicators and details of the estimation procedures followed by the Department of Commerce are given in two supplements to *Survey of Current Business: National Income* (1954) and *U.S. Income and Output* (1958). Recent changes in definitions are discussed in *Survey of Current Business* (August, 1965).

sonable to regard as "productive" any activity that in some way satisfies the individual or collective *wants* of the community. The quantity of "production" ought (in principle, anyway) to be measured in terms of the degree of satisfaction provided, rather than in tons or bushels or other physical units. In this sense, production is not an engineering term but a purely economic concept.

However, it is not possible to measure the satisfaction of wants directly. Instead, the prices that buyers are willing to pay and the quantities of commodities they buy at these prices have to be taken as indicating how much satisfaction they expect to obtain. There are objections to this; for example, it may be argued that a dollar spent by a wealthy man will not represent the same expected satisfaction as a dollar spent by a poor man — if, indeed, it is possible even to compare the satisfactions enjoyed by two different persons. But for practical purposes of statistical measurement, prices must be used for lack of a better indicator. Accordingly, the "production" of a given commodity over any particular period of time is defined as the physical quantity of its output multiplied by its price per unit; and in cases where physical units of output are hard to identify (as with the various services mentioned above) the total payment made by the buyers is taken as the value of production.

This procedure assumes the existence of markets in which buyers are free to buy as much or as little as they wish, and in which the price is both a condition of supply and a reflection of the intensity of the buyers' desire for the commodity. But there are some goods and services that are not bought and sold in markets, even though they clearly satisfy wants and therefore ought to be counted as part of the nation's output. The obvious example is public services such as defense, education, the administration of justice, and the maintenance of law and order. Here the normal practice is to provide the service without collecting a direct charge from the recipients and to meet the cost from taxes, payment of which is compulsory, but whose amount in the case of each citizen is not necessarily equal to the value of the services rendered to him. Because public services have no market prices, it is not possible to value them on the lines described in the previous paragraph; instead, government "production" is measured in terms of the costs incurred in providing these services. Thus, if local governments spend $1,600 million a year on fire protection, it is assumed that this sum represents the extent to which the desire for that particular "commodity" is satisfied.

Another case is that of owner-occupied houses, which provide their owners with services for which, had they been tenants of houses owned by other people, they would have had to pay rent. Although no money is in fact paid (it would be merely a transfer from one pocket to another for the homeowner), the value of the service can be assessed in money terms by assuming it equal to the rent paid by tenants who occupy houses of similar size and amenities. Here the existence of a market for such services allows their value to be "imputed" in cases where the market is bypassed.[2] Logically, no doubt, the same procedure should be adopted with all other kinds of "consumers' durables" used by their owners — automobiles, furniture, perhaps even clothing and footwear; but in these cases rental markets are too small, relative to the total stock of durables, for their prices (*e.g.*, the cost of rent-a-car service) to be used safely to impute values.

The services rendered by housewives to their families present a similar problem. By raising children, cooking, and cleaning, housewives are obviously rendering valuable services, which should logically be treated as production and included in aggregate output.[3] But it seems impossible to set a satisfactory money value on them, since the labor of housewives is not sold for wages in a free market. So for lack of information, this important form of "production" is omitted altogether in practical calculations of the nation's output.

3. Which Products Should Be Included?

So far, it seems that to compute aggregate output it is necessary to multiply by their prices the quantities of goods and services that are

---

[2] The amount of "imputed" rent on owner-occupied nonfarm dwellings was $40.9 billion in 1967 (*Survey of Current Business*, July, 1968, Table 7.3). Other "imputed" items include food and fuel that farmers withhold from the market for their own consumption and food and clothing furnished directly by employers to their employees; but none of the other items is very large in itself, and all of them together were less than $15 billion in 1967.

[3] There are probably no fewer than 35 million full-time housewives in the United States, if widows and divorcées looking after young families are included. If their services are valued at $4,000 a year each (and less than $80 a week is surely a conservative estimate in view of the hours worked), the total value of housewives' "output" works out at $140 billion; if this were added to Gross National Product, it would increase it by nearly one-fifth.

being sold through markets; to include government services at cost; to include the services of owner-occupied houses at their imputed rents; and to neglect cases in which no satisfactory valuation of production can be made. But now another difficulty arises. If the full value of *all* goods and services is aggregated, the total will overstate the nation's output because some commodities are used in the making of others. The price of a loaf of bread, for example, must include the value of the flour from which it was made; the price of the flour must include the value of the wheat that was milled to make it. To add together the value of the wheat grown, flour milled, and bread baked would be to count the value of the flour twice and that of the wheat three times, unless some of the flour or wheat happened to be left unused instead of being absorbed in the next stage of production. The output of textile fabric would be counted twice if it were included along with the value of the garments made from it; to aggregate the production of automobiles with the steel used to make them would have a similar effect. Another anomaly would arise in the case of goods manufactured from imported materials; the price of the finished commodity obviously would include an amount representing its "import content," yet this amount would not be part of the nation's production at all. Unless this kind of "double counting" is somehow eliminated, the total value of national output will obviously be greatly exaggerated.

Two methods suggest themselves for dealing with the problem. The first is to count only products that are not used for making others in the course of the year [4] — *i.e.*, to exclude all those that are "intermediate" in the production process (like the flour, the steel, and the textile fabric just mentioned) and to include only "final" products. Of course, the category of final products will include some services as well as material output; although most services count as "intermediate" (the services of a textile firm's legal counsel, for example, are "absorbed" into the output of cloth), those rendered directly to consumers, such as domestic service, count as "final" and are therefore included in the aggregate output. Government services are all counted as "final products," even though some of them, like the protection of property by the police and the enforcement of contracts by courts of law, might well be regarded as "intermediate" since they are prerequisites for the undertaking of production rather than ends in themselves. But it is impossible to make a satisfactory separation between

---

[4] Or any other time period; however, "year" is a less cumbersome term than "the accounting period," and it will be convenient to use it from now on.

public services that satisfy wants directly and those that merely assist other kinds of production, and so the entire value of such services is included in aggregate output.

"Final" products need not be commodities in a form suitable for consumption. Certainly, all consumers' goods and services are to be counted as "final," but so also are any "producers' goods" that have not been used up during the year. If, say, 5% of steel production is stockpiled instead of being used to make other commodities, it must be included in "final" output. Similarly, all machinery, buildings, and other durable means of production newly constructed during the year must be regarded as "final" products; so, too, must work-in-process that is still in the pipeline at the year's end — the materials that, like the pig during its journey through the sausage machine, have ceased to be "input" but have not yet become "output." On the other hand, since only production attributable to the current year is to be counted, the amount of work-in-process at the beginning will have to be deducted, as will the value of whatever inventories existed at the start of the year and have been used up in the course of it. These materials have already figured as part of the "final output" of the previous year, so that to include their value in that of the "final" goods that now embody them would be to overstate the current year's production. Finally, the value of imported goods and services must be deducted, since these are part of other countries' aggregate output.

The second way of dealing with the problem of double counting is the "value added" method; that is, to estimate the increase in value that each sector of the economy imparts during production to the inputs it receives from other producing sectors, and then to add up the value increases over all sectors. The economy is likened here to an enormous assembly line. At its starting point, domestic agriculture and mining (along with imports from abroad) provide primary materials; as these move down the line, they pass from one industry to another, undergoing successive processes until they emerge at the end in the shape of clothing, bicycles, loaves of bread, and so on — and in the shape, too, of machine tools, blast furnaces, and other durable instruments of production. At each stage, the materials increase in value as they are brought nearer to some ultimately usable shape.

To find the value added by each process to the commodities passing through it during a given period, it is necessary to take the value of all the products leaving the process and then deduct the value of those intermediate products and business services entering it. The net difference indicates what portion of the product is attributable to the process at hand as distinguished from what can be attributed to earlier processes through which it has already passed.[5] Thus, if the steel industry produces output worth $20 billion in any year, using pig iron, coal, manganese, and other inputs worth $10 billion all together, its *net* contribution to aggregate output — its "value added" — is $10 billion.

The process need not change the form of the commodities: transport, for example, by carrying them from less to more convenient places, increases their value just as surely as the hewing and hammering at other points on the assembly line. The delivery by railroad of a consignment of steel to an automobile plant means that the automobile industry is receiving an input of "transportation services" from the railroad industry as well as an input of steel from the steel industry. So, also, the operations of wholesale and retail distribution contribute to value added by breaking bulk and holding the inventories from which consumers can choose. When some branch of retail trade sells for $15 billion commodities that cost $10 billion wholesale, its "value added" is $5 billion; this is the value of the services rendered by store proprietors and sales clerks to their customers. Outputs, too, may consist wholly of services, as in the case of banking and other financial institutions, which, though not handling physical commodities, provide subsidiary services to ease the passing of commodities down the line.

Government services are not sold in markets, but since, by convention, government output is valued at input cost, value added would include total government expenditure less the cost of intermediate goods — or, what is the same thing, value added by government may be measured by its expenditure on "factors of production." Value added in households, primarily by domestic servants, is handled in the same manner. Provided that no industry or activity is left out of account and that no overlapping of industries causes some firms to be counted more than once, the addition of value added (*i.e.*, gross output minus intermediate inputs) over all sectors ought to give a correct estimate of aggregate output.

---

[5] At each stage of production, the difference between the value of gross sales and the cost of intermediate products and business services represents payments to the "factors of production" (*e.g.*, wages and salaries paid to workers, interest on capital, rent paid to the landlord, and profits accruing to the owner of the business) plus indirect business taxes paid to the government, an allowance for depreciation of capital equipment, and several additional minor charges to be introduced below.

It is not necessary to deduct the value of imported goods and services; since these are intermediate inputs, they have already been offset against the output of the industries using them. By the same token, all goods slated for export have been included in the gross sales at each stage of production, up to the point where they leave the country. The accumulation and subsequent use of inventories have also been allowed for; inventory accumulated during the year is part of current output, while any inputs from inventories held at the beginning of the year are considered as intermediate products and have been automatically deducted from the outputs of the sectors in which they were used.

Logically, it makes no difference whether the "final products" method or the "value added" method is used to eliminate double counting. This may be shown by a simple example. Suppose a 39-cent loaf of bread was made with flour costing 25 cents, which in turn was milled from wheat costing 10 cents; the wheat was grown from seed costing one cent, using imported fertilizer also costing one cent. The "final products" approach would take the value of the end product (the loaf of bread) and deduct the cost of the seed (since this came from inventory carried over from the previous year) and the fertilizer (because it was imported), so that "final output" would be valued at 37 cents. The "value added" method, deducting input from output at each stage, would give the wheat farmer's contribution to the loaf of bread as 8 cents, the miller's as 15 cents, and the baker's as 14 cents; when these values are totaled, the result is exactly the same as that found by the "final products" method.

4. National Product and Expenditure

The national accounts of most countries rest on the same conceptual basis, but the techniques of measurement and the exact way in which the various accounts are compiled differ from country to country depending on the nature of political and economic institutions, the data available, and the history of the individual nation's accounting bureau. In some countries, separate summary accounts are made up for production and expenditure. In the United States, however, estimates are made of the product originating in each of four sectors of the economy — business, government, households, and the rest of the world — but the final National Product totals are classified by the type of purchaser, *i.e.*, by *expenditure* categories.

Recall that National Product is the flow of goods and services produced by the economy; and, by definition, it must be equal to the flow of spending that comes forth to buy it. But though the totals are necessarily equal in money value, production and expenditure are different economic activities, coming together from different sides of the market. Their subdivisions may not correspond at all — for example, the output of consum-

Table 2.1

U.S. Gross National Product by Sector and by Industry, 1967

		Billions of Dollars
Business		681.5
Agriculture, forestry, and fisheries	26.2	
Mining	14.3	
Contract construction	36.2	
Manufacturing	224.6	
Transportation	33.1	
Communication	17.6	
Electric, gas, and sanitary services	18.9	
Wholesale and retail trade	129.5	
Finance, insurance, and real estate	106.9	
Services	63.5	
Government enterprises	10.7	
General government		84.8
Households and institutions		22.3
Rest of the world		4.6
Statistical discrepancy		−3.5
Gross National Product		789.7

ers' goods will be much larger in value than the amount of consumers expenditure in a country that exports a large part of its production of this group of commodities and imports none. As a matter of practical measurement, however, it is possible to compile the estimate of National Product by totaling the various expenditure flows that buy it, and this is in fact done by the Department of Commerce when it presents estimates of National Product allocated according to purchasers.[6] The official tabulation is liable to give the impression that National Product *is* the total of consumption, government outlays, and other forms of expenditure; but logically it is necessary to keep production and expenditure distinct for the purposes of economic analysis. Accordingly, the term "National Expendi-

---

[6] As in *Survey of Current Business*, Table 1.1; also see Table 2.2 on p. 24 below.

ture" will be used to refer to the flow of spending, and "National Product" to refer to the flow of output of goods and services, though the reader must be warned that the term "National Expenditure" is not used at all in the official accounts.

Table 2.1 shows the relative contributions of the different sectors to U.S. National Product in 1967.[7] Approximately 86% of National Product originates in the "business" sector of the economy. In addition to the transactions normally associated with private business, certain other businesslike activities are included within this sector. Homeowners are considered to be in the "business" of providing themselves with shelter, and so the imputed rental on owner-occupied housing is introduced here. Other nonmarket transactions are included as well; for example, the imputed value of food and fuel consumed on farms is introduced, as are certain nonmonetary product flows occurring in financial businesses. Also, in the construction of the accounts a distinction is made between the general activities of government, which are financed by tax revenues and borrowing, and "government enterprises" whose operating costs are, to a substantial degree, financed by the sale of goods and services. Public power utilities and the Post Office are examples of this type of government business; for purposes of estimating gross product by sector of origin, these activities are considered to take place within the business sector.

Since the services of federal, state, and local governments are valued at cost, the contribution of this sector to gross product is total government expenditure excluding all purchases of intermediate products; *i.e.*, the value added by government is the total payment to labor, its primary input factor.[8] For example, when a local government supplies the services of a police force, the total *expenditure* on this service includes the officers' salaries and payments for uniforms, cars, radios, and the like. But the uni-

---

[7] The figures in Table 2.1 are adapted from Table 1.22 of *Survey of Current Business* (July, 1968). The figures are given for illustrative purposes only, and it should be noted that these estimates are, in fact, derived indirectly from data concerning incomes rather than by the direct "value added" or "final products" methods described in the text. The "statistical discrepancy" is the difference between this estimate of gross product originating by industries and the estimate of Gross National Product measured as the sum of expenditures on final products.

[8] Interest payments on the public debt are not counted as remuneration for factor inputs; the bulk of this debt was incurred in financing past wars, and the magnitude and fluctuations of these payments bear slight relation to the current value of production. No attempt is made to impute the rental value of government property as is done for owner-occupied housing.

forms, cars, and radios were produced by business firms; the contribution of the local government to the *production* of this service is the payment made to the policeman himself. Approximately 10% of Gross National Product is attributable to "general government" operations (see Table 2.1). The personal sector, on the other hand, includes households and other nonbusiness institutions such as foundations and churches; and their output is also estimated in terms of the total payment of wages and salaries.[9] The personal sector as such accounts for less than 3% of the national total.

The word "national," too, requires a few words of explanation. If the nation were defined in a purely geographical sense, National Product would be the output produced within the physical boundaries of the United States.[10] By the official definition, however, the nation is the collection of people who live here,[11] and National Product is the output arising from the use of the labor and property that they own. But some of this property is located in other countries — for example, the overseas installations of the U.S. oil corporations — and, on the other hand, some of the means of production located on American soil belong to foreigners. Accordingly, National Product must include the output of American-owned property overseas and exclude that of foreign-owned property in the United States. In 1967, the former exceeded the latter by $4.6 billion. In the official terminology, this was the output of the "rest-of-the-world" sector of the United States economy, and, as can be seen in Table 2.1, it contributes less than 1% of the National Product total.

Finally, the term *Gross* National Product means that no allowance has been made for "capital consumption," *i.e.*, depreciation and accidental damage to fixed capital. But some portion of gross output must be applied to making up for the wear and tear and obsolescence that the econ-

---

[9] Interest payments by the personal sector — referred to as "interest paid by consumers" in the accounts — are not regarded as reflecting output. Since most of the debt of the personal sector was incurred to finance consumer purchases, the interest payments are not considered to reflect the contribution of capital assets to production in the sense that wages and salaries reflect the contribution of labor. For a more complete discussion of the handling of government and consumers' interest in the accounts, see *Survey of Current Business* (August, 1965).

[10] In some countries, aggregate output within the national territory is designated by a special term: in Britain and Canada, for example, it is called "Domestic Product," while in France and Italy it is "Internal Product."

[11] Governmental bodies and various corporate institutions, as well as individuals, count as "U.S. residents" for the purposes of this definition. Note, too, that U.S. residents are not necessarily U.S. citizens, while some citizens may not be U.S. residents.

omy's capital stock has sustained in the course of a year's activity; in 1967, this was estimated at $69.2 billion. When this amount is taken away from Gross National Product, the remaining $720.5 billion is a measure of *Net* National Product.

In principle, Net National Product is a better measure of aggregate output than Gross National Product, because until capital consumption has been deducted it cannot be said that double counting has been completely eliminated. To the extent that durable capital equipment is partly worn out in the process of production, it is just as much an "input" as the nondurable materials that are wholly used up, and its value ought therefore to be deducted from the value of the output it helps to produce. In practice, however, it is difficult to estimate the amount of capital consumption. The simplest method is to divide the original cost of each piece of equipment by the number of years of its expected life: if a $10,000 machine takes ten years to wear out, it is being "consumed" (or "depreciated") at the rate of $1,000 per year. But how can its life be known in advance? It may turn out that the machine continues to be capable of producing for fifteen years, in which case the allowance of $1,000 a year is an overestimate. On the other hand, the machine may become technically obsolete and have to be scrapped after only five years, and the allowance is then inadequate. Even if the machine *does* last for precisely ten years, the allowance is incorrect if the cost of replacement (*i.e.*, the price of a new machine) has changed during that time; for example, if it has risen to $20,000 by the tenth year, it will appear that the allowance ought to have been $2,000 a year instead of the original $1,000. For all these reasons, the calculation of capital consumption is subject to an appreciable margin of error, and estimates of Net National Product must consequently be regarded as less reliable than those of Gross National Product.[12]

5. Expenditure on National Product

After aggregation, the sum of the gross outputs produced by each of the four sectors of origin is termed Gross National *Product* (see Table 2.1). As noted earlier, however, in preparing the final summary account

---

[12] From this point onward, the more general term "National Product" will be used when the distinction between Gross and Net National Product is not of importance.

for national output, the data are presented not by sector of origin but by category of expenditure: personal consumption, private expenditures on capital goods and addition to inventory, exports minus imports, and government purchases of goods and services. Total output, broken down in this fashion, is more conveniently referred to as "Expenditure on Gross National Product" or "Gross National Expenditure"; although it should be pointed out once again that this latter term is a departure from official Department of Commerce terminology.

Table 2.2

Expenditure on U.S. Gross National Product, 1967

			Billions of Dollars
Personal consumption expenditures			492.2
Gross private domestic investment			114.3
Fixed investment		108.2	
Producers' durable equipment	55.7		
Nonresidential structures	27.9		
Residential structures	24.6		
Change in business inventories		6.1	
Net exports of goods and services			4.8
Exports		45.8	
Less: Imports		−41.0	
Government purchases of goods and services			178.4
Gross National Expenditure			789.7

Details of actual expenditure on United States Gross National Product in 1967 are given in Table 2.2.[13] It is important to note that all of these are categories of "final" expenditure. Because of the way the underlying sector accounts are set up, they exclude any purchases that are "intermediate" in the sense of being offset within the same accounting period by the resale of the commodities bought, either in the same form or after processing into other products. That is, consumers' expenditure on shoes is "final," whereas that of the shoe manufacturers on leather, glue, and so on is "intermediate" unless some of these materials are added to inventory instead of being made into shoes.

----

[13] The figures are taken from Table 1.1 of the National Income Issue of *Survey of Current Business* (July, 1968). This publication gives detailed statistics of U.S. National Income and Product for 1964–67. Figures for earlier years are to be found in *The National Income and Product Accounts of the United States, 1929–65*, a supplement to the *Survey of Current Business* published in 1966.

Of the total consumers' spending shown at the head of Table 2.2, about 45% was on nondurable goods such as food and clothing, 40% was on services of various kinds, and 15% was on durables such as kitchen appliances and automobiles. Expenditure on new housing is not included, since this is treated as "investment" and appears lower in the table under "residential structures." Goods bought on installment credit are included at their full value, even though consumers appear to be spending only the amount of the down payment at the time of purchase. In some cases where consumers provide *themselves* with goods and services, such as accommodation in owner-occupied homes, the value is reckoned as part of their expenditure, even though no money payments are involved.

"Gross private domestic investment" includes all purchases of newly produced capital equipment and structures, and all additions to inventories, made by business firms and individuals for use within the United States. The word "investment" can easily be misunderstood, since it is often used in a loose everyday sense to mean the purchase of stocks and bonds and other assets of a purely financial nature, as well as the acquisition of "real" (*i.e.*, physical) assets such as machinery and buildings. For the nation as a whole, however, the exchange of financial assets among its members can of itself add nothing to total wealth; neither can dealings in real assets that were constructed in the past and do not form part of current output, nor dealings in land, which never had to be produced at all. Transactions of that sort only redistribute ownership of the nation's wealth; to increase it, the quantity of real assets must be increased by producing additional capital goods and adding to inventories, and by acquiring financial claims on other countries. In the present context, "investment" (or "capital formation" as it is also termed) is defined as expenditure undertaken for any of these last three purposes. "Domestic" investment is expenditure on new capital goods and additions to inventory located within the United States; [14] "gross" means that it includes purchases of equipment and structures to replace those worn out during the year

---

[14] It must be emphasized that "domestic investment" does *not* mean only expenditure on domestically produced capital goods. In 1967, the United States imported machinery worth $3 billion, the purchase of which is included in the item "producers' durable equipment" shown in Table 2.2. The word "domestic" does not refer to the *origin* of the goods bought, but to their *location* once they have been acquired and installed; the essential distinction is between the purchase of currently produced real assets within the United States ("domestic investment") and the acquisition by U.S. residents of assets located elsewhere in the world ("foreign investment").

(*i.e.*, to provide for capital consumption). If replacement expenditures were deducted from the total, the remainder would be "*net* domestic investment"; but because of the difficulty of making reliable estimates of capital consumption, investment is customarily left "gross" in the official statistics.

The gross private domestic investment shown in Table 2.2 is divided into "fixed" (*i.e.*, durable) investment and additions to inventories. "Producers' durable equipment" includes mainly expenditure on machinery and transportation equipment; the term "nonresidential structures" refers to industrial and commercial building and public utility installations; while "residential structures" is expenditure on the construction of new houses and apartments, whether for rent or for sale to owner-occupiers. Between them, the three categories of fixed investment account for nearly nine-tenths of all gross private domestic investment.

The $6.1 billion spent on "increase in business inventories" is the value of the change in the volume [15] of inventories that occurred during 1967. These include not only "input materials" that firms had bought but not used during the year, but also any outputs that had not yet been sold and therefore were still in the hands of the firms that produced them. It may seem paradoxical to count the value of unsold products as part of investment *expenditure*; but it is so counted, under a convention by which the producers are regarded as having "bought" the goods themselves. Artificial though this may appear, it is not unreasonable in the case of firms that have *planned* to increase their holdings of their own products; had they not wished to do so, presumably they could have sold this part of their output and used the proceeds for other purposes. When a firm keeps part of its current output back from the market, it is, in effect, employing the money it would have earned in order to improve its capacity to meet sudden and unexpected demands for its products; its action is

---

[15] Note that it is the "value of the change in volume," not the "change in value," that is being counted here. If prices had risen, say, 10% during 1967, the value of inventories at current prices would have increased by that much even if their volume had been unchanged. But in that case, the increase in value would not represent any physical output, and if it were counted, it would cause Gross National Product to be overestimated. To avoid this, an "inventory valuation adjustment" is applied, which has the effect of eliminating the part of the change in value due solely to price movements during the year. A similar adjustment would be necessary if the general price level fell during the year — though it would, of course, cut in the opposite direction to an adjustment offsetting price *increases*.

tantamount to an expenditure. This approach is much less convincing when firms are "buying" their own output solely because they have been unable to induce anyone else to do so; but it is very difficult to make a practical distinction between planned and unplanned increases in inventory. The simplest procedure, therefore, is to regard *all* such increases as part of business investment expenditure.

Federal, state, and local governments contribute approximately 23% of total expenditure on Gross National Product (Table 2.2). Government spending includes purchases from domestic business and from abroad, along with the compensation of employees. In addition, when national output is aggregated according to expenditure categories, all expenditure by government enterprises on "final product" is included under government purchases of goods and services. Thus all "public" (as opposed to "private") fixed investment and inventory changes are contained in this general category.[16]

The Table 2.2 items examined so far — consumers' spending, fixed investment and the increase in business inventories, and government purchases — are the expenditures of individuals, enterprises, and institutions located within the United States. Since the purpose of the account is to tabulate *all* the categories of expenditure that together purchase the National Product, it is necessary also to include the spending done by foreigners on United States output — the value of *exports* — and to deduct that portion of the expenditure of the various domestic sectors that goes for the output of other countries — *imports*. It should be noted that imports and exports include not only trade in merchandise but also payments for services — the so-called "invisible" exports and imports. For example, when a United States shipping firm conveys cargoes for foreign merchants, or when a New York bank performs financial services for foreigners, this results in the earning of foreign currency. And when French hotels supply meals and accommodation to American tourists, a service has been sold to (*i.e.*, imported by) U.S. residents involving the payment of dollars to France.

---

[16] Some countries do, in fact, keep a separate account of government investment, and in limiting the normal definition of investment to include only "Gross *Private* Domestic Investment," a substantial portion of United States domestic capital formation is omitted. In 1967, for example, federal, state, and local expenditure on "structures" totaled $25 billion — an amount roughly one-fifth the size of total private domestic investment.

6. The Relationship Between Product and Income

The third important magnitude referred to in Chapter 1, which is now to be more rigorously defined, is that of "aggregate income." In the economy as a whole, it will be remembered, incomes provide a link between aggregate supply and demand; the production and sale of goods and services puts money in the hands of those concerned with production, so that they, in turn, can appear as spenders on the demand side of the market. The next step, therefore, must be to elucidate the concept of income and its relationship with production.

For an individual, income can be defined as whatever receipts he can spend or give away over a specified period of time without becoming poorer than he was to start with. The receipts may be in money or in kind, as in the case of a worker given a free lunch at the company cafeteria in addition to his wage. The income need not be received from others; it includes, for example, the imputed rent of a house occupied by its owner. "Without becoming poorer" means that the individual's holding of money, goods, and other assets, less his debts, must have a value at the end of the period at least equal to its value at the beginning. He may, of course, change the *form* of his holdings — for example, he may sell his house and buy stock with the proceeds, or he may buy a car on credit and thus acquire both an asset and a liability at the same time. But whatever changes he makes, he must not finish up with a smaller value of *net* assets than that with which he began.[17] He must keep his capital intact or, if he is on balance a debtor, his net debt must not increase. His income, therefore, must come from sources other than loans and the running-down of assets; it must come from his labor, or from the use of his property, or from "transfers" (*i.e.*, current receipts other than those from goods or services rendered or money lent). Income from his labor may

---

[17] This raises the question of how the assets and liabilities ought to be valued: should a house be regarded as being worth whatever the owner paid for it (less depreciation if he has had it for long) or as being worth whatever price it would bring if sold now? If house prices are rising, and the owner finds he could sell at the end of the year for 10% more than he would have got at the beginning, should he regard the 10% as part of his income? Would the answer be "yes" if only house prices are rising, but "no" if *all* prices are rising? See J. R. Hicks, *Value and Capital*, 2d ed. (London: Oxford University Press, 1946), Chap. XIV, for a discussion of the difficulties of defining income.

take the form of wages or fees. If his property is in securities, such as government bonds or corporate stock, the income will be as interest or dividends, while if his property is in physical form (for example, an apartment house or an ice cream truck) income will accrue as rent or profit. Transfers may include unemployment compensation, other social security benefits, or private gifts.

The National Income can be regarded in almost exactly the same way, since the nation is being treated for this purpose as a single entity, albeit a very complex one. The nation's income, therefore, must be the yield of the factors of production that its members own, plus any transfers received from other nations. In practical calculations the transfer element is excluded from the income estimate (in any case, it is very small), so that National Income is the sum of the yields of the nation's factors of production — that is to say, the National Product. This can be illustrated in another way. The National Product is the sum of the "values added" over a given period by the various branches of economic activity, and the "value added" is the difference between the total value of the output of each branch and the value of its inputs from other branches. For an individual firm, it appears as revenue from sales minus expenditure on materials and "outside" services (*e.g.*, transportation), plus the value of any increase (or minus any decrease) in inventories that occurs during the period. Out of the sum remaining, the firm must pay wages and salaries, rent for land and buildings, interest on borrowed money, and remuneration (such as fees to surveyors) for any other services it receives. What remains after these payments have been made is profit. So the whole of the "value added" by the firm becomes income of one kind or another. The same principle must apply to all economic entities, whether firms, households, or the government; and therefore the total of "values added" in the whole economy — the National Product — must be equal to the total of incomes paid in return for the services of labor and property — the National Income.

Because of some of the special activities of business and government, the fundamental identity of Income and Product is slightly more complex than the description in the previous paragraph might indicate. According to the official Department of Commerce definition, National Income is the aggregate earnings of labor and property from current production of goods and services; *i.e.*, it is the total *factor cost* of the commodities produced by the economy. But because of the necessity of covering certain "nonfactor charges" associated with productive activity, not all of *Gross*

National Product is available to be paid to the owners of factors of production. The first of these charges is the "capital consumption allowance" or depreciation; this portion of the returns from production is devoted to the maintenance of the economy's stock of capital and thus is not paid out as factor incomes. When this item has been deducted, the remainder represents the net receipts from productive activity, or *Net* National Product, as shown in Table 2.3.[18]

Table 2.3
Relation of U.S. Gross National Product
and National Income, 1967

		Billions of Dollars
Gross National Product		789.7
Less:	Capital consumption allowances	−69.2
Equals:	Net National Product	720.5
Less:	Indirect business tax	−69.6
Less:	Business transfer payments	− 3.2
Plus:	Subsidies less current surplus of government enterprises	1.6
Less:	Statistical discrepancy	− 3.5
Equals:	National Income	652.9

Besides allowances for capital consumption, there are three additional items that are considered as charges against National Product but do not constitute the income of factors of production as defined in the U.S. accounts. It should be noted that National Product is valued "at market prices" — *i.e.*, in terms of the prices actually paid by the buyers of the various goods and services that make up aggregate output. But some of these prices include indirect business taxes such as sales taxes, property taxes, and the like. For example, out of the average dollar spent by consumers on cigarettes and other tobacco products in 1967, more than forty cents went to federal and state taxes, leaving less than sixty cents to pay for the services of the workers and enterprises engaged in producing the commodities. In other cases, market prices are actually *less* than the cost of production because of the payment of government subsidies (which are, in effect, negative indirect taxes). If all indirect taxes were deducted from market prices (and subsidies added back into them), the effect would be to value goods and services at factor cost, *i.e.*, the cost of

---

[18] Table 2.3 is adapted from Table 1.9 of *Survey of Current Business* (July, 1968).

remunerating the labor and capital (the factors of production) that produce them. In 1967, indirect taxes (net of subsidies) totaled $69.6 billion, as Table 2.3 shows.

The last two minor items also are corrections from market prices to factor cost. An adjustment is made to National Product at market prices to account for "business transfer payments," *i.e.*, payments from business to persons or institutions for which no factor service is received in return. Consumer bad debts are one example of such a payment to individuals; gifts to nonprofit foundations are another. Finally, a correction is made to account for the activities of government enterprises. Recall that, for purposes of calculating Gross National Product by sector of origin, government enterprises are included in the business sector. An evaluation of the outputs of these activities at market prices will include the influence of any profits (or losses) they might have made, and logically this profit would be considered to accrue as income to the owner of the business. But in this case the government is the owner; and rather than treat the government as a "supplier" of the factor of entrepreneurship, the net surplus or loss of government enterprises is treated as a nonfactor charge against National Product.

If a government enterprise runs a surplus, the prices of its products reflect the influence of this "profit": prices are higher than they would have been had the enterprise just broken even, and the surplus must be *deducted* from National Product to obtain the value of output "at factor cost." If, on the other hand, the enterprise is subsidized, output prices do not reflect the full cost of input factors, and the amount of the subsidy must be *added* to National Product at market prices in order to convert the estimate to factor cost. In 1967, state and local government enterprises ran a current surplus of $3.2 billion, but this was outweighed by the net subsidy of $4.8 billion paid to federal enterprises; the net result was the $1.6 billion item for "subsidies less current surplus of government enterprises" shown in Table 2.3.

With the deduction of indirect business taxes and business transfer payments, and with the addition of the net subsidy to government enterprises, the conversion to National Product at factor cost is complete. For some purposes it is more appropriate to value output at factor cost than at market prices; for example, if indirect taxation on a particular commodity is increased between one year and the next, market price valuation will make it appear that the output of the commodity has risen even though it is unchanged in physical terms. In this case, factor cost valuation would be more reliable. Normally, however, market price measures of output are used in calculating national output, and when figures of Gross National Product and Net National Product are quoted, they are always understood to be "at market prices" unless otherwise specified.

According to the argument presented earlier, Net National Product at factor cost should equal National Income; and Table 2.3 indicates that they are very nearly equal, except that Net National Product at factor cost is derived from data on output and expenditure, while the figure for National Income is the result of a separate estimate using different data sources. The difference between the two estimates is the "statistical discrepancy" shown in Table 2.3.

7. National Income

The independent estimate of incomes paid to owners of the factors of production, although based on different sources of information, is compiled according to the same sectors of origin used in preparing the National Product figures. Aggregation of the incomes originating in each of the sectors yields the total *National* Income. As in the product estimates, the business sector is the largest contributor; in the United States over four-fifths of National Income originates in business. These incomes accrue in the form of the compensation of employees, proprietors' incomes, rental income, corporate profits, and interest. A wide variety of sources is used in preparing these estimates, with extensive use being made of the records of the Internal Revenue Service.

Furthermore, it may have been noted that all the nonfactor charges against national output really relate to the activity of the business sector; they are allowances for indirect *business* taxes, *business* transfer payments, and the *business*like activities of government. In addition, capital consumption allowances are made for the productive assets of the business sector only.[19] If these nonfactor charges are added to the factor cost

---

[19] Recall that only *private* investment is segregated in the accounts; all government purchases are classified as current expenses, and therefore no depreciation is charged against production either in general government activities or in government enterprises. Since homeowners in their capacity as landlords to their own families are counted within the business sector, the depreciation on owner-occupied housing does appear in this sector.

incurred in business activity (*i.e.*, to the portion of National Income originating in the business sector), the total exhausts that part of Gross National *Product* originating in this sector. On the other hand, each of the other three sectors of origin makes an identical contribution to National Income and to Gross National Product. Because the gross output originating in the government and household sectors is evaluated in terms of the compensation of employees, these payments are precisely the contribution of government and households to National Income. Finally, the contribution of the rest-of-the-world sector to national output is estimated, as noted earlier, in terms of a net international flow of factor incomes.

Table 2.4

U.S. National Income, 1967

			Billions of Dollars
Compensation of employees			468.2
Wages and salaries		423.4	
Employer contributions for social insurance		21.5	
Other labor income		23.3	
Proprietors' income			60.7
Rental income of persons			20.3
Corporate profits and inventory valuation adjustment			80.4
Profits before tax		81.6	
Profits taxes	33.5		
Dividends	22.9		
Undistributed profits	25.2		
Inventory valuation adjustment		−1.2	
Net interest			23.3
National Income			652.9

Aggregation of these four sectors for the United States in 1967 yields the figures shown in Table 2.4.[20] Slightly over 70% of the National Income accrues to labor as a factor of production, as summarized in the total "compensation of employees." "Wages and salaries" include payments in kind — for example, food and housing provided by the employer — as well as monetary remuneration. Also included under factor income to labor (or factor cost to the producer) are "employer contributions for social insurance" and "other labor income," such as employers' contributions to private pension funds, insurance plans, and other fringe benefits.

---

[20] The figures in Table 2.4 were taken from Table 1.10 of *Survey of Current Business* (July, 1968).

The next three items — "proprietors' income," "rental income of persons," and "corporate profits and inventory valuation adjustment" — all refer to incomes that accrue within the private enterprises making up the business sector of the economy. Some portions of these income flows accrue directly to persons or are paid out to persons by the businesses they own, and some portions are retained within the enterprises themselves. "Proprietors' income" refers to the activity of unincorporated businesses, individual ownerships, partnerships, farmers, and certain professions; their incomes often are called "mixed incomes" because it is usually impossible to say to what extent they are the equivalent of wages for work done rather than profit from the ownership of the enterprises. "Rental income of persons" is distinguished from proprietors' income and consists of the rents paid to landlords who are not primarily engaged in the real estate business; this category also includes the imputed rent of owner-occupied houses as well as royalties from natural resources, copyrights, patents, and the like.

The income accruing to the owners of corporations is divided into "dividends," "undistributed profits," and federal, state, and local corporation "profits taxes." It will be noted that in these accounts a distinction is made between indirect and direct business taxes. Indirect business taxes are introduced as a nonfactor charge against national production, while corporation profits taxes are treated as a factor cost. With indirect taxes, firms are deemed to act as "agents" for the government in collecting the tax revenue, so that what they collect is not part of their own business receipts. With direct taxes, they are paying the tax due out of their own profits, which would (by assumption) be the same even if there were no direct taxes.

The definition of the incomes of proprietors and corporations does not take capital gains and losses into consideration. What is desired is a measure of the payments to the factors of production; and a capital gain, if not carefully omitted, would show as an income payment for which no factor service had been provided. One item of the nature of a capital gain or loss does show up in figures for business profit, however; it is the profit or loss on inventory, *i.e.*, the change in income that is attributable to variation in the prices of goods held in inventory rather than to increased or reduced quantities of factor inputs. A correction must be made, and the "inventory valuation adjustment" shown in Table 2.4 is negative, indicating that prices were rising during 1967; business profits would be overstated without this correction.

Finally, "net interest" is the excess of interest payments by the business system over the interest received, and thus it is the net factor payment to property owners for interest-earning capital assets they have contributed to the productive process.

Since, in United States accounting practice, the term "National Income" is limited to payments to the factors of production,[21] it is useful to introduce the term "Gross National Income" as a companion concept to Gross National Product and Gross National Expenditure. *All* of the nonfactor "charges against National Product" constitute incomes in the larger sense of a distribution of the returns from production among the various sectors of the economy. Business transfer payments contribute to the incomes of individuals and nonprofit foundations, and thereby contribute to the spending capacity of the personal sector. Indirect taxes and the surplus of (or subsidy to) government enterprises become a part of the current revenue or "income" of government, and thus add to potential expenditure in the public sector. Even allowances for depreciation can be considered as part of the returns from production; it is just that this portion of gross income is automatically committed to be spent on the maintenance of the existing capital stock, and thus is never paid out. Quite often, therefore, the total of all these charges is referred to as Gross National Income; by the nature of the definition over any accounting period it is identical to Gross National Production and Expenditure.

8. Other Income Concepts

In addition to the concepts of National Income and Gross National Income, it is useful to give names to certain other income aggregates that are required for particular purposes. In order to help clarify the definitions, Table 2.5 presents, in a revised format, the income data introduced earlier.[22] In the first column, National Income is broken down according to the initial income recipient. Factor incomes to persons (as in

---

[21] Since this aggregate does not include depreciation, it might more conveniently be termed *Net* National Income. This, however, would be a departure from the official U.S. national income accounting terminology.

[22] Table 2.5 is adapted from Tables 1.9, 1.10, and 2.1 of *Survey of Current Business* (July, 1968).

Table 2.5

Initial Receipts and Disposable Incomes, 1967

	Factor Incomes	Non-factor Charges*	Taxes and Transfers†	Disposable Incomes
	Billions of Dollars			
Personal Incomes				
From employment	468.2 ⎫		− 41.9 ⎫	
From self-employment	60.7 ⎬		− 82.5 ⎪	
Rentals, dividends, net interest	66.5 ⎭		⎬	533.2
Government and business transfers and government interest			+ 62.2 ⎭	
Interest paid by consumers				(13.1)
Corporations				
Profits less dividends	58.7		− 33.5 ⎫	25.2
Business transfer payments		3.1	− 3.1 ⎭	
Government				
Indirect taxes less net subsidy to government enterprises		68.0		
Taxes on incomes			+157.9 ⎫	
Interest on public debt			− 10.5 ⎬	166.8
Transfers to persons			− 48.6 ⎭	
Inventory valuation adjustment and statistical discrepancy	−1.2	− 3.5	0.0	− 4.7
National Income	652.9	652.9		
Total Charges Against Net National Product		720.5	0.0	720.5

* The first three items in the column are nonfactor charges against National Product; the addition of National Income yields "Total Charges against Net National Product."

† Net receipts (+) and payments (−) of taxes and transfers.

Table 2.4) include income from "employment" and "self-employment," *i.e.*, proprietors' income. In addition, persons receive income from "rentals," the "dividends" paid out by corporations, and the "net interest" payments of the domestic business system. With dividends shifted to the category of personal income receipts, corporations are credited with "profits less dividends." In order to simplify the presentation, the "inventory valuation adjustment" is shown near the bottom of the table on the same line with the statistical discrepancy. The government earns no factor income, and thus the total of factor incomes received by persons and retained within corporations (plus the inventory valuation adjustment) exhausts the National Income.

In the second column, other charges against National Product are entered; they include "business transfer payments" and "indirect taxes *less* the net subsidy to government enterprises." The "statistical discrepancy" is introduced here as well. When these figures are added to National Income, the result is the figure for "total charges against Net National Product." The addition of capital consumption allowances would yield the value of total charges against *Gross* National Product.

The third column shows the various taxes and transfer payments that serve to redistribute the returns from productive activity from the initial recipients to the persons and institutions who have ultimate discretion in their disposal or expenditure. Out of the income that persons earned from employment and self-employment, $41.9 billion was paid in contributions to social insurance; in addition, out of the total factor income accruing initially to persons, $82.5 billion was taken by income taxes. On the other hand, $62.2 billion was distributed back to persons in the form of government and business transfer payments and government interest. Of the income remaining in corporations after dividends had been deducted, $33.5 billion was paid in corporate income taxes. Business firms also paid out $3.1 billion in transfer payments to persons, including gifts to foundations, churches, etc. The government was the recipient of $157.9 billion in contributions to social insurance and in personal and corporate income taxes; and, in turn, it distributed $48.6 billion in transfer payments to persons and $10.5 billion in interest on the public debt.

No new income can be generated in this process — note that the third column totals to zero — and the only returns available are those originally accruing to the owners of the factors of production or charged as nonfactor costs. But the redistribution is nevertheless of great importance when the spending of income comes to be considered; insofar as spenders are influenced by the sizes of their incomes in deciding their outlays, they will consider disposable incomes — shown in the final column — rather than their factor earnings.

The first of the special income concepts is *Personal Income*: it is the total income received by persons from all sources. It includes all factor incomes accruing to persons *less* all contributions for social insurance. Also included are transfer payments to persons — such as the benefits from federal social insurance (*e.g.*, old-age, survivors, disability, and Medicare benefits), state unemployment insurance payments, and veterans' benefits, along with business transfers to persons – and government interest. Finally, Personal Income includes the total "interest paid by consumers," shown in parentheses in column 4. It will be recalled that interest paid by consumers is not regarded as reflecting production, and therefore it is not included as a contribution to National Product or National Income. These payments are viewed as income from the standpoint of the lender, however, and thus they are included as a component of Personal Income. Although Personal Income does not appear in Table 2.5, it can be calculated from the figures presented: $595.4 billion in factor incomes accruing to persons, *less* $41.9 billion in payments for social insurance, plus $62.2 billion in transfers and government interest and $13.1 billion in consumers' interest – for a total of $628.8 billion in 1967.

Personal Income, however, is not equal to the amount of income over which persons have complete command, to spend or save or give away at their own discretion. Income taxes represent a use of income over which the recipient of the income has no control – an obligatory rather than a discretionary outlay, so to speak. When income taxes ($82.5 billion in 1967) are deducted from Personal Income, the result is *Disposable Personal Income* – a figure that can be seen in column 4 as the total of factor incomes plus transfers and minus taxes ($533.2 billion), plus $13.1 billion in consumer interest, a total of $546.3 billion.[23] Disposable Personal Income still includes contributions to private pension schemes, which may be a condition of employment and therefore compulsory. Also, individuals have fixed commitments, such as the repayment of savings and loan mortgages and installment credit notes, which further reduce the part of their incomes over which they have complete and immediate discretion in the short run. When all possible outlays of this sort have been taken away, the remainder may be called "discretionary income" – although this is not official usage and no estimate of it is provided in the U.S. national income statistics.

As a companion concept to Disposable Personal Income, it may be useful to have the concept of *Disposable Corporate Income, i.e.,* the income remaining at the discretion of corporate managers once dividends and direct taxes have been paid. Table 2.5 shows this to have been $25.2 billion in 1967. Finally, in the public sector, a total of $166.8 billion remained at

---

[23] Disposable Personal Income, in turn, is equal to the total of *Personal Outlays* – which in 1967 consisted of $492.2 billion in personal consumption expenditures, $0.8 billion in transfer payments to foreigners, and the $13.1 billion in interest – plus $40.2 billion in *Personal Saving.*

the disposal of government authorities after the payment of the interest on the public debt and transfer payments to persons.[24]

9. Summary of the Principal Concepts

To conclude this chapter, it may prove useful to summarize the definitions of the magnitudes that have been described and to set forth the relationships between them. For convenience in later argument, a set of symbols is adopted for these aggregates; the symbols are conventional abbreviations.

Gross National Product (GNP) is the market value of the output of goods and services produced within the nation's economy. *Net National Product* (NNP) is GNP less depreciation and other allowances for the consumption of capital goods. NNP "at factor cost" is NNP less indirect taxes and other minor nonfactor charges against output. Often, in the discussion to follow, the distinction between GNP, NNP, and NNP at factor cost is not important; at these times, reference will be made simply to National Product or Output, which will be represented by the symbol pQ where Q is the national output in physical units and p is the price level.

Gross National Expenditure (GNE) is the sum of the expenditures that purchase the GNP, and therefore GNP $\equiv$ GNE.[25] It consists of consumers' expenditure (C), gross private domestic investment (I), government expenditures (G) and the difference between imports (M) and exports (E). GNE is not an official U.S. national income accounting term, although it will be used a good deal in the following chapters. With the deduction of depreciation, GNE becomes "Net National Expenditure" (NNE); and with the further deduction of nonfactor costs, NNE becomes "Net National Expenditure on factor inputs." The distinction between net and gross expenditure is seldom important in the text to follow, and the aggregate will normally be termed "National Expenditure."

National Income (NI) is the total earnings of labor and property (*i.e.*,

---

[24] Government purchases of goods and services, shown in Table 2.2, exceed the government's disposable income calculated in Table 2.5 by $11.6 billion. This is attributable to the fact that in 1967 the government ran a deficit of $13.8 billion in the Income and Product Accounts while expending $2.2 billion in transfer payments to foreigners.

[25] The symbol $\equiv$ denotes identity.

payments to the factors of production), which result from the production of goods and services by the nation's economy. These earnings include the compensation of employees, the profits of corporate and unincorporated enterprises, net interest, and the rental income accruing to persons.

Gross National Income (GNI) is the sum of incomes earned by the factors of production (the National Income) plus other production costs — *e.g.*, depreciation, indirect taxes, net subsidy to government enterprises, and business transfer payments. Although the latter costs are not payments for factor services, they nonetheless are components of the gross income of participants in the productive process. Since all final expenditure must be financed from income, gross national expenditure is identical to gross national income. Or, taking another view, all net returns from the sale of final products must be distributed either to the factors of production (including profit paid to owners) or to some nonfactor cost, and therefore Gross National Product is identical to Gross National Income. In symbols,

$$GNP \equiv GNI \equiv GNE.$$

If all nonfactor charges are deducted from gross product, expenditure and income, then

$$NI \equiv NNP \text{ at factor cost} \equiv NNE \text{ on factor inputs.}$$

Or, alternatively,

$$NNP \equiv NNE \equiv NI \text{ plus nonfactor costs.}$$

Once again, in much of the discussion to follow it is not necessary to draw a distinction between Gross National Income and income net of depreciation and nonfactor payments; where this is the case, the term "National Income" will be used, and this aggregate will be represented by the symbol Y. Wherever the term "National Income" is used in the sense of its official definition — that is, as the sum only of payments to the factors of production — special note will be made.

Disposable Personal Income is the sum of incomes from employment and self-employment, dividends, rent, and interest received by persons, *plus* all transfer payments to persons, *minus* all forms of social security and personal income taxes. It is a measure of the overall spending power of persons, and it will be denoted as Y_d.

With the aid of the concepts defined above, it is now possible to discuss in more detail, and with greater precision, the nature of macroeconomic equilibrium; and that is the subject of the following chapter.

CHAPTER 3

Aggregate Demand, Output, and Equilibrium

1. Aggregate Demand and Supply

In Chapter 1, the equilibrium of the economy was roughly described in terms of aggregate demand and supply. It was said that when the amount of money everyone wishes to spend is equal to the value of the goods and services currently being made available for purchase, the economy is in equilibrium in the sense that the situation will not itself cause changes in the general level of prices, in the level of output, or in anything else. But the concept of equilibrium implies the possibility of disequilibrium: aggregate demand *may* be equal to aggregate supply, but it may also be larger or smaller at any particular time. In this, there is a marked contrast with the relationship between National Expenditure and National Product, since these are identical in amount at all times and under all circumstances; they can never be said to be in equilibrium, because they can never differ. Nonetheless, the concepts defined in the previous chapter can be used to throw light on the conditions of equilibrium between aggregate demand and supply.

For the time being, the notion of aggregate supply will be likened to that of National Product. This does not mean that the two are to be regarded as identical; National Product is simply a numerical measure of the flow of output, whereas the concept of supply involves the idea of volition — it is the quantity that sellers *wish* to sell, rather than the amount that they merely happen to have available from current production. Firms will be content to produce a given level of output only if they believe that they could not improve their profits by either increasing or reducing it. It will be shown in a later chapter [1] that production decisions depend on the current relationship between prices and wages; if labor costs are low in relation to sales revenue, firms are likely to feel that it would be profitable to expand output, while in the opposite case they will wish to contract it. Moreover, the prices/wages relationship itself may alter as the volume of output changes. It follows that a given level of National Product can be identified with aggregate supply only if prices and wages happen to bear the appropriate relationship to one another. In this and the next few chapters, however, it will be convenient to make the simplifying assumption that this condition is satisfied at all levels of

---

[1] See Chapter 10, page 235.

National Product; firms will then be willing to provide whatever volume of output is needed to satisfy aggregate demand, and their only concern will be to avoid excesses or shortfalls between production and sales. This assumption will be relaxed at a later stage, but for the time being it means that aggregate supply coincides with the current level of National Product, whatever it happens to be.

The original definition of equilibrium – that aggregate demand should be equal to aggregate supply – can then be restated in three ways. First, aggregate demand (including, of course, the demand for additional inventories [2]) will be equal to National Product. Second, aggregate demand will be equal to National Income when equilibrium exists, since National Income is necessarily equal to National Product; all income recipients must between them be willing to spend on currently produced goods and services the whole of their combined incomes, no less and no more. It is not necessary, of course, that each individual income recipient spend the exact amount of his *own* income; some may spend a good deal less, while others may borrow or use previously accumulated funds in order to spend more than the amount of their current incomes. Business firms, in particular, are likely to be in the second category; but as long as spending plans are such that the underspending of the first group exactly offsets the overspending of the second, the sum of all incomes will be equal to aggregate demand, and the economy will be in equilibrium. Third, the equilibrium of aggregate demand and supply can be restated in terms of equality between aggregate demand and National Expenditure: the total amount of money that everyone *wishes* to spend on goods and services must be equal to the amount that actually *is* spent.

From the last statement, it is clear that the concept of aggregate demand will have to be retained when the equilibrium of the economy is under investigation. As has been seen, the concepts of National Product and National Income can be used without modification. However, National Expenditure cannot be used in place of aggregate demand, since they are quite distinct concepts and are equal only when the economy is in equilibrium. The total of National Expenditure is necessarily identical with National Product, because nothing can be sold without being bought; such an identity can therefore tell us nothing about the conditions of equilibrium. But the total of aggregate demand need not be

---

[2] This demand, as has already been observed, may be either positive or negative.

equal to National Product, just as demand need not equal supply in the market for a single commodity; there is no reason why buyers should always wish to buy exactly the quantity that sellers wish to sell, and indeed the two sides of the market will find that their respective intentions are mutually compatible only when equilibrium exists. For the equilibrium of the whole economy, then, aggregate demand is the significant magnitude, not National Expenditure.

Nevertheless, this does not mean that the attention given to National Expenditure in the previous chapter was wasted. When aggregate demand is submitted to more precise definition, it must fall into the same mold as the details of total "Expenditure on National Product" or National Expenditure were found to do. Just as it was necessary to eliminate expenditures on intermediate products and to count only purchases of final goods and services, so also in the case of demand double counting must be eliminated by including only "final" demands in the total. The demand for fixed capital formation can be taken as gross or net, according to whether it is made to include or exclude depreciation, just as *actual* expenditure may be gross or net. The classification of demand into categories — consumers' demand, government demand for goods and services, and so on — follows logically exactly the same pattern as that adopted for expenditure.

If statistics of demand were available, they could be tabulated in a form precisely similar to that of Table 2.2 (p. 24), in which particulars of total expenditure on National Product are given. If the demand figures were then placed beside the expenditure figures, both sets would show the same layout of items; and the details of definition would be exactly the same for each set, except that one column of figures would show *actual* spending while the other would show *intended* expenditures. The parallel is so close that many writers have preferred to retain the word "expenditure" for both aggregate demand and National Expenditure — referring to the former as "intended" or "planned" expenditure, the latter as "actual" or "realized" expenditure. Swedish economists [3] have applied the terms *ex ante* and *ex post* to make a similar distinction: *ex ante* ("as of before the event") expenditure is what everyone expects to spend when looking forward at the beginning of a period, while *ex post* ("as of afterward") expenditure is what people find they have spent when they look back on the period after it has ended. The "before and after" conno-

---

[3] The terms were first used by Gunnar Myrdal in 1927.

tation of these terms, however, may be misleading in the present context:[4] intended expenditure, or aggregate demand, should be thought of as coexisting with actual expenditure — at the same time as spenders are attempting to buy $x billion worth of commodities, they may in fact be succeeding in buying only $y billion worth. Indeed, it is when spenders *simultaneously* are wishing to do one thing and in fact doing another that disequilibrium exists in the economy.

If aggregate demand is to be regarded as a more significant magnitude than National Expenditure, it would seem to be a serious disadvantage that no comprehensive statistical information is available about it. Wishes are less amenable than actions to observation and measurement, so it is hardly surprising that there are no official figures of *intended* expenditure comparable to those published for National Expenditure.[5] But this is not a fatal objection to the use of the concept of aggregate demand, any more than it is when a demand schedule is assumed in the case of a single commodity's market. Very often the objective of economic reasoning is not to make detailed predictions in a particular case but to establish general relationships that can reasonably be expected to hold true whatever the precise details of the situation. To say, for example, that X is bigger than Y, or that Q gets bigger whenever R increases, may be quite possible even without a precise knowledge of the magnitudes of X and Y, or Q and R at any particular time. If the statistical information is available, it is useful in verifying such relationships, but the relationships themselves are usually asserted to exist on other than purely statistical grounds. Since the concept of aggregate demand is required for this kind of purpose rather than for detailed factual prediction (in the present context, at any rate), the lack of detailed information about it need not prevent it from being extremely useful.

It can be argued, moreover, that in a good many situations there will be a very close correspondence between the figures of National Expenditure and those that would appear (if they were known) in a detailed

---

[4] As used by the Swedish writers, *ex ante* and *ex post* have a dynamic significance that is not relevant to the present description of *static* equilibrium. See B. Ohlin, "Some Notes on the Stockholm Theory of Saving and Investment," G. Haberler, ed. for American Economic Association, *Readings in Business Cycle Theory* (Homewood, Ill.: Irwin, 1944).

[5] This does not mean that there are no official figures at all. For example, the Department of Commerce conducts quarterly surveys of planned investment in plant and equipment and of manufacturers' inventory and sales expectations; the results are published in *Survey of Current Business*.

statement of aggregate demand. Consumers, for example, can be assumed to spend whatever amounts they wish (given the prices of commodities, their own incomes, and so on) unless for some reason the available quantities of the commodities they desire are inadequate to meet their demands — in which case some of the spending that consumers wish to do will not in fact be done. If, on the other hand, commodities are in plentiful supply, consumers will buy what they want and leave the rest of the available commodities in the hands of the sellers. In short, consumers' *actual* expenditure conceivably may fall short of their *intended* expenditure, but it cannot exceed it. This is true also of government expenditure, of the purchase of imports and exports, and of expenditure on fixed capital equipment; in all these cases, buyers may have to make do with less than they would have liked to purchase, but they cannot be made to buy more than they want. Therefore, unless demand in all these categories is so high that it causes great difficulties of supply, it can be supposed that the statistics of National Expenditure coincide with those that would have existed for demand had it been possible to obtain them.

Table 3.1
Total Demand and Supply in an Imaginary Economy

Demand	$ billions	Supply	$ billions
Consumers' demand	520	Gross National Product	800
Government demand	180	Imports	40
Fixed investment demand (gross)	110		
Demand for increases in inventories	10		
Demand for exports	40		
Total demand	860	Total supply	840

The single category of expenditure for which this does not hold true is increases in inventories; there actual spending may exceed intended expenditure because of the convention by which firms are regarded as buying from themselves any unsold accumulation of their own products. Firms may produce a certain output, hoping that it will be bought from them by consumers, government, and so on, except perhaps for a certain quantity of their products that they themselves wish to retain as additional inventory. If, however, demand is less brisk than was expected, the firms will find that a larger part of their output is left on their hands than the increase in inventories they had originally intended. The firms' *de-*

mand is the originally planned increase; their *expenditure*, on the other hand, is the increase that in fact occurs. If other sectors' demands were unexpectedly strong, firms might find their existing inventories drained away in the effort to keep their customers supplied; and the result would be that the firms' expenditure would be *less* than their demand for additional inventories.[6] Unless the excess of aggregate demand over National Product is so great that all the inventories held by firms are inadequate (when added to current output) to meet the demands of other sectors, it seems that the difference between demand and output in the whole economy is likely to be concentrated wholly in the "increase in inventories" item.

2. Symptoms and Effects of Disequilibrium

Other possible consequences of disequilibrium between aggregate demand and National Product may be seen when the constituent elements are tabulated in detail, as in Table 3.1. Imaginary annual figures are used for purposes of illustration, though it may be observed that the order of magnitude is not much different from that of the authentic 1967 figures used in previous tables. The left-hand column includes all the elements of demand that come forward over the year in search of the various goods and services available in the country; the right-hand column summarizes what is supplied — Gross National Product (which might be called "internal supply of goods and services" on the argument given on pages 42–43) and imports, which appear here as a flow of commodities into the domestic market from abroad, rather than a deduction from the left-hand side as in the conventional presentation of Expenditure on Gross National Product (Table 2.1).[7]

If equilibrium existed, the two totals would be equal; if the symbols

---

[6] Of course, firms may plan to *decrease* inventories, but if the amount by which they actually fall is larger than the planned reduction, demand would still exceed expenditure in this respect — though both would be negative.

[7] The shift of imports from the category of a (negative) demand to that of supply is for convenience in presentation. It involves the assumption that the "rest of the world" supplies exactly the quantity of goods and services demanded by domestic purchasers.

introduced at the end of Chapter 2 are brought into use,[8] this would mean that

$$C + G + I + E = \text{GNP} + M$$

(where C is consumers' demand, G government demand, I the demand for investment and increased inventories, E the demand for exports, and M the supply of imports.) In the situation imagined in the table, however, total demand exceeds total supply; the left-hand side of the equation is larger than the right-hand side.

It is clear that, as things stand in the table, all spenders cannot be fully satisfied; they wish to spend $860 billion, while the value of goods and services available to be purchased is only $840 billion. An "excess demand" of $20 billion exists. But actual expenditure cannot exceed the value of goods and services purchased; perusal of Table 3.1 suggests that there are six ways in which the equality of expenditure and supplies may be brought about.

(i) Firms may satisfy other sectors' excess demand by throwing into the breach their accumulated inventories, as described on page 46. If these are large enough (*i.e.*, at least $20 billion in this case) and if the firms are prepared to use them in this way, their action may permit all other sectors to satisfy demand to the full — although of course the firms' own demand for increased inventories will be completely frustrated.

(ii) If firms' inventories are too small for this, or if they are not prepared to give them up in the necessary quantities, demand in *all* sectors may be frustrated: the "excess" $20 billion will go a-begging. Consumers will find themselves faced with shortages; government departments will be unable to procure all the supplies called for by their spending programs for the year; export customers will be told that their orders are being placed on waiting lists; and so on.

(iii) Instead of a general shortage of supplies arising in all sectors, export customers may be made to take the strain because of the diversion to the domestic market of commodities originally produced for export. The likelihood of this occurring depends on many things — for example, if the country's exports normally consist of commodities adapted to the special requirements of foreign customers (such as icebreakers, narrow-gauge railway locomotives, and fezzes), it may not be possible to sell

---

[8] The symbols are given the sense of "intended" rather than "actual" expenditure in the above context: *ex ante*, rather than *ex post* as they were in Chapter 2.

these things at home, and exports will continue as before; if, on the other hand, overseas markets are generally regarded as overflow for products that are mainly sold domestically, it will be easy to divert the entire supply to customers at home.

All of the first three possible outcomes of this imagined disequilibrium are concerned with the *demand* side of Table 3.1. The remaining three possibilities appear as possible changes on the *supply* side.

(iv) The converse of (iii) is an increase in the quantity of the country's imports. If overseas suppliers can easily increase their consignments to domestic buyers, all of the excess demand may be met in this way; instead of demand being frustrated, the supply of imports will rise to meet it.

(v) However, the volume of imports may already be at a maximum; this could be the case if foreign producers are working at full capacity to produce the particular commodities that the country imports and, for technical reasons, are unable to expand production further. It may be, also, that the government of the country is apprehensive of possible ill consequences from a surplus of imports over exports and therefore takes steps to prevent such a surplus arising; for example, by controlling imports by a system of licenses. The quantity of commodities supplied can then increase only by a rise in domestic production — that is, in Gross National Product. If the economy is initially in a state of underemployment, with many of its workers unemployed and a good part of its plant and equipment lying idle, it will be quite possible to increase output very quickly simply by calling back into use some or all of these unemployed resources. The $20 billion of excess demand will quickly be met by a rise in the physical quantity of output of equal value.

(vi) However, there may be no reserve of temporarily idle resources available to expand the quantity of output; the economy may be already at full employment. In that case, the physical quantity of output can be increased only by giving the fully employed labor force more equipment or by improving the productivity of available resources; how feasible this is depends on the increase in production required and on the length of time within which it must be provided. If the time is too short for additions to plant and equipment through capital formation to make much difference in the volume of output, the only remaining way in which supply can increase to match demand is by a general rise in prices. The "excess" $20 billion can all be spent if the same physical quantities of goods and services are made $20 billion dearer. The increase in prices is almost certain to extend to any imported commodities that are being sold along-side similar domestically produced goods, if it is not possible for the *quantity* of imports to rise as in (iv). How far the prices of other imports will rise depends on the reactions of foreign suppliers. As the original market value of all supplies, both domestic and imported, was $840 billion, an average rise in market prices of 2.4% will suffice to bring the figure up to one of equality with aggregate demand.

These, then, are the immediate consequences that may result from the "excess demand" situation imagined in Table 3.1, a situation that might be described as "inflationary" — though nothing has yet been said on the subject of inflation, so that the word is not here intended in a very precise sense. The six possible outcomes are by no means mutually exclusive; they can all operate simultaneously. For example, an average increase of 1% in prices would raise the value of supplies by $8.4 billion; a rise of 1% in the physical quantity of domestic production would contribute a further $8.08 billion;[9] an increase in imports of $1 billion, a decrease in exports of $1 billion, and an increase in inventories of only $9 billion, instead of the $10 billion originally planned, would between them offset all but $0.52 billion of the $20 billion of excess demand. This small remainder might then be the degree of frustration experienced by consumers, government authorities, and business firms seeking to obtain new plant and machinery. Exactly how much of the impact will be borne in each of the six ways would depend on the circumstances. Obviously price increases are more likely if there is no possibility of quickly increasing the physical quantity of output — if, that is, the economy is already fully employed. But even then, much depends on the attitude of business management. Some may feel that taking advantage of buoyant demand to raise their products' prices could damage their goodwill in the long run and may therefore keep prices unchanged even when it is quite clear that they could be increased without reducing sales; other firms, taking a shorter view, may put up their prices as soon as opportunity offers. The net result for the price level in general will depend on which of these attitudes is more prevalent among policymakers in industry and commerce.

Such questions as these will have to be considered in detail later. At present it is more important to observe that the various possible effects of excess demand will not immediately lead to the restoration of equilib-

---

[9] At the original price level, it would have been just $8 billion, but this figure must itself be increased by 1% because prices have been assumed to rise by that much.

rium in the economy. The three possibilities on the demand side — (i), (ii) and (iii) above — merely leave part of aggregate demand unsatisfied; either it is partially frustrated in all sectors, or the frustration is concentrated among business firms seeking to hold a particular level of inventories, or among export customers. This blocking-off of demand may be the main consequence in the current period (the figures were assumed to refer to an imaginary year), but it will presumably mean that excess demand will be carried over into the next year, so that when the current year is finished, the disequilibrium situation will be reproduced and further effects brought about.

Alternatively, the effects on the supply side will cause incomes to increase where there is a rise in output and/or prices (possibilities [v] and [vi] above), though not, it should be noted, when the main consequence is an increase in imports (as in [iv] above). When output or prices increase, additional remuneration in money terms is paid out to the owners of the factors of production or to the recipients of various nonfactor charges such as indirect taxes, business transfers, or the surplus of government enterprises; National Product is always equal to National Income.[10] Every dollar paid in exchange for goods and services must be received by someone, and these payments, after the elimination of double counting, are incomes; whether more is paid because a larger quantity of commodities is being bought or because the same quantity is being bought at higher prices makes no difference in the fact that more money is being received as income. Whether the extra income takes the form of higher corporate profits, increased wages, or larger farm incomes must depend on a number of circumstances; but no matter who actually receives it, it will become available, after the usual processes of taxing and transferring, as disposable income to be used by the recipients as the basis for further demands for goods and services. Even if prices and domestic output do not go up, but imports increase to the full extent of the excess demand, the increase will bring about a rise in incomes for the

---

10 Recall that, under the official definition, National Income is the total of payments to the factors of production and thus does not include nonfactor charges or depreciation. National Product, on the other hand, is normally stated "at market prices" (*i.e.*, including nonfactor charges) and may be expressed either gross or net of depreciation. In this discussion, it is not specially important to distinguish between evaluation at market prices and at factor costs — or between aggregates gross or net of depreciation — and so the terms National Product and National Income are used in a general sense without further specification. See Chapter 2, pp. 28–32.

people overseas who produce the imported commodities. They, in their turn, may increase their demand for the exports of the original country — but this feedback will be less direct than that resulting from increased domestic incomes, and may be much weaker. If it is negligible (for example, because foreigners spend their additional income entirely on their own products) the original country will have "exported," as it were, the whole of its excess demand.

Unless the excess demand is channeled off through the purchase of extra imports, then, it will pass into domestic incomes and reappear on the demand side; if *all* of the increase in income reappears as additional demand, both aggregate demand and the value of supplies will have been increased by $20 billion, leaving demand in excess of supply by just as much as before. If this were to happen, the excess demand would once again pass round the circuit, increasing the value of supplies, augmenting incomes, and consequently raising demand yet again by $20 billion; which in turn will reproduce itself, leading to an infinite series of further increases in incomes and demand. Equilibrium, it would seem, will never be attained; it is not possible for aggregate demand to come into equality with the value of available supplies if the *whole* of the original excess of demand circulates at every turn of the circuit. If, however, the adding of $20 billion to incomes results in an addition of *less* than that amount to aggregate demand, then the increase in incomes that occurs on the next round will be only, say, $18 billion; if less than this is added to demand on the next turn of the circuit, the following increase in incomes will again be smaller. Further turns of the circuit will be made by successively smaller amounts, until in the end the addition to demand will be negligible and equilibrium will at last be reached.

The relationship between incomes and demand is therefore crucial for the attaining of equilibrium. It is necessary to know how each of the categories of spenders will react to changes in income. Suppose, for example, that in the imaginary situation of Table 3.1, it is known that none of the $20 billion of excess demand will have the effect of increasing imports, and that Gross National Product will be made to rise by exactly $20 billion through rises in prices, or in output, or a mixture of both; then Gross National Income will rise by the full $20 billion. Now suppose that four-fifths of this becomes the disposable income of *persons* and that, on the average, people try to spend on consumption three-quarters of any rise in disposable income; this will mean an addition to consumers' demand of $12 billion at the next stage. Suppose, further, that business firms try to spend on capital formation exactly the amount of their disposable undistributed profits, which happen to be a tenth of the increase in Gross National Income; this means that $2 billion of further demand will arise in this sector. Finally, suppose that government authorities and export customers do not react at all to the change in Gross National Income. Then the income increase of $20 billion will cause an increase in demand of $14 billion altogether — that is, seven-tenths of the rise in income will be passed on in increased demand to the next stage. When the $14 billion then emerges as a further increase in Gross National Income, and seven-tenths of *that* is added to the demand, only $9.8 billion will be passed on at this further turn round the circuit. It will generate yet more demand equal to seven-tenths of $9.8 billion, and so on.

The successive additions to demand can be written as a series (the figures are in billions of dollars) — 14, 9.8, 6.9, 4.8, 3.4, 2.4, and so on. Though aggregate demand was at first $20 billion higher than the value of supplies, the excess is gradually whittled away. Both demand and supply increase (in monetary terms) with each tour of the circuit, but demand does not maintain its lead; eventually, the excess demand will be reduced to an amount so insignificant as to be hardly worth counting, and equilibrium will have been achieved.[11]

In the above example, the possibility of equilibrium existed because the relation between incomes and demand was assumed to be such that only seven-tenths of any rise in income was translated into further demand for goods and services. As long as less than the whole of income is passed on in this way, equilibrium can be attained. If, on the other hand, the spending habits of the various sectors were such that a rise in income would lead to attempts to increase spending by *more* than the amount of extra income — if, for example, the $20 billion of extra income imagined earlier were to cause consumers to raise their demands by $18 billion and business· firms to attempt extra capital formation of $3 billion — then not only would equilibrium not be possible, but the original excess of aggregate demand over supply would become steadily greater and would go on growing without limit. So everything depends upon the way in which

---

[11] It should be noted that this is "static" equilibrium, as defined in Chapter 1, pp. 6–7. It is assumed that there are no important time lags in the process of circulation described above: demand causes the value of supply to increase, incomes rise, and demand rises further, all in too short a time for the process itself to produce any important changes in the system. The "time path" of the circuit is at this stage deliberately ignored; but the effect of time lags will be explored in Chapter 6.

the various categories of spenders react to changes in their incomes; it is a matter of such importance that several subsequent chapters will be devoted to exploring the connection between income and demand. Meanwhile, however, some further points must be made regarding the nature of the equilibrium of the economy as it has so far been outlined.

3. The Saving-Investment Relationship

The first of these points concerns *saving*, which has not so far been mentioned and which may be defined in a general way as the part of disposable income that is not spent on consumption. In the case of individuals, this seems a fairly straightforward concept.[12] Whatever is left of a man's income after he has paid his taxes will be available to him for outlay in various ways. He may spend it on commodities that he consumes — in which case nothing will be left behind as wealth to be carried over into the future — or he may use it in some other way that will leave him better off. He need not accumulate cash, of course; he may buy government bonds or common stock; he may acquire a house; if he is the owner of a small business, he may use part of his income to increase its equipment or its inventory. Saving is thus not the opposite of spending, but merely the alternative to the spending of income on consumption. Consumption and saving together will account for the whole of the individual's disposable income.

For the nation as a whole, the definition of saving is slightly more complicated. It would not be correct to subtract consumers' expenditure from National Income and call the remainder "saving," because no allowance is made for the "collective consumption" represented by government expenditure on goods and services. When local governments, for example,

---

[12] A word of clarification is in order here, however. Under the official definition, Disposable Personal Income includes consumers' interest payments, and these same payments show up as an item of personal "outlay" along with personal consumption expenditures and personal saving. But though it is a part of the internal accounting of the personal sector, consumer interest is *not* reflected in the national aggregates of income, product, and expenditure (see p. 38). Therefore, in this discussion of the division of income between consumption and saving, Disposable *Personal* Income is considered *net* of consumer interest. In effect, this interest payment is an internal transfer within the personal sector and does not play a direct role in the determination of aggregate demand output, and equilibrium.

spend money on street lighting and sewage disposal, they are satisfying their citizens' wants in a way that uses up resources without leaving any assets to be carried over into the future; they are doing things that might have been part of private consumers' expenditure had it not been found more convenient to provide such services publicly. To calculate the saving of the whole nation, then, it is necessary to deduct from National Income both private consumers' expenditure and the expenditure on goods and services by government authorities. When this is done, it will be seen that the nation's saving is exactly equal to capital formation at home (including increases in stocks as well as expenditure on fixed capital equipment), *plus* exports, *minus* imports of goods and services.

This is because Gross National Expenditure consists of the spending of consumers and government, plus investment, plus exports, and minus imports; or, using the conventional symbols,

$$\text{GNE} = C + G + I + E - M.$$

Gross National Income, on the other hand, equals consumers' and government spending plus saving (which may be denoted by the symbol S),

$$\text{GNI} = C + G + S.$$

Gross National Expenditure and Gross National Income are always equal — that is, $\text{GNE} \equiv \text{GNI}$ — so that

$$C + G + I + E - M \equiv C + G + S.$$

If public and private consumption are subtracted from both sides, the remainder — investment, plus exports, minus imports in the case of National Expenditure; saving in the case of National Income — must necessarily be equal:

$$S \equiv I + E - M.$$

Expenditure and income are both shown gross of depreciation, so that saving here includes allowances set aside for replacing assets; and this part of saving must be equal to the actual expenditure on making good depreciation, which is included in gross investment. If depreciation were to be deducted from both, the result would show the equality of "net" saving and "net" domestic investment *plus* exports *minus* imports. Since the difference between exports and imports is the amount of the country's overseas investment,[13] capital formation at home *plus* exports *minus* im-

---

[13] The influence of transfer payments abroad is omitted in this discussion. Overall consumers' and government outlays include, in addition to the purchase of goods and

ports can be called simply "investment"; it is the total of capital formation at home and abroad. In this sense, the nation's investment is necessarily equal to its saving at all times. The only way in which the whole
nation can carry over current income into the future is by creating new
capital equipment, piling up inventories of commodities, and acquiring
claims on the rest of the world. Saving and investment, indeed, appear to
be the same thing.

From this, it might appear that the concept of saving is an unnecessary
one; if it is always the same as investment, why not keep only the latter
concept and discard the concept of "saving"? The answer is that the "saving" defined above is *actual* rather than *intended*; it is the difference between income and whatever expenditure is in fact made on private consumption and government goods and services. But, as has been seen,
these expenditures may not be the same as the spending that consumers
and public authorities planned to do; if *intended* consumption (both private and public) is subtracted from income, the result is *intended* saving —
and this may not be the same as either actual or intended investment.
Saving, in this *ex ante* sense, can be regarded as that part of income
which consumers and government authorities are content to leave available for other purposes; since National Income equals National Product,
saving is also equivalent to the quantity of goods and services not required for public and private consumption. If the plans of business firms
for capital formation at home and abroad happen to call for exactly the
quantity of goods and services left over from consumption — if, that is,
intended investment equals intended saving — then equilibrium will
exist; aggregate demand will be in balance with aggregate supply.

But it could easily happen that the desired amount of investment differs from the amount of intended saving; by planning to consume too little, consumers and government authorities may leave for capital forma-

---

services, transfer payments to foreigners such as gifts to family members overseas and
foreign aid. These payments thus do not constitute saving; by the same token, these
transfers must be subtracted from the excess of exports over imports to get a true
figure for net investment abroad. In the equations presented above, M may be considered to include these transfers in addition to the import of goods and services.

The *form* of overseas investment does not matter in the present context: the export
surplus may bring in a holding of foreign currency or be used to buy stock in foreign
corporations or actual physical equipment situated overseas. All possible uses of
the export surplus, however, represent an increase in the country's wealth. If there
were a surplus of imports over exports, this would be "overseas disinvestment" — the
country would be reducing its wealth.

tion purposes a larger part of output than is wanted. The result of this excess of saving over investment will be that producers will fail to sell as much of their products to others as they had expected; inventories will pile up higher than was called for in the firms' own plans to increase them. When firms attempt to work off these excess inventories by reducing current output, or by cutting prices, or by a combination of both, the effect will be to reduce the money value of National Product. If the fall in National Product (and in National Income, which is always equal to it) causes changes in both the amount of intended saving and the demand for investment at home and abroad, in such a way that saving and investment (in the *ex ante* or "planned" sense) become equal to one another, equilibrium will be reached and there will be no further fall in National Product.

A similar sequence of events could be imagined if intended saving were to fall short of intended investment; in that case, the demand for consumption would not leave available a large enough slice of the economy's output to satisfy the demand for new capital equipment, additions to inventories, and overseas investment. When firms respond to this situation by attempting to increase the quantity of output, or by increasing prices, or by a mixture of both, the value of the National Product will rise; it will continue to increase until the willingness to save becomes great enough to provide for investment purposes a sufficiently large part of output to satisfy the demand. Saving and investment, when taken in the *ex ante* sense, will therefore be equal to one another only in equilibrium; though *actual* saving and investment must always be equal, *intended* saving and investment may very well differ.

That decisions to save should at times be incompatible with plans for investment is hardly surprising when it is observed that these decisions and plans are made by different groups of people. An individual whose income accrues as a wage or salary, or as dividends or interest, may save part of it, but will hardly be likely to put the saving into the form of industrial machinery or inventories of commodities; instead, he will accumulate cash, lend his savings to someone else by buying bonds, or acquire an interest in some corporation by buying stock. A business firm, on the other hand, need not rely only on its own undistributed profits when it wishes to expand its productive capacity by installing new machinery or to increase its inventory; it can borrow from a bank or issue new bonds or stock to borrow from the public at large. When the firm sees an investment opportunity that it thinks will be profitable, it may first decide on its program of plant expansion and then seek a means of financing it.

It is true, of course, that corporate undistributed profits have for some time been a major source of finance for capital investment; and in some cases the decision as to how much of current profits should be retained instead of given out to stockholders in dividends must have been made in the light of the firm's requirements for new capital equipment and inventory. Here the link between saving and investment is as close as possible; plans for capital formation are made, in such cases, by the same people who decide how much shall be saved from the corporations' profits. In the same way, an individual who is running his own business may plan to save part of his profits in order to buy new machinery, letting his desire for capital formation determine his decisions regarding saving. To this extent, saving and investment plans will be kept in line with one another because the same people are making both types of decision; but as long as only a part of the nation's saving is decided on in this way, and as long as the capital formation planned to be made from firms' own savings is only a part of the whole nation's intended investment, there will be sufficient dissociation between saving decisions and investment decisions to make it possible for the nation's intended (or *ex ante*) investment to differ from its intended saving — giving the disequilibrium situation, described earlier, that will lead to changes in the value of National Product and Income.

For the economy as a whole, then, the condition of equilibrium is that intended saving must equal intended investment. This is merely another way of saying that aggregate demand must equal aggregate supply, since investment (in the *ex ante* sense) is aggregate demand *minus* the demands of consumers and government authorities, while saving is the part of income (and therefore of National Product or aggregate supply) not required to meet the demands of public and private consumers. Is there any advantage in restating the equilibrium condition in terms of saving and investment? It must be admitted that it would be quite possible to give a fairly complete account of macroeconomic theory without saying much about saving, because saving is merely the difference between income and consumption, and all the various influences that determine the level of consumption automatically determine the level of saving also. If, for example, people decide to spend four-fifths of their incomes on consumption, they are *ipso facto* deciding to save one-fifth of their incomes;

consequently, it makes no difference whether the causes of their decisions are investigated as influences on consumption or influences on saving. It may even be thought undesirable to eliminate consumption from the picture by discussing equilibrium entirely in terms of saving and investment; as the influence of consumers' and government demands is felt only negatively in such a formulation, consumption demand may appear to be somehow less important than the demand for capital formation. Such an impression would not, of course, have any logical basis, but it could nonetheless cause a misplacement of emphasis in the analysis of particular situations.

On the other hand, the savings-investment approach does focus attention on the aspect of equilibrium that is most important from the point of view of *monetary* theory and policy. Where savers are not the same people as those who make decisions about capital formation, questions of finance must be important. For investment purposes, business firms must somehow or other get control of funds sufficient to allow them to buy the goods and services not wanted for consumption; the simplest and most obvious method is for the firms to borrow the savings of income recipients, in which case the rate of interest offered on loans and the dividend rate expected on corporate stocks become important. It may be that savers are not prepared to part with their money even when offered attractive inducements in the way of interest and dividends; if they prefer to accumulate their savings in cash, it may be necessary for the monetary authorities to increase the quantity of money in circulation so that firms bent on capital formation can still obtain the necessary funds. The powers and policies of those authorities will then be important. If it is considered (for reasons that need not be detailed at this stage) that the government ought to rely mainly on monetary policy in controlling the economy, its pre-occupation will be with such matters as the quantity of money and the level of interest rates; and the part played by these things in the working of the economy may be more conveniently studied in terms of the savings-investment relationship.[14]

---

[14] This argument has lost some of its force in present conditions. If all new borrowing were by business firms and government authorities seeking the means of financing capital formation, the savings-investment approach would obviously be appropriate. But the August, 1968, *Federal Reserve Bulletin* shows that in 1967 *consumers* borrowed around $12 billion for house purchases as well as contracting over $4 billion in new credit for other personal expenditures. The financing of consumption clearly involves a good deal of borrowing and lending, and there is a risk that its

The second matter to be discussed in connection with the equilibrium of the economy is the general price level. The point was made above [15] that one of the consequences of an excess of aggregate demand over supply (and therefore, of course, of intended investment over saving) may be a general increase in prices. If there are plenty of unemployed men and machines, additional demand may induce business firms to put them to work to increase the physical *quantity* of output. If, on the other hand, there are practically no reserves of labor and equipment available, an increase in the quantity of production may be impossible for the time being; and an increase in demand will then tend to force up prices.

But how are increases in the quantity of output to be distinguished from increases in the value of output due to price changes? It was pointed out in Chapter 1 that in calculating *aggregate* output it is necessary to add together the money values of all the different goods and services produced in a period of time. It is not possible to add together physical quantities of different commodities, but the total of aggregate output may nevertheless be found if the quantity of each commodity's output is multiplied by its price and all the resulting "value of output" figures are added together. Also, since production is to be thought of as the satisfaction of wants rather than the fabrication of objects, the use of prices in aggregating output will have the effect of putting different commodities into the total in the right proportions — the "weight" given to a ten-cent article will be one-tenth of that given to something priced at one dollar. But suppose it should be necessary to compare one year's output with another, when both are calculated in money terms. If it is important to say what part of the difference between them is due to increases in the quantities of commodities produced, and what part is due to changes in prices, a means must be found of separating the two while still permitting aggregate output to be valued in terms of money.

Again suppose the reactions of income recipients to an increase in

---

importance may be overlooked if attention is restricted to the finance of capital formation by business and government, as it tends to be in the savings-investment approach.

[15] See pp. 49–50.

National Income are being investigated. Any increase in the value of National Product, whether it arises from price changes or quantity changes, will bring about a rise in incomes, as has been seen above; but will consumers, business firms, and others react to an increase in money income that accrues from higher production in the same way as they will to one that accrues from higher prices? If a consumer, for example, finds that his income has gone up 10% but that he must spend it on commodities whose prices have also gone up 10%, his "real" income (that is, his income valued in terms of the quantities of goods it will buy) is unchanged. Unless he is unduly impressed by the fact that he is getting more money and unduly forgetful of the rise in prices — unless, in other words, he is suffering from what has been called "money illusion" — he will no doubt go on buying much the same quantities of commodities as he did before, and the amount of his money expenditures will rise 10%. If, on the other hand, he were to enjoy a 10% rise in income while the prices of goods and services remained the same as before, he might very well increase his spending so as to enjoy greater consumption; but there is no reason to think he would increase his spending by exactly 10%. If, then, consumers' behavior differs according to the nature of the rise in income, it is important to know whether the increase is in the quantity of goods and services available, or whether it is in terms only of money.

For this purpose, it is necessary to use "index numbers." If the general price level in a given year (say, 1965) is taken as 100, the price levels of other years can be shown as numbers larger or smaller than 100 according to their relation to average prices in 1965. For example, if all prices are one-fifth higher in 1966, that year's index number will be 120; if, by 1970, prices are one-quarter *below* the 1965 level, the index number will be 75. The year whose number is taken as 100 is called the "base year," and the rise or fall of the price level is thus shown as a percentage change from the level in the base year. Given a set of such index numbers, the money value of output over a number of years can be adjusted to show only changes in the physical quantity of goods and services produced. For example, if the Gross National Products in 1965, 1966, and 1967 were respectively $700 billion, $756 billion, and $851 billion, and if the index numbers of prices in the three years were 100, 105, and 115, all that is necessary is to divide each year's GNP by the year's index number and then multiply by 100. This will change "GNP at current prices" into "GNP at 1965 prices," with the results shown below:

Year	Index of Prices	Gross National Product, $ billion	
		at current prices	at 1965 prices
1965	100	700	700
1966	105	756	720
1967	115	851	740

In place of a series of GNP figures in which changes in prices are mixed up with changes in the quantities of commodities produced, there is now (in the last column of the table) a series showing how much GNP would have been if prices had remained unchanged — GNP "at constant prices." The procedure by which price changes are eliminated is called "deflating" in this case, because prices were rising as the years passed; had prices been falling, it would have been necessary to "inflate for price changes."

This procedure, of course, assumes that a suitable set of price index numbers is already at hand, and that these numbers can be accepted as an authentic representation of movements in the general price level. Unfortunately, no index of this kind is free of ambiguity.[16] To measure the "general level" of prices, some sort of averaging is necessary; for example, if there are only three commodities, A, B, and C, whose prices have risen 10%, 20%, and 30%, respectively since last year, it would be simple to average these percentages and say that the general price level has risen 20%. Taking last year's prices as 100, this year's index will then be 120. However, this will be clearly unsatisfactory if the commodities are not equally important objects of expenditure; if they happen to be, say, bread, meat, and salt, it would be absurd to give the price of salt the same weight as the prices of meat and bread — but that is what a simple average does. Obviously, it is necessary to make an adjustment. If half of total expenditure is on commodity A, two-fifths on B and only one-tenth on C, their price increases can be weighted according to the number of tenths of expenditure made on each of them. This means multiplying A's

---

[16] Table 1.2 in *Survey of Current Business* (July, 1968) shows GNP in constant (1958) dollars for the years 1964–67. Table 8.1 gives "implicit price deflators" (with 1958 as the base year) for 1964–67. The fact that prices of consumers' durables are shown as having remained very nearly constant between 1964 and 1967, while those of consumers' services rose by about 9% and those of producers' durable equipment by over 6%, suggests the difficulty of indicating changes in the "general level" of prices.

10% increase by 5, *B*'s 20% by 4, and *C*'s 30% by 1, adding the results together and dividing by 10. The "average" price increase now appears to be 16% – a good deal less than the 20% found earlier.

Here, however, a fundamental difficulty may arise; this year's pattern of expenditure may not be the same as last year's. Suppose that this year the fractions of total expenditure allotted to *A*, *B* and *C* are one-fifth, two-fifths, and two-fifths respectively; this implies weights of 2, 4 and 4 instead of last year's 5, 4 and 1. Applying this year's weights gives 22% as the rise in the general price level (*i.e.*, 10% × 2, *plus* 20% × 4, *plus* 30% × 4, the whole divided by 10), giving a price index of 122 instead of the 116 found previously by using last year's weights. If last year's National Product was $800 billion and if this year's is $960 billion at current prices, deflating by the "last-year's-weights" price index of 116 will make National Product appear to have risen by about $27.6 billion "at constant prices"; deflating by the "this-year's-weights" index of 122 will make it seem to have *fallen* by $13.1 billion. The two methods of weighting thus lead to very different results, yet there is no reason to prefer either as being more "correct" or "valid" than the other; nor is there any logical superiority in a compromise that splits the difference between them.[17]

This index number problem is not a mere matter of the incompatibility of different statistical methods; an issue of economic significance is involved. The way in which spenders choose to spend their money is assumed to provide some indication of the satisfaction they obtain (or at least expect) from the commodities they buy. Production, it will be remembered, is essentially the satisfying of wants, not the making of physical objects; the measurement of National Product involves the assumption that spenders preferred the pattern of outlays they actually made in a given period to any other they could have chosen at that time, given the purchasing power at their disposal. But as time goes by, tastes are liable to change; when this happens, the same collection of commodities will not give the same satisfaction as before – whether less or more depends on the way in which preferences have altered. Consequently, a given proportionate change in the quantities of goods and services received cannot be assumed to represent an equivalent change in the satisfaction of wants; the "base year" quantities may now have a different sig-

---

[17] The above account of the matter is extremely crude; for a full-length explanation of index numbers, see Croxton, Cowden and Klein, *Applied General Statistics*, 3d ed. (Englewood Cliffs, N.J.: Prentice-Hall, 1967), Chaps. 17 and 18.

nificance in terms of the satisfaction they afford. Because it is not possible to measure and compare degrees of satisfaction, estimates of changes in the "real" National Product have to be made in terms of commodities, and so they inevitably involve logical difficulties of this sort.[18] In subsequent chapters the word "real" will be used to mean that the magnitude to which it is applied has been "deflated" (or, where necessary, "inflated") by the use of some appropriate price index; but it should be borne in mind that such procedures impart a certain haziness and ambiguity to the "real" quantities involved.

Finally, a third aspect of macroeconomic equilibrium must be investigated before the relations between income and aggregate demand are explored. This aspect is employment. Whatever the level of National Product, some particular number of man-hours must be worked in order to produce it; if unemployment exists, it may be because aggregate demand calls for a National Product too low to require the employment of all the workers who would be willing to provide their services, and official policies aimed at reducing or preventing unemployment must seek to do so by influencing the level of aggregate demand. The connection between National Product and employment is thus of great importance, and the following chapter will be devoted to examining it.

---

[18] It was the consideration of these difficulties that led Keynes to work in terms of "wage units"; see the *General Theory*, Chap. 4, esp. pp. 40–41.

CHAPTER 4
The Level of Employment

1. The Relationship Between Output and Employment

To increase the flow of goods and services that make up the National Product, more labor and capital equipment must be brought into use, or else existing resources must be employed more efficiently through improvements in the methods of production. But improved methods are the result partly of chance discoveries and partly of sustained applied research, which takes time to carry out and whose outcome cannot be guaranteed in advance; even when better methods have been devised, time will still be needed for the modification of processes at "shop-floor" level, for getting workers used to the new methods, and for consulting labor unions about changes in working conditions. If it is necessary to increase output quickly, changes in production techniques cannot be counted on to help very much; over a short period of time, they must be accepted as temporarily fixed.[1] Higher output can then come only as a result of larger inputs of the factors of production — more labor, more capital equipment, or a combination of both.

But, considering the economy as a whole, an increase in the quantity of capital equipment will also take time. An individual firm may be able to obtain plant quickly by buying existing machinery from someone else; but this merely redistributes equipment between owners — it does not increase the total amount at the nation's disposal. That can be done only by constructing additional plant. Machines must be produced, buildings must be erected to house them, sources of power must be installed, and provision must be made for various ancillary services. A rough estimate suggests that the productive capacity of the United States can be increased by 2 to 4% a year [2] through fixed capital formation: if, then, it

---

[1] In practice, improvements in methods and investment in new equipment tend to go together; the separation made here is a logical distinction only. But if, as often happens, the introduction of new methods must wait for the installation of a new type of machine, this is another reason for regarding methods as unchangeable in the short run.

[2] *Survey of Current Business* (December, 1967) gives estimates of the stock of fixed business capital (*i.e.*, producers' durable equipment and nonresidential structures) for 1925–1966. The figures are in constant 1958 dollars and are presented both gross and net of depreciation. The estimated gross stock of fixed business capital in 1966 was approximately $800 billion, and over the decade 1956–1966 the average annual rate of increase in the capital stock was 3.3%; for industrial equipment, the rate was 3.8%.

should be necessary to raise output by 10% in three months, very little help could be expected from the additions to capital equipment made in that time. Like the methods of production that are in use, the stock of fixed capital must be assumed to be practically constant over a short period.

This leaves labor as the only input that can be rapidly increased. To raise production quickly, more workers can be employed, or those already at work can be asked to work longer hours, or both. Conversely, if output is to be reduced, the number of man-hours worked can be cut down at very short notice by dismissing some workers altogether and putting others on a part-time basis. Thus, within the short period during which capital equipment and productive techniques are virtually unalterable, changes in output will be associated exclusively with changes in employment. The number of man-hours worked will be uniquely related to the quantity of goods and services produced.

The objection may be made, however, that labor and capital are not being treated here in comparable fashion: if the input of labor can be varied by the working of more or fewer man-hours, cannot the input of the *services* of capital equipment be similarly altered by the use of more or fewer machine-hours? Fixed capital has been regarded as a stock of productive capacity; if labor were dealt with on the same basis, it would appear as a stock of "labor power" rather than as a flow of services. Just as the extent of employment of the country's total labor power is measured by the number of man-hours worked, so also the stock of capital could be regarded as being used less or more intensively according to the number of machine-hours involved. Closing down a factory is, therefore, analogous to the unemployment of labor; working machines harder (for example, through the introduction of multiple shifts that permit machinery to be used round the clock) is analogous to the labor force's working overtime. On this view, production does not vary uniquely with the input of labor, but with man-hours and machine-hours taken together. A given increase in the employment of labor, without any increase in the quantity of equipment in use, will obviously add less to output than it would if each newly employed worker could be provided with capital equipment that had previously lain idle.

This argument is not unreasonable; nonetheless, it need not invalidate the original conclusion that, in the short run, the volume of output depends entirely on the input of labor. The enterprises whose managers decide the quantities to be produced are also the owners of the nation's capital equipment; whether they make full use of it or not, their plant remains in their possession and they must meet the various costs involved in its upkeep. They are not, however, the owners of the labor power they employ; they can hire as much or as little as they choose within the limits of what is available. And however many man-hours the workers themselves wish to work, it is still their employers who decide how much use shall be made of their capacity to produce. Neither the owners of capital equipment nor the owners of labor power have any reason to want their resources to remain unused; but since it is the owners of the fixed capital who are in control of production, it can be expected that they will work their plant as fully as possible even when they have decided on a low level of output, by employing relatively little labor and spreading it thinly over all the available equipment. In such a situation, output per worker may be fairly low because the amount of labor is too small to take the best advantage of the plant and machinery available; if more man-hours are worked, output will increase in a greater proportion because equipment is now being used on a scale nearer to that for which it was designed. Finally, if still more labor input is employed, the plant will be working above its capacity, and output, though still increasing, will not rise in proportion to the increase in man-hours; in the end, there may come a point at which further labor will add nothing to output at all.

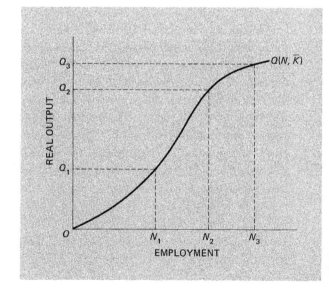

Fig. 4.1

The aggregate production function given a fixed capital stock

This sequence exemplifies the "law of variable proportions," according to which successive equal additions of one factor of production (in this case labor) to fixed quantities of other factors (capital and natural resources) will bring first increasing, then constant, then diminishing, and finally zero marginal returns. A situation in which the technical relationship between labor and equipment is very rigid (for example, where each machine requires exactly one operator) merely presents a special case of the general "variable proportions" principle; instead of a smooth transition from increasing to diminishing marginal returns, there will be constant returns falling immediately to zero returns when all machines are in use. Even though it is technically impossible, in such cases, to bring all capital equipment into action when the employment of labor is low, the equipment can still be regarded as a fixed factor of production; it is not necessary to invoke the concept of "machine-hours" to treat the input of capital as variable. The technical restrictions imposed by the nature of the capital equipment influence the relationship between labor input and commodity output, but they do not make it necessary to invoke a second relationship, *i.e.*, between capital and output, alongside the first.

For the economy as a whole, then, employment determines output in the short period within which capital equipment and methods of production can be assumed not to change to any significant degree; the greater the input of labor, the greater the quantity of goods and services produced. This characteristic of the economy can be summarized in symbolic terms by means of an aggregate "production function":

$$Q = Q(N, \bar{K})$$

where the Q on the left-hand side is aggregate output, N is the number of man-hours worked, and $\bar{K}$ is the capital stock (a "bar" above the symbol indicates that K is considered constant), while the Q on the right-hand side stands for the relationship between them.[3]

---

[3] Most readers will have encountered the word "function" before, but it may be convenient to have a rough definition. Where a quantity y varies with another quantity x in some definite way, y is said to be a function of x, and the relationship can be represented symbolically as $y = y(x)$. In the production function shown above, N is the independent variable and Q is the dependent variable that is "determined" by N according to the functional relationship, $Q(\ldots)$.

In Chapter 2 (p. 39) the symbol Q was defined as the gross output in physical units; the total value of output was defined as pQ, where p is the price level. In this chapter prices are considered fixed (*i.e.*, $p = \bar{p}$), and in order to simplify notation the $\bar{p}$ is dropped and the symbol Q is used to denote gross product measured in constant dollars.

The law of variable proportions suggests that the relationship will be something like that shown by the line $Q(N, \bar{K})$ in Figure 4.1. At a fairly low level of employment, such as N_1 man-hours, output is low at Q_1, and output per man-hour is Q_1/N_1; as employment increases to N_2, output rises to Q_2, and the proportionate increase in output is obviously greater than the proportionate increase in employment (*i.e.*, $Q_1Q_2/0Q_1$ is greater than $N_1N_2/0N_1$). When N_2 man-hours are worked, output per man-hour is Q_2/N_2, and this clearly exceeds Q_1/N_1. When employment increases still further to N_3 man-hours, output rises to Q_3, but this represents a *smaller* proportionate increase than that in the number of man-hours — $Q_2Q_3/0Q_2$ is smaller than $N_2N_3/0N_2$. Meanwhile output per man-hour has fallen to Q_3/N_3 (which can be seen to be smaller than Q_2/N_2). The leveling out of the curve $Q(N, \bar{K})$ as it moves to the right-hand side of the graph suggests that further man-hours will increase output, but by smaller and smaller amounts. Because the amount of capital equipment is fixed, only one level of employment will bring labor and equipment into their most productive relationship (*i.e.*, where output per man-hour is at its maximum); this level is at N_2. Where employment is lower than N_2, the number of man-hours is too small to make the best use of the available plant; where more than N_2 man-hours are worked, the plant becomes inadequate in relation to the labor being used.

It should be noted that these different employment-output situations are not to be thought of as succeeding one another over a period of time, but rather as a set of alternative possibilities, all of which are present at a given moment of time. The economy *could* use N_1 man-hours, and if it did, output would be Q_1; or it could employ N_3 man-hours and get Q_3 as its output. These alternatives, and all the others shown by the line $Q(N, \bar{K})$, are available only during the short period in which capital and productive methods do not change significantly. The curve $Q(N, \bar{K})$ does not trace out a path of development occurring over time, but merely shows the amount of labor required to produce each possible level of output.

If the time perspective were lengthened beyond the short period, it would be necessary to take account of possible changes in the economy's stock of capital equipment and in its methods of production. This would give rise to a whole family of curves, as shown in Figure 4.2. Each curve shows the employment-output relationship for a given stock of capital used according to given techniques. As the stock of capital grows and methods of production improve, a given quantity of labor becomes capable of producing more and more output; a given level of output requires less and less labor. The greater the amount of equipment and the better the methods of production, the higher the curve; $Q(N, \bar{K}_2)$ shows output produced by labor that has more plant to work with than is assumed in $Q(N, \bar{K}_1)$; $Q(N, \bar{K}_3)$ implies still more equipment than $Q(N, \bar{K}_2)$, and so on. If the stock of capital were assumed always to grow and never to diminish, and if techniques were assumed always to improve, $Q(N, \bar{K})$ would then move up the diagram; in this case, the time factor would be important, since each curve relates to a different point in time. A capital stock of K_2 refers to a later date than one of K_1; K_3 to a later date than K_2, and so on. The actual length of time taken to get from one position of the curve to another must depend on the rate at which the nation's capital equipment is being increased and the speed with which its techniques are being improved. This will be an important consideration when the long-period growth of the economy comes to be investigated.

Meanwhile, the short-period employment-output relationship presents another feature that must be noticed. In Figure 4.1, the vertical axis does not measure numbers of physical units of a single commodity, but "output" in the National Product sense; the man-hours shown on the horizontal axis are assumed to be the labor input of *all* industries, and the output

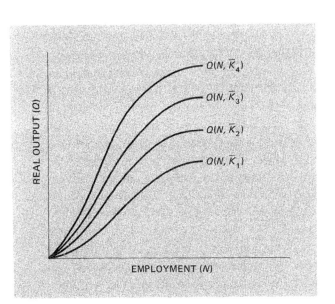

Fig. 4.2

The aggregate production function with changes in the capital stock and in methods of production

is therefore a mixture of many different goods and services, added together in terms of their money values and adjusted for changes in the general price level so that the total is given in "constant dollars." This particular mixture, however, is only one of many possible combinations of commodities that could have been produced with the same number of man-hours. If labor had been differently distributed among industries, total output might have contained more armchairs and fewer automobiles, more beef and less wheat, and so on; had some other combination of products been produced, its total value (in constant dollars) would not necessarily have been the same as that of the combination shown. In a given situation it may happen that the strength of demand for certain commodities causes many man-hours to be allocated to their production, even though output per man-hour is not particularly high. If the pattern of demand shifts so as to encourage the transfer of labor to the production of commodities for which output per man-hour is higher, the increase in the value of production for the second group of commodities may exceed the reduction for the first group, and aggregate output will then be greater even though exactly the same number of man-hours are being worked as before. Thus in Figure 4.1, Q_2 is not the only possible level of output that can be produced by N_2 man-hours, even under the "static" conditions of unchanging capital and techniques; a different pattern of preferences, giving a different distribution of demand among the various commodities, could cause the output from N_2 man-hours to be either larger or smaller than Q_2.

Similar considerations apply to *changes* in the volume of employment within the short period. In Figure 4.1, N_2N_3 extra man-hours give rise to an increase in output of Q_2Q_3. But Q_2Q_3 is a conglomeration of many different goods and services, the demand for which determines the quantities produced. If the commodities most in demand happen to be those whose production has reached the stage of sharply diminishing returns, the rise in aggregate output (Q_2Q_3) is likely to be less than it would be if the main weight of demand called for further output of commodities whose producers were still operating under increasing or constant returns. The increase in aggregate output, therefore, depends not only on the additional man-hours worked, but also on the distribution of demand among the commodities produced by those man-hours. Both the height and shape of the curve $Q(N, \bar{K})$ in Figure 4.1 are affected by the pattern of demand; different patterns give different curves. This means that any particular curve, like $Q(N, \bar{K})$, is drawn on the assumption of a given —

and, for the time being, unchanging – distribution of demand among commodities.

The assumption that the pattern of demand does not change in the short period during which the capital stock and methods of production are also fixed does not seem to be unrealistic; over a longer period, however, it is unlikely to hold true. This means that the employment-output relationship will change over time, not only as a result of investment and improved techniques as shown in Figure 4.2, but also because of changes in demand. As the curve $Q(N, \bar{K})$ in Figure 4.2 moves higher and higher, some part of its movement may be due to alterations in the allocation of demand among commodities – an influence that may cause $Q(N, \bar{K})$ to move either faster or slower, further or less far, than it would have if its movement had depended only on additions to the stock of capital equipment and on changes in technique. For present purposes, however, these dynamic possibilities will be left unexplored and attention directed back to the short period in which, by assumption, only one employment-output curve – such as $Q(N, \bar{K})$ in Figure 4.1 – can exist.

Given this static relationship, the actual level of employment will be determined by the strength of aggregate demand and the efforts of enterprises to meet that demand. At any particular time, the forces described in the previous chapter will be interacting in such a way as to cause a certain volume of goods and services to be produced: this need not be "equilibrium output" in the sense that it exactly satisfies demand, but it will tend to approach the equilibrium level as enterprises make efforts to adjust their production to meet the desires of their customers. The actual level of employment will then be the number of man-hours required to produce this volume of output. If aggregate demand falls, so that enterprises find their production is more than enough to meet demand (including, of course, their own demand for increased inventories), they will attempt to reduce output by an appropriate amount and will therefore employ fewer man-hours. If demand increases, more employment will be offered so that output can be stepped up.

However, the level of demand may be so high that it is not possible to raise production sufficiently to meet it, because of the physical limits on the employment of labor. There must be some number of man-hours that represent the maximum possible effort of the economy's labor power – when every individual, young or old, male or female, rich or poor, is working every minute not required for eating and sleeping, the limit will have been reached, and the number of man-hours available in such circumstances will be "maximum employment." Given the employment-output relationship, there will be some level of output that corresponds to maximum employment; it is the utmost of which the economy is technically capable in the short period. On the other hand, there is no such obvious physical limit to aggregate demand; spenders may be prepared to buy a much larger quantity of commodities if they could be supplied, and in that case the economy could not attain an equilibrium of aggregate demand and supply.

Maximum employment, however, merely sets a *technical* upper limit to the input of labor; it is hard to imagine a situation in which the community would be willing to work so hard. The desire for leisure is strong enough to make workers wish to limit the working day and cease work altogether on weekends and holidays. The community as a whole insists on keeping children out of the labor force by means of compulsory school attendance laws, which are designed to insure that children receive a certain minimum number of years of formal education. Elderly people expect — and are expected — to retire from employment after a certain age. In a community where people are free to work as much or as little as they choose, and where most labor is sought and offered for wages in a market, a man who is well paid may feel he can afford more than the usual amount of leisure; a man who is rich may decide to do no work at all; a husband with ample earnings may insist that his wife and daughters not take employment even though the housework is not enough to occupy them fully.

In almost any conceivable circumstances, even when everyone is working as many hours as he wishes, the amount of work done will fall far short of "maximum employment." The practical limit on the input of labor, in fact, is determined by people's desire for lesiure as well as by their capacity for work: this limit is "full employment," which may be roughly defined as the number of man-hours that are worked when everyone is enjoying as much leisure as he wishes, and no more, given the prevailing cost of leisure in terms of real wages forgone.

2. Demand and Supply in the Labor Market

If all units of labor were exactly alike, if workers were highly mobile between places and occupations, and if there were perfect competition in the buying and selling of labor, it would be possible to define full employment as the number of man-hours at which there is equilibrium between demand and supply in the labor market. On these assumptions, the supply of labor at any given real wage rate would depend on its marginal disutility. Work entails fatigue, boredom, and the loss of leisure, and the oppressiveness of these things increases more than proportionately to the number of hours worked; a man working a thirty-hour week will find an extra hour of work less onerous than he would if he were already working sixty hours. To persuade workers to supply a given number of man-hours, the wage rate must be high enough (in terms of the goods and services it will buy [4]) to compensate for the disadvantages to workers of the "marginal man-hours" — the additional labor that brings the total hours worked up to the given number. If still more man-hours were required, the wage rate would have to be raised to offset the greater disutility of the extra labor; if fewer hours were wanted, the wage could be reduced, since marginal disutility would be less for a smaller number of man-hours.

Workers' views as to the disadvantages of labor are likely to be modified, however, by the fact that wages are normally their only source of income; a reduction in the hourly wage will cause total earnings to fall unless hours are proportionately increased. The prospect of lower earnings will no doubt diminish the attractions of leisure, and workers may therefore respond to a cut in wage rates by offering *more* labor, not less. Similarly, a rise in the wage rate gives workers the opportunity to enjoy more leisure in which to spend their extra income. This "income effect," then, may make the supply of labor vary *inversely* with the wage rate, even though the "marginal disutility" considerations mentioned earlier would by themselves cause the supply to vary *directly* with the wage rate. Because of this, it is not possible to attribute any characteristic shape to the supply curve of labor; on balance, the number of man-

---

[4] This assumes that wage earners have no "money illusion," or in other words, they are influenced not by the "nominal" wage rate (*i.e.*, the number of dollars and cents per hour) offered them, but by its purchasing power in terms of commodities. However, changes in the purchasing power of money due to movements in the general price level are hard to assess (as was shown in the section on index numbers at the end of Chapter 3), while the nominal wage rate, by contrast, is a precise and unambiguous quantity. It is natural that workers should pay more attention to the latter than to the former, so that they sometimes ignore relatively small movements in the general price level. It may, at times, seem that "money illusion" is present, even though wage earners are well aware that rising prices may erode their "real" earnings.

hours that workers are willing to work may either rise or fall when a higher wage rate is offered.[5]

The demand for labor is usually said to depend on its marginal productivity (though, as will be seen presently, this is subject to an important qualification). If, at a given level of production, additional labor would increase output by more than the real wages that would be paid in exchange for it, firms will find it profitable to increase employment. As more man-hours are used, diminishing returns will cause the successive additions to total output (*i.e.*, the marginal product of labor) to become smaller and smaller, since the additional labor is not accompanied by any increase in the quantities of other factors of production. When the level of employment has risen to the point at which the marginal product no longer exceeds the real wage, firms have no further incentive to increase the input of labor.

At a given real wage, then, the most profitable level of employment from the point of view of the enterprises hiring the labor is the number of man-hours at which labor's marginal product equals the wage rate.[6] Because the marginal product falls as more labor is employed, the quantity of labor demanded will be greater, the lower the wage rate; where the amount demanded is equal to the amount supplied, the market will be in equilibrium. Since the supply depends on the marginal disutility (conditioned, as has been seen, by the income effect), the equilibrium wage rate will be equal both to the marginal product of labor and to the marginal disutility of labor.

The argument is illustrated in Figure 4.3. The demand curve for labor, $N_d(W)$, shows the amount of the marginal product at different levels of

---

[5] In symbols, this can be expressed as

$$N_s = N_s(W)$$

where N_s represents the supply of labor in terms of man-hours, W is the hourly wage rate in real terms (it could also be written w/p, *i.e.*, the money wage rate w divided by the general price level p), and $N_s(W)$ indicates that N_s is a function of the real wage rate W.

[6] In symbols, the condition for profit maximization is

$$\frac{w}{p} = \frac{dQ}{dN}$$

where w/p is the real wage (W), and the right-hand term represents the rate at which output is changing in response to the input of labor, *i.e.*, the marginal product of labor. If this condition is maintained, the demand for labor may be stated as a function of the real wage: $N_d = N_d(W)$.

employment. The supply curve, $N_s(W)$, shows the value set by workers on the marginal disutility of labor at each level of employment. The intersection shows the equilibrium of demand and supply, where N_2 man-hours are worked at an hourly real wage rate of W_2. The demand curve can occupy only the single position $N_d(W)$ as long as the short-run assumptions of unchanging capital stock, given techniques, and a fixed demand pattern are valid. The marginal product of labor is given by the slope of the curve $Q(N, \bar{K})$ in Figure 4.1 (since movement along a straight line tangent to $Q(N, \bar{K})$ at any point approximates the addition to total output that would be caused by the working of an extra man-hour), and as long as $Q(N, \bar{K})$ is fixed in position, the curve $N_d(W)$ in Figure 4.3 must also be fixed. The supply curve $N_s(W)$ will also be fixed in position as long as workers' preferences between earnings and leisure remain unchanged. If the income effect were very strong, it would make the supply curve downwards from left to right, so that it could conceivably occupy the same position as the demand curve; in that case, *every* level of employment would be an equilibrium level. Another possibility is that $N_s(W)$ might be parallel with $N_d(W)$; if that were so, no equi-

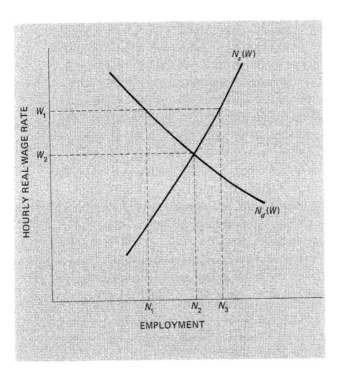

Fig. 4.3

Demand and supply in the labor market

librium would be possible at *any* level of employment. Apart from such extreme cases, however, it appears that there will normally be only one position of equilibrium, which will be that of full employment; at wage levels lower than W_2, there will be "over-full" employment in the sense that demand will be in excess of supply; at wage rates higher than W_2, unemployment will exist in the sense that the supply of labor will exceed the demand for it.

The picture of the labor market presented in Figure 4.3 may, however, be misleading in a number of ways. The first problem concerns the interpretation of the $N_d(W)$ curve, which has so far been referred to as "the demand curve for labor." In the typical market of *micro*analysis, the demand curve normally indicates a straightforward causal relationship between price and quantity demanded; to increase or diminish the amount of a commodity people wish to buy, it is sufficient to lower or raise the price. But the curve $N_d(W)$ in Figure 4.3 cannot be read in this sense. For the demand for labor to be N_1, it is not enough that the real wage should be W_1; another condition must be fulfilled as well. With a fixed stock of capital equipment and with given methods of production, there will be a unique relationship between the input of labor and the output of commodities, so that each level of employment is associated with a particular level of production, as shown by the $Q(N, \bar{K})$ curve in Figure 4.1. In deciding whether or not to employ a given number of man-hours, firms will have to consider whether or not they can *sell* the resulting output. If they produce the exact quantity needed to satisfy demand (that is, if they are not prepared to accumulate inventory by producing more than they can sell nor to run down existing inventories in the opposite case), their labor requirements will depend on what the volume of aggregate demand for their output happens to be; in symbols, $N_d = nD$ where D is the aggregate demand for commodities, N_d is the demand for labor, and n is the number of man-hours needed to produce a unit of output.[7] It follows that, for N_1 units of labor to be demanded, it is necessary for aggregate demand to be exactly enough to absorb the output they produce, and for the hourly real wage to be W_1.

If both these conditions are not satisfied simultaneously — for example, if the real wage happens to be W_2 when aggregate demand calls for the output of only N_1 man-hours — the implication is that supply is not

---

[7] The value of n (the inverse of the *average* product of labor) will, of course, be likely to vary with the level of output, as explained on pp. 69–70 above.

matched by demand in the market for commodities. Aggregate supply is the volume of output that firms would *like* to sell because it is the most profitable; since profit is maximized when the marginal product of labor equals the real wage, the most profitable output when the real wage is W_2 is one that requires the employment of N_2 man-hours. But if aggregate demand is satisfied by the commodities produced by only N_1 man-hours, there will be an excess of supply over demand[8] equal to the output of $N_2 - N_1$. To eliminate this excess supply, the real wage and/or the level of aggregate demand must change until they are consistent with one another. Equilibrium can exist in the market for commodities only when the real wage is equal to the marginal product of labor at the level of employment needed to satisfy aggregate demand; the $N_d(W)$ curve in Figure 4.3 merely expresses this equilibrium condition.[9]

The second problem in the interpretation of Figure 4.3 concerns the results of disequilibrium between the demand and supply of labor at a given real wage. Suppose, for example, that the aggregate demand and supply of commodities are balanced at a level of output that requires the employment of N_1 man-hours at a real wage of W_1. However, the supply of labor is N_3, so that there is unemployment of $N_3 - N_1$ man-hours. In the market for a single commodity, such a situation would cause the commodity's price to be forced down to the equilibrium level; sellers would underbid one another in the effort to sell more, the price reductions would elicit more demand, and the process would continue until supply and demand were balanced. It might seem reasonable to expect similar competitive forces to operate in the labor market, reducing the real wage from W_1 to W_2 and bringing about full employment at N_2 man-hours; but this

---

[8] This does not necessarily mean that firms will actually be producing the output that requires N_2 man-hours: they may, in fact, restrict output to the quantity they can sell, employing only N_1. But at a real wage of W_2, they will certainly *wish* that the demand for commodities would allow them to produce and sell the ouptut of N_2. To say that supply exceeds demand merely means that sellers *wish* to sell more than buyers are prepared to buy, whatever the *actual* level of production happens to be.

[9] Because the $N_d(W)$ curve cannot be interpreted as showing that the demand for labor is determined solely by the level of real wages, some writers have urged that it is inappropriate and misleading to call it "the demand curve for labor" and prefer to call it merely "the marginal-product-of-labor curve." See P. Davidson and E. Smolensky, *Aggregate Supply and Demand Analysis* (New York: Harper & Row, 1964), pp. 175–177; and E. J. Mishan, "The Demand for Labor in a Classical and Keynesian Framework," *Journal of Political Economy*, Vol. 72 (December, 1964), pp. 610–616.

assumption would be a mistake, since it does not take full account of the significance of the $N_d(W)$ curve. A fall in the real wage will certainly mean that firms will wish to employ more labor and thus supply a larger quantity of commodities; however, unless the aggregate demand for commodities increases in step with supply, an expansion of output will merely result in an excess of supply over demand in the market for commodities, as a result of which the real wage is likely to be forced up again.[10]

But there is no obvious reason why aggregate demand *should* increase by precisely the amount needed to maintain equilibrium. It is true that if firms expand output and employment to the level consistent with profit maximization at W_2, incomes will rise by an amount equal to the additional output; but to keep aggregate demand equal to aggregate supply, the community would have to be willing to spend *all* of its additional income, however large that happened to be. In the previous chapter,[11] a hypothetical example was given in which aggregate demand rose by only seven-tenths of any increase in income; if spenders were to behave in a similar way in the present case, it would not be possible to achieve a new equilibrium at the full-employment level of N_2 man-hours, because there would be excess supply in the market for commodities. Further consideration of this question must be postponed until after the investigation of the relationships between income and aggregate demand made in the next few chapters; for the time being, it must be noted that it is not possible for a disequilibrium in the labor market to be corrected without an appropriate change in the market for commodities.

It has been assumed here that the existence of unemployment in a competitive labor market will normally exert downward pressure on the real wage. But it must be remembered that workers and employers bargain in terms of *money* wages (w), whereas the *real* wage (W) is the money wage divided by the general price level of commodities (*i.e.*, $W = w/p$). Excess supply in the labor market will cause w to fall; if prices remain unchanged, there will be an equivalent reduction in W. However, if firms respond to this by expanding output and employment to the point where W once again equals the marginal product of labor, and if the aggregate demand for commodities has not increased sufficiently to absorb this in-

---

[10] For example, if firms reduce their selling prices in the attempt to dispose of excess output, this will automatically raise the real wage again, since the latter is the money wage divided by the average level of prices (w/p).

[11] On pp. 52–53 above.

crease in supply, the resulting excess supply of commodities will cause the general price level to fall, thereby wholly or partially offsetting the original fall in money wages. The original pressure on money wages in the labor market will be renewed, and both commodity prices and money wages will continue to decline. An important consequence of this decline will be a reduction in the amount of money needed to effect the economy's purchases and sales, both in the labor market and in the market for commodities; if the amount of money in existence is not reduced, there will now be an imbalance between the supply of money and the demand for it. The effects of this imbalance may alter the situation in the market for commodities — for example, by making it easier to borrow money and thereby stimulating aggregate demand. These possibilities, however, cannot be traced in detail until the monetary side of the economy has been examined; they do, however, provide yet another indication that the working of the labor market cannot be considered in isolation from the rest of the economy.

It was assumed earlier that the employment-output relationship was of the kind represented by the curve $Q(N, \bar{K})$ in Figure 4.1, which holds true only during the short period within which the stock of capital and the technique of production can be taken as fixed. As time passes, techniques will improve and capital will increase, so that any given level of employment will produce a larger and larger volume of commodities; the employment-output relationship will be changing in the way illustrated by the upward shifting curves in Figure 4.2. If employment is not to fall as productivity increases, aggregate demand must grow enough to absorb the increasing output; in addition, the real wage may have to change so as to remain equal to the marginal product of labor.

How much the marginal product of labor itself will change depends on precisely what is happening to the employment-output relationship. The position and shape of the $N_d(W)$ curve in Figure 4.3 are determined not by the height of $Q(N, \bar{K})$ in Figure 4.1, but by its shape; the marginal product, which in Figure 4.3 is measured by the *height* of $N_d(W)$ at any given level of employment, is indicated in Figure 4.1 by the *slope* of $Q(N, \bar{K})$ above the corresponding point on the employment axis. If $Q(N, \bar{K})$ shifts upward in such a way that its slope is unaltered along most of its length, the corresponding section of $N_d(W)$ in Figure 4.3 will remain completely unchanged; although the average product of labor will have risen, the marginal product will be the same as before, so that the employment of, say, N_1 man-hours will still be consistent with a real wage of W_1. On the other hand, if $Q(N, \bar{K})$ rises in such a way that it becomes steeper at every level of employment, the $N_d(W)$ curve will also rise, and the real wage appropriate to any given number of man-hours will increase.

If the supply curve of labor retains the position and shape of the $N_s(W)$ curve in Figure 4.3, the upward-shifting $N_d(W)$ curve will intersect it further and further to the right. To maintain full employment, the aggregate demand for commodities must grow faster than the productivity of labor increases, so that the demand for labor will remain equal to the number of man-hours indicated by the rightward-moving intersection of $N_s(W)$ and $N_d(W)$. However, it has already been argued that $N_s(W)$ may in fact slope downward from left to right because of the "income effect"; in that case, full employment can be maintained even if the demand for labor is diminishing over time. Of course, it is also likely that the $N_s(W)$ curve itself will shift as time goes by, due to population growth and to changes in workers' preferences that affect the marginal disutility of labor. The upshot of all these considerations is that the number of man-hours worked at full employment may either rise or fall as time passes, but that it is unlikely to remain constant. If it is public policy to maintain full employment, avoiding both shortages and surpluses of labor, the policymakers will find that they have to aim at a moving target.

3. Types of Unemployment

In the labor market described above, full employment appears to be (at any particular time) a precise quantity of labor that could be calculated to the nearest man-hour if sufficient information about demand and supply were available. This impression, however, is the result of the assumptions made in the first instance; though useful in simplifying and sharpening the analysis, all of them do violence to the facts in greater or lesser degree, and when they are removed the concept of full employment becomes much less clear-cut. Some of the difficulties that arise in practice can be seen from the following brief description of the way statistics of employment and unemployment are collected in the United States.

Each month, the Bureau of Labor Statistics, in cooperation with the Bureau of the Census, conducts a sample survey of more than 50,000 households; the sample is designed to cover each of the states and the

District of Columbia and to reflect the major geographic and rural-urban divisions in the country. Each civilian sixteen years of age or older who lives in one of the households surveyed is classified as either employed, unemployed, or not in the labor force. A person is classified as "employed" if he does any work *for pay* during the week in which the survey is taken or if he works fifteen hours or more in a family business. A person is "unemployed" if he is currently available for employment and has actively sought a job within the past four weeks, but does no remunerative work within the week of the survey. The total of all persons who are classified as "employed" and "unemployed" is considered to be the nation's labor force. Persons who do not work during the week of the survey and who have not actively sought work within the past four weeks are classified as "not in the labor force."

It may be noted that these definitions are different from those that underlie the model of the labor market shown in Figure 4.3; the official statistics are based on a concept of employment and unemployment that is more social than economic. Employment is measured in terms of the number of persons gainfully employed, not the number of labor hours worked; the housewife who works a few hours at a local boutique is counted the same as her husband who may be putting in forty or more hours a week building houses. Their teen-age son, if he decides to work during the summer vacation, enters the labor force in June — perhaps to join the ranks of the unemployed for a period — and then again disappears from the labor force when he returns to school in September. Furthermore, if an unemployed worker has been unable to find a job for so long that he finally gives up hope, he drops out of the labor force and off the unemployment rolls as soon as he goes four weeks without looking for a job. If, some time later, new opportunities appear, he may be induced to try again, thereby reentering the labor force.

The existence of this type of in-and-out movement means that the size of the labor force is not insensitive to the overall level of economic activity, even apart from the response of the supply of labor to the level of real wages. The supply of labor responds to the demand for it. Thus, as economic activity increases, so does the demand for labor; more jobs become available. As a result of this increased opportunity, more people enter the labor force. The formerly discouraged worker goes back to the employment bureau for another try; the housewife decides she can ease the family's budget difficulties without having to put forth too much effort in finding a suitable job. The creation of a million new jobs, therefore, will not lower unemployment by an equal amount because more workers will be attracted into the labor market by the new opportunities. In a business downturn, on the other hand, the labor force shrinks; because of layoffs or normal job turnover, individuals find the job hunting more difficult and either give up hope or decide that securing a new job just isn't worth the effort.[12]

This pool of workers who drop out of the labor force due to a perceived lack of job opportunities is often called "disguised unemployment." Such in-and-out behavior is particularly characteristic of what is termed the "secondary labor force," *i.e.*, women and teen-age males who usually take employment to supplement the earnings of the husband or father who is the primary breadwinner. The "primary labor force" — males aged 25 to 65 — is much less sensitive to swings in overall economic activity. If a man in his prime working years finds himself unemployed, he is likely to continue job hunting for a considerable length of time; the phenomenon of the "discouraged" male worker is concentrated in pockets of chronic unemployment such as are found in depressed rural areas and in urban ghettos.

The elasticity of the labor supply to the demand for it is only one of the phenomena that make the concept of "full employment" somewhat more complicated than Figure 4.3 might indicate. Next, the concept of a single labor market for the whole economy must be abandoned. In reality, workers are not perfectly mobile between places and between occupations; their labor is not homogeneous in the sense of being equally adaptable to all forms of production. It is therefore not legitimate to regard all types of labor as entering one general market. Instead, there are many separate markets, each with its own demand and supply curves; conditions in any one of them are no doubt connected with those in others, but they are nonetheless distinct because each is dealing in a different commodity. Labor in the electronics industry is clearly not the same thing as labor in coal mining; bricklayers, actors, and accountants sell their services in quite separate

---

[12] There is a reverse moment at the same time. In a downturn, additional family members may seek work in order to compensate for the declining or interrupted income of the breadwinner. This is particularly likely to be the case in low-income families, who do not have a cushion of savings to sustain them through difficult periods. Current evidence shows, however, that in the aggregate the influence of the "push" of necessity is outweighed by the "pull" of opportunity. See J. Mincer, "Labor-Force Participation and Unemployment: A Review of Recent Evidence," in R. A. Gordon and M. S. Gordon (eds.), *Prosperity and Unemployment* (New York: Wiley, 1966).

markets; the man-hours available in Seattle cannot readily be added to the supply of labor in New Orleans. Obviously, it goes against the facts to lump all workers together by ignoring the differences between their products and the difficulties of moving labor from one industry or locality to another.

But if the buying and selling of labor is regarded more realistically as taking place in a large number of separate markets, the earlier definition of full employment becomes ambiguous. It might mean that employment is full only when the demand and supply of labor are equal in each separate market. This definition, however, is severely restrictive. In the economy as it exists in real life, changes in production methods and in the demand for products are constantly altering the pattern of demand for labor, and workers are responding by moving from old industries into new ones and from one place to another. The response normally takes time, so that in each separate labor market today's demand is faced with yesterday's supply. At any particular moment, the imperfect meshing of supplies and demands will cause some unemployment to exist, so that full employment in this restricted sense can never be reached.

A second definition might be that full employment exists when the *sum* of demands in all markets equals the *sum* of supplies, even though there may be an excess of supply over demand (or demand over supply) in two or more of the separate markets for particular types of labor. If data were available on job vacancies, a comparison of the number of vacancies with the number of job-seekers would provide a rough guide to whether full employment exists or not. For the United States, however, no such vacancy statistics exist on a national level.[13]

Still a third definition of full employment might be based on the relation between a high level of employment as an objective of macroeconomic policy and other national goals, such as price stability or a healthy balance of payments situation. Employment could be said to be full at that point where attempts to reduce unemployment still further would take an unacceptable toll in terms of other objectives of national policy. It is in this last sense that the term "full employment" is normally used in the United States, and the very nature of the definition makes it the subject of considerable dispute.

Full employment, thus defined, is therefore compatible with the existence

---

[13] There have been several pilot efforts to gather such data; see the National Bureau of Economic Research volume on *The Measurement and Interpretation of Job Vacancies* (New York: Columbia University Press for the NBER, 1966).

of *some* unemployment, which is conventionally called "frictional" or "structural" to distinguish it from that which exists when employment is less than full. The latter type has been called[14] "involuntary" unemployment, on the ground that no possible effort on the part of jobless workers can find employment for all of them when the *overall* demand for labor is less than the supply. Since it arises when aggregate demand fails to match the output forthcoming if employment is full, it has also been called "demand-deficiency" unemployment.

Quite often a distinction is made between frictional and structural unemployment, although it is not easy to draw a neat division between the two. "Frictional" unemployment normally refers to that portion of the labor force which is out of work at any particular time due to the normal turnover in the job market. Over any period of time, some workers either quit or are released from their jobs, and although almost all may take up new employment, there generally is some delay in job hunting or perhaps in moving to a new location. Also, new entrants in the labor market may have to search for some time before finding a job; and some types of work — e.g., agricultural labor — are seasonal in nature, and workers may be unemployed several months of the year.

The term "structural" unemployment, on the other hand, is usually applied to workers who cannot find positions because technological change or geographical shifts in economic activity either have done away with the jobs for which they are trained or have severely cut the demand for labor in their local area. For example, when industries automate, their total demand for labor may remain roughly the same, but jobs for unskilled workers are eliminated and the new openings are for clerks, skilled technicians, and computer programmers. Firms may be actively seeking to hire additional workers, but the unskilled are no longer "in the market." Or, if the major industry of a region goes into a decline, the overall regional economy suffers, and the local demand for labor is severely reduced. In the short run, at least, there may be significant personal and economic barriers to the

---

[14] Keynes, *General Theory*, pp. 15–16. It should be noted that the "voluntary" unemployment that seems to be implied as the logical opposite of "involuntary" is not the same as "frictional" or "structural" unemployment. The term has traditionally been applied to situations where some artificial restriction keeps employment lower than the level that would be established by competitive forces — for example, where labor union action keeps wages so high that employers cannot afford to employ all who would be willing to work at those wages; or where there is an outright restriction on the number of new entrants into a given occupation.

movement of workers to other parts of the country where jobs are more plentiful.

In a sense, the difference between frictional and structural unemployment is one of severity; unemployment becomes "structural" when the friction is particularly great. If an industry with excess demand for labor can draw in workers recently dismissed from an "excess supply" industry where their functions have been fairly similar to those they will now have to perform, the transition should be easy and quick, and little unemployment will arise. If, on the other hand, the "excess demand" industry requires skills quite different from those lately practiced by the unemployed, or if it is far removed geographically from the areas where the surplus labor happens to be, the unemployment may persist long enough to be termed "structural." If the pace of economic development is such that the pattern of demand and output is constantly changing in fairly radical fashion, fresh numbers of "structurally"[15] unemployed workers will be continually replacing those who are at last finding work, and there may be a great deal of this type of unemployment.

In some countries, indeed, there is no doubt that structural unemployment is a more serious problem than demand-deficiency unemployment, because it is fed continuously by strong dynamic forces such as population increase, industrialization, and rapid technological advance. A country setting out on the path of economic growth may develop what has been called a dual economy, in which an "advanced" sector, using modern plant and techniques, coexists with a "backward" sector where productive

---

[15] Where workers are dispaced through the introduction of labor-saving machinery or as a result of new methods that raise productivity in other ways, they are sometimes said to be suffering "technological" unemployment. This term must be received with caution, because it has been given several distinct senses in past usage; it has been made to mean the following:

(a) structural unemployment of the kind discussed above: workers are no longer needed in the technically revolutionized industry, but there are vacancies elsewhere even though the workers' skills are unsuitable for them.

(b) demand-deficiency unemployment, which arises because aggregate demand fails to keep pace with rising productivity: new inventions cause $Q(N, \bar{K}_1)$ to rise to $Q(N, \bar{K}_2)$ in Figure 4.2, but demand fails to rise and unemployment ensues.

(c) unemployment that results from a "flattening" of the $Q(N, \bar{K})$ curve. If the new inventions change the shape of the employment-output relation so as to push to the left the point where diminishing returns begin, the demand curve for labor will fall. If *real* wages are "inflexible" downward (*e.g.*, because labor unions resist reductions) there will then develop some unemployment of the type that pre-Keynesian writers would have called "voluntary."

methods are still primitive and relatively little capital equipment is employed. To expand the advanced sector and reduce the backward sector may require widespread social as well as economic changes — the transformation of a peasantry into a mass of urban wage earners, the supplanting of independent crafts by factory production, and so on. If, in addition, capital equipment in the advanced sector happens to have, for technological reasons, rigid labor requirements of the "one man, one machine" sort, it will not be possible to shift surplus labor from the backward sector into the advanced sector at a rate faster than that permitted by current capital formation. As a consequence, unemployment may be massive and chronic. Under the definition given earlier, it may be entirely frictional or structural; but to say that a state of full employment exists because there is no "demand-deficiency" unemployment,[16] would seem highly anomalous — so much so, that some writers have preferred to reserve the terms "frictional" and "structural" for the relatively small margin of unemployment that it usually represents in advanced economies, and to speak of "non-Keynesian"[17] unemployment in the case just described.

Even in advanced economies, the distinction between demand-deficiency unemployment, on the one hand, and structural or frictional unemployment, on the other, is not as clear as the terms might indicate. Demand-deficiency unemployment, it will be recalled, presumably could be eradicated if the nation's level of economic activity were increased, but the pool of frictionally and structurally unemployed would not be significantly affected by such aggregate measures. But the "full-employment target" — that is, the unemployment level that can be reasonably attempted with aggregate demand policy — is (as noted above) a subject of considerable debate, with most discussion ranging between target un-

---

[16] In fact, there will probably be some of this in a "dual" economy. Its absence would imply a tremendous pressure of excess demand on the advanced sector, which, if only it had the necessary capital equipment, would offer employment to the excess labor in the backward sector. But the lack of equipment prevents the advanced sector taking on more workers, and its output cannot increase quickly in response to demand; the result may be continuous price increases in the advanced sector, giving an inflationary character to the whole economy in spite of the unemployment in the backward sector. In these circumstances, the authorities might take action to reduce aggregate demand until the advanced sector is in equilibrium; but this would imply demand deficiency in the backward sector.

[17] For example, K. Kurihara, *The Keynesian Theory of Economic Development* (New York: Columbia University Press, 1959), Chap. 6. "Keynesian" unemployment, by implication, is the "demand-deficiency" unemployment with which the *General Theory* was chiefly concerned.

employment rates from 3% to 5%. With sufficiently high aggregate demand, the bulk of those conventionally classified as structurally unemployed could be put to work. If demand and expected profits from increased output were high enough, firms would have an incentive to seek out more workers, perhaps training the unskilled and transporting those who live far from the job.

The difficulty, of course, is that labor is not homogeneous, nor is the increased demand for different types of skills necessarily matched to the supply. As aggregate demand increases, bottlenecks appear in certain skill categories and geographical areas long before all the unemployed are taken up. Where these bottlenecks appear, employers have several possible modes of adjustment. They can try to attract additional workers by offering higher wages or by stepping up recruitment efforts. In expanding the work force, employers naturally prefer to hire the more skilled and better educated prospects. But as the level of economic activity increases, skilled workers may be hard to find or may be bid away from their present jobs only at very high wages. As an alternative to seeking already skilled employees, firms can work their way down the queue of unemployed workers, taking those with less education and fewer skills and increasing in-firm expenditure on training. Or, of course, the firm can choose to operate with unfilled vacancies, perhaps putting the existing work force on overtime. In any case, the labor cost per unit of output goes up, and soon this is reflected in higher output prices. As noted above, at some point attempts to reduce unemployment by increasing aggregate demand produce an unacceptable level of price inflation; the social cost of increased inflation is deemed to be higher than the social gain of a lowered unemployment rate. The dispute over what constitutes "full employment" originates in disagreements about how much inflation would be associated with a lower unemployment rate and, more importantly, in differences of opinion about what rate of price inflation is acceptable.[18] Whatever level is chosen, public efforts can continue to be devoted to lowering "structural" barriers to the employment of those who make up the remaining pool of the unemployed. Special federal, state, and local training programs and improved systems for disseminating information about job openings are examples of this type of activity.

---

[18] For further discussion of this point, see R. G. Lipsey, "Structural and Demand-Deficient Employment Reconsidered," in A. M. Ross (ed.), *Employment Policy and the Labor Market* (Berkeley: University of California Press, 1965).

One of the major focal points of current efforts to remove "structural" barriers and reduce "friction" is the critical problem of the urban slum-dweller. It is necessary to look behind the global unemployment figures to see the special problems of this group, many of whom have been recently displaced by mechanization in agriculture. A 1966 study by the Department of Labor[19] revealed that one out of ten workers in the slums of thirteen major cities was unemployed, a rate three times the national average; of the nonwhite teen-agers, one in four was unemployed. Furthermore, close to 7% of those employed had only part-time work (the national average was then 2.3%), and one out of five persons working full time made less than $60 a week. As might be expected, the "discouraged worker" phenomenon was more pronounced among this group; a high proportion of slum residents were not in the labor force either because they were convinced they could not find jobs or because the jobs available were not attractive enough to overcome the lure of alternative sources of income as welfare and crime.

There is a complex web of "structural" reasons for this special problem — e.g., inadequate education and training, isolation from the zones where new jobs are opening up, increased health problems, poor work habits, and racial discrimination both by some employers and by certain labor unions. With a high level of economic activity, employers move further down the labor queue in search of workers; and with the relaxing of some of the "structural" barriers, Negroes and members of other disadvantaged minority groups are able to improve their position. The conditions of this part of the population should improve as a result. If, however, the demand for labor slackens, these workers tend to be among the first who drop back into the unemployment pool — a tendency enforced by the "last hired–first fired" policy followed by most employers and encouraged by representatives of organized labor, and by the fact that these workers tend to be concentrated in industries that are more sensitive to swings in economic activity.

Thus, within a few percentage points more or less in the national unemployment rate, and in efforts to deal with certain special "structural" aspects of unemployment, lie important keys to some of the nation's more pressing social problems.

To decide which kind of policy to adopt in a given situation, however, government authorities must first determine which type of unemployment

---

[19] See the *Manpower Report of the President* (April, 1967).

exists — and, as has been seen, this is not easy. Indeed, when there is significant movement in and out of the labor force, there may even be some difficulty in actually identifying unemployment as such. For example, if a country has a large peasant agriculture, workers losing their jobs in the towns may return to their ancestral farms instead of registering themselves as unemployed; their families may accept them and let them share the farm work, even though there was previously no shortage of labor; in extreme cases, they may add nothing to agricultural output. Official statistics would then show a fall in industrial production but no increase in unemployment. The same thing could occur if craftsmen, shopkeepers, and small businessmen brought unemployed relatives into their enterprises. Among the self-employed, lack of demand may leave them with little to do — but unless they actually give up their businesses and register themselves as seeking wage employment, they will not be included in the statistics of unemployment.

The importance of this "disguised" unemployment depends, of course, on the economic and social structure of the country concerned; in the United States, where the majority of the occupied population are urban wage and salary earners, it will obviously not be as great as in many less-developed countries.[20] These considerations may serve to obscure the statistical picture for governments seeking to discover the level of employment that is "full" in the sense that aggregate demand for labor is brought as close as possible to aggregate supply without causing disruptive price increases.

4. Market Imperfections and Wage Rigidity

Even this theoretical criterion of "fullness" may, however, be far from clear in a modern economy. Not only will the labor market be divided into many separate ones, separated from one another by the "frictions" described above; but the markets themselves may contain "imperfections"

---

[20] Even in a predominantly industrial, wage-earning community, however, it may take the form of a diminution in the intensity of labor: workers may find ways of reducing productivity so as not to work themselves out of their jobs. The amount of "disguised" unemployment will then equal the difference between the number of workers employed and the number who would have been needed if productivity had not been reduced.

that make it impossible to assume that the equilibrium number of man-hours bought and sold in each market must be that for which the marginal disutility of labor equals its marginal product.[21] An individual worker may be ready to put in 50 hours a week at a given hourly wage rate, but his factory may be open only 45 hours a week. Employers may be obliged, for technical reasons, to take on workers in groups of given size, so that there can be no close adjustment of marginal product to wage rate. Firms are unlikely to have precise knowledge of the marginal productivity of labor; they will, no doubt, be led by the desire for profit to seek by trial and error the point where real wage and marginal product are equal — but trial-and-error processes take time. Employers may not always be guided solely by the profit motive, but may retain certain workers on grounds of long service even though their productivity is low. Workers may be employed on a contractual basis that prevents their employers from discharging them in order to reduce labor input. Even in the same occupation, man-hours are seldom homogeneous, and instead of a simple "price of labor" in the shape of a uniform wage rate, a great many trades have complicated provisions for overtime rates, production bonuses, and the like. Above all, there is the fact that wages in many industries are not determined by the interplay of competitive forces in free markets, but by the processes of "collective bargaining" between labor unions and employers, under which the latter agree not to pay less than an agreed "standard rate" in the industry to which they belong.

Because such rates are stated in dollars and cents, they appear to be minimum *money* wages, which will fall in real terms if the general price level rises. But when this rise does happen, unions normally try to negotiate fresh agreements under which standard rates are increased to offset the rise in prices; in some industries the agreements contain "escalator clauses" that automatically raise wage rates in step with an index of prices and thereby maintain minimum rates of *real* wages in the industries concerned. Where their bargaining power is strong enough, unions may go further and attempt to raise standard rates in real terms by claiming increases that are more than enough to compensate for current price rises. If, on the other hand, the price level happens to be falling, a successful defense of the existing money wage will be enough to bring about a rise in the real wage. The choice between alternative union policies — *i.e.*, whether to seek higher real wages or merely to maintain the existing real

---

[21] See pp. 75–77 above.

wage — depends on such factors as the size of a union's membership in relation to the whole labor force in its industry and its estimate of the degree of resistance employers are likely to offer to fresh wage claims.

The implications of all this for the labor market can be seen, in highly simplified terms, in Figure 4.3. It is assumed that there are no market imperfections other than those arising from the existence of labor unions, so labor is taken to be homogeneous and perfectly mobile. The curve $N_s(W)$ represents the supply curve of labor as it would have been if there were no collective bargaining; but workers are now assumed to belong to a single large union that negotiates a standard money wage for all of them. At a given price level, this wage corresponds to the real wage rate W_1; since no labor can be hired at a lower rate, the horizontal line at W_1 now replaces the part of the $N_s(W)$ curve which lies below it. Firms can employ any number of man-hours they like, up to a maximum of N_3, at a real wage of W_1. If they want to hire more than N_3 man-hours, they will have to pay higher real wages [22] as indicated by the part of the $N_s(W)$ curve that lies above W_1. On the other hand, if they want to use fewer man-hours than N_3, they cannot take advantage of the fact shown by the part of $N_s(W)$ below W_1 that there are some workers who, rather than be unemployed, would work for a real wage lower than W_1; the existence of the labor union insures that no one can be paid less than this.

The effect of the wage-agreement, then, is to put a "floor" on the market. Firms will now find that the most profitable level of output is that which is produced with N_1 man-hours, at which the marginal product of labor is equal to the real value of the standard wage; and if this happens to be the output that satisfies the aggregate demand for commodities, the demand for labor will be N_1, and there will be unemployment of $N_3 - N_1$ man-hours. Here, however, the excess supply of labor will not be able to push down the money wage as it might be expected to do in a competitive market. It was suggested on p. 80 above that a fall in money wages could have repercussions that might change the level of aggregate demand for commodities; in the present case, none of these consequential changes can occur, since the existence of the standard rate prevents the money wage from falling in the first instance.

---

[22] This ignores the possibility that employers may have agreed among themselves not to pay *more* than the standard rate, treating the latter as a maximum wage in the same way that the union regards it as a minimum. In that case, employment could not exceed N_3 man-hours.

The fact that the standard rate is fixed in money terms means that the real wage will remain at W_1 only so long as prices do not change. An upward movement of the price level will, of course, bring about a proportionate reduction in the real wage, causing it to fall to, say, W_2; it will remain at this level unless the money wage is automatically adjusted by the operation of an "escalator clause," or until the union negotiates a new standard rate that is high enough to offset the price increase and restore the real wage to W_1. If the union always presents the necessary wage claims promptly, and if it continues to be strong enough to get them conceded quickly, the real wage W_1 will persist as the market "floor" except during temporary lapses while negotiations are in progress.[23] With a more aggressive policy, and the strength to carry it out, the union will go further and push the real wage up to levels even higher than W_1; such levels could, of course, also be reached if prices fell and the union successfully maintained the existing standard money wage.

It will be noticed in Figure 4.3 that the real wage rate W_2 is at the level of the intersection of the $N_d(W)$ and $N_s(W)$ curves. Here, the labor input that is most profitable to business firms is exactly equal to the amount of labor that workers are willing to supply; if, in addition, the aggregate demand for commodities is satisfied by the output produced by this number of man-hours, the labor market will be in equilibrium at full employment. However, reducing the standard wage in real terms to W_2 will not in itself suffice to bring about full employment if the level of aggregate commodity demand remains inadequate; in this respect, the

---

[23] If the union leaders are under "money illusion" (see p. 75 and footnote 4 above), they will regard any rise in the standard money wage as bringing an improvement in their members' livelihood and think them no worse off as long a money wages are not reduced; thus, a nonaggressive union would be content to leave the real wage at W_2 and would ignore the price increase that forced it down from the original W_1 level. However, the fact that the real wage may at times fall to W_2 before the union has been able to negotiate a higher money wage is not evidence of money illusion in the union leadership. It should be noted that if the workers (as distinct from their union leaders) harbor money illusion, the $N_s(W)$ curve will be defined with reference to *money* wages — i.e., $N_s = N_s(w)$ — and in Figure 4.3 it will shift downward when the price level rises. If the union leaders, but not the individual workers, are under money illusion, the $N_s(W)$ curve will stay put and the *standard* rate will shift down when prices rise. Keynes, writing in the depressed England of the 1930's, seemed to suggest that both workers and unions entertained money illusion (though he did not himself use the term; see the *General Theory*, pp. 14–15), but experience in the more inflationary conditions since World War II suggests that few unions, in any country, are under money illusion nowadays.

union-dominated labor market is exactly like the competitive market described earlier.

In the economy that exists in real life, wages are never so rigidly fixed as in the foregoing discussion. Instead of a single all-inclusive labor union, there are many; many workers do not belong to unions at all; and the unions that exist differ greatly in size and bargaining power. Though a few of them have a high degree of control over money wages and other conditions of work in the industries in which they operate, their influence on the average level of wages in the economy as a whole is necessarily diluted. If mass unemployment existed in all the labor markets of the economy, it is unlikely that the unions could prevent a downward movement of the overall level of money wages, but they could certainly cause the movement to take place more slowly than it would otherwise have done; in this sense, they can be said to make money wages "sticky" or "inflexible" in a downward direction.

For the purposes of the next few chapters, however, it will be convenient to assume that money wages are completely inflexible – *i.e.*, that labor unions are strong enough to prevent even the slightest reduction in them, no matter how much unemployment exists. It will also be assumed that the marginal product of labor is the same at all levels of employment, so that variations in the level of output will not cause changes in the prices at which firms are willing to sell their products.[24] The price level will, of course, rise when aggregate demand becomes so great that even full-employment output is insufficient to satisfy it; but short of that, prices will remain constant as supply is adjusted to the level of demand. These are convenient assumptions to make when the determination of aggregate demand is being investigated, but they will be relaxed at a later stage of the analysis.

----

[24] Since a competitive firm's most profitable level of output is where $w/p = $ MPL (*i.e.*, where the real wage equals the marginal product of labor), the price that will induce it to supply this output is $p = w/$MPL. If both w and MPL are constant, p will be constant also. A constant MPL means that the curve $Q(N, \bar{K})$ of Figure 4.1 is a straight line through the origin (so that labor input and the output of commodities rise in the same proportion as employment expands); the $N_d(W)$ curve of Figure 4.3 will then be a horizontal line, implying that firms are ready to produce any output, up to the full-employment level, at the level of real wages (*i.e.*, the ratio of money wages to prices) indicated by the height of the line.

CHAPTER 5

Income and Consumption

1. The Consumption Function

In Chapter 3, the short-period equilibrium of the economy was presented in terms of a balance between aggregate demand and output. Consumers, government, capital-forming enterprises, and export customers wish to spend money on goods and services; if the total amount, less the value of imports, equals the value at current market prices of the National Product, the economy is in equilibrium; if not, changes will occur in the physical quantity of output, or in the price level, or in both. To explain why the economy is in equilibrium at a given level of National Product, it is necessary to examine the various components of aggregate demand and to discover what causes them to be what they are. For reasons already indicated in Chapter 3,[1] it will be necessary to pay special attention to the level of income as a possible determinant of demand; in the case of each component, two questions must be answered. First, how important is the influence of income on demand, as compared with the strength of other forces? Second, if that influence is important, what exactly is its nature?

---

[1] See pp. 51–54.

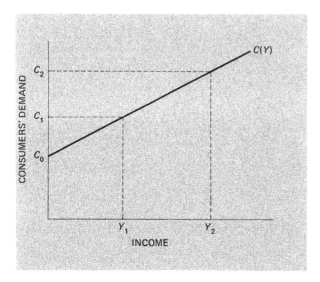

Fig. 5.1

The consumption function, expressing consumers' demand as a function of current income. Both quantities are measured at constant prices.

In the case of consumers' demand, these questions may be restated in terms of the concept of the "consumption function." This is simply a name for the general income-consumption relationship.[2] Just as a demand curve shows what quantity of a commodity will be demanded at each possible price, so the consumption function shows what expenditure consumers will wish to make on consumers' goods and services at each possible level of income. In Figure 5.1, the function is represented by the curve $C(Y)$, from which it can be seen that if income is Y_1, consumers will wish to spend C_1; if income is Y_2, they will wish to spend C_2; for all levels of income, the curve shows what consumers' demand will be. As drawn in the diagram, $C(Y)$ shows that if income is nil, consumers' expenditure is C_0 — instead of starving at zero income, they draw on past savings, borrow, sell property, and so on in order to buy consumer goods. Also, the fact that $C(Y)$ is a straight line implies that as income rises, consumers' demand increases by an amount that always is in the same proportion to the increase in income, whatever the size of the increase and whatever the original income level. Whether this is a correct representation of con-

---

[2] Keynes originally called it "the propensity to consume" (*General Theory*, p. 90), but subsequent usage has established the term "consumption function" in its place. Following the notation introduced earlier (p. 69), consumption as a function of income is expressed as $C = C(Y)$.

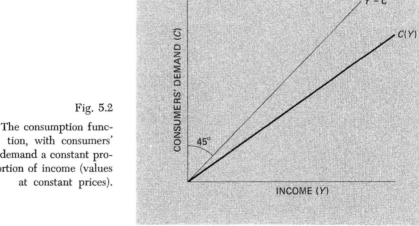

Fig. 5.2

The consumption function, with consumers' demand a constant proportion of income (values at constant prices).

sumers' preferences, however, is a question of fact about which evidence must be sought; there are many conceivable shapes that the consumption function can take.

Two further possibilities are shown in Figures 5.2 and 5.3. In Figure 5.2, $C(Y)$ is a straight line starting at the origin of the diagram, implying that consumers spend more as income rises, but always spend the same proportion of income, however large or small it may be. The broken line marked "$Y = C$" shows the position $C(Y)$ would occupy if the consumers' expenditure were always 100% of income; the fact that $C(Y)$ slopes less steeply than the broken line implies that the proportion of income consumed is always less than 100%. In Figure 5.3, a completely different pattern of behavior is shown by the curve $C(Y)$. Consumers make a minimum expenditure C_0 even when income is zero, and this level of consumption remains the same so long as income is not greater than Y_1. At higher income levels, consumption rises as income rises, but it rises by less than the increase in income; the diminishing slope of the curve beyond Y_1 implies that the proportion of income consumed falls progressively as income rises.

To ask — as did the second of the questions posed earlier — about the nature of the relationship between income and consumption is, therefore, to ask what the shape and position of the consumption function are. Whatever the answer, it will still leave in the air the first of the original ques-

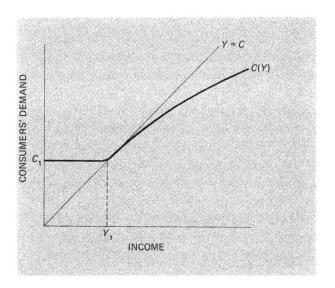

Fig. 5.3

The consumption function may take many forms, depending on individual patterns of behavior.

tions, *i.e.*, how strong is the influence of income on consumers' demand? Even if the consumption function is correctly evaluated, it does not imply that income is necessarily the main determinant; its influence may be submerged under those of other and stronger forces. Diagrams such as Figures 5.1, 5.2, and 5.3 are drawn on the assumption of *ceteris paribus* ("other things being equal"); the relationship between income and consumption is the only one considered, while every other possible influence on consumption is held constant. But if, for example, interest rates were known to be much more powerful than income in determining consumers' demand, it would be necessary to show a separate consumption curve for each possible level of interest; instead of a single curve, like $C(Y)$ in Figure 5.1, there would be a family of curves. In such a case, the "other things equal" assumption could not reasonably be made, and the consumption function would have little importance; the direct relationship between interest rates and consumption would take priority as an object of investigation. To justify the use of the consumption function, therefore, it is important to produce evidence to show that income is, if not the sole determinant of consumers' demand, at least the most important of the many factors that can be held to influence it.

2. Properties of the Function: the Marginal Propensity to Consume

So far, then, the consumption function is merely a piece of theoretical apparatus, an "empty" concept waiting to be filled with a content of fact. Before proceeding, however, it will be useful to note some further aspects of the concept as such.

(i) The relationship is normally presented in terms of *real* income and *real* consumption; the amounts measured along the axes of Figures 5.1, 5.2, and 5.3 are "at constant prices." Consumers may be expected to respond differently to a rise in income depending on whether or not it is accompanied by a rise in the price level; if a simultaneous doubling of both income and prices leads consumers to double their spending, while a doubling of income at unchanged prices causes them to raise expenditure by only 75%, both reactions cannot be described by a single curve such as $C(Y)$ in Figure 5.1. Unless prices are assumed to remain unchanged, the horizontal axis will be attempting to measure not one independent variable, but two — real income and the price level. To avoid confusion, the latter must be removed to the *ceteris paribus* bag. This is not to say that consumers' decisions will remain unaffected by price changes, but rather that those effects should be investigated separately from the effects of changes in real income.

(ii) The relationships shown in Figures 5.1, 5.2, and 5.3 can be expressed as equations using the notation introduced earlier; this form is sometimes more convenient than diagrammatic representation. The equation of $C(Y)$ in Figure 5.1 is

$$C = C_0 + bY,$$

where C stands for consumers' demand, Y for income, and C_0 and b are constants. For example, if C_0 were \$100 million and b were 0.8, the equation would mean that consumers wish to spend \$100 million even when their income is zero; when they *are* receiving income, they wish to spend four-fifths of it in addition to the basic \$100 million. Thus, if income were \$1,000 million, consumers' demand would be \$100 million plus $0.8 \times$ \$1,000 million — *i.e.*, \$900 million. The C_0 of the equation is the amount measured on the consumption axis at the point where $C(Y)$ cuts the axis; b is the slope of $C(Y)$.

The equation of $C(Y)$ in Figure 5.2 is simpler. Because $C(Y)$ starts from the origin of the diagram, there is no C_0; in this case,

$$C = bY,$$

where b is a constant equal to the slope of $C(Y)$. The curve $C(Y)$ in Figure 5.3 is less easy to put into equation form because the part beyond Y_1 is not a smooth continuation of the segment between zero and Y_1. For the horizontal section where income is equal to or less than Y_1, consumption is of a fixed amount; in symbols,

$$C = C_0 \quad \text{when } Y \leq Y_1.$$

When income exceeds Y_1, consumption rises, but at a diminishing rate; because the slope of $C(Y)$ is not constant, the equation cannot be "linear" (*i.e.*, giving a straight-line relationship) but takes a rather more complicated form, such as

$$C = C_0 + b\sqrt{Y - Y_1} \quad \text{for } Y > Y_1.$$

Here, if Y_1 and C_0 were each equal to 100 and if b were 2, income of 150 would give rise to consumers' demand of about 114; $Y = 200$ would give $C = 120$; $Y = 250$ would give $C = 124$ (approximately), and so on.

(iii) Sometimes it is less important to ascertain the general income-consumption relationship than to discover how consumers respond to a given *change* in income; the concept then required is the "Marginal Propensity to Consume" (hereafter abbreviated to MPC), which is the ratio between a change in consumers' demand and the change in income that brings it about. In symbols, it is $\triangle C/\triangle Y$, where $\triangle$ stands for a change in the quantity it precedes.[3] If an increase of $10 million in income is accompanied by an increase of $8 million in consumers' expenditure, the MPC is $\frac{8}{10}$ (or 0.8). If the change in income is extremely small, the MPC is the slope of the consumption function at a given point. When the function is a straight line, as in Figures 5.1 and 5.2, the MPC has the same value along the whole length of the line; in the equations of these curves ($C = C_0 + bY$ and $C = bY$), it is equal to the constant b. When the function is nonlinear, as in the right-hand section of $C(Y)$ in Figure 5.3, the MPC varies with the level of income, and its value is different at every point along the curve; in the corresponding equation there is no single term that represents it.

(iv) The consumption function implies a "saving function." Since saving is the part of income not consumed,[4] a decision to consume, say, three-quarters of income is also a decision to save one-quarter. In the diagrams given earlier, a "saving curve" can be deduced by subtracting from each level of income the consumption indicated by the consumption function. The equations of the curves can be adapted by putting

$$S = Y - C.$$

For example, if the consumption function is of the form

$$C = C_0 + bY,$$

then

$$S = Y - C_0 - bY = Y(1 - b) - C_0.$$

Here $(1 - b)$ is the Marginal Propensity to Save (MPS); the MPS always equals $1 -$ MPC, and is symbolized as $\triangle S/\triangle Y$. When convenient, therefore, all propositions about consumption may be translated into propositions about saving.

---

[3] It is the $\triangle$ that makes the MPC *marginal*. C/Y can be called the average propensity to consume — the proportion of *all* income that is spent on consumption.

[4] This statement, of course, assumes appropriate definitions of income and consumption. See above, pp. 54–55.

3. The Logic of Consumer Behavior

Is the consumption function thus defined a useful concept? As already noted, its usefulness depends on whether income is the main determinant of consumers' demand; if so, it is worthwhile inquiring what the shape of the function is likely to be. On these questions evidence is needed; to see what is relevant, it will be convenient to start by considering the individual consumer.

In the ordinary microeconomic theory of consumer behavior, the individual has a certain sum of money with which he can buy various commodities at given prices; he decides what quantities to purchase by comparing the satisfactions to be derived from them. The more he has of a particular good, the less will another dollar's worth add to his total satisfaction, and eventually a point will be reached where an extra dollar spent on the good will give less satisfaction than if it were spent on something else. If his expenditure on each commodity stops just short of this point, he will be obtaining "equimarginal" returns: the last dollar spent on any one good will bring the same satisfaction as the last dollar spent on any other, and he cannot switch expenditure from one good to another without a net loss of satisfaction. Such a distribution of resources will maximize the consumer's satisfaction, and this is the pattern of expenditure that he will choose if he is (as he is assumed to be) a rational person trying to satisfy his wants as fully as possible.

On this principle, an individual's decision to leave some resources unconsumed is explained in terms of the satisfaction he obtains by doing so. If he can spend $100, but buys only $75 worth of goods for immediate consumption, it is because a 76th dollar's worth of consumption would give less satisfaction than the 25th dollar of "sparing" (as the nonconsumption of resources may be called; "saving" is appropriate only if the consumer has nothing but his current income to spend). The object of sparing may be to postpone consumption to a time when unusual needs will arise or when resources will otherwise be inadequate — marriage, old age, and next summer's vacation are obvious examples. Or the object may be one that does not necessarily envisage future consumption, as with a man who spares in order to bequeath property to his heirs or to build up a reserve for unforeseen emergencies. Achieving these aims by sparing satisfies present wants; in addition, the individual will obtain satisfaction from any income accruing from his unconsumed resources — for example, he will receive interest if he continues to hold bonds instead of selling them to finance consumption. In allocating his resources, then, he must balance the satisfaction from sparing against that derived from consumption in such a way as to get equimarginal returns.[5] Exactly where the balance will be struck depends partly on the individual's temperament — if he is of a thrifty disposition, he will no doubt spare more than a less provident person; partly on his family circumstances — the head of a family must consider his dependents' consumption wants as well as his own; and partly on his age, since this determines the "time horizon" in his plans for future consumption. The balance will also depend on the amount of the individual's resources: the smaller they are, the larger the proportion he will consume; the greater they are, the greater the proportion that will be spared.

This relationship between the amount of resources and the proportion consumed follows from the obvious fact that some minimum of consumption is necessary to sustain life. If an individual can afford only this minimum, he would be acting irrationally by sparing anything at all, unless he is ready to die of starvation in order to bequeath to his heirs; there is no point in providing for his own future consumption if he cannot survive to enjoy it. Up to the level of resources needed for minimum subsistence, there can thus be no question of sparing. But as the level rises, enabling the individual to consume more if he wishes, the satisfaction obtained from consumption will rise more and more slowly relative to the expenditure on it, until a point is reached where a dollar of sparing gives more satisfaction than an additional dollar of consumption; thereafter, additions to the individual's resources will be divided between consumption and sparing in proportion to the additional satisfactions afforded by them.[6] It is conceivable that when the individual's resources reach some very high

---

[5] For a more rigorous account of the logic of this choice, see G. Ackley, *Macroeconomic Theory* (New York: Macmillan, 1961), pp. 249–251.

[6] The individual will still be devoting a larger proportion of his *total* income to consumption than to sparing. If he had to choose between consuming *all* his income and sparing all of it, he would choose consumption, because the satisfaction given by the, say, 50th dollar of consumption (when no sparing is done) must be greater than that from the 50th dollar spared (when no consumption is taking place). This is the idea behind Irving Fisher's concept of "time preference," defined as the proportionate "excess of the present marginal want for one more unit of *present* goods over the *present* marginal want for one more unit of *future* goods." See his *The Theory of Interest* (New York: Macmillan, 1930; reprinted by Kelley, 1965), p. 62. The argument in the text implies that time preference varies according to the level of individual's resources.

level, *all* his consumption wants will be completely satisfied, so that further expenditure on consumption will be pointless; additional sparing, on the other hand, will always give *some* satisfaction — a man can provide for larger bequests to his children or build up a larger reserve. At this point, all additional resources will be spared and none consumed; the proportion of total resources spared will be high. As the level of resources rises from the minimum subsistence level, at which no sparing is done, towards the very high level just mentioned, it seems that the proportion spared must increase; obversely, the proportion of resources consumed will fall as resources increase.

This is not to say that the proportions will always change *steadily* with the level of resources. There may be ranges of resource levels over which the proportions change hardly at all, or they may change sharply at certain points. Between the two extreme positions of minimum subsistence and the complete saturation of consumption wants, there is for most people an intermediate level of consumption — the "normal standard of living" to which they are accustomed. It is common experience that cutting consumption a little below the normal standard causes a loss of satisfaction much greater than the gain from an equal increase above the normal standard. The attractions of consumption, in relation to those of sparing, will be high when resources are only sufficient to procure the normal standard and will decrease sharply when the level of resources rises above this critical level; the ratio of consumption to resources will be "kinked" at this point. But standards can be changed; given time, an individual can get used to a lower or higher consumption norm if some change in his circumstances makes it necessary; the influence of this discontinuity will be greater in the short run than in the long.

4. The Consumer's Assets and Liabilities

An individual's expenditure on consumption in any period, then, will depend on his temperament, his family circumstances, his age, and the total resources at his disposal during the period. There is an a priori expectation that his consumption will rise with the level of resources, though it will not rise in proportion — the larger the resources are, the smaller the proportion used in consumption. This relationship, however, implies a modification of the consumption functions introduced above, for they were written as if current income were the only resource available to the consumer. This assumption may be more or less true for many consumers, but clearly it does not hold for all. In addition to his income, the individual may have a stock of money on which he can draw; he may have made loans that he can call in; he may possess bonds and stock or physical assets such as real estate, which can be sold to finance consumption. In the analysis of macroeconomic equilibrium, the primary focus is on the influence of income on consumers' demand, but it is evident that this relationship may need to be expanded to take account of the effect of other resources that the individual may have.

All consumer-owned assets are not alike, of course. For example, if assets may have to be sold to finance consumption, the price the assets would fetch is important. If they would have to be offered much below their original cost to attract buyers, their owner may be disinclined to reckon them among his "resources" when deciding how much to consume. Other nonmoney assets may not be realizable at all for the time being. For example, a loan that has been made for a specified period cannot be "called" before the period ends, and in the meantime the lender may not be able to raise money by getting someone else to take his place as creditor; such assets cannot be used to finance consumption until they mature. Because of this, the individual's consumption decisions may be influenced less by his *total* assets than by the part that is "liquid"—that is, can be turned into money quickly without loss. However, liquidity is not an all-or-nothing quality, but one that assets may possess in different degrees; as will be seen later,[7] it is a quality that may vary with circumstances, so that the same assets may have greater liquidity at some times than at others. This makes it difficult to divide an individual's assets neatly into liquid and illiquid parts.

Even if assets could be divided, it would be unwise to assume that illiquid assets do not influence consumption decisions at all. For example, the owner of a house may find it hard to sell quickly without loss and so will not count its value among his consumable resources—but the fact of possessing a house eliminates the need of saving to buy one, so that he may consume more than he would have otherwise. What is true of house ownership must also apply to other "consumer capital": a man who already has a car, a television set, and a houseful of furniture will no doubt consume more than one whose income and liquid assets are the same

---

[7] See Chapter 11, pp. 256–257.

but who owns none of these things. However, the inclusion of consumer durables among the individual's assets means that the purchase of new ones must not be counted as part of his consumption expenditure; only the part of their value consumed during the year (*i.e.*, their depreciation) can be regarded as consumed, the remainder being counted as saving — a procedure not followed in the official statistics of consumption.[8]

Against the individual's assets must be set his liabilities. He may have borrowed money by outright loan in the past; he may be buying a car on installment credit or a house on mortgage; he may have unpaid bills outstanding. The greater his liabilities, the less he can spend on consumption. Just how much less, however, depends on the nature of the liabilities. If a debt need not be repaid for many years, the debtor need not for the moment set aside funds for repaying it and may devote all his resources to consumption if he so wishes; but if repayment is falling due, he must divert the whole amount from resources that would otherwise have been available for consumption. The latter kind of debt may be called "liquid," the former "illiquid"; the greater the liquidity of an individual's liabilities, the more they will restrict his ability to spend on consumption.

If liabilities are deducted from assets, the result is the individual's "net assets" or "net worth"; this amount, along with his income, is available for consumption if he wishes. But this need not be the limit of his resources. He may, in addition, be able to count on credit if he needs it; he may know that his bank will lend him up to, say, $10,000, or that he can buy goods up to a certain value on installments, or that he can run up a bill at the department store. The ability to borrow allows him to anticipate future income; instead of gradually accumulating funds by saving, he can obtain money now and earmark his future saving for repayment of the loan. Even when the loan must be secured by an existing asset, his power to consume will be increased if he offers an illiquid asset as security; the overall liquidity of his assets will thereby be increased. Anything that increases the individual's borrowing power (such as a general extension of installment buying facilities or a bank's more generous assessment of his credit-worthiness) will increase his ability to consume and may lead him to spend more on consumption.

His maximum possible outlay during a given period will therefore be

---

[8] See above, p. 15. In some formulations of the consumption function, durable goods are treated as being consumed over time in this manner; see p. 112 below.

the sum of (a) the value of his net assets at the beginning of it, (b) the amount he could borrow if he so wished, and (c) the income accruing to him during the period — though this, of course, will be his "disposable income" rather than his total receipts, since some of the latter will be preempted for tax payments and will consequently not be available for spending on consumption.[9] In symbols, this budgetary constraint can be expressed as

$$C \leq Y_d + A$$

where Y_d is disposable income and A is net assets plus borrowing power. The proposition that the consumer's expenditure depends on his total resources can be written

$$C = C(Y_d, A)$$

— subject, of course, to the condition that C cannot exceed the value given by the budgetary constraint just mentioned. As long as his net assets and potential borrowing remain unchanged at some fixed amount $\bar{A}$ (as might reasonably be expected over a short period), variations in consumption will occur only as a result of changes in disposable income, and the relationship will be equivalent to the consumption function defined earlier. As the amount of A changes over time, however, the effect will be to alter the income-consumption relationship in the way shown in Figure 5.4. With net assets and borrowing power initially at the level $\bar{A}_1$, the consumption function is $C(Y_d, \bar{A}_1)$; but subsequent increases in the value of A, to $\bar{A}_2$ and $\bar{A}_3$, push the curve vertically upwards, indicating that at a given level of income larger and larger expenditures on consumption will be made as assets and borrowing power increase. Here, the value of $\bar{A}$ is said to be a "parameter" of the consumption function, in the sense that the relationship between C and Y_d is conditioned by $\bar{A}$, and alters when $\bar{A}$ changes.[10]

So long as the individual is saving anything, he is adding to his net assets. If, on the other hand, his expenditure on consumption exceeds current in-

---

[9] See p. 38 on Disposable Personal Income. If the individual is paying interest on past borrowing, these payments should also be deducted, leaving "discretionary" income (as defined on p. 38). However, if his consumer durables, such as his car, are being treated as assets that by their services give him income in kind, and if those durables were originally bought with borrowed money, the interest on those loans must not be deducted from income, since it is, in effect, a precommitted consumption expenditure that is "buying" the services of the durable assets.

[10] On the definition and usage of the term "parameter," see Miles Fleming, *Introduction to Economic Analysis* (London: Allen and Unwin, 1969), p. 76.

come, then the consumer is running down his assets or adding to his liabilities, *i.e.*, he is "dis-saving." The value of an individual's assets may change significantly over a short period; for all consumers taken as a body, however, total asset value is much more stable, and growing steadily over time.

To treat income as the main determinant of consumers' demand, then, is to imply that the influence of nonincome resources can usually be left out of account, either because they are small in relation to income or because they do not change very rapidly for the average consumer. Some relevant evidence is contained in a survey undertaken by the Federal Reserve Board.[11] The survey found that in 1962 the average net assets per "consumer unit"[12] were about $21,000, which was a little over three times the average income ($6,400). But *liquid* assets per consumer unit were only $2,700 — one eighth of total assets and 42% of average income. For most units, the largest single asset was the equity they held in their own

---

[11] D. S. Projector and G. S. Weiss, *Survey of Financial Characteristics of Consumers*, Federal Reserve Technical Papers (August, 1966).

[12] For purposes of the survey, consumer units were defined as consisting of "families," *i.e.*, groups of two or more persons related by blood, marriage or adoption and residing together, and "unrelated individuals," which refers to persons not living with any relatives.

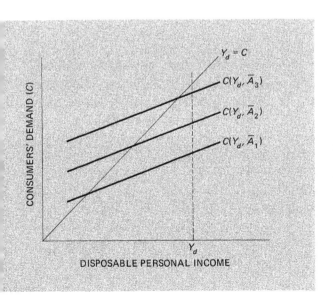

Fig. 5.4

The consumption function, showing the influence of consumer-owned assets (A) on expenditure out of Disposable Personal Income.

homes; 57% of all consumer units owned some assets of this type, and the value of owned homes was 27% of total consumer wealth. The largest item among the different types of assets, however, was investment portfolios. Investment assets totaled 33% of the total wealth covered by the survey, although this type of asset was held by only 31% of the consumer units.

As this last figure suggests, asset ownership was found to be highly concentrated. A mere 2.5% of consumer units owned more than 40% of the total net assets, while 15% had net assets of less than $1000. Twenty percent of all income units had no *liquid* assets at all; a quarter of those with incomes less than $5000 had none. It would seem that, for many consumers in the United States in the early 1960's, the influence of net assets on consumption decisions must have been slight compared with that of income, though it must be remembered that the figures quoted do not include estimates of the consumer units' borrowing power.

For that proportion of consumers whose net assets are substantial, however, changes in the value and liquidity of assets may be important. The causes and effects of such changes will be examined in later sections; another question must be considered first.

5. Lags, Expectations, and Experience

In the foregoing account of the consumer's behavior, the "income" considered was his *current* income, *i.e.*, the income that accrues during the same period in which his consumption spending is done. But most people receive their incomes in arrears — wage earners at the end of the week, stockholders at the end of the quarter, and so on. Obviously, money cannot be spent until it has been received; if the wage earner is spending last week's wages this week, should not the consumption function relate the consumption of a given period to the income of the preceding period?

It is true that an individual who cannot borrow and cannot realize any of his assets cannot spend more than the income he received at the end of the last period. But to say that current consumption is *limited* by last period's income is not to say that it is *determined* by it; it is a constraining, not a causal, relationship. During the period, the individual's income accrues in the form of debt owed to him by someone else (*e.g.*, the wage earner's employer); at the end of the period the debt is liquidated by a cash payment. If he knows that his income is accruing at a higher rate than in the previous period, he may very reasonably decide to spend more on consumption because his resources are increasing; in that event, the amount of his current, not last-period, income has determined his consumption. He may be prevented from consuming as much as he wants by the fact that his resources include too little cash and too much credit, but this is a matter of the *composition* of his resources, not their total amount. If he is, after all, assumed to be able to borrow, there need be no difficulty; for example, he may run up bills with his grocer and other suppliers, to be settled at the end of the period when his income is paid to him in cash.

The presence of an income-payment lag, then, does not mean that consumption decisions are necessarily determined by last-period income. Nevertheless, past income may influence current consumption in another way. The individual may not know precisely what his current income is (stockholders, for example, must wait for dividend announcements to know what their shares have earned); he may therefore proceed on the assumption that it will be the same as in the previous period and decide his consumption accordingly. Alternatively, he may take an average of the incomes received in the last five or six periods, or he may add to last period's income the average increase over the last few periods. Whatever his procedure, he will be using past experience as a means of estimating present income. Even if he does know his current income, he may wish to compare it with those accruing in past periods in order to decide whether it is unusually high or low. Should it seem abnormally high, he may think it unwise to increase consumption to a level he may not be able to sustain; if it is abnormally low, he will not reduce consumption if he expects his income to regain its normal level soon. In this case the individual will decide his consumption not in the light of current income but by considering some estimate of "normal" income based on past experience.

His consumption may also be influenced by expectations as to what his income will be in the future. If he has reason to think it will be larger (for example, because he expects a promotion in his job or because he has a salary arrangement that provides for automatic raises), he may consume more than if he expects it to continue at its present level. If he takes a really long view, he will look ahead to his prospective income for the rest of his working life and try to arrange his consumption so that it is smoothed out over his life span in the most satisfactory way. This is, indeed, the *Life*

Cycle Hypothesis proposed by F. Modigliani, R. Brumberg and A. Ando [13] (from whose initials the convenient label "MBA theory" is derived); they argue that consumption in any period is "a facet of a plan which extends over the balance of the individual's life, while the income accruing within the same period is but one element which contributes to the shaping of such a plan."

A very simple example would be that of a man of forty who believes he will die at seventy; he expects to retire from work at sixty, but until then he will be earning $10,000 a year; at present, his net assets are worth $40,000, and he does not wish to bequeath anything at death. It is assumed that neither his existing assets nor his future saving will yield any interest. His present position, then, is that he can count on a total of $240,000 (*i.e.*, $200,000 in prospective earnings plus $40,000 in assets) to finance his consumption during the rest of his life. If he wishes to consume the same amount in each of the thirty years that remain to him, he will spend $8,000 a year: in symbols,

$$C_t = c_t W_t$$

where W_t is his total existing assets and future prospective earnings at time t, c_t is the fraction he wishes to consume at time t (in this case one-thirtieth, or 0.033), and C_t is the amount of consumption at t. A more realistic formulation would allow for uncertainties about the dates of the individual's retirement and death, for possible variations in earnings expected in future years, and for the fact that he might not wish to consume the same amount each year during the rest of his life. If, after all, he wishes to provide for his heirs, he must plan his consumption so that some of his resources are still unconsumed at his death; and he must take account of interest and the yield of future services from his consumer durables.[14] Even in the simple case just given, however, it is clear that a rise in current in-

---

[13] F. Modigliani and R. Brumberg, "Utility Analysis and the Consumption Function: An Interpretation of Cross-section Data," in K. K. Kurihara (ed.), *Post-Keynesian Economics* (New Brunswick, N.J.: Rutgers University Press, 1954); A. Ando and F. Modigliani, "The 'Life Cycle' Hypothesis of Saving: Aggregate Implications and Tests," in R. A. Gordon and L. R. Klein, eds. for the American Economic Association, *Readings in Business Cycles* (Homewood, Ill.: Irwin, 1965).

[14] MBA allows for the last point by defining C_t as outlays on nondurables plus the rental value of durables. Interest affects the calculation of the "present value" of future earnings included in W_t; on this see p. 159 below. The consumption plan involves maximizing a utility function $U(C_t, C_{t+1}, \ldots, C_{t+n})$, where n is the number of years of life remaining, subject to the constraint that the consumption planned over all n years cannot exceed W_t.

come will affect current consumption only through its effect on W_t; for example, an unexpected rise in earnings to $13,000 this year will increase W_t to no more than $243,000 if earnings in future years are still expected to be at the $10,000 rate, and consumption will therefore rise by only $100 to an annual figure of $8,100.

The "life-cycle" approach has a good deal in common with Milton Friedman's *Permanent Income Hypothesis*.[15] Given an individual's earning capacity and assets (in Friedman's terms, his "human" and "non-human" wealth) there will be some level of income that he regards as normal or "permanent"; he may not calculate it over his whole life span, but he may be supposed to have a planning horizon some years ahead, which will be relevant to his estimate of the average income he can expect in the long run. Unforeseen excesses or shortfalls of actual income over permanent income are termed "transitory." Thus,

$$Y = Y_p + Y_t$$

where Y_p and Y_t are permanent and transitory income respectively, and Y is the total (or measured) income actually received during a given year or quarter. Thus, Y_p includes both normal earnings from labor and the average long-run yield from real or financial assets; its difference from $Y - i.e., Y_t -$ will be due to such unexpected events as a spell of unemployment or an unusually high stock dividend. Similarly, actual (measured) consumption, C, has permanent and transitory components C_p and C_t so that

$$C = C_p + C_t;$$

C_p consists of the outlays needed to maintain the standard of living the consumer thinks appropriate to his permanent income level, while C_t would include such items as unexpected medical bills and spur-of-the-moment gifts. It is, of course, possible for C_t to be negative, for example when the individual has an unexpected chance to buy at unusually low prices; and as in the MBA formulation, C is defined as including the rental value of durables rather than outright purchases of them.

Friedman's hypothesis is that permanent consumption is proportional to permanent income, *i.e.*, that

$$C_p = c^* Y_p$$

---

[15] M. Friedman, *A Theory of the Consumption Function* (Princeton, N.J.: Princeton University Press for the NBER, 1957).

where c^* is a constant determined by the individual's preferences, by the rate of interest, and by the ratio of human to nonhuman wealth. By contrast, C_t and Y_t are not systematically related to one another, and the Marginal Propensity to Consume out of transitory income is zero. It follows that estimates of the MPC for measured consumption and income will give a value less than that of c^*, and Friedman suggests that this may explain certain discrepancies in the empirical evidence about the income-consumption relationship. For the purposes of economic analysis, permanent income is a much more important magnitude than measured income; an increase in the latter will cause a rise in consumption only to the extent that it causes the recipient to change his views as to the level of income which is to be regarded as "permanent."

An obvious difficulty is that the hypothesis cannot be tested by direct comparisons of C_p and Y_p, since the available statistics are of measured income and consumption only. Instead, Friedman applies a number of ingenious indirect tests to show that his theory is consistent with the statistical data. There has, however, been a good deal of controversy both with regard to the tests and also over the formulation of the theory itself,[16] and it cannot be claimed that the permanent income hypothesis, any more than the MBA life-cycle theory, has gained universal acceptance as yet. Even so, they are particularly instructive in showing possible ways in which consumers' decisions may be affected by expectations as well as by current income, and they have provided a useful stimulus to research on the nature of the consumption function.

6. Changes in the Price Level

The consumption function was defined earlier (p. 100) in terms of *real* income and consumption, not in terms of money values, which may alter solely because of price changes. Since National Product is necessarily equal in value to National Income, a rise in prices must increase both in the same proportion. It may seem, therefore, that a 10% rise in the general price

---

[16] For a summary treatment of these issues, see M. J. Farrell, "New theories of the Consumption Function," in *Readings in Business Cycles, op. cit.*; and R. Ferber, "Research on Household Behavior," in *American Economic Review*, Vol. 52 (March, 1962), pp. 19–63.

level will give consumers 10% more money income to spend on commodities that are 10% more expensive on the average, and so they may be expected to consume the same *proportion* of income as before, leaving the situation unchanged in real terms. Nevertheless, price changes are likely to affect consumers' decisions in a number of ways.

To begin with, a change in the general price level is unlikely to involve an equal proportionate change in the price of each single commodity; for example, food prices may rise only 5% while clothing prices rise 15%. If consumers react by buying less clothing (because it is relatively, as well as absolutely, more expensive) but go on buying about the same quantity of food (even though it is relatively cheaper), total consumption will fall in real terms.

Second, a change in National Income does not necessarily mean an equal change in personal disposable incomes. When prices rise, firms receive more money for the commodities they produce; but they retain it (for the time being, at any rate) as undistributed profits, so that it does not get into the hands of personal consumers. Even if it does all pass into personal incomes, the recipients may find themselves pushed into higher tax brackets under a system of progressive income taxation; their disposable incomes will then rise by a percentage smaller than the rise in National Income. When prices fall, these effects will of course be reversed.

Third, changes in the general price level may give rise to what has been called [17] the "Pigou effect" or "real-balance effect." Individuals who possess money balances will feel worse off when prices rise and better off when prices fall, because of the change in the real value of their money. When prices fall, it is as if their money balances had increased while prices remained the same; with greater real resources, they will now spend a higher proportion of income on consumption. The same considerations apply to individuals holding assets such as bonds, which entitle the holders to a fixed money interest payment and to a fixed sum on redemption. On the other hand, those who have contracted fixed-interest debts in the past will now find that the real burden of their obligations has increased; they may reduce consumption accordingly. If all the fixed-interest assets owned by consumers were the liabilities of other consumers, the higher con-

---

[17] The terms were coined by D. Patinkin in "Price Flexibility and Full Employment," *American Economic Review*, Vol. 38 (September, 1948), pp. 543–64; and in his *Money, Interest and Prices*, 2d ed. (New York: Harper and Row, 1965), p. 19.

sumption of creditors could be offset by the reduced consumption of debtors, and the net effect of the fall in prices would be nil.

But the most important single debtor in the community is not an individual at all; it is the government. If the government does not alter its behavior in response to the fall in prices, its creditors' increased consumption will not be canceled out by a reduction in anyone else's. Corporations, too, are fixed-interest debtors, whose creditors (*i.e.,* the owners of their bonds) may raise their consumption when the price level falls. But because lower prices have reduced the money value of firms' turnover and profits, the necessity to pay the same amount of bond interest as before may induce corporations to cut dividends proportionately even more than prices have fallen; this cut in dividends will lead to a reduction in stockholders' consumption — and this will offset the increased expenditure of bondholders. If, however, corporations were to maintain the level of dividends unchanged in real terms,[18] there would be no such offset; and the consequences of the fall in prices would include the rise in bondholders' consumption along with that of the owners of government securities and money balances. If the community's real income is assumed to have remained unchanged, the consumption function will have been shifted upward.[19] Conversely, a rise in the price level — by reducing the real value of money balances and of fixed-interest assets — will push the function downward. The strength of this Pigou effect will depend on the proportion that such assets bear to the total of consumers' resources; it has been suggested earlier (p. 109) that for most consumers this proportion is probably small, so that for the community as a whole the effect is unlikely to be very important.

Finally, changes in the price level may set up expectations of further movements in the same direction. A fall in prices, for example, may lead consumers to expect further reductions and so to postpone some consumption in the hope of getting more for their money later on; the consumption function will be shifted downward. Conversely, the expectation of rising prices may cause consumption to increase, and the consumption function will be pushed up. These expectational effects of price changes work in opposition to the Pigou effect and will tend to neutralize it.

---

[18] This would, of course, reduce their undistributed profits in real terms, and they might reduce their demand for investment in consequence. But this is by no means certain; they might decide to maintain their original investment plans and to finance them by borrowing.

[19] See above, p. 108, and Figure 5.4.

7. The Influence of Interest Rates

A rise in interest rates makes lending more remunerative; if consumers are induced to save a higher proportion of income so as to have more to lend, the consumption function will shift downward. Conversely, a fall in interest rates will reduce the attractions of saving and lending, and the consumption function will move upward.

But will consumers necessarily react in this way? If an individual wishes to secure income of a fixed amount in the future, a rise in the rate of interest will enable him to do so by lending *less* than before; and the proportion of income he consumes may therefore increase rather than diminish. It is conceivable that the increased consumption of people who behave like this ("Sargant men," as D. H. Robertson called them[20]) may exactly offset the increased saving of those who respond to higher interest rates in the opposite way; the community's aggregate consumption function would then remain unchanged.

If there are no "Sargant men," a rise in interest rates will reduce the proportion of income consumed, but the reduction will not necessarily be very great. The prospect of earning interest is, after all, only one of the considerations that induce people to leave resources unconsumed; even if no interest were obtainable, the desire to provide for emergencies, for old age, and for bequests to heirs would lead some individuals to save. If these motives were very strong compared with the desire for interest, a very large change in interest rates might be needed to produce even a small shift in the consumption function.

For people whose resources include a high proportion of interest-bearing assets, however, changes in interest rates may be important in another way. The income from a bond is a fixed percentage of its "nominal" value, *e.g.*, a 4% $1000 bond gives $40 per annum. But if new loans are being made at a rate of 8%, $40 per annum can be obtained by lending $500, and no one will give more than that for the 4% bond. Because the market value of fixed-interest assets changes inversely with current interest rates, their owners will feel poorer when rates rise; they will also feel less willing to consider

---

[20] In "Some Notes on the Theory of Interest," in *Money, Trade and Economic Growth, Essays in Honor of John H. Williams* (New York: Macmillan, 1951), p. 196. Robertson was referring to Marshall's *Principles of Economics*, 8th ed. (London: Macmillan, 1920), p. 235.

selling them, because of the capital loss involved – *i.e.*, the liquidity of such assets will be reduced. The reduction in the value and liquidity of their resources will induce individuals to cut consumption. Conversely, a fall in interest rates, by making resources more valuable and more liquid, will increase consumption. The results here are similar to the Pigou effect described in the preceding section and are subject to the same limitations: they may be neutralized by expectational effects.

On the whole, the conclusion must be that the influence of interest rate changes on the consumption function is unlikely to be very marked, except perhaps in the case of people who own many fixed-interest assets.

8. Emulation: the "Relative Income" Hypothesis

So far, the individual's consumption has been assumed to depend on preferences formed independently of other people's choices – preferences that may be called (in sociological terms [21]) "inner directed." But observation suggests that much consumption is "other directed" – people are influenced by what they see of their neighbors' and fellow workers' spending. Also, consumption standards are often taken to be an indication of income, which in many societies determines status; by keeping up with the Joneses' consumption, the Smiths hope to share their status and the esteem it brings. In view of this, J. S. Duesenberry has suggested [22] that an individual's consumption does not depend on the absolute amount of his income, but on its size in relation to other people's – *i.e.*, on his position in the income scale. His response to a change in income will differ according to whether others' incomes have changed by a like amount; if they have, his consumption will change in the same proportion as his income; if they have not, his consumption will change less.

A rise in aggregate income, if it leaves everyone in the same relative position as before, will therefore be associated with an equal proportionate rise in aggregate consumption; the community's consumption function will be a straight line like $C(Y)$ in Figure 5.2 (p. 98), even though

---

[21] David Riesman, *The Lonely Crowd*, 2d ed. (New Haven, Conn.: Yale University Press, 1961), Chapter 1.

[22] J. S. Duesenberry, *Income, Saving and the Theory of Consumer Behavior* (Cambridge, Mass.: Harvard University Press, 1949).

each individual's function taken by itself may be like those shown in Figures 5.1 and 5.3. Statistical testing of the "relative income" hypothesis has not shown that it explains the facts better than the theory that consumption depends on absolute income,[23] but it is instructive in drawing attention to the importance of the distribution of incomes in determining the aggregate consumption function — a matter that must now be considered.

9. The Aggregate Consumption Function and the Distribution of Incomes

The list of possible influences on the individual's consumption is already long, yet even now it is by no means complete. Advertising, for example, may cause him to consume more than he otherwise would; moral attitudes about "the virtue of saving" may restrain his expenditure. But no statistical evidence has so far been presented on these matters; investigations of the cross-section type, in which a sample of individuals is asked to give details of income, assets, expenditure, and so on, seem to show that current income is the chief determinant of consumption, with asset holdings the next strongest. Age and number of dependents also play a part, though the direction and importance of their influence is not very clear.[24]

The object of investigating individual consumer behavior, however, is to draw conclusions about the determination of *aggregate* consumption; as was seen in Chapter 3, it is important to know how the community's total consumption will react to a change in National Income. This may seem a mere matter of addition; if, say, three men are each known to consume seven-eighths of their disposable income, it is clear that their collective consumption will be seven-eighths of their combined incomes. But it is obvious only because they were assumed to have identical consumption functions. If *A* consumes three-quarters of his personal disposable income, *B* seven-eighths, and *C* nine-tenths, and if their combined dis-

---

[23] See J. Tobin, "Relative Income, Absolute Income and Saving," in *Money, Trade and Economic Growth, op. cit.*, pp. 135–156.

[24] For a thorough review of research on these questions, see R. Ferber, "Research on Household Behavior," *op. cit.*

posable incomes are $30,000, it is not possible to say what their total consumption will be unless their individual incomes are also known. If, for example, A's income is $16,000, B's $8,000, and C's $6,000, their combined consumption will be $24,400. But if it had been C who received $16,000, while A had $8,000 and B $6,000, their combined consumption would have been $25,650. Here the aggregate consumption function is a weighted average of the individual functions, the weights being the individuals' incomes; the change in income distribution has shifted the aggregate consumption function by altering the weights.

The effects of redistributing incomes may be shown with the aid of a diagram. In Figure 5.5, the consumption functions of two income groups A and B are shown as $C^A(Y_d)$ and $C^B(Y_d)$, and their disposable incomes as Y_d^A and Y_d^B respectively. If their incomes are equalized [25] so that each receives Y_d^E (B's loss of $Y_d^E Y_d^B$ being equal to A's gain of $Y_d^A Y_d^E$), it appears from $C^A(Y_d)$ that A will consume C_2^A and save the remainder of their income (*i.e.*, $Y_d^E - C_2^A$); previously A consumed C_1^A and saved nothing,

---

[25] The following argument will still hold true, even if incomes are not completely equalized — *e.g.*, if the B group is taxed to provide transfer incomes for A, but in such a way as to leave A's income less than B's.

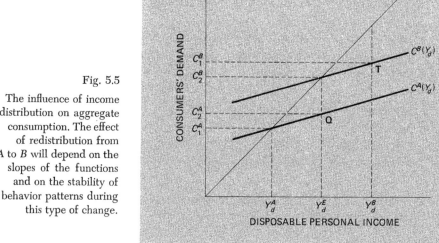

Fig. 5.5

The influence of income distribution on aggregate consumption. The effect of redistribution from A to B will depend on the slopes of the functions and on the stability of behavior patterns during this type of change.

because C_1^A lies on the line $Y = C$. Group B, on the other hand, formerly saved $Y_d^B - C_1^B$ but now saves nothing, since C_2^B is where $C^B(Y_d)$ cuts the $Y = C$ line.

After equalization, *total* income is unchanged, and saving is $Y_d^E - C_2^A$ instead of $Y_d^B - C_1^B$. If $C^A(Y_d)$ and $C^B(Y_d)$ are parallel, then $Y_d^B - C_1^B = Y_d^E - C_2^A$. In this case, saving (and therefore consumption) is unchanged, because the MPC of A — the slope of $C^A(Y_d)$ — equals the MPC of B — the slope of $C^B(Y_d)$ — over the range of income between Y_d^A and Y_d^B. The same result would occur if $C^A(Y_d)$ were identical with $C^B(Y_d)$ or if each group's consumption function were the same straight line running through the origin of the diagram — like $C(Y)$ in Figure 5.1, p. 97. Redistributing income will change aggregate consumption only if (i) the groups' functions are straight lines differing in slope — in Figure 5.5, $Y_d^B - C_1^B$ will exceed $Y_d^E - C_2^A$ if the slope of $C^B(Y_d)$ is less than that of $C^A(Y_d)$;[26] or if (ii) the groups' functions, even if identical or parallel, are curved so that they slope more steeply above point Y_d^A on the income scale than above Y_d^B.

Even these conclusions depend on both groups staying on their respective consumption functions, but this may not happen. Income tends to be associated with social status, though there is a good deal of overlapping; different social classes have different norms of consumption expenditure. If redistribution gives more income to members of a "lower" class, they may respond by joining a higher one and thereby change their consumption standards. In Figure 5.5, the members of the A group may jump from $C^A(Y_d)$ to $C^B(Y_d)$ instead of moving from C_1^A to C_2^A when their incomes are increased. If the B group insists on remaining on $C^B(Y_d)$, merely moving from C_1^B to C_2^B when their incomes fall, the result will be to increase consumption considerably. Nothing can be taken for granted about the results of income redistribution; it is necessary to know something about the MPC's of the income groups concerned and to assess mobility between the social classes.

The position and shape of the aggregate consumption function thus depends on the distribution of incomes as well as on the individual func-

---

[26] If the slope of $C^B(Y_d)$ were *greater* than that of $C^A(Y_d)$, the combined consumption of A and B would fall when incomes were equalized. The usual assumption is that the higher income groups have smaller MPC's than the lower groups; but it is not impossible to imagine a community in which the poor are so hidebound by custom that extra income hardly changes their consumption, while the rich are eager to increase theirs when a rise in income occurs.

tions of the members of the community. Similar considerations arise regarding the distribution of nonincome resources (*i.e.*, net assets plus borrowing power) among consumers. A transfer of assets from rich to poor would be likely to raise the poor's consumption and reduce that of the rich, the net outcome depending on the relative importance of assets in their respective consumption functions. Population structure may play a similar part; if age and family size influence individuals' consumption, a change in the age grouping of the community or in the number and size of families will alter the proportion of aggregate income consumed. All these things are parameters of the aggregate consumption function — that is, a given position of the income-consumption curve, as in Figures 5.1, 5.2, and 5.3, implies a given state of income distribution, age grouping, and so on; should any of them change, the effect would be to move the entire curve bodily up or down.

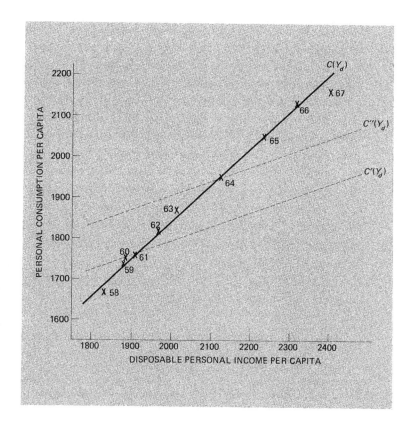

Fig. 5.6

A consumption function for the United States for the years 1958–1967. All figures are in 1958 dollars.

Finally, it must be noted that the aggregate consumption function has been defined so as to relate consumers' demand to the total of personal disposable incomes, not to National Income. It will be recalled that personal disposable incomes are equal to National Income *minus* undistributed corporate profits, *minus* personal income and social security taxes, *plus* transfer payments to persons along with consumer and government interest. If the relationship between National Income and consumption were under consideration, it would be necessary to observe whether any of these items tends to show a systematic variation with the level of National Income. An obvious example is progressive income taxation, under which the proportion of income taken for taxes rises with the level of income; if this were the only variable item among those just mentioned, the higher the level of National Income, the greater would be the difference between National Income and personal disposable incomes. If consumers' expenditure were to be plotted against each level of National Income in a diagram, the resulting consumption function would lie below that plotted against personal disposable income; it would slope less steeply, and its slope would tend to diminish – *i.e.*, it would be curved like $C(Y)$ in Figure 5.3, p. 99 – even if the "personal disposable income" consumption function were a straight line.

10. Statistical Measurement of the Consumption Function

If income *is* the chief determinant of consumption, outweighing all the other influences mentioned in the last few pages, it is reasonable to expect a close correlation between their recorded values. In Figure 5.6, these have been plotted [27] for the years 1958–1967. Each cross shows, for

---

[27] Quarterly figures of per capita disposable personal income in 1958 dollars, seasonally adjusted, were taken from the *Survey of Current Business* (September, 1967, p. 52; July, 1968, Table 2.1). Quarterly personal consumption expenditures in 1958 dollars, seasonally adjusted, were taken from Table 1.2 of the July, 1968, *Survey* for the years 1964–1967, and from Table 1.2 of *The National Income and Product Accounts of the United States, 1929–65* for the years 1958–1963; these were divided by the population figures implicit in the disposable personal income series to give personal consumption per head. To keep Figure 5.6 simple, only the ten pairs of *annual* values of income and consumption are actually shown, but all forty pairs of values

the year indicated by its accompanying number, the amount of Disposable Personal Income per capita and the amount of consumption expenditure per capita, measured in dollars of constant (1958) purchasing power.[28] The line $C(Y_d)$ shows the average relationship between income and consumption implied by the distribution of the crosses. The equation for $C(Y_d)$ is of the "$C = C_0 + bY$" type described on p. 101, and is calculated to be

$$C = 139.7 + .849 \; Y_d.$$

The fact that the crosses all lie close to the line suggests a very strong association between income and consumption. To assess the strength of such relationships, statisticians use a "correlation coefficient" denoted by the symbol r, whose square (which they call the "coefficient of determination") measures the extent to which changes in one variable can be attributed to changes in the other. If, in Figure 5.6, all the crosses lay precisely on the line $C(Y_d)$, r^2 would have a value of 1.0; and this value would be consistent with the hypothesis that consumption is determined solely by the level of income. If, on the other hand, the crosses were scattered at random over the diagram, the value of r^2 would be close to zero, implying that the influence of income on consumption is almost negligible.[29] In the present case, the arrangement of the crosses suggests that the value of r^2 is much closer to 1.0 than to zero; when calculated, it turns out to be 0.99.

However, the fact that per capita consumption and income were both rising throughout the period 1958–1967 (both rose by approximately 30% over the ten years) would of itself produce a certain degree of correlation even if there were no causal connection at all between the two

---

were used in calculating the equations and the values of r^2 that appear later on in the text.

[28] Prices rose by 14% between 1958 and 1967. This would have caused current price valuations of income and consumption to rise in step with one another, even if both had remained unchanged in real terms. A systematic relationship would have appeared to exist, but it would have been due not to the influence of income on consumption, but to the fact that both variables were affected by a third factor, namely rising prices. To avoid spurious correlation of this sort, it is necessary to express both variables in terms of constant (1958) prices. Population growth (16% over the whole period 1958–1967) could produce a similar effect by causing *real* income and consumption to increase simultaneously, and it is to eliminate this that per capita figures have been used.

[29] For a full explanation of the concepts and methods of calculation, see Croxton, Cowden, and Klein, *Applied General Statistics*, 3d ed. (Englewood Cliffs, N.J.: Prentice-Hall, 1967), Chapter 19.

variables.[30] Consequently, the very high value of r^2 is not satisfactory evidence of the strength of the income-consumption relationship, and it is necessary to find a method of estimating it that will eliminate the effect of the rising trend. One such method is to compare quarterly *changes* in income and consumption instead of their absolute values. When this is done, the value of r^2 is found to be 0.43, which implies that only about two-fifths of the variation in consumption can be explained as being due to variations in current income — a result that hardly seems to permit much reliance to be placed on the consumption function in further analysis.

This outcome, however, is attributable to an overly simple formulation of the consumption function; the several influences other than current income that were discussed above have yet to be introduced. It will be recalled that this function was deduced from statistics of income and consumption extending over a period of ten years. The consumption function presented at the beginning of this chapter is not a concept describing consumers' behavior over a considerable length of time. It indicates a set of simultaneously existing possibilities that arise from consumer preferences at a particular moment. To accept the line $C(Y_d)$ in Figure 5.6 as an estimate of "the consumption function" in this sense is to assume that the function remained unchanged in shape and position for a whole decade — but this is a very dubious assumption.

It is not unreasonable, for example, to assume that consumers' assets may remain unchanged during a period of six or even twelve months. Over several years, however, saving may cause personal wealth to grow sufficiently to make consumers feel that they can afford to consume a larger proportion of income, and the consumption function will then have shifted bodily upward. In Figure 5.6, the broken line $C'(Y_d)$ might represent the consumption function that existed in 1960–1961, while the line $C''(Y_d)$ shows the function as it might have been during 1964, the upward shift being due to increasing wealth, to consumers' becoming accustomed to higher living standards, and to similar long-run influences. Other lines, more or less parallel to $C'(Y_d)$ and $C''(Y_d)$, might be supposed to run through each of the crosses representing the consumption and income of other years; the resulting family of curves would show how the short-run function had moved throughout the whole period. The line $C(Y_d)$ cuts

---

[30] This is by no means the only possible pitfall in the interpretation of r^2. Another consideration, for example, is whether the number of observations, from which the r^2's have been calculated, provides too small a sample to justify accepting conclusions drawn from it. See Croxton, Cowden and Klein, *op. cit.*, pp. 395–410.

through this set of curves, since it is derived from a series of *successive* observations, each of which may have referred to a point on a different short-run consumption function; its equation is merely a summary statement of the way in which amounts actually spent on consumption were associated with amounts of income received during 1958–1967.

It may be thought that the association is sufficiently systematic to justify calling $C(Y_d)$ a "long-period consumption function," but it will obviously differ from any short-run function in being affected by influences (such as the growth of assets) that remain practically constant in the short run but change considerably over a number of years. It is hardly surprising, therefore, that the value of r^2 deduced earlier for changes in income and consumption should have been found to be fairly low; the logical presumption is that the influence of current income on consumers' demand was much stronger in the short run.

When the short-period function is distinguished from the long-period one, it has to be admitted that the characteristic shape of the former is difficult to discover. The statistical material cited above provides, for any single year, only four pairs of quarterly values of Y_d and C from which to deduce curves of the type of $C'(Y_d)$ in Figure 5.6; to use two or three years' quarterly values would violate the short-run assumptions on which such curves are drawn. It might be thought that this difficulty could be overcome by the use of cross-section data from sample surveys of consumer units.[31] Such surveys show the incomes and the consumption expenditures of a large number of different individuals within the same short period, so that a curve fitted to these observations might appear to be an approximation to the short-run consumption function. However, this would hold true only if all the individuals covered by the survey could be assumed to occupy points on the same short-run function. If the situation were similar to that depicted in Figure 5.5, with each income group on a separate function of its own, the survey would merely have revealed a number of points like Q on $C^A(Y_d)$ and T on $C^B(Y_d)$. To draw a line between Q and T and call it "the consumption function" would clearly be illegitimate. Because of this possibility, estimates derived from cross-section data may be misleading. Nonetheless, it should be noted that they do at any rate provide evidence of a reasonably strong correlation between income and consumption and that they agree with time series analysis in showing consumption to be an increasing function of income —

---

[31] See, for example, D. S. Projector, *Survey of Changes in Family Finances*, Federal Reserve Technical Papers (November, 1968).

which, indeed, is often all that needs to be assumed for many purposes of short-run theoretical analysis, as will be seen in Chapter 6. Insofar as it becomes necessary to estimate the short-period function more precisely, it may be possible — paradoxical as it may seem — to do so by means of a somewhat different (and, unfortunately, less simple) approach to the long-period relationship.

When the statistical evidence was considered earlier, it was presented in terms of a straightforward confrontation between income and consumption, using simple equations of the $C = C_0 + bY_d$ type; but this failed to give a complete explanation of changes in consumption, since influences other than current income were left out of the reckoning. It should be possible to improve on this explanation by bringing these other influences explicitly into the relationship. For example, if there are reasons for thinking that consumers' decisions are affected not only by their present incomes but also by incomes received in the recent past,[32] the earlier equation could be amended to

$$C_t = bY_{d,t} + cY_{d,t-1},$$

where the subscript t refers to any given short period and $t - 1$ to the period immediately preceding it. Thus, if b is 0.5 and c is 0.25, and if $Y_{d,t-1}$ is \$2000 and $Y_{d,t}$ \$2200 (per capita and at constant prices), C_t will be \$1,600. Here $cY_{d,t-1}$ replaces the constant C_0 of the original equation. If income is regularly rising from one period to the next, the effect will be that of a continuous increase in the value of C_0. If drawn in a diagram, the function will appear as a set of curves, each higher than the preceding one, instead of a single line like $C(Y_d)$ in Figure 5.6. Each of the curves will be associated with a particular income period, and its slope, b, will measure the short-run MPC; but the equation will also trace the growth of consumption over time. A curve relating the successive values

---

[32] This may happen because people regard past income as "normal," and suspect that current changes in income may not be lasting — a "Friedman" approach. It may also arise from inertia: having become accustomed to their previous level of income, consumers take time to respond fully to a new one. In this case, it may be the last period's consumption, rather than the income itself, to which they have become habituated; in the next period, they will repeat that consumption plus or minus a proportion of any change in income, so that

$$C_t = C_{t-1} + b(Y_{d,t} - Y_{d,t-1}).$$

If the proportion between C_{t-1} and $Y_{d,t-1}$ is a, and if $(a-b)$ is equal to the c of the expression in the text above, the two equations are merely different ways of saying the same thing; but it may be useful to distinguish in this way between "consumption inertia" and "income habituation."

C_t, C_{t+1}, C_{t+2}, etc., to those of income in successive periods will have a slope steeper than b and will thus overestimate the short-run MPC.

In the same way, if the amount of consumers' assets is an important influence on their spending, the relationship can be made explicit in the form

$$C_t = bY_{d,t} + gA_t$$

where A_t is the amount of personal assets (per capita, at constant prices) at the beginning of period t. Assets are accumulated through saving; if consumption has been less than income during previous periods, A_t will be larger than A_{t-1} (assets at the beginning of period $t-1$), which will, in turn, have been larger than A_{t-2}, and so on. This growth of assets will give a rising trend to consumption, causing it to go on increasing even when income remains unchanged. Since one period's assets are those of the previous period plus the saving done in that period, *i.e.*,

$$A_t = A_{t-1} + Y_{d,\,t-1} - C_{t-1},$$

and since

$$C_{t-1} = bY_{d,\,t-1} + gA_{t-1},$$

the earlier equation can be rewritten

$$C_t = bY_{d,\,t} + g(1-b)Y_{d,\,t-1} + g(1-g)A_{t-1}.$$

Thus the influence of assets on consumption is seen to imply a relationship between consumption and past income,[33] similar in form to that discussed in the previous paragraph.

The connection with past income would be less simple if (for reasons indicated earlier, on p. 106) consumers were influenced by the amount of their *liquid* rather than their total assets. The last equation would then have to include a term representing the proportion of liquid assets in consumers' total wealth, and there is no obvious reason to suppose that

---

[33] Past income refers not only to the $Y_{d,t-1}$ that appears explicitly in the equation, but also to $Y_{d,t-2}$, $Y_{d,t-3}$, and so on. This is because

$$A_{t-1} = A_{t-2} + Y_{d,t-2} - C_{t-2}$$
$$= A_{t-2} + Y_{d,t-2} - bY_{d,t-2} - gA_{t-2}$$
$$= Y_{d,t-2}(1-b) + A_{t-2}(1-g).$$

When this is substituted for A_{t-1} in the equation in the text, it becomes

$$C_t = bY_{d,t} + g(1-b)Y_{d,t-1} + g(1-g)(1-b)Y_{d,t-2}$$
$$+ g(1-g)^2 A_{t-2},$$

and A_{t-2} could in turn be expressed in terms of $Y_{d,t-3}$ and A_{t-3}. The original A_t, in fact, implies a series of terms involving income during *many* previous periods.

this proportion will either remain fixed or change at some regular rate over time.[34] In spite of this, liquid assets have often been used as a "proxy variable" to represent total assets, simply because of the extreme difficulty of obtaining statistical information about the latter.[35]

In addition to income and consumers' wealth, the consumption equation can also be made to include the terms for the distribution of incomes, the age-structure of the population, the cost and availability of credit, the amount of advertising expenditures, and anything else that may be thought to exert a significant influence on consumers' behavior, with appropriate subscripts to indicate any time lags that may be involved. So far, all the lags that have been mentioned have been of fixed length. Some writers, notably J. S. Duesenberry, have suggested a different type of lag in the case of past income; instead of consumption depending on income received, say, two periods previously, it may be affected by the highest level of income attained at *any* time in the past. Consumers (it is supposed) have adjusted their spending to the last peak of income and are reluctant to reduce it when income falls again; thus

$$C_t = bY_{d,t} + cY_{d,0}$$

where $Y_{d,0}$ represents the last highest level of income. As long as income is increasing from one period to the next, $Y_{d,0}$ will equal $Y_{d,t-1}$. If, on the other hand, it falls for several periods in succession, $Y_{d,0}$ will denote the income of the period before the recession began and will continue to do so until it is replaced by a new peak when income rises again. When income falls, the fact that $cY_{d,0}$ retains a constant value means that the equation is then equivalent to

$$C = C_0 + bY_d$$

instead of the form

$$C_t = bY_{d,t} + cY_{d,t-1}$$

that it assumes when income is rising.

---

[34] Changes in the proportion could occur in a number of ways; for example, the distribution of assets between the various "sectors" of the economy (personal, corporate and public) may alter so that the personal sector holds more cash and fewer long-term bonds. Or there might be an increase in the total amount of money and other liquid assets relative to total assets in the economy as a whole, with the personal sector getting a proportionate share.

[35] For an excellent discussion of the influence of liquid assets, and of other factors, on the consumption function, see D. B. Suits, "The Determinants of Consumer Behavior: A Review of Present Knowledge," in Commission on Money and Credit, *Impacts of Monetary Policy* (Englewood Cliffs, N.J.: Prentice-Hall, 1963).

In diagrammatic terms, this means that the function can be represented by a series of curves like $C'(Y_d)$ and $C''(Y_d)$ in Figure 5.6, but with the special condition that only upward shifts are possible. That is, successive increases in income will move the short-period function from $C'(Y_d)$ to $C''(Y_d)$ and so on up the diagram, but a subsequent fall in income will not shift it back again. The presence of $Y_{d,0}$ in the equation acts as a ratchet, holding the curve at the highest position so far attained. Thus, a point relating consumption and income will travel up Figure 5.6's line $C(Y_d)$ as long as income is rising, but when income falls it will move to the left along whichever curve of the $C'(Y_d)$ family happens to intersect $C(Y_d)$ at the peak level of income. A function of this sort was shown by Duesenberry to be consistent with the United States' experience in the years 1929–1940.[36]

In spite of their differences with respect to the number of variables to be included, all the functions examined so far have one thing in common — they seek to explain the level of consumption as a whole, as though it were a single homogeneous quantity rather than the total of expenditures on many separate commodities. Although demand can reasonably be supposed to be related to incomes, assets, etc. in a different way for each community, it is implicitly assumed that the differences are not such as to invalidate the procedure of aggregating all forms of consumption into a single magnitude. Where there is reason to question this assumption, it becomes necessary to disaggregate total consumption into an appropriate number of subcategories, each with its own consumption function. A good example of this is to be found in the Brookings Institution's *Quarterly Econometric Model of the United States*, which includes five such functions.[37]

The commodity groups in the Brookings model are automobiles, other durables, food, other nondurables, and services. For example, the equation

---

[36] Duesenberry's function was

$$S_t/Y_{d,t} = 0.25 \, (Y_{d,t}/Y_{d,0}) + 0.196 \quad (r^2 = 0.81)$$

in dollars of constant purchasing power per head of population. This is equivalent to

$$C_t = 0.804 Y_{d,t} - 0.25 \, Y_{d,t} (Y_{d,t}/Y_{d,0}),$$

which is somewhat more complicated than the expression in the text above. See his *Income, Saving, and the Theory of Consumer Behavior, op. cit.*, pp. 89–92.

[37] D. B. Suits and G. R. Sparks, "Consumption Regressions with Quarterly Data," in Duesenberry, Fromm, Klein and Kuh (eds.), *The Brookings Quarterly Econometric Model of the United States* (Chicago: Rand McNally, 1965). The consumption equations are simplified slightly for presentation here.

for quarterly consumption of nondurables (except food), $C_{N,t}$, was of the form

$$C_{N,t} = 4.27 + 0.169Y_{d,t} + 0.074L_{t-1},$$

where L_{t-1} is total liquid assets at the end of the last quarter. In this equation, the liquid assets variable very likely captures a number of influences mentioned earlier. Since the holding of liquid assets is related to holding other assets, this variable would represent the influence of the consumers' total wealth, as discussed earlier on pp. 105–110. Liquid asset holdings are also indicative of the longer-run economic condition of households and thus tend to reflect the stabilizing influence of current wealth and future prospects, which play such a predominant role in the consumption hypotheses developed by Friedman and by Modigliani, Brumberg and Ando.

The equation for food, on the other hand, places emphasis on two influences not encountered in the discussion of aggregate functions, *i.e.*, the size of the population to be fed, P, and the price of food p_F relative to that of consumer goods in general, p_C. The estimated equation is

$$C_{F,t} = 21.1 + 0.66\,Y_{d,t} - 10.9\,\frac{p_F}{p_C} + 0.189\,P_{t-1}.$$

Thus if the relative price of food goes up, the consumption of food declines.

The consumption of durables (excluding automobiles), $C_{D,t}$, is best approximated by a function similar to that for nondurables, except that a term is added for the stock of durable goods at the end of the last period, $K_{D,t-1}$. The expenditure equation is

$$C_{D,t} = -26.2 + 0.162Y_{d,t} - 0.178\,K_{D,t-1} + 0.049\,L_{t-1}$$

As expected, consumption of durables is positively related to Disposable Personal Income and liquid assets. The negative relationship between the demand for durables and last period's stock of them, however, is still another phenomenon that did not appear in the earlier discussion of aggregate functions. The explanation for this effect is that consumers seem to desire a particular stock of durables, depending upon their current circumstances; the larger the stock carried over from last period, the smaller the current expenditure on these items. Conversely, the smaller the stock carried over, the greater the expenditure required to approach the desired level. A similar relationship involving the stock of cars appears in the equation for expenditure on automobiles.

The function developed to describe the consumption of services $C_{S,t}$, on the other hand, stresses the importance of habit by introducing a term for average expenditures on services over the past four periods, $\bar{C}_{s,t}$. The expression used is

$$C_{s,t} = 2.68 + 0.055\, Y_{d,t} - 13.65\, \frac{p_s}{p_c}$$

$$+ 0.801 \bar{C}_{s,t} + 0.057 L_{t-1},$$

where, as in the case of food, the consumption of services is influenced by their price level, p_s, relative to that of consumption goods in general, p_c.

These consumption functions from the Brookings model, of course, are only a sample of the types of relations that have proved useful in the analysis of disaggregated categories of consumer expenditure. The degree of dissaggregation, the selection of variables to be included, and manner in which the calculations are carried out must depend on the circumstances and on the use that is to be made of the results. The function most appropriate to the United States, for example, may be very different from one that gives the best "fit" in Britain or France. Even within the same country, the development of the economy may make it necessary to bring in new variables that were not important previously, so that no particular function can be expected to retain its relevance from one decade to the next. Different functions may be preferred, depending on the structure of the broader framework of the macroeconomic analysis of which they form a part. In any case, statistical information is lacking in most countries about many variables with a good claim to be included on a priori grounds. Certainly, no function is generally accepted as *the* consumption function for the United States in the 1960's and 1970's. What *is* generally agreed, however, is that the dependence of consumption on current income is sufficiently great in the short run to justify the use of such a relationship in theoretical analysis; if this can be taken for granted, certain results follow with regard to the equilibrium of the economy as a whole, and the next chapter will be devoted to a consideration of them.

CHAPTER 6
The Multiplier

1. The Consumption Function and Equilibrium

If consumers' demand is related to income through a consumption function of some kind, there are certain consequences for the equilibrium of the economy. The condition of equilibrium — that aggregate demand shall equal aggregate supply — was amplified in Chapter 3[1] into

$$C + I + G + E - M = \text{GNP},$$

where all the symbols on the left-hand side of the equation stand for *ex ante* quantities, and where (in accordance with the assumption of constant prices made at the end of Chapter 4) all are in real terms. This relationship may be simplified, for the time being, by assuming an economy that has no general government expenditure or government enterprises, no foreign trade, and no indirect business taxes or business transfer payments. Also, capital consumption is subtracted from both sides of the equation, so that investment (I) becomes net instead of gross, and GNP becomes *Net* National Product (NNP), which, in the absence of indirect taxation and special business transfers, is identical in value to National Income, Y. Accordingly, the equilibrium condition may now be rewritten as

$$Y = C + I.$$

If, further, it is assumed that there are no personal income or corporate profits taxes, no social security taxes or transfer payments to persons, no undistributed corporate profits, and no consumer or government interest, Y will be identical with the total of personal disposable incomes. If the consumption function is $C = cY$, where c is some fraction that does not change with the level of income, it can be substituted in the last equation, giving

$$Y = cY + I$$

or

$$Y = \frac{I}{1 - c}.$$

For equilibrium to exist, therefore, Y must take whatever value will make the excess of income over consumers' demand equal to the demand for investment. If (as is assumed at present) I is not influenced at all by the

---

[1] See above, p. 48.

level of income, then it is investment demand that determines income. Thus, if c is 0.75 and investment demand is $100 billion,

$$Y = \frac{100}{1 - 0.75} = 400$$

— where the units are billions of dollars. Similarly, if I were $150 billion, Y would be $600 billion; and so on.

This relationship can also be stated in terms of saving. Saving has been defined as income minus consumption; the latter is defined by the consumption function $C = cY$, so

$$S = Y - C = Y - cY = Y(1 - c).$$

This is the "savings function," which could also be written

$$S = sY \qquad \text{(where } s = 1 - c\text{).}$$

The equilibrium condition is that

$$I = sY; \quad \text{that is,} \quad Y = \frac{I}{s}.$$

Investment demand must equal the amount the community wishes to save, but because the latter is dependent on income and the former is not, income must adjust itself to the level of investment if equilibrium is to exist.

If the consumption function were $C = C_0 + bY$ instead of $C = cY$, the equilibrium condition

$$Y = C + I$$

would become

$$Y = C_0 + bY + I$$

so that

$$Y = \frac{C_0 + I}{1 - b}.$$

If $C_0 = \$50$ billion, $b = 0.8$, and $I = \$100$ billion, the value of Y must be $750 billion in equilibrium. Here, income is determined not only by I and b, but also by C_0, which is the part of consumers' demand independent of the level of income. Similarly, any element of aggregate demand that is "autonomous," in the sense that it does not depend on the level of income, will play a part analogous to those of C_0 and I: if government expenditure (G) and foreign trade $(E - M)$ are assumed to be autonomous and are brought back into the equilibrium condition, this becomes

$$Y = \frac{C_0 + I + G + E - M}{1 - b};$$

equilibrium income equals the sum of autonomous demands divided by $(1 - b)$, where b is the marginal propensity to consume.

This is illustrated in Figure 6.1, which resembles Figure 5.1 (p. 97) in showing the consumption function $C(Y)$ as a straight line starting from a point on the vertical axis. The latter, however, measures not only consumers' demand but aggregate demand in general. Income is measured on the horizontal axis; the line $Y = D$, passing through the origin at 45°, indicates all the possible positions of equilibrium where aggregate demand is exactly equal to income. If the nonconsumption elements of demand (I, G, etc.) are Z_1 and are assumed autonomous, they can be added to consumers' demand at all levels of income to give an "aggregate demand function" $C(Y) + Z_1$ that is parallel to $C(Y)$. The function $C(Y) + Z_1$ cuts the $Y = D$ line at an income level of Y_1; at that position, aggregate demand D_1 equals income Y_1 and the equilibrium condition is fulfilled. If autonomous nonconsumption demand were Z_2, the aggregate demand function would be $C(Y) + Z_2$ which cuts the $Y = D$ line at an equilibrium income of Y_2. In fact, income is in equilibrium wherever the vertical distance between $C(Y)$ and the $Y = D$ line is exactly filled up by Z, the sum of nonconsumption demands.

The same principle applies when the consumption function is not

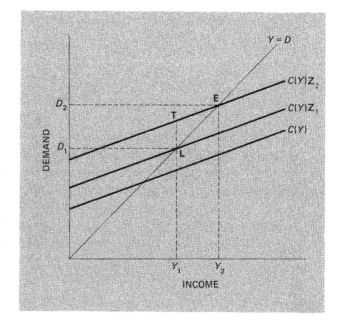

Fig. 6.1

Equilibrium levels of income and demand, and the "multiplier" effect of a shift in the aggregate demand function (quantities expressed in real terms).

linear — *i.e.*, when it is not a straight line but a curve with diminishing slope, as it would be if its equation were, say, $C = C_0 + bY - cY^2$. The principle also applies even when nonconsumption demands are not wholly autonomous. If, for example, investment were responsive to the level of income, getting larger at higher income levels, the aggregate demand function would not be parallel to $C(Y)$, but would diverge from it toward the right-hand side of the diagram, opening up an ever-increasing gap between itself and $C(Y)$. Equilibrium would still require that the gap between $C(Y)$ and the aggregate demand function be equal to that between $C(Y)$ and the $Y = D$ line. These more complicated situations, however, will be set aside for the moment.

2. The Static Multiplier

In Figure 6.1 two equilibrium levels of income are shown: Y_1 when nonconsumption demand is Z_1, and Y_2 when it is Z_2. If these positions are compared, it is clear that Y_2 exceeds Y_1 by an amount greater than the difference between Z_2 and Z_1. The horizontal distance Y_1Y_2 equals the vertical distance D_1D_2, since the $Y = D$ line slopes at 45°; but D_1D_2 is greater than the difference between Z_1 and Z_2 (the latter value being indicated by the length of the line LT in Figure 6.1). Obviously, the effect of a change in Z on the equilibrium level of D and Y will be greater the steeper the slope of the consumption function $C(Y)$.

In economic terms, this means that a given autonomous change in investment (or in any other form of demand) will be associated with a change in income larger than itself; how much larger depends on the Marginal Propensity to Consume (MPC). In the numerical example given on p. 135 above, income was $400 billion when investment was $100 billion; with investment at $150 billion, income was $600 billion; that is, a difference of $50 billion in investment was associated with a difference of $200 billion in income, the MPC being 0.75 throughout.

If the consumption function is $C = C_0 + bY$, a given level of investment I_1 will be associated with a certain level of income Y_1; a higher level of investment I_2, with higher income Y_2. The two equilibria are

$$Y_1 = C_0 + bY_1 + I_1$$

and

$$Y_2 = C_0 + bY_2 + I_2.$$

The difference between the two situations is found by subtracting the first equation from the second giving

$$(Y_2 - Y_1) = b(Y_2 - Y_1) + (I_2 - I_1)$$

from which

$$(Y_2 - Y_1) = \frac{(I_2 - I_1)}{1 - b}.$$

The difference between the income levels (which for brevity may be written $\triangle Y$) is equal to the difference between the levels of investment ($\triangle I$) multiplied by $\frac{1}{1 - b}$. The ratio between $\triangle Y$ and $\triangle I$ is thus

$$\frac{\triangle Y}{\triangle I} = \frac{1}{1 - b} = \frac{1}{s},$$

where b is the MPC and $(1 - b)$ is the Marginal Propensity to Save, s. This ratio is called the Multiplier and is conventionally represented by the symbol k. Its value is automatically defined when the MPC is known: *e.g.*, if the MPC is 3/4, the MPS is 1/4, and k (which is the reciprocal of the MPS) is 4. The higher the MPC, the higher the value of k; a MPC of 1.0 would give k equal to infinity — that is, there would be no possible equilibrium of income if a change in investment were to disturb the original equilibrium. Conversely, a MPC of 0 gives $k = 1$: the change in income would be equal to the multiplicand, $\triangle I$. The lower the value of the Multiplier, the less will a given $\triangle I$ alter the level of income.

The multiplicand has so far been assumed to be a change in investment. But it could just as well be a change in government spending, or in the demand for exports, or in any other element of aggregate demand — provided the change is autonomous, not induced by a change in income itself. It could even be a change in the autonomous part of consumption (the C_0 in $C = C_0 + bY$) since C_0 does not vary with the level of income. If the consumption function was initially $C = 40 + 0.75Y$, and if it changes to $C = 50 + 0.75Y$ (*i.e.*, the value of C_0 rises from 40 to 50), income will rise by 40, thus,

$$\triangle Y = (50 - 40) \times \frac{1}{1 - 0.75} = 40.$$

It may sometimes be convenient to speak of a "consumption multiplier" or an "investment multiplier" according to the nature of the multiplicand in a particular case, but the numerical value of the multiplier will be the same whatever the multiplicand is.

It is possible that not only consumption but also other elements of demand may be responsive to the level of income. For example, investment may consist of an autonomous part (I_0) and a part that rises as income rises (iY), so that $I = I_0 + iY$ where i is the "marginal propensity to invest." Equilibrium is then

$$Y = C + I = C_0 + bY + I_0 + iY.$$

If autonomous investment rises by $\triangle I_0$, income rises by

$$\triangle Y = b\triangle Y + i\triangle Y + \triangle I_0$$

(there being no change in C_0), and the multiplier is

$$k = \frac{\triangle Y}{\triangle I_0} = \frac{1}{(1 - b - i)}.$$

This has been called the "compound" Multiplier to distinguish it from the "simple" Multiplier $\frac{1}{1-b}$. If b and i are added together in an inclusive "marginal propensity to spend" (which could also include marginal propensities in other elements of demand), the multiplier principle can be generalized into the proposition that any autonomous rise in demand ($\triangle Z$) will be associated with a rise in income ($\triangle Y$) whose size will depend on the marginal propensity to spend (σ) in such a way that

$$\frac{\triangle Y}{\triangle Z} = \frac{1}{1 - \sigma}.$$

So far, income and all other magnitudes have been assumed to be at constant prices; for example, the difference between Y_1 and Y_2 in Figure 6.1 represents a physical quantity of goods and services, not a change in money income only. The Multiplier has, in fact, been defined in real terms: a change in the volume of goods and services demanded necessitates a multiple increase in the physical quantity produced. A difficulty seems to arise here, however, since there is an obvious limit to increases in *real* income; no matter what the size of the Multiplier, income and output cannot exceed the physical quantity the economy is capable of producing at full employment. When full employment prevails, a rise in autonomous demand may very well cause *money* income to rise through effects on the general price level, but it cannot bring about a rise in *real* income. It may seem, therefore, that the Multiplier should have a value of zero at full employment;

if $\triangle Y = 0$, $\dfrac{\triangle I}{\triangle Y}$ must also be 0. This is false reasoning, however; the Multiplier does not show what level of income will *actually* be reached, but the level that must be reached to attain equilibrium. It shows the overall change in aggregate demand that results from an autonomous change in a particular element of demand; it could be symbolized as $\dfrac{\triangle D}{\triangle Z}$ where D is aggregate demand and $\triangle Z$ is the multiplicand. Putting $\triangle Y$ in place of $\triangle D$ simply assumes that the equilibrium condition is satisfied. If this is physically impossible, the Multiplier will simply indicate the extent of the disequilibrium resulting from a change in demand.

The Multiplier so far described is a *static* concept. It gives little insight into the process by which the economy tries to achieve a new equilibrium. The process by which output adjusts itself to a new level of demand is assumed to take place instantaneously, or at least so quickly that none of the parameters of the system have time to change — consumers' preferences remain unchanged, the distribution of incomes stays as before, and so on. In real life, it is very unlikely that this would hold true. But if lapses of time are introduced into the working of the Multiplier, it ceases to be a comparison between two different positions of equilibrium; attention must be directed to the sequence of events by which the economy moves from one position to the other, and this inevitably brings in the time factor.

3. The Dynamic Multiplier

The "multiplier process" was crudely sketched in Chapter 3.[2] An initial rise in, say, investment demand gives rise to expenditure on new plant; the incomes of those concerned in supplying these facilities are increased, and they in turn increase their expenditure according to their "marginal propensities to spend." If investment does not rise any further, and if other kinds of demand remain unchanged, subsequent rounds of spending will be on consumption only, and each round will bring less spending than the last if the MPC is less than 1.0. To satisfy the increase in demand at each

---

[2] See above, pp. 51–53.

stage, production must be increased. If, for example, retailers meet a rise in consumers' demand by running down inventories, it is assumed that they order replacements, since their willingness to hold lower inventories would amount to a reduction in investment demand, which has been assumed not to change after its initial rise. The increase in production will then take the form of replacement of retailers' inventories. Rising demand may also be met by increases in prices; but these will merely increase the money incomes of those who charge the higher prices, causing the next stage of the process to be transacted in higher values. The physical quantities involved will be the same, unless the change in prices has affected the consumption function to a significant extent.[3]

If the MPC remains, say, 0.8 throughout, an increase of $10 billion in investment demand will first raise income and output by $10 billion as the initial increase in demand is satisfied; the recipients of the $10 billion will wish to spend eight-tenths of it on consumption, and satisfying *this* demand will raise income and output by $8 billion; at the next stage, $6.4 billion of income and output will be added, causing consumers' demand to rise by a further $5.1 billion — and so on. At the tenth round, the increase in income will be only $1.07 billion; at the twentieth, $0.115 billion; at the thirtieth, $0.01 billion. Eventually the repercussions will become virtually imperceptible. In symbols, the initial rise in income, $\triangle Y_1$, equals the rise in investment $\triangle I$; in the next period, the increase in income[4] $\triangle Y_2$ is equal to c (the MPC) times $\triangle Y_1$, or $c\triangle I$. In the third period, $\triangle Y_3$ is $c^2\triangle I$; and this process continues in such a way that in the nth period,

$$\triangle Y_n = c\triangle Y_{n-1} = c^{n-1}\triangle I.$$

If Y_0 is the income of the period before the one in which the initial investment took place, then the sum of the series of increases in income over n periods, $Y_n - Y_0$ or

$$\triangle Y_1 + \triangle Y_2 + \triangle Y_3 + \ldots + \triangle Y_n,$$

is equal to

$$\triangle I + c\triangle I + c^2\triangle I + \ldots + c^{n-1}\triangle I.$$

---

[3] See above, pp. 114–116.

[4] In this and the following paragraphs, $\triangle Y$ stands for the difference between current income and the income of the previous period, *not* between current income and the income of the period before the multiplier process began; for example, $\triangle Y_4 = Y_4 - Y_3$, not $Y_4 - Y_0$ (where the subscripts stand for periods equal in length to the rounds referred to earlier).

If n is a large number, this expression can be reduced[5] to

$$\triangle I\left(\frac{1}{1-c}\right)$$

and consequently

$$\frac{Y_n - Y_0}{\triangle I} = \frac{1}{1-c},$$

which appears to be the same as the "static" multiplier described in the previous section, except that n periods are required for the full effect to be experienced.

The resemblance is due to the fact that the rise in investment demand is assumed to be permanent — having risen by $\triangle I$ in the first period, investment remains at its new level throughout the rest of the process. But that is by no means the only possibility. Investment may increase only during the first period, falling back to its original level in the second and remaining unchanged thereafter. In this "single-injection" multiplier process, the initial increase in income, $\triangle Y$, is $\triangle I$ as before; but in the next period the consequential rise in consumption, $c\triangle I$, will be accompanied by a reduction in investment offsetting the initial increase, so that $\triangle Y_2 = c\triangle I - \triangle I$. In the third period, the second round of consumption spending due to the original rise in investment will take place, but there will also be a *fall* in consumption because of the reduction in investment that occurred in the previous period; thus $\triangle Y_3 = c^2\triangle I - c\triangle I$. If c is less than 1, $\triangle I$ will be greater than $c\triangle I$, and $c\triangle I$ will be greater than

---

[5] The series can be written $\triangle I(1 + c + c^2 + \ldots + c^{n-1})$. Let the sum of the terms inside the brackets be denoted S; that is,

$$S = 1 + c + c^2 + \ldots + c^{n-1}.$$

Now multiply both sides of this equation by c, giving

$$Sc = c + c^2 + c^3 + \ldots + c^n,$$

and subtract the second equation from the first; on the right-hand side, all terms cancel out except 1 and c^n, so that

$$S(1 - c) = 1 - c^n.$$

Because c is a fraction, c^n will be very small if n is very large; it can therefore be omitted without making any serious difference to the solution of the equation, so that

$$S = \frac{1}{1-c}.$$

Thus,

$$\triangle I(1 + c + c^2 + \ldots + c^{n-1}) = \triangle I\left(\frac{1}{1-c}\right).$$

$c^2 \triangle I$; so $\triangle Y_2$ and $\triangle Y_3$ will both be negative if $\triangle Y_1$ was positive. During the first period, income rose by the amount of additional investment, but in the second and third periods it has been falling; the decline will continue until, in the nth period,

$$\triangle Y_n = c^{n-1} \triangle I - c^{n-2} \triangle I.$$

If n is a large number, both c^{n-1} and c^{n-2} will be so small as to be negligible, and the difference between them will be smaller still; for practical purposes, $\triangle Y_n = 0$. Income will now have returned to its original level. The sum of the income changes that have occurred is

$$\triangle I + c \triangle I - \triangle I + c^2 \triangle I - c \triangle I + \ldots + c^{n-1} \triangle I - c^{n-2} \triangle I,$$

in which all the terms cancel out except $c^{n-1} \triangle I$, which is assumed to be so small that it can be neglected; so $Y_n - Y_0 = 0$. The original stimulus $\triangle I$ has at last been completely offset by subsequent reductions in income.[6]

Whether the rise in investment is sustained or not, the whole multiplier process is likely to take a considerable time to work itself out, even if each of the n periods is fairly short. Strictly speaking, the process will *never* finish; though $\triangle Y_n$ will be very small if n is very large, it will never quite reach zero value,[7] and how small it must be before it can be regarded as negligible is obviously a matter of judgment. It may happen, however, that only the first few periods are really of interest; well before the nth period is reached (and, consequently, well before the value of $\triangle Y$ becomes negligible), it may be important to see how far the process has gone and to compare the current level of income with that existing before the initial stimulus was given. If the series $\triangle I$, $c \triangle I$, $c^2 \triangle I$ . . . (which occurs when investment rises to a new level and remains there) is carried only as far as the tth period, where t is not a large number, the sum of the increases in income will be[8]

$$\triangle I \left(\frac{1 - c^t}{1 - c} \right).$$

---

[6] The "single-injection" multiplier might well be regarded as a combination of two processes of the "repeated-injection" type described earlier. Thus, Multiplier A starts off in period 1 with $\triangle I$, and continues $c \triangle I$, $c^2 \triangle I$, etc.; in period 2, Multiplier B starts with $-\triangle I$ (so as to reduce investment to its original level) and continues $-c \triangle I$, $-c^2 \triangle I$, and so on, but always one period behind A; the process described in the text results from the addition of A and B in each period. In this approach, the repeated-injection sequence may be considered the *basic* multiplier process, all other multipliers being merely variations caused by the introduction of fresh sequences.

[7] In mathematical terms, $\triangle Y_n$ approaches zero as n approaches infinity.

[8] The derivation is the same as in Footnote 5, p. 142, except that c^t now appears

For example, if $\triangle I$ is \$10 billion, $c = 0.8$ and $t = 6$, the level of income will rise by \$36.89 billion over the six periods, and the value of the multiplier, $(Y_t - Y_0)/\triangle I$, will be approximately 3.7. This incomplete, or "truncated," multiplier is obviously less than the "full" multiplier, which in this case is 5.0 since the total increase in Y over all n periods will be \$50 billion; but knowing the values of the former may be more useful.[9] If the whole n-period process would take two or three years to work itself out, the more distant repercussions will be irrelevant to analysis that seeks to forecast developments during the coming six months; moreover, the longer the time taken by the n periods, the greater the likelihood that the later rounds will be distorted and even overwhelmed by the consequences of changes in consumers' preferences, in the distribution of incomes, and in other parameters of the system.

The one-period "consumption lag" in the above sequences (often called the "Robertsonian lag"[10]) implies a consumption function of the form $C_t = c(Y_{t-1})$ or $C_t = C_0 + c(Y_{t-1})$. But, as was seen in the previous chapter, the function may be more complicated than this. If consumers' demand depends partly on their "net worth," and if this is growing from period to period, an additional element will enter into aggregrate demand in each period. Changes in income distribution, caused by the change in aggregate income, may affect consumers' demand in subsequent periods; rising income may alter the expectations on which consumers' decisions are based. If c (the MPC) changes from period to period, it may be impossible to reduce $\triangle Y_n$ to a simple multiple of $\triangle I$ as was done in the last two sequences worked out above. As time goes by, the chances of further autonomous changes in demand will become greater, so that the sequence may be disturbed by the injection of a fresh change in, say, investment demand, which will set up subsequent reactions of its own concurrently with those persisting from the original sequence.

In the examples given above, it is assumed that the level of output adjusts itself immediately to changes in aggregate demand; this was shown

---

in place of c^n. Because t is not large enough to make c^t negligible, the latter term cannot be discarded from $S(1 - c) = 1 - c^t$, and must therefore be retained in the expression given in the text.

[9] See F. Machlup, "Period Analysis and Multiplier Theory," in G. Haberler, ed. for American Economic Association, *Readings in Business Cycle Theory* (Homewood, Ill.: Irwin, 1944).

[10] After D. H. Robertson; see his *Banking Policy and the Price Level* (London: P. S. King & Son, 1926), p. 59.

by setting the change in income $\triangle Y$ (which is identical with the value of output) equal to the change in demand for consumption and investment occurring in each period. If output lags behind the change in demand, this lag will have effects of its own, which are investigated in the next section.

4. The Effects of an "Output Lag"

When demand rises, firms may need to train additional workers and re-plan processes before they can increase output to meet it. When demand falls, it may be cheaper to finish work in progress than to abandon it. Producers may be unwilling to alter their output until convinced that the new level of demand is going to last. In the meantime, they may use their inventories as a buffer, drawing on them if sales are rising or adding to them if sales fall; if the rise in demand finds their inventories low, they may simply let buyers wait, so that demand is frustrated, or they may allow prices to alter appropriately. Whatever the ultimate consequences of the change in demand, output will remain the same for the time being.

Suppose it takes one period for output to catch up with demand: $pQ_t = D_{t-1}$ where D is money expenditure or demand and pQ is the value of output, Q being output in physical units and p being the price level (as-sumed constant at this point). The subscript t denotes any given time period and $t-1$ the preceding period. Excess demand ($D_t - pQ_t$ or, what is the same thing, $D_t - D_{t-1}$) is met from inventory, excess output is put into it, and firms try to readjust their inventories to normal in the following period. Their demand for inventory replacements is a form of investment demand (which may, of course, be negative if excess output occurred in the previous period); total investment demand in period t, then, will be $A_t + (D_{t-1} - D_{t-2})$, where A_t is autonomous investment. Consumption is assumed to depend on current income; that is, $C_t = cY_t$. Here Y_t is actual income generated by, and identical to, current output pQ_t. Because $pQ_t = D_{t-1}$, $C_t = cY_t$ implies $C_t = cD_{t-1}$. Aggregate de-mand D_t consists of consumption and investment, so

$$D_t = cD_{t-1} + A_t + D_{t-1} - D_{t-2}$$
$$= D_{t-1}(1+c) - D_{t-2} + A_t.$$

If D_{t-1} and D_{t-2} are both 100, and if $A_t = 20$ and $c = 0.8$, D_t will be $100(1.8) - 100 + 20 = 100$. Now let autonomous investment rise by 10, giving $A_{t+1} = 30$, and then return to its original level, so that A_{t+2}, A_{t+3}, etc., are all 20. Then

$$D_{t+1} = D_t(1 + c) - D_{t-1} + A_{t+1}$$
$$= 100(1.8) - 100 + 30 = 110;$$

$$D_{t+2} = D_{t+1}(1 + c) - D_t + A_{t+2}$$
$$= 110(1.8) - 100 + 20 = 118.$$

By a similar calculation, $D_{t+3} = 122.4$. Now, however, demand falls again: $D_{t+4} = 122.3$ and $D_{t+5} = 117.8$. The decline continues until period $t + 10$, when $D_{t+10} = 77.6$, after which demand begins to rise once more.[11]

The presence of the output lag (or "Lundbergian lag" as it is sometimes called[12]) has thus enabled the rise in autonomous investment to set up a *cyclical* movement in aggregate demand. From one period to another, demand increases not only through the simple multiplier effect of the rise in investment, but also by the carrying over of a backlog of demand for inventories. As output approaches the level at which the backlog of demand begins to be satisfied, the very act of catching up on the backlog will eliminate it from the next period's demand, so that eventually demand will fall again. But a fall in demand must mean the accumulation of surplus inventories if output is not immediately reduced; the effort to work these off will cause demand to fall further — and so on through the cycle.

When firms merely leave excess demand unsatisfied, instead of meeting it from inventory, the effects should be exactly the same; but the backlog of demand will be accumulated by final buyers instead of by producers whose inventories are depleted. If, however, the excess of demand over supply in the opening periods causes prices to be driven upwards, the pattern of demand may be changed through the expectational and Pigou effects described in the previous chapter,[13] thus complicating the cycle.

So far, it has been assumed that the output lag is of fixed length, but in

---

[11] The reader may carry on the calculation, if he wishes, by inserting numerical values; unfortunately, this is a laborious procedure. A shortcut is to find a general solution for such a series of equations (which are known as *difference equations*); for methods, see W. J. Baumol, *Economic Dynamics*, 2d ed. (New York: Macmillan, 1959), Chaps. 9, 10, and 11; or T. Yamane, *Mathematics for Economists: An Elementary Survey*, 2d ed. (Prentice-Hall, 1968) Chap. 9.

[12] After E. Lundberg, *Studies in the Theory of Economic Expansion* (Stockholm, 1937; reprinted by Kelley, 1954).

[13] See above, pp. 115–116.

real life this would hardly be true. A pronounced upward or downward trend in demand may induce firms to alter output quickly, perhaps even to anticipate the trend; small changes may leave them in a "wait-and-see" frame of mind, so that the lag will increase as the multiplier effects taper off. If a rise in demand calls for output at or near the full employment level, the physical difficulties of increasing output will be much greater than if there are plenty of idle resources available; the lag will therefore increase as output rises. No such difficulty will arise when it is a question of reducing output to match falling demand, and since the embarrassment of piling up an accumulation of unsold goods is greater than that of not being able to satisfy demand fully, firms may be expected to cut output more quickly than they increase it. In general, then, the output lag is likely to be shorter when demand is falling than when it is rising.

The practical measurement of output lags is difficult. If differences between demand and output were always met from (or put into) inventory, and if inventories never changed for any other reason, then a rise or fall in inventories would signal a lag of output behind demand. But firms may stockpile raw materials when they think their prices will rise in the future or run down inventories if they think price reductions will allow cheaper replacement later. A rise in demand may sometimes be directed mainly to industries (*e.g.*, transportation) that cannot store their output, sometimes to industries that can. Firms whose inventories run down may be spurred into finding ways of economizing them, so that a rise in their customers' demand for finished products will be partly offset by a permanent fall in the firms' own demand for inventory.

5. Corporate Saving and the Multiplier

Up to this point, it has been assumed that all returns to the factors of production were paid out immediately as individuals' incomes. In particular, it was assumed that all corporate profits were paid out in dividends to stockholders, *i.e.*, that there were no undistributed corporate profits. From their gross income (which includes certain nontrading receipts as well as gross profits on sales) corporations must pay taxes, provide for depreciation, and service whatever fixed-interest debt they have contracted; whatever remains after these payments have been made (the net profit after taxes, or "discretionary income," of corporations) is used partly for distribution as dividends and partly for retention within the firm. This latter undistributed portion of corporate profits constitutes corporate saving. In 1967, for example, U.S. corporations retained 52% of their $48 billion of after-tax profits.

Each year, corporate managers must determine how much to distribute in dividends, and indications are that these decisions are made in the light of a "target" — an ultimate desired rate of dividend payment stated as a percentage of net profit or of net profit plus depreciation (the so-called "cash flow").[14] As profits rise and fall, firms adjust their dividend payments in an attempt to maintain the desired pay-out percentage; they do not, however, attempt a complete adjustment to the target percentage every year. Stockholders appear to have a strong preference for a reasonably stable and smoothly growing rate of dividend payment on their shares, and most corporate managements seek to avoid introducing dividend increases that might have to be cut back if the higher profit level is not maintained. Therefore, corporations follow a policy of "partial adaptation" of dividends to changing profit levels; that is, in any year they revise the dividend pay-out percentage by some fraction of the gap between the existing level and the target. As a result, when corporate profits are rising, increases in dividend payments lag behind; likewise, when profits fall, dividends are slow to respond to lower profit levels and may even keep rising for a time. Thus dividends tend to remain stable in the face of fluctuating corporate profits, which means that the corporate short-run marginal propensity to save can be quite high.

A recent study of the dividend behavior of U.S. corporations[15] from 1920 to 1960 found that the target dividend pay-out ratio was around two-thirds of net profits, but that the short-run (annual) marginal propensity to pay dividends out of profit was as low as 0.15 to 0.2. This implies a corporate short-run marginal propensity to save of 0.8 or more. By retaining profits in this fashion, corporations are saving on behalf of their stockholders; the question is, however, whether the stockholders would have saved the same proportion if the *whole* of corporate discretionary income had been distributed in dividends. If they would not in fact have

---

[14] See J. Lintner, "Distribution of Incomes of Corporations among Dividends, Retained Earnings, and Taxes," *American Economic Review*, Vol. 46 (May, 1956), pp. 97–113; and J. A. Brittain, *Corporate Dividend Policy* (Washington, D.C.: Brookings, 1966).

[15] J. A. Brittain, *op. cit.*

done so, it becomes necessary to modify the earlier formulation of the Multiplier.

Instead of the consumption function $C = cY$ (where Y is National Income, *i.e.*, the sum of factor incomes), the function $C = cY_d$ (where Y_d is the sum of personal disposable incomes) will be used. The equilibrium condition $Y = C + I$ then becomes $Y = cY_d + I$. If taxes and transfer are neglected, Y_d is National Income *minus* undistributed profits (U). The relationship of U to corporate profits P may be stated as

$$U = U_0 + uP$$

where u is the corporate marginal propensity to save — say, 0.8. Then, if total profits are normally 15% of National Income,

$$U = U_0 + .80\,(.15Y) = U_0 + .12Y.$$

Let the symbol j stand for the corporate propensity to save (u) multiplied by the share of profits in National Income, so that $U = U_0 + jY$; then

$$Y_d = Y - U = Y - U_0 - jY$$

or

$$Y_d = Y(1 - j) - U_0.$$

The equilibrium condition $Y = cY_d + I$ now becomes

$$Y = cY(1 - j) - cU_0 + I.$$

If autonomous investment[16] rises by $\triangle I$, income increases by

$$\triangle Y = c\triangle Y(1 - j) + \triangle I$$

(there being no change in U_0), and the static multiplier will be

$$k = \frac{\triangle Y}{\triangle I} = \frac{1}{1 - c + cj}.$$

Thus, the greater the corporate marginal propensity to save and the greater the share of corporate profits in National Income, the smaller the value of the Multiplier.

Similar modification of the dynamic Multiplier, with a one-period Robertsonian consumption lag and no output lag, will give the following series

---

[16] It should be emphasized that this argument assumes that the level of investment is independent not only of changes in National Income but also of the level of corporate saving. As noted below in Chapter 7, the quantity of available undistributed corporate profits is, in fact, an important factor in the determination of corporate investment. Inclusion of this additional influence would tend to dampen the impact of corporate saving on the multiplier.

of income changes in response to an initial rise in investment which is not repeated after period 1:

$$\triangle Y_1 = \triangle I_1$$
$$\triangle Y_2 = c\triangle I_1(1 - j) - \triangle I_1$$
$$\triangle Y_3 = c^2\triangle I_1(1 - j)^2 - c\triangle I_1(1 - j)$$

leading in the nth period to

$$\triangle Y_n = c^{n-1}\triangle I_1(1 - j)^{n-1} - c^{n-2}\triangle I_1(1 - j)^{n-2}.$$

Here, the "corporate marginal propensity to save" (if positive) reduces the proportion of income handed on from each period to the next, causing total income to rise less at first and then to taper off more sharply and quickly than if all profit had been distributed in dividends.

Bringing corporations' behavior into the Multiplier sequence naturally increases its realism; it is obviously unlikely that an increase in autonomous expenditure will bring about an immediate increase of the same magnitude in personal disposable incomes. It would indeed do so if the multiplicand were expenditure on a project involving only an increase in labor employed — for example, the digging of a system of irrigation ditches by hand. But most investment projects involve the purchase of machinery and the placing of contracts, for which payments are made to corporations in the first instance; they in turn[17] pay out wages, buy materials from other firms, pay dividends out of whatever profit they make, and retain the rest undistributed. If the distribution of dividends comes some time after the payment of wages, the subsequent effects of a rise in investment will be complicated by an earning lag. For example, if w is the share of wages in any increase in income and z is the share of dividends, and if the MPC's wage earners and stockholders are c_1 and c_2 respectively, then the response of consumption to a change in income would be

$$\triangle C_t = c_1 w\triangle Y_{t-1} + c_2 z\triangle Y_{t-2}$$

in a situation in which dividends lag one period behind wage payments. If c_1 and c_2 happen to differ from one another, further complications will be added to the sequence.

---

[17] The actual order of payments may very well be the other way round: contractors may not receive payment until the project is finished and in the meantime will pay for labor and materials by borrowing or by using funds of their own. But this means that they *behave* as though payment had been made when the order was first placed, and the sequence of income generation then proceeds in normal multiplier fashion.

6. The "Multi-Sector" Multiplier

Unfortunately, the more "realistic" the account of the Multiplier, the more complicated it becomes; this, if nothing else, should be clear from the last two sections. The original version given on p. 138 owed its apparent simplicity to the fact that income, consumption, and investment were treated as large aggregates, with no distinction being made among component elements of each one. But in fact, consumption may change much or little in response to a rise in income, depending on how the latter is distributed among groups of consumers; for example, if Marylanders have a lower MPC than Virginians, a rise in investment north of the Potomac will produce a different effect from one south of it. When de-

Table 6.1

Sample Input-Output Matrix

Paid By ↓	Received By →	Industries			Con- sumers	Totals
		A	B	C		
Industries: A		—	40	60	100	200
B		50	—	50	150	250
C		50	100	—	250	400
Consumers		80	100	220	—	400
Totals		180	240	330	500	1250

mand increases, the response of output may be quick or slow depending on which industries are called upon to produce more; if consumers want more clothing, labor and materials will be required to meet the demand, whereas if they wish to go to the theater more often, it may be possible to accommodate them merely by filling empty seats. Some industries may carry large inventories that can be used to meet a rise in demand; others may not. To increase the output of industry A, it will be necessary to employ more labor, but relatively little extra capital equipment will be needed, while in industry B it may be the other way around, so that a good deal will depend on whether a rise in demand is directed towards A's product or B's. Obviously, there will be a considerable gain in realism if the aggregates are "disaggregated" in order to allow for such differences between industries and between groups of consumers.

For this purpose, transactions between the various sectors of the economy can be set out in a *matrix*, of which Table 6.1 is a simple example. Each entry (except for the totals) shows the amount paid by the sector named at the left to the sector named at the head of the column. All transactions are for currently produced goods and services; "capital transfers," such as the purchase of stocks and bonds, are excluded. Thus, payments by consumers to the various industries represent purchases of the industries' products; payments by industries to consumers are wages, dividends, and interest. Transactions between industries represent the purchase of materials; for example, the $50 billion in the second row of the first column is Industry *B*'s purchase from Industry *A* of goods to be processed into the output *B* sells to other sectors. Transactions *within* sectors are cancelled out. Because consumers' total receipts are $500 billion and their total payments $400 billion, personal saving is $100 billion. Industry *A* pays out $20 billion more than its receipts, Industry *B* $10 billion, and Industry *C* $70 billion; these amounts represent the purchase of plant and buildings and the accumulation of inventory — *i.e.*, the investment undertaken by the two industries. Total investment, of course, equals total saving. If saving (a capital payment) and investment (a capital receipt) were explicitly shown in an extra column and row, each sector's total payments would equal its total receipts.

Such matrices (often called "input-output tables" or "Leontief systems" [18]) can be made more detailed, with extra rows and columns for imports, exports, and government transactions, and with a larger number of industries.[19] Ideally, there should be a separate row and column for each sector within which spenders' behavior is much the same; for example, if rich consumers have a different consumption function from poor ones, they should be divided accordingly. Regardless of how numerous the rows and columns, however, the principle is the same as in Table 6.1, which has been restricted to four sectors for the sake of simplicity.

Altering any one of the figures (or elements) in Table 6.1 will obviously change the relevant column total, the row total, and the grand total in the bottom right-hand corner. But it will do even more than that. The proportions in which an industry's payments are divided among the other sectors

---

[18] After W. W. Leontief, who pioneered this approach: see his *The Structure of the American Economy, 1919–1939*, 2d ed. (New York: Oxford University Press, 1951).

[19] See *Survey of Current Business* (September, 1965) which presents an input-output table for the United States with 86 industrial sectors.

are determined by the nature of its product and by its technique of production. Just as the manufacture of a given quantity of steel requires certain definite quantities of pig iron, fuel, and labor, so Industry *A* cannot produce its output without buying inputs from *B*, from *C*, and from consumers (who contribute labor and the use of their property) in amounts 40:60:100 respectively. The distribution of consumers' payments to *A*, *B*, and *C* is determined by their preferences, and the consumption function relates the total of consumers' payments to their total receipts. The proportions between the individual elements and the grand total (the so-called "technical coefficients") thus form a pattern that gives a set of equilibrium conditions for the system; if the coefficients are simple percentages, an autonomous change in any single element must cause equal proportionate changes in all of the others.

However, the coefficients may not be simple percentages. Because consumers spend four-fifths of their receipts when the latter are $500 billion, it does not follow that an addition of $100 billion to their receipts will cause their spending to rise by $80 billion — this is a matter of the marginal, rather than the average, propensity to consume. Similarly, the proportions between the *extra* inputs needed for a given increase in an industry's output may not be the same as those between the *total* inputs shown in Table 6.1; the distinction here is between marginal and average cost of production. Thus, when an autonomous change in expenditure occurs, the results will depend on the *marginal* values of the technical coefficients, some of which may even be zero. When the system is completely adjusted and a new equilibrium has been established, the multiplier effect will be disclosed by a comparison of the figures appearing in the table before and after the disturbance occurred. This version of the Multiplier, working through the transactions relationships of the various sectors, may be called the "Multi-Sector" or "Matrix" Multiplier. Introducing time lags (which need not, of course, be the same for all sectors) will make it dynamic, raising the possibility of oscillations as it did in the Lundbergian case. Further analysis, however, would require the use of matrix algebra, with which the reader is not assumed to be familiar; in the present text, therefore, the matter will be left at this point.[20]

---

[20] For an introduction to input-output methods, see W. H. Miernyk, *The Elements of Input-Output Analysis* (New York: Random House, 1965); for a more advanced treatment, see H. B. Chenery and P. G. Clark, *Interindustry Economics* (New York: Wiley, 1959).

7. The "Employment" Multiplier

So far, the Multiplier concept has been presented in terms of *output*: an autonomous change in demand induces further changes, leading to a multiple rise in the equilibrium level of National Product. It should be noted, however, that the Multiplier was first introduced (by R. F. Kahn in 1931[21]) as a ratio between levels of *employment*: an initial rise in investment creates "primary" employment for workers engaged directly on new capital projects, and their spending then gives rise to "secondary" employment in the industries producing consumer goods; the ratio between the overall rise in employment and the primary employment is the "Employment" Multiplier.

If the proportion between output and employment — *i.e.*, the productivity of labor — were the same for all levels of output, there would be no difference between the value of the Employment Multiplier (k^*) and the ordinary multiplier (k). But, as was argued in Chapter 4 (pp. 69–70), output per unit of labor may be expected to fall as output increases toward the full-employment level; if this happens, k^* should be larger than k when the Multiplier is working to increase output and employment, but smaller when it is working in the opposite direction. In the notation introduced in Chapter 4, physical output as a function of labor input is expressed as $Q = Q(N)$, and output per man-hour may be denoted as

$$\frac{Q}{N} = Q'(N).$$

The value of output is Q times the price level (p), but for simplicity's sake it can be assumed that prices are constant and, furthermore, that $p = 1$. Then any level Y of income and output must be equal to N, the

$$Y = N \cdot Q'(N),$$

and the ratio between two levels of output Y_2 and Y_1, therefore, is

$$\frac{Y_2}{Y_1} = \frac{N_2 \cdot Q'(N_2)}{N_1 \cdot Q'(N_1)},$$

so that

---

[21] R. F. Kahn, "The Relation of Home Investment to Unemployment," *Economic Journal*, Vol. 41 (June, 1931), pp. 173–178.

$$\frac{N_2}{N_1} = \frac{Y_2 \cdot Q'(N_1)}{Y_1 \cdot Q'(N_2)}.$$

If $Y_1 = 100$ and $Y_2 = 110$, while $Q'(N_1) = 100$ and $Q'(N_2) = 90$, then $N_2/N_1 = 1.22$; that is, a rise of 10% in the level of production, accompanied by a 10% fall in output per man-hour, requires an increase of 22% in the level of employment. In this case, k^* is more than twice as large as k.

If time lags are introduced into the Employment Multiplier, its value may be reduced by improvements in labor productivity over time. If the economy's capital equipment is being improved and increased through investment, output per man-hour will be rising, for *all* levels of output, between one period and the next. The fall in productivity due to diminishing returns will then be offset by the rise due to investment, and the *dynamic* Employment Multiplier will be a good deal smaller than the static one. In addition, input-output analysis may be used to investigate employment multipliers. Different patterns of demand imply differing output levels among industries, and the ultimate impact on employment of any change in autonomous demand will depend on the labor productivity within each of the industries in the table.

With these adjustments for changes in labor productivity, the Employment Multiplier is completely analogous to the "output" Multiplier, and everything that has been said about the latter applies also to the former. In all Multipliers, the basic principle is that changes in the level of activity (whether in terms of output or employment) are initiated by changes in the autonomous elements of demand. In addition to those aspects of the multiplier that have been introduced in this chapter — *e.g.*, different forms of the consumption function, output lags, corporate saving — subsequent chapters will consider other influences such as international trade and various types of direct and indirect taxes. For simplicity's sake, each is taken up separately, although the calculation of multipliers when several of these influences are operating at once is the same in principle — only the algebra is more cumbersome.

Investment has traditionally been regarded as the chief autonomous element of demand. The next chapter, therefore, will be devoted to the subject of investment and its determinants.

CHAPTER 7

The Determinants
of Investment

1. The Categories of Investment

The first thing to notice about investment is its multifarious character. Of the $114 billion spent in the United States in 1967 on gross private domestic investment, $6.1 billion (*i.e.*, about 5% of the total) represented increases in business inventories. Of the remaining $108.2 billion of fixed investment, almost exactly half was spent on "producers' durable equipment," mostly machinery of various kinds; another $27.9 billion was spent on "nonresidential structures" (*i.e.*, industrial and commercial building and public utility installations); the remaining $24.6 billion was spent on new homes and other forms of residential construction.[1] In addition to these private expenditures, government authorities spent $25.5 billion on construction (of which the leading items were $8.5 billion on highways and $6.0 billion on educational buildings) and $25.8 billion on other durables.[2] When this "gross public investment" is added to the private investment already detailed, it gives a total investment in 1967 of $165.6 billion. The fact that private capital consumption was $69.2 billion means that about three-fifths of expenditure on private fixed investment was merely to replace equipment worn out during the year, so that only $45.1 billion represented a net addition to the stock of privately owned durable means of production. The figures refer, of course, to *actual* expenditure in 1967, not to demand; but it seems reasonable to suppose that the pattern of intended (*ex ante*) investment must have been roughly similar.

With so many different forms of investment, it is hardly to be expected that a single theory will satisfactorily explain them all. The criteria by which a manufacturing corporation decides to build new plants are obviously different from those by which an individual decides to buy a new home or those by which a city government decides on a program of school construction. Increasing inventories serves one set of purposes, installing new machinery serves another; firms' decisions to replace their equipment may involve different considerations from decisions to expand it. In general, no doubt, each kind of investment expenditure can be assumed to envisage a future yield of some sort, which the spenders wish to maxi-

---

[1] *Survey of Current Business* (July, 1968), Tables 1.1, 5.2, and 5.4.
[2] *Ibid.*, Tables 1.4 and 5.2.

mize; but general resemblances may be overwhelmed by particular differences. This chapter will therefore deal with each of the main catgories of investment separately when trying to discover their determinants.

As earlier with consumption, so now with investment, special attention must be paid to the relationship with income. If changes in investment demand normally arise from causes other than changes in income, they will bring about multiplier effects of the kind described in Chapter 6, and the level of investment demand will determine the equilibrium level of income. It is therefore particularly important to decide how far each category of investment demand is autonomous, and how far it is responsive to changes in income.

2. The Marginal Efficiency of Investment

The category most frequently discussed in the literature of the subject (sometimes, indeed, as though it were the only category) is the net fixed investment of business firms. The general aim of such enterprises is to maximize profits; accordingly, they may be expected to judge investment projects by their expected profitability. Suppose, then, that a given firm is considering whether or not to buy a new machine costing, say, $10,000, which will be a net addition to its existing stock of equipment. How is it to decide?

Installing the machine will give a physical output that will be sold to provide the firm with a revenue, the amount of which will depend on the price of the product. If that product is something quite new, the firm will have to estimate the price at which it can be sold when it comes on the market. If the product is already on sale, some estimate must be made as to what its price is likely to be during the period over which the machine will be operating. It may not be easy to foresee how long that period will be; no doubt the machine's makers can forecast its "life" from an engineering point of view, but there is always the possibility of sudden obsolescence if technological progress should make new and better types of machinery available. Obviously, the assessment of prospective revenue from the machine will be subject to a large margin of uncertainty.

Against the revenue must be set the various expenses of operating the machine. It will use materials, fuel, and lubricants; it may require the employment of additional labor, and it will occupy floor space. The physical quantities of these inputs will be known to the firm, just as will the quantity of its output capacity; but the firm cannot be sure what the costs of the inputs will be during the life of the machine, since these will depend on the future course of prices and wages. However, the firm must make the best guess it can. Having decided on the most probable level of input cost, the firm can subtract it from its estimate of revenue to obtain estimates of the net yield to be expected from the machine during its life; the annual yield can then be expressed as a percentage of the current price, giving a *rate* of yield.

This is analogous to compound interest on a loan of money. If a principal sum P is lent for n years at compound interest, it will accumulate to a sum A such that $A = P(1 + r)^n$, where r is the interest rate. If P, r, and n are given, A can be calculated. Alternatively, if A, r, and n are known, the value of P is given as

$$P = \frac{A}{(1 + r)^n} \; .$$

Here future receipts A are "discounted" by r to give a "present value" P. The term r appears as a rate of interest when the reckoning is forward (from the present to the future), and as a rate of discount when reckoning is backward (from the future to the present).

If a firm buys a machine for \$10,000 expecting a lump-sum net yield of \$15,000 five years hence, the annual rate of yield, indicated by the symbol ρ, can be deduced from the formula

$$\$10,000 = \frac{\$15,000}{(1 + \rho)^5} \; .$$

That is,

$$\rho = \sqrt[5]{\frac{\$15,000}{\$10,000}} - 1 = 0.084 = 8.4\% \; .$$

More typically, yields accrue continuously over the life of the machine, rather than all at once; the series of annual net yields is $A_1 + A_2 + A_3 + \ldots + A_n$, where the subscripts stand for years and n is the number of years for which the machine is expected to last. This is as though a number of loans had been made simultaneously, each accumulating at compound interest over a different number of years: P_1 for one year, P_2 for two years, and so on, so that

$$P_1 = \frac{A_1}{(1+\rho)} \ , \ P_2 = \frac{A_2}{(1+\rho)^2} \ , \ P_3 = \frac{A_3}{(1+\rho)^3} \ , \ \text{etc.}$$

Adding these gives P, the total sum laid out; and

$$P = \frac{A_1}{(1+\rho)} + \frac{A_2}{(1+\rho)^2} + \frac{A_3}{(1+\rho)^3} + \cdots + \frac{A_n}{(1+\rho)^n}.$$

If the machine costs \$10,000, if each year's net yield is expected to be \$3,000, and if $n = 5$, the value of ρ that satisfies the equation is approximately 0.15 or 15%. The annual net yield need not be the same in each year – the series may run \$2,000, \$2,600, \$2,900, and so on – but whatever the values of A_1, A_2, etc., some value of ρ will satisfy the equation,[3] and this will be the rate of yield. It should be noted that the analogy with compound interest lending requires that the depreciation of the machine shall not be counted as an expense of production; just as a lender of money receives back his principal at the end of n years as part of the accumulated sum A, so the investing firm will recover the original outlay on the machine as part of the series of yields received during its life.

The rate of yield ρ is conventionally called the *Marginal Efficiency of Investment* (MEI). The word "marginal" must be emphasized: the MEI is the ρ of an additional machine, and may be quite different from the average rate of yield on the amount of current investment as a whole. Keynes[4] originally called it the "Marginal Efficiency of Capital" (MEC), but this term has the disadvantage of directing attention to the capital stock as a whole rather than to current investment.[5] The MEI must also be distinguished from the marginal product of capital, which is the increase in *current* output arising from the addition of one more unit of capital to the currently employed factors of production. Obviously, the marginal product of capital is a physical quantity analogous to the marginal product of any other factor (whereas the MEI is a percentage

---

[3] This burkes a mathematical point. If any of the A's are negative, as they might where a firm was prepared to face losses in some stages of an operation, the equation may give *several* values for ρ. See H. Bierman and S. Smidt, *The Capital Budgeting Decision*, 2d ed. (New York: Macmillan, 1966), Chapter 3. In the text, this possibility is ignored for the sake of simplicity.

[4] J. M. Keynes, *The General Theory of Employment, Interest and Money* (New York: Harcourt, Brace & World, 1936), pp. 135–136.

[5] A. P. Lerner has a formulation that uses both the MEC and the MEI in different senses; see Chapter 25 of his *Economics of Control* (New York: Macmillan, 1944), and his "On Some Recent Developments in Capital Theory," *American Economic Review*, Vol. 55 (May, 1965), pp. 284–286.

rate) and, unlike the MEI, it does not involve expectations about the yield from the unit of capital during the remainder of its life.

A firm considering the purchase of a new machine may be supposed to compare the MEI with the cost of the funds required to buy the unit. If the firm does not itself possess the necessary funds, it must acquire them by borrowing,[6] in which case the cost of funds is the rate of interest on the loan. If the firm already has the money in hand, the cost is the return that could have been obtained by making some other use of the money; here the choice is between employing the funds within the business to get an "internal rate of return" and lending it out to get an external rate. If the MEI is greater than the rate of interest to be paid or forgone, the machine is worth buying.

This may be put in another way. If money can be borrowed or lent at an interest rate r, the series of expected yields A_1, A_2, etc., can be discounted by r to give their present value, *i.e.*, the sum of money which, if lent at interest r, could produce the given yields. The present value V is

$$V = \frac{A_1}{(1+r)} + \frac{A_2}{(1+r)^2} + \frac{A_3}{(1+r)^3} + \cdots + \frac{A_n}{(1+r)^n} \, .$$

If V is greater than the price of the machine, P, it is obviously profitable to make the investment; in buying the machine, a firm is giving up a sum of money smaller than the present value of the yields obtainable from the use of the machine.[7]

If *one* machine is worth buying, why not two, or three, or still more? If the firm can borrow any amount at the prevailing rate of interest r, it will be profitable to buy new machines as long as the MEI exceeds r; if investment is to be limited, the MEI must fall as more machines are bought. Such a fall may occur because the firm expects the price of the product to be depressed as output rises in consequence of the installation of new equipment; the firm may foresee rising input prices in response to the increasing pressure of demand for labor and materials. Between falling product price and rising output prices, the values of ρ associated with additional numbers of machines — and thus the MEI — will be reduced.

A small firm, of course, may not fear such an outcome. If its output is small relative to the market as a whole, it may be confident that even a

---

[6] The possibility of issuing stock is for the moment neglected, but is considered later (pp. 167–169).

[7] See A. H. Hansen, *Business Cycles and National Income*, 2d ed. (New York: Norton, 1964), p. 125.

sizable rise in its own sales would not disturb the market price; and it may feel sure of obtaining all the inputs it expects to need without creating price-raising shortages in the markets for labor and materials. Nevertheless, such a firm would still be obliged to limit its investment for another reason. The interest it must pay is certain because it is fixed by contract, whereas the rate of yield from the machine is a matter of estimation and could turn out to be less than expected. The greater the investment, then, the greater the loss the firm stands to take if things turn out badly. A small loss might be met from the original resources of the firm, but a large one might ruin it. On M. Kalecki's [8] "principle of increasing risk," therefore, the firm should make a greater allowance for risk, the greater the investment it undertakes; set against the firm's original yield calculations, this will cause the MEI to fall with each additional machine bought.

The MEI, then, falls as investment increases, and the limit to the demand for new machines will be reached when the MEI is reduced to equality with the rate of interest. The inverse relationship between the MEI and the level of investment is illustrated in Figure 7.1. For any level of investment demand (measured on the horizontal scale) there is some value of the MEI (indicated on the vertical scale) that is consistent with it. A line passing through all such points associating values of I with values of the MEI may be called the "MEI schedule" or "MEI curve." For any rate of interest measured on the vertical scale, the MEI schedule shows the level of investment demand at which the MEI will be brought into equality with that rate of interest; the schedule is thus a demand curve for investment, and is denoted $I(r)$ in the figure. Summing the MEI schedules of all firms gives the demand for investment in the economy as a whole.

3. Investment and Interest Rates

The foregoing account of the MEI concept seems to imply that investment demand depends almost entirely on the level of interest rates; for

---

[8] M. Kalecki, *Essays in the Theory of Economic Fluctuations* (New York: Farrar and Rinehart, 1939), Chapter 4. Kalecki prefers to include an allowance for risk in the cost of finance by adding it to the rate of interest; but since risk is here a matter of subjective calculation, it seems better to bring it into the MEI.

example, in Figure 7.1 it appears that a reduction in interest from r_1 to r_2 would raise demand from I_1 to I_2. In practice, of course, the decision to undertake new investment is a much more complex process than this simple diagram indicates. Surveys of business behavior reveal that there are many factors that influence investment choices and that most firm managers do not consider the market interest rate a particularly important datum when making plans to acquire new plant and equipment. For example, in summarizing the results of several studies based on interviews with corporate decision makers, Robert Eisner mentions "numerous reports that current interest rates have no direct connection with investment decisions. These are documented by various statements by businessmen indicating that they never consider interest rate changes at all, or simply that such considerations never influence investment decisions."[9]

Thus the conclusion that emerges from inquiries into the investment policies of individual firms is that the MEI of Figure 7.1 is near vertical, *i.e.*, that investment is inelastic with respect to the rate of interest. There is, in fact, some reason to believe that the elasticity is not so low as this,

---

[9] R. Eisner, "Interview and Other Survey Techniques and the Study of Investment," National Bureau of Economic Research, *Problems of Capital Formation*, Studies in Income and Wealth, Vol. 19 (Princeton, N.J.: Princeton University Press, 1957), p. 563.

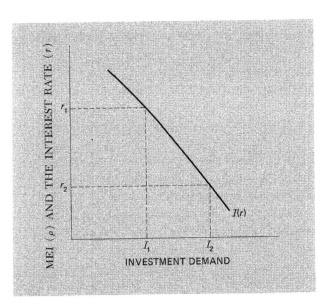

Fig. 7.1

The Marginal Efficiency of Investment schedule indicates investment demand as a function of the interest rate.

but the survey results do call attention to those influences that tend to reduce the importance of the interest rate, and highlight those factors that, when they change, shift the whole MEI curve.

Among these factors, the most obvious is the state of expectations. It was assumed earlier that firms take definite views about the most probable level of revenue and cost, and make precise assessments of the life of equipment. But expectations may be much vaguer than this. A firm may feel fairly sure that the rate of yield will be within certain limits — say, between 5% and 30% — but may find it impossible to decide which rate within these extremes is most likely to be realized. In such a case, only really large changes in interest would alter a decision to go ahead with investment. In addition to being uncertain, expectations may also be very volatile; they may change quickly and drastically in response to the general mood of the business community. Rumors, news of technical developments, political events, even the vice-president's ulcers, may cause a sudden rise or fall in the expected rate of yield.

A particular source of uncertainty is the possibility that plant may become technologically obsolete sooner than had been expected and well before it is worn out physically. This is one reason why firms often work in terms of a "pay-out period" for new investment. Instead of the rate of yield over its whole life, they calculate the rate that must be obtained if the plant is to cover its original cost in, say, four years; in the fifth year and subsequently, all yields will be net gain. Thus, a four-year pay-out period implies a rate of yield of 25% of the cost of the plant; if a firm thinks it cannot obtain this, it will not undertake the investment, even though the necessary funds could be obtained at 5%. If it turns out that the plant goes on yielding 25% per annum for ten years, it will *then* appear to have been worth buying even with money borrowed at much more than 5%. The essence of the investment decision, however, is that the firm may have no notion, at the time when the plant is acquired, of how long the yield will continue.

Some machines, it is true, have a fairly short expectation of life. When it is a question of forecasting yield not over ten years but only over two or three, uncertainty will be less, and it might seem that such investment ought to be more interest-elastic than that in longer-lived equipment. But here another consideration arises. It was seen earlier (p. 161) that the prospective yields of a machine may be discounted by the interest rate r to give a present value V; if this value exceeds P, the price of the machine, it is profitable to buy it. A rise in r means that yields are being discounted more heavily, so that V will fall; when V falls below P, the machine is no longer worth buying. But the nearer the yield in time, the less will a change in r alter its present value. For example, $100 receivable two years hence, discounted [10] at 5%, has a present value of $90.07; at 6%, $89; at 7%, $87.3. The same $100 receivable ten years hence, discounted at 5%, has present value of $61.4; at 6%, $55.9; at 7%, $50.8. Thus, V for a given machine will be altered relatively little in response to changes in interest if the yields extend only over the next two or three years. For maximum sensitivity, V must include many distant yields — that is, the machine must be long lasting.

Insensitivity to current interest rates may also arise from long "gestation periods" for new projects. If a new plant will take some years to build, all the necessary funds need not be available when the decision to build is first taken; if financing is to be spread out over a long period, and the firm expects interest rates to be lower during that time than they are at present, a high *current* interest rate will not affect its decision. It can, indeed, wait for the moment when a long-term loan can be obtained on favorable terms, borrowing on short term in the meantime, and repaying short loans out of its later long-term borrowing. In this case, the expectational factor will involve not only the prospective yield from the investment but also forecasts about future levels of the rate of interest itself.

Even if individual projects can be completed fairly quickly, it may not be at all easy to cancel or postpone them. Large firms tend to formulate expansion programs extending several years ahead, in which the project undertaken in any particular year is merely one link in a chain of developments; to give up any of the current year's investment might disorganize the whole program. In such a case, the prospective losses might be greater than the saving in interest payments.[11] Cutting current investment may

---

[10] The present value is calculated as

$$V = \frac{A_2}{(1+r)^2} = \frac{100}{(1.05)^2} = 90.7 \ .$$

The other calculations involve increasing r to 0.06 and 0.07, and for the more distant yield A_{10}, discounting by $(1+r)^{10}$ instead of $(1+r)^2$. For a mathematical demonstration of the general relationship between present value, rate of yield, and length of yield series, see G. L. S. Shackle, *Uncertainty in Economics* (London: Cambridge University Press, 1954), Chapter XI.

[11] See R. Eisner, *op. cit.*, pp. 557–561. Because of this inflexibility in investment plans, any influence that interest rate changes may have on investment demand will be observed only after some time lag.

also prevent the realization of expected yields from past investment, if that investment represented a previous stage of an integrated program.

Another reason why large firms may pay relatively little attention to the cost of finance is that they may have considerable control over their markets. If a firm is a leading supplier of a commodity, it is not obliged to accept the price that would be settled in a competitive market by supply and demand. It may, therefore, be able to meet higher costs of borrowing simply by increasing the price of its product. When an entirely new commodity is to be made, the firm will treat interest charges as just another item among its overhead costs; the margin of error in its estimate of what consumers will pay for the new product may be so great that the level of interest makes little difference. The interest elasticity of the MEI schedule may therefore depend on the nature of markets in the economy: the less competitive they are, the lower the interest elasticity.

For all these reasons — uncertainty of expectations, long gestation periods, long-range planning, and market imperfection — investment decisions may be insensitive to the cost of borrowing. Insensitivity may appear greater than it really is, however, because of the difficulty of identifying the borrowing cost that is relevant to the firms' calculations. To relate investment spending to "*the* rate of interest" is too drastic a simplification; there are many rates of interest, differing according to the duration and conditions of loans, the degree of risk, and so on.[12] Whatever the average terms of borrowing may be, potential lenders will assess the prospects and risks of a particular loan in the light of what they believe to be the borrower's present circumstances and past record, and these considerations may cause the relevant rate of interest for a given firm to depart from the average. The average could conceivably change without altering a particular firm's relevant rate, so that the firm would have no reason to alter its investment. The firm would then appear insensitive to borrowing costs if these were measured by the average rate, even though such costs were actually an important factor in its investment decisions.

Whatever the rate a firm is prepared to pay, there will be a limit to its power to borrow. Large firms may, to some extent, succeed in obtaining

---

[12] See J. S. G. Wilson, "Credit Rationing and the Relevant Rate of Interest," *Economica*, Vol. 21 (February, 1954), pp. 21–31. As Wilson has written, "no two entrepreneurs will have access to financial resources on exactly the same terms, and . . . even the same entrepreneur will generally find that these costs will be conditioned by the *purpose* for which he borrows."

more financing by offering better terms; small ones, however, may find that they can borrow at a given rate up to some maximum amount, but cannot exceed that maximum no matter what they are ready to pay. Banks, for example, decide advances according to the "credit-worthiness" of borrowers; having assessed (in the light of a firm's cash flow, assets, and so on) the amount that can be safely lent to it, a bank charges an almost standardized interest rate on borrowing up to that limit, but will lend nothing beyond it. A firm might therefore be obliged to limit investment not because the rate of yield from a further unit would not meet the cost of borrowing, but because its credit limit had been reached. Its decisions about investment would then depend on the availability rather than the cost of finance; a rise in interest rates would not necessarily affect those decisions.

For firms proposing to finance investment from internal funds accumulated in the past from undistributed profits, the relevant interest rate is not the one at which it can borrow, but the highest rate at which it can lend. If the firm is prepared to buy shares of stock in other enterprises, it may get a high return; but this means a sacrifice of liquidity, since the stocks may someday fall in price. Most firms are unwilling to take this risk except when they are acquiring stock giving them control over firms engaged in similar lines of business. These investments in other firms, in any case, are usually a means of gaining control of additional plant, *i.e.*, a roundabout method of buying plant and equipment. The expected return from them is itself an MEI rather than a measure of the cost of finance.

If the firm wishes to retain reasonable liquidity when it lends out its funds, it may acquire Treasury Bills, short-term government bonds, or negotiable certificates of deposit in commercial banks, on which the yield is normally less than that on corporate stock. When these "lenders' rates" are low, the firm will forgo so little revenue by using its funds internally that it can virtually ignore the cost of financing capital expansion; even though "borrowers' rates" may be relatively high, they will not be relevant to the firm's investment decisions. Thus, a firm that might pay more careful attention to interest rates if it were obliged to contract external debt may appear insensitive to them.

So far, the terms "cost of borrowing" and "interest rates" have been used as though they were synonymous. But firms may also obtain funds by issuing stock, on which the holders are not entitled to regular fixed-interest payments. Dividends can be made large or small according to the corporation's profit earnings, and can be cut out altogether if earnings are low. Stockholders are part owners rather than creditors of the firm, and as such they share the risks as well as the gains; by recruiting more stockholders, a firm avoids the dangers associated with fixed-interest borrowing. What, then, is the cost of financing a new project if no fixed-interest charge is incurred?

If the firm is taken to be the original body of "old" stockholders, the cost of finance is the part of the new project's yield that accrues to the new stockholders. Conceivably, this could be the whole of that yield. Suppose a new company owns equipment and other assets worth $1 million, earns annual profit of $100,000, and distributes all of this to the owners of its one million $1 shares of common stock; the dividend rate is 10%. If it issues 200,000 new shares for $1 each, buys machinery worth $200,000 with the proceeds,[13] and earns an extra $20,000 that is distributed in dividends, the dividend rate remains 10% and the original shareholders have gained nothing.

If the old stockholders are to benefit, the extra machinery must increase the firm's earnings by more than $20,000, or else the new shares must be sold for more than their nominal value of $1 each. With the second alternative, suppose the 200,000 new shares are sold at $2.50. The $500,000 thus raised buys equipment yielding additional earnings of $50,000; distributing this raises the dividend to 12½%; the dividend rate is a percentage of the nominal value of the shares ($1), so each share now receives 12.5¢ instead of 10¢ as previously — a gain of 2.5¢ for the owner of each "old" share. But 12.5¢ is a return of only 5% on the $2.50 paid for each newly issued share. Here, then, the rate of yield is 10% ($50,000 earned on $500,000 worth of new equipment), and the cost of finance is 5%. Earnings and dividends may, of course, change in the future; if next year the dividend rate is 20%, each new share will obtain 8% on the $2.50 paid for it, and the benefit accruing to the old shareholders will be less than if the additional $500,000 had been raised by the issue of fixed-interest bonds at 5%. The possibility of such "earnings dilution" thus makes share issues a potentially costly method of financing investment.

In the first place, however, the company must induce prospective stockholders to pay $2.50 per share. Its chances of doing so will be small if $2.50 put into other corporate stock, or into government bonds, would

---

[13] The expense of issuing the stock is ignored.

return much more than 12.5¢ per year. If buyers see prospects of higher dividends in the future, they may pay more than they would for fixed-interest bonds paying 12.5¢ per year, or for the stock of corporations with dimmer prospects. On the other hand, they will not pay as much if they think the returns are riskier than those obtainable elsewhere. The firm will thus get a price that the buyers think will give them the average rate of return on loanable funds (the market rate of interest), plus or minus some "risk and prospects" margin. Subject to this margin, the market rate of interest thus sets the terms on which firms obtain funds by issuing stock, just as it does in the more obvious case of fixed-interest bond issues.

For old stockholders, earnings dilution is a reason for avoiding finance by stock issues. But firms are in practice controlled by managers who may not themselves have large holdings of stock. For them, the main disadvantage is the threat of "control dilution": the votes of the new stockholders may be used to impair the managers' command, perhaps even to unseat them. Bond issues, on the other hand, have been seen to entail the "principle of increasing risk": the more bonds issued, the greater the risk that the firm may be unable to meet the interest charge, in which event the bondholders could insist on a reorganization of the corporation, including perhaps the dismissal of the managers. If lenders' rates happen to be low, it would seem that managers have strong incentives to avoid the use of outside funds and to rely as far as possible on using the firm's own resources, *i.e.*, its holdings of liquid assets. It may therefore be the amount of these assets, rather than the level of interest rates, that determines a decision to undertake investment.

Nevertheless, the rate of interest may exert an indirect influence; if the firm holds interest-bearing securities, a rise in interest rates will depress capital values [14] so that it will sustain a loss if the securities are sold. The liquid assets will have become less liquid than before. The firm may hesitate to incur the loss by selling the securities; even if it does, it will have less money than it could count on before interest rates rose; its power to buy new equipment will be diminished. However, on the whole, corporations tend to hold more cash than securities — and, in any case, not to hold large quantities of either [15] — so this indirect effect of interest rate changes cannot be strong.

---

14 See above, p. 117.

15 The net working capital of corporations is made up of current assets (cash, securities, accounts receivable, and inventories) less current liabilities (accounts payable and

The main source of internal finance, however, is not the liquid assets held at a given time, but the inflow of profit earnings throughout the year. Some of these earnings must be distributed in dividends to stockholders; although there is no legal obligation to distribute any particular amount, corporate executives may create unmanageable dissatisfaction among stockholders by setting dividends exceptionally low. Also, low dividends often mean a low stock exchange price for a company's shares, creating the possibility of a "take-over bid" by which other interests can obtain control of the company.[16] But as long as directors recommend a dividend rate no lower than stockholders will tolerate, they will be able, when earnings are high, to dispose of a mass of undistributed profits for investment purposes.

Table 7.1

Annual Changes in Corporate Profits and Dividends
Billions of Dollars

Changes over Previous Year		1959	1960	1961	1962
Profits after Tax		+ .1	−1.9	+ .1	+3.8
Dividends Paid		+ .8	+ .9	+ .1	+1.3
Changes over Previous Year	1963	1964	1965	1966	1967
Profits after Tax	+1.8	+4.8	+7.9	+4.6	−3.3
Dividends Paid	+1.4	+1.1	+1.8	+2.0	+1.0

Statistics of profits and dividends in recent years show much smaller fluctuations in dividends than in earnings; in bad years, dividends were maintained at the expense of retained profits, while in good years most of the increased earnings were withheld from distribution. In Table 7.1, corporate profits after taxes (*i.e.*, the amount of profit available for distribution) are compared with annual changes in dividends paid during the

---

accrued taxes). At the end of 1967, total working capital of U.S. corporations was $200 billion; corporate cash holdings totaled $52 billion; and only $12 billion was invested in securities. See any issue of the *Federal Reserve Bulletin,* p. A-47.

[16] The price in this case is that of old shares, not newly issued ones; old shareholders are selling their holdings without changing the original number of shares in the company. If the market price of old shares were, say, $1 while the net assets of the company divided by the number of shares were $3, it would pay someone to bid $2 per share to acquire a controlling interest in the company.

years 1959–1967.[17] It is noteworthy that dividends continued to rise throughout the period, even in years when profits fell. On the other hand, substantial increases in profits, as in 1962 and in 1964–1966, were not matched by comparable increases in dividends. Even in 1967, when dividends were raised in spite of a significant reduction in profits, the total amount of dividends paid was only 48% of corporate distributable income; and in 1960 this proportion was as low as 42%. It has already been noted (on p. 148) that the corporate short-run marginal propensity to save has been around 80% in recent years. For the corporate sector as a whole over this 1959–1967 period, *gross* retained earnings (*i.e.*, undistributed corporate profits plus capital consumption allowances) were sufficient to finance approximately four-fifths of gross private domestic investment.[18]

In these circumstances, the amount of retained earnings should be an important determinant of the level of investment undertaken; this, indeed, is the essence of what is known as the "residual funds" theory of investment demand.[19] If firms try to pursue a policy of keeping dividends stable, retained earnings will fluctuate with the level of total profits earned in the recent past. Thus this theory holds that, while the expectation of future profits creates the motive for investment, the level of past and current profits, by providing the means, will significantly influence the extent to which that motive can be indulged.

It is evident, then, that the market interest rate is not the only factor affecting the cost of finance, and that the cost of funds for new capital expansion is but one of several considerations that influence investment decisions. This being the case, what importance should be attached to the interest rate? A partial answer to this question is to be found in the results of several econometric studies of the determinants of fixed business

---

[17] Figures derived from Table 1.14 of the *Survey of Current Business* (July, 1968) and *The National Income and Product Accounts of the United States, 1929–65*.

[18] See Table 7.1 of the *Survey of Current Business* (July, 1968). Though this was true of all corporations taken together, it was not true of each individually. In 1967, for example, various industrial and commercial corporations acquired external finance to the amount of $33 billion by the issue of new stocks and bonds; but this was partially offset by the retirement of $10 billion in securities on the part of other firms whose internal resources exceeded their capital formation requirements. Data on corporate securities are presented in each issue of the *Federal Reserve Bulletin*, p. A-45.

[19] See J. R. Meyer and E. Kuh, *The Investment Decision* (Cambridge, Mass.: Harvard University Press, 1957). The interest rate is accorded a minor role under this approach — the interest cost being of concern only during periods of investment boom when internal funds may be insufficient to finance desired levels of capital outlay.

investment.[20] Almost all statistical analyses of investment include the market interest rate as one of the factors to be investigated. Most of these efforts also consider one or more of the other influences mentioned earlier — *e.g.*, the level of retained earnings or the state of business expectations. And almost all studies emphasize the importance of recent trends in sales as an important determinant of investment behavior. This last point will be discussed further in the next two sections.

The various studies differ considerably in their estimates of how strong an influence interest rates have on aggregate business investment. One of the key assumptions that distinguishes the different empirical approaches, and affects the estimates of the significance of the cost of finance, concerns the lag that is presumed to exist between the time of an interest rate change and the resultant influence on aggregate investment. Despite these differences, however, current evidence seems to indicate that the elasticity of investment to the interest rate is significant (though certainly less than unity), given sufficient time for the various lags to work themselves out.[21]

4. Autonomous and Induced Investment

From the last section, it appears that the existence of a relation between interest and investment is well established, but that there is some question as to how strong the relationship is. A glance ahead to Table 7.2 (p. 177) will show that there were considerable year-to-year changes in investment during the years 1957 to 1967 — yet during this period long-term interest rates were relatively stable. The implication is that investment demand was responding to other forces, which were more powerful than the rate of interest. One of these may have been the level of National Income. In the previous chapter, it was suggested that part of aggregate

---

[20] For an excellent survey of empirical research on investment behavior through about 1960, see R. Eisner and R. H. Strotz, "Research Study Two: Determinants of Business Investment," in Commission on Money and Credit, *Impacts of Monetary Policy* (Englewood Cliffs, N.J.: Prentice-Hall, 1963).

[21] For a critical review of recent econometric research on investment behavior, see M. K. Evans, *Macroeconomic Activity* (New York: Harper and Row, 1969), Chapters 4 and 5. Evans concludes that current knowledge indicates that a one point change in the long-term interest rate (say, from 4% to 5%) will reduce aggregate investment by approximately 5 to 10% over a two-year period.

demand is *autonomous* of the level of income, while part is *induced* by it. If the demand for investment is largely income induced, then the MEI schedule will change its position every time National Income changes, so that investment could vary considerably even with a constant rate of interest.[22]

Many of the influences mentioned in the last section, however, have the effect of making investment autonomous of income. Long-range planning, for example, implies that firms have formed a view of market demand for their products some years ahead, and are readying themselves to meet it. A firm may invest to keep up with its competitors; its policy will then depend on what other firms are doing, rather than on the level of National Income. Firms producing for export markets may invest in order to meet higher demand abroad; such demand may be due to income growth in other countries, but not to changes in the level of domestic income. Technological progress is yet another factor that may lead firms to invest without regard to the level of income. A firm may equip itself to market an entirely new product, confident that its attractiveness will cause sales to justify the venture, whatever the state of the economy when the product is offered for sale. New methods of making existing products may require investment in new plant, which firms may feel obliged to install for fear their competitors may do it first. Increasing business concentration (large firms swallowing small ones, groups of firms merging), by making the average firm larger, may increase investment if greater resources and easier access to finance make firms more able and willing to face the risks of capital development.

There are many reasons, then, why much investment is autonomous of income. But there are also reasons for thinking that another part may be strongly influenced by it. A situation of high output and full employment diffuses a senses of prosperity, causing firms to assess future returns more optimistically than if the economy were suffering from underemployment of labor and equipment. The residual funds theory suggests that when income is high and corporations are earning good profits, they will spend a good part of them on investment; at depression levels of incomes, most, if not all, profits will be required to maintain dividend distributions, and

---

[22] This would be consistent with the findings of the empirical studies just mentioned, that changes in the volume of sales are an important determinant of investment behavior. Business sales account for a very large part of GNP, so that their variations closely reflect changes in National Income.

investment plans may be held up by the resulting lack of internal finance. When demand is so high that a shortage of labor exists, firms in despair of obtaining additional workers may attempt to expand output by install-ing labor-saving processes, and this usually means ordering more equip-ment. The effect of all these considerations will be to shift the MEI curve of Figure 7.1 upward and to the right when income is high, downward and to the left when income is low. At a given interest rate, this shift will cause investment to rise and fall with the level of income.

The result will be a positive Marginal Propensity to Invest of the sort mentioned on p. 139. The curve that relates investment demand to income will no longer be horizontal like I_1 in Figure 7.2 (as it would be if all in-vestment were autonomous), but will slope upward from left to right after the manner of the line $I(Y)$. This curve is analogous to the consumption function $C(Y)$ in Figure 5.1 (p. 97) and may be called the *Investment Function*. The vertical distance I_0 measures autonomous investment, and the slope of $I(Y)$ is the Marginal Propensity to Invest (MPI). The condi-tion of equilibrium is that investment demand shall be equal to intended saving, as shown by the *Saving Function* $S(Y)$; this occurs where $S(Y)$ intersects $I(Y)$, giving Y_1 as the equilibrium level of income. A rise in au-tonomous investment will shift $I(Y)$ upward so that it intersects $S(Y)$ to the right of Y_1, and the level of income will then be higher; there will be

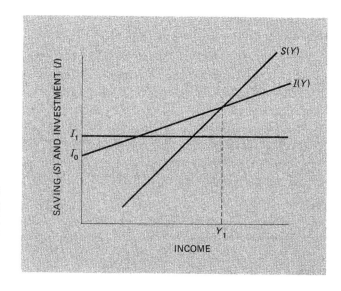

Fig. 7.2

The investment and saving functions and equilibrium income

a multiplier effect whose size will depend not only on the slope of $S(Y)$ (which is, of course, the MPS) but also on the slope of $I(Y)$. It will be, in fact, the Compound Multiplier given earlier on p. 139.

A steeply sloping $I(Y)$ curve, however, could give *unstable* equilibrium. In Figure 7.2, income is in stable equilibrium at Y_1; if a momentary disturbance pushes the level of income to the right, saving will exceed investment, implying a deficiency of aggregate demand that would reduce income back to the Y_1 level. Similarly, at any income to the left of Y_1 there will be an excess of investment over saving, which would force the income level back toward equilibrium. If, however, the curve $I(Y)$ slopes more steeply than the curve $S(Y)$, all these conditions are reversed: if income is dislodged from Y_1 toward the right, investment will exceed saving and income would increase further instead of returning to Y_1; if it is dislodged to the left, saving will exceed investment, and income would decline further.[23]

If the slope of the curve $S(Y)$ is slight (implying a small Marginal Propensity to Save and a high MPC), even a fairly small MPI gives instability of this sort. On the other hand, it is not completely inconceivable that the MPI could be negative. For example, if a firm must suspend or reduce normal output while reconstructing its plant to take additional machinery, it may carry out plant extensions during lulls in demand and may postpone them when demand is brisk; if the demand for its product rises or falls in line with National Income, the firm's own MPI is negative. If all firms were to behave thus, the line $I(Y)$ in Figure 7.2 would be downward-sloping; even if only a minority do so, their behavior will make the general MPI lower than it would otherwise be, and this will make for stability of income equilibrium.

---

[23] In this case, the compound Multiplier of p. 139 will be negative. The formula

$$k = \frac{1}{1 - b - i} \, ,$$

where b is the MPC and i is the MPI, may be rewritten

$$k = \frac{1}{MPS - MPI} \, ,$$

since the marginal propensity to save is 1 *minus* the MPC. If the value of the MPS were 0.1 and that of the MPI 0.2, the value of k would be $1/- 0.1$ or -10. A rise in autonomous investment would cause the equilibrium level of income to be *lower* than before — but because the additional investment is pushing income up, the economy will move *away* from this equilibrium instead of toward it.

The foregoing analysis has assumed that induced investment depends on *current* income. But firms may take time to form impressions and collect information (for example, the amount of residual funds will not be known until the end of the accounting period), and their decisions to invest may involve more or less lengthy planning processes. In either case, the lag will have the effect of making investment depend on the income of a previous period. The investment function (which was first given on p. 139 as $I = I_0 + iY$, where I_0 is autonomous investment and i is the MPI) would then have to be represented as

$$I_t = I_0 + iY_{t-1}$$

(where the lag is assumed to be of one period's duration).

Still another possibility is that investment depends not on the absolute level of present or past income, but on current or recent *changes* in income. If firms are continually attempting to adjust their productive capacity to the level of demand for their products, any rise in demand will necessitate investment for this purpose whatever the absolute level of demand happens to be. The equation of the investment function will then be

$$I_t = I_0 + i(Y_{t-1} - Y_{t-2}) \; ,$$

where it is assumed that a one-period lag elapses before firms become aware of, and respond to, the change in income. The lag may, of course, be longer than this, and it may be a more complicated one: some firms, for example, may consider the *average* change in demand over several past periods when they are deciding how far to adjust their capacity. Moreover, there is no obvious reason why all firms should behave in precisely the same fashion in this respect, so that induced investment in the economy as a whole may very well be determined in all of the ways just mentioned, with one part depending on current income, another on past income, and yet another part on past changes in income. Because of this possibility, it is hardly to be expected that a clear pattern of response will emerge from a statistical comparison of investment and GNP; nevertheless, some relevant figures are presented in Table 7.2.[24]

---

[24] Data from Table 1.2 of *Survey of Current Business* (July, 1968) for 1963–67, and from Table 1.2 of *National Income and Product Accounts of the United States, 1929–65* for 1957–62. It should be noted that column (2) relates to *gross* investment; for present purposes, it would be more useful to compare GNP with *net* investment to show the extent to which changes in GNP induced business firms to make net additions to their capital equipment, but unfortunately, official estimates of capital consumption

Those in column (2) exclude expenditure on residential construction and increases in inventories as well as all public investment, and therefore represent the "business fixed investment" that may be supposed to be influenced by the level of income. When the figures in column (2) are compared with the GNP series in column (1), it certainly seems that there is a strong association between them; but this may be a misleading impres-

Table 7.2

The Relation of Investment to GNP

Billions of 1958 Dollars

Year	(1) Gross National Product	(2) Gross Private Nonresidential Fixed Investment	(3) Change from previous year in GNP	(4) Change from previous year in Investment
1957	452.5	47.4	—	—
1958	447.3	41.6	− 5.2	−5.8
1959	475.9	44.1	+28.6	+2.5
1960	487.7	47.1	+11.8	+3.0
1961	497.2	45.5	+ 9.5	−1.6
1962	529.8	49.7	+32.6	+4.2
1963	551.0	51.9	+21.2	+2.2
1964	581.1	57.8	+30.1	+5.9
1965	617.8	66.4	+36.7	+8.6
1966	657.1	73.8	+39.3	+7.4
1967	673.1	73.7	+16.0	−0.1

sion arising from the fact that both series, even though expressed at constant prices, show a marked upward trend. It may therefore be better to compare annual *changes* in GNP and business investment, as set out in columns (3) and (4). The fluctuations in these series still suggest some sort of relationship between business investment and GNP, but it is clearly a very imperfect one. In 1961 and 1967, investment actually fell while GNP was rising; in the other years, though the response of investment to GNP is positive, it seems to vary considerably in strength. There is little appearance of a lagged relationship between columns (3) and (4). If it is assumed that investment depends on the way GNP is *changing* rather

are not sufficiently detailed to allow the column (2) figures to be shown net of depreciation. It should also be observed that the investment figures refer to actual, rather than to planned, expenditure; if, for any reason, firms were unable to spend the amount they had intended, the figures will have understated the response of investment demand to GNP and changes therein.

than on its absolute amount, the appropriate comparison is between columns (2) and (3); in this case, the relationship shown during the years 1963–1967 appears to be quite different from those exhibited in earlier years.

These results may appear to be rather disappointing, but it would indeed be surprising if a series of annual statistics of the kind given in Table 7.2 were to give precise confirmation of any theory of induced investment. Apart from the fact, noted earlier, that behavior may differ considerably between firms and between industries, it must also be remembered that variations occurred in the cost and availability of finance during these years, that there were changes in taxation which probably affected investment decisions, and that technological innovation was going on throughout the period. Whatever may have been the underlying connection between income and investment, it must have been considerably complicated by these additional factors. More detailed statistical inquiry provides little support for hypotheses linking investment with the absolute amount of current or past income, but it does suggest that past *changes* in income may have had some influence on current investment. As this theory (known as the *Acceleration Principle*) also has a good deal to be said for it on a priori grounds, it will now be examined at greater length.

5. The Principle of Acceleration

Suppose a firm produces a commodity X, for which the annual demand over the past few years has been 1,000 units. The firm uses machines that produce 100 units per year and last for ten years. To satisfy demand, the firm thus needs ten machines, of which (it is assumed) one becomes due for replacement each year. This is the initial situation in Year 1. In Year 2, let the demand for X rise by 100 units; to satisfy it, an extra machine must be installed, so that the firm will now buy two new machines (one additional plus one replacement) instead of the customary single one. Next year (Year 3), let demand rise again by 100X; the firm must install yet another machine, so that it will again buy two instead of the usual single replacement. In Year 4, let demand stay unchanged at 1,200X; the firm now need only its customary replacement, so that its order for new machines will be halved. In Year 5, let demand for X fall by 100 units; this time, since the firm's requirement for machines has fallen from twelve to eleven, it need not even replace the machine that ends its "life" during the year, and so it will now order no new machines at all.

In this sequence, the initial rise of demand for X creates a proportionately much larger demand for machinery; thereafter, a steady rise in X demand is required to maintain machine demand at a constant level. Even a levelling-off of X demand causes machine demand to fall, while a reduction in X demand wipes it out altogether. To give a steady annual rise in machine demand (say 1, 2, 3, 4, . . .), the demand for X would have to increase at an accelerating rate — from 1,000 in Year 1 to 1,100 in Year 2, 1,300 in Year 3, 1,600 in Year 4, and so on. This can be expressed in the formula

$$M_t = m(X_t - X_{t-1}) + R ,$$

where M_t is the number of new machines ordered in Year t, X_t and X_{t-1} are the demand for X in years t and $t-1$ respectively, R is replacements, and m is the number of machines needed per unit of X.

If *all* firms behave in this way, aggregate investment will depend on changes in aggregate demand.[25] These aggregates are, of course, in terms of money, so all the values of M, R, and X must be multiplied by their prices. The total money value of X will be aggregate demand, which will be equal to National Income (Y) if the economy is in equilibrium throughout; thus investment I in the year t is

$$I_t = v(Y_t - Y_{t-1}) + R .$$

Here the physical machine/product relationship m is replaced by v, which is the number of dollars' worth of machinery needed to produce $1 worth of output per year. For example, if m were $1/100$ as in the example above, and the price of machines were $200 and that of X $1, v would be $200 ÷ $100 or 2. The ratio v is a "capital-output ratio" or "capital coefficient" expressed in terms of money; in this context it is conventionally called the Accelerator.

It should be noted that the size of v depends not only on the capacity of the machines but also on the period of time over which output is mea-

---

[25] Some accounts of the Acceleration Principle have made investment depend on changes only in *consumers'* demand. But an autonomous rise in demand for new machinery will mean that the firms producing it require more equipment themselves — machines are needed to make machines. Thus the Principle will operate whatever the nature of the rise in demand.

sured. A machine worth $200, which can produce $100 worth of output in a year, will produce $50 worth in six months and $25 worth in a quarter. So if v is measured on a half-yearly basis, it will be $200 ÷ $50, or 4, while if quarterly output is taken, it will be $200 ÷ $25, or 8. Similarly, a two-year span would make v equal 1.0. Which, then, is the appropriate time dimension? It must depend on how quickly firms wish to equip themselves to meet the increased demand for their products. Suppose the typical firm, having decided to expand its capacity, plans to complete the process within three months. Its investment demand will then be concentrated into that period, and if all other firms behave in the same way, the I_t of the equation in the last paragraph will represent a single quarter's investment in the economy as a whole; Y_t and Y_{t-1} will be the values of output in successive quarters, and v will be 8. If, on the other hand, firms plan to adjust capacity over a twelve-month period, the subscripts t and $t-1$ will refer to successive years, and I_t will represent the amount of *annual* investment demand. The length of time over which firms plan to carry out their investment decisions may be called the *investment period*; the longer it is, the lower the value of v. It will be convenient to assume for the time being that the investment period is always exactly twelve months, so that all measurements — output, investment, and the rate of replacement — are on an annual basis; but it must be borne in mind that this is an arbitrary assumption that may have to be altered.[26]

In the above equation, I is *gross* investment; to show *net* investment, R must be deducted from both sides. If Y_{t-1} exceeds Y_t (*i.e.*, if income is falling), net investment will be negative; but disinvestment cannot exceed R unless firms dismantle equipment that is not yet worn out. Replacement demand appeared to be constant in the example discussed above — the firm always replaced one machine per year; however, an extension of the sequence would have changed this. Machines were assumed to last ten years, so the additional machines added in Years 2 and 3 become due for replacement ten years later; because no machines at all were bought

---

[26] The capital-output coefficient v is an example of a stock-flow ratio. When two flows are being compared — for example, annual consumption and annual income — the ratio between them is independent of the time span over which both are measured. Similarly, the ratio between two stocks — for example, the figure of capital per worker found by dividing the number of workers at a given moment of time into the volume of capital existing at that moment — will also be a pure number. In a stock-flow ratio, however, where one quantity has a time dimension and the other does not, it is essential to specify the length of time over which the flow quantity is being measured.

in Year 5, no replacement will be needed in Year 15. The original sequence, in fact, will produce an "echo effect" distorting the replacement pattern in the next decade. This gives replacement demand for the economy as a whole, as

$$R_t = v(Y_{t-10} - Y_{t-11}) + R_{t-10} .$$

In turn, R_{t-10} will echo the gross investment of ten years previously, and so on back into the past.

For the moment, however, replacement will be ignored, leaving I_t as net investment; dropping R_t from the earlier equation gives

$$I_t = v(Y_t - Y_{t-1})$$

plus whatever autonomous investment exists. If firms take time to react to the changing pressure of demand for their output, so that they do not make their decisions to adjust capacity until the end of the year in which demand has altered, there will be a lag[27] such that induced net investment is

$$I_t = v(Y_{t-1} - Y_{t-2}).$$

But lagged or unlagged, the theory of investment embodied in these equations is valid only if firms behave as the original X-producing firm was supposed to do at the beginning of this section; and this is very much open to question.

It would certainly appear that the firm *need* not have ordered more machines when faced with higher demand. Had it expected demand to relapse in Year 3 to its original level, it could have met Year 2's increase by working existing equipment more intensively; overtime work or the introduction of a shift system would have increased output for the time being. Though machines were assumed to last ten years, it is unlikely that they would be completely useless at the end of that time; last year's superannuated equipment could have been kept in operation, perhaps even the previous year's if it were the firm's practice to keep old machines as a reserve of standby capacity. It would not have been necessary to increase output at all if the firm had had an inventory of X large enough to meet

---

[27] This lag must not be confused with the investment period defined in the previous paragraph. Given a change in demand for its product, a firm will take time to become aware of the change and decide what action to take; having decided whether or not to adjust its stock of capital, the firm must then decide on the date by which the adjustment is to be completed. The investment period is the length of time involved in the second decision; the lag referred to in the text is that involved in the first decision.

the extra demand; had demand risen by only 40, not by 100, it would clearly have been preferable to run down inventories rather than buy an extra machine producing 100 units. Lacking an inventory, a cautious firm might even let the additional demand go unsatisfied rather than buy an extra machine.

On the other hand, the firm might well have installed *more* than one extra machine in Year 2; the initial rise in demand might have appeared to indicate the beginning of a considerable expansion, for which the firm might have tried to equip itself in advance. To order precisely the number of machines needed to produce the increased output currently demanded implies a gross lack of imagination on the part of businessmen, who will in fact, in view of the risks of investment, consider very carefully whether a current rise in demand augurs further expansion or not. The response of investment to demand changes thus depends on expectations as well as on the current value of the Accelerator v.

Before ordering extra equipment, cautious firms may wait to see whether demand increases are sustained; if they do wait, a time lag will operate. They may look back over the last few periods to discover what trend, if any, is shown by demand, and then decide investment accordingly; in this case a "distributed lag" will be present.[28] The gestation period of new plant may also complicate the picture. If a factory takes three years to build, investment demand in the first year will be only one-third of that induced by annual changes in demand for the firm's product — that is, the value of v will be reduced by the existence of a three-year "investment period." When new equipment is installed, it may not be the same type as the old; it may be technologically more advanced, perhaps of different size, and may give a greater output per $100 worth of machinery. Here the Accelerator v would itself be changing.

There are, then, many reasons why the Acceleration Principle should not work with the mechanical precision implied in the original sequence.[29] Nevertheless, the principle contains a strong element of truth. If a firm tries to expand output with an inadequate volume of equipment, the strain on its capacity will increase costs; overtime work, for example, costs more

---

[28] For example, instead of $I_t = v \triangle D_t$, suppose investment depends on the average change in demand during the last three periods, giving

$$I_t = .33v(\triangle D_{t-1} + \triangle D_{t-2} + \triangle D_{t-3}) \ .$$

The time lag is "distributed" over periods $t-1$, $t-2$ and $t-3$.

[29] See A. D. Knox, "The Acceleration Principle and the Theory of Investment: A Survey," *Econometrica*, Vol. 19 (August, 1952), pp. 269–297.

in wages than normal time. Adjusting capacity to the new level of production will thus reduce costs. A sequence of net yields A_1, A_2, A_3, etc., which was earlier (p. 159) described as resulting from the introduction of a new machine, will here arise from cost reductions; and if the MEI implied by the yields is greater than the interest cost of the machine, it will pay the firm to install it. Buying a new machine will be cheaper than incurring extra costs in other directions in the effort to produce more finished goods.

Much depends on how the firm's costs change with the level of output. If any attempt to produce above capacity would sharply increase the per-unit cost of labor and materials, the cost reduction from new machinery will be great. If "capacity" is a *range* of possible levels of output, at each of which the per-unit cost is the same, the incentive to install new equipment will be nil as long as demand changes stay within the range. But for sizable changes in demand that are expected to persist in the future, it will almost certainly profit a firm to enlarge its capacity. Conversely, when demand falls, costs will rise because output is *below* capacity; the firm will cut its costs if it reduces its stock of equipment by disinvesting.

Thus, changes in income can be expected to induce some investment, though in less rigid proportions than the original statement of the Acceleration Principle implied. The latter, indeed, can be regarded as a special case of what has been called the *Capital Stock Adjustment Principle*.[30] This principle asserts that investment will vary positively with the level of income and negatively with the quantity of capital in existence at the end of the last period, that is,

$$I_t = aY_t - bK_{t-1} ,$$

where a and b are constants.[31] Or, if the response is lagged one period,

$$I_t = aY_{t-1} - bK_{t-1} .$$

This approach is equivalent to the Acceleration Principle if a is replaced by v and b is equal to 1. The capital-output ratio v, multiplied by Y_t, gives the amount of capital required to produce the current level of output; and if this differs from existing capital K_{t-1}, firms try to make up

---

[30] See R. C. O. Matthews, *The Business Cycle* (Chicago: The University of Chicago Press, 1959), pp. 40–43.

[31] For an early application of this approach, see H. B. Chenery, "Overcapacity and the Acceleration Principle," *Econometrica*, Vol. 20 (January, 1952), pp. 1–28. Almost all recent empirical studies of investment incorporate some form of acceleration influence; see Eisner and Strotz, *op. cit.*, pp. 122–124 and 138–178.

the difference by new investment (or, of course, by *disinvesting* when K_{t-1} exceeds vY_t). Insofar as expectational and other factors are incompatible with this behavior, they can be incorporated into the values of a and b, which will then differ from v and 1.

6. Inventory Investment

The investment-determining forces described in previous sections — profit expectations, the level of National Income and changes in that level, the cost and availability of internal and external finance, and the stock of capital — have so far been considered in the light of their effects on the *fixed* investment of the private sector of the economy. But, as was noted at the beginning of the chapter, this is only one of the categories of investment; it remains to be seen what determines other forms of investment demand. In this section, the demand for increases in inventories of materials and finished products is examined.

On the whole, it appears that interest rates affect the demand for inventories very little. In the past, the reverse has often been argued. By holding inventories, firms are "locking up" funds that could be realized if the inventories were sold off. If firms use their own money for this, they lose the interest it could have earned; if they use borrowed funds, they pay interest. Either way, they must weigh the interest cost against the advantages of holding the existing quantities of inventory. Having a reserve of finished products allows them to meet unexpected demands; with an inventory of materials, they are in a position to step up output at short notice; but these facilities become relatively less attractive when their cost rises, and more so when their cost falls. However, this does not mean that firms will actually vary their inventories when holding costs change. They may have found by experience that some minimum amount is essential, and they also may see no point in exceeding that minimum. Their demand for inventories will be inelastic with respect to holding costs.

Even if inventory demand *is* elastic, it is so with respect to *total* holding cost; if a firm maintains warehouses, insures them and their contents, and employs watchmen, these expenses may be so much greater than the interest cost of the inventories that a small change in interest rates will make almost no difference. A substantial rise might be a different matter, spurring firms to find more efficient ways of utilizing inventories so as to hold less; but this would be a once-for-all effect — when interest fell again, firms would obviously not resume the less efficient arrangements they had before.

For many firms, the relevant rate of interest affecting inventory decisions is not that on bank loans but the charge (if any) for *commercial credit*. The latter commonly takes the form of a discount on bills for goods supplied, if the bills are paid within a certain period. If trade discounts are left unchanged when other short-term interest rates rise, firms may not experience any rise at all in the cost of holding inventories, and erstwhile bank borrowers may turn to commercial credit as a cheaper form of finance unless their suppliers enforce strict limits.

The most important influence on the demand for inventories, however, is the level of output or sales. If the demand for a firm's products is liable to rise on short notice by, say, 5% of the normal level of sales, then the firm will carry an inventory to allow for this contingency. A rise in the normal sales volume will automatically increase the desired level of inventories; over some period of months, the firm will proceed to augment its stock of goods until the desired level is attained. The result is an Accelerator process similar to that discussed in the previous section.

To state this "Accelerator" model of inventory demand in symbolic terms, let H_t denote the level of inventory actually held in any period, and let H^d_t be the *desired* level. The inventory that firms desire to hold is likely to depend on current sales and on recent trends in sales; for example, the relation may be of the form

$$H^d_t = aS_t + b\triangle S_t \,,$$

where S_t is current sales, $\triangle S_t$ is the change in sales since last period, and *a* and *b* are constants. Due to lags in decision, and because of the time required to build up or run down inventory once a decision to change it has been made, firms may not adjust their holdings completely within each period; they may accomplish only some fraction of the desired change in inventory. In this case, the expression for inventory investment, $\triangle H_t$, would be of the form

$$\triangle H_t = g(H^d_t - H_t) \,,$$

where *g* is the fraction of the gap between desired and actual stocks that is closed in any period.[32] When $aS_t + b\triangle S_t$ is put in place of H^d_t, and $S_t - S_{t-1}$ in place of $\triangle S_t$, the last equation becomes

---

[32] For more detailed coverage of the theory of inventory investment and empirical research in this area, see M. C. Lovell, "Determinants of Inventory Investment" in

$$\triangle H_t = g(a + b)S_t - gbS_{t-1} - gH_t \ ,$$

meaning that the current demand for investment in additional inventory will vary positively with recent increases in sales and negatively with the volume of inventory already held. There is an obvious affinity with the Capital Stock Adjustment Principle described on p. 183 above.

If, as these equations indicate, firms raise inventories in response to increased sales, this action will itself add to aggregate demand. But the satisfying of inventory demand will eliminate it from aggregate demand, which will now be less than the level of output that has been reached, and so output will start to contract. Thus, an original change in autonomous demand could set in motion an "inventory cycle" even if output is keeping pace with demand all along; if, in addition, there is an output lag, the "Lundbergian cycle"[33] will be superimposed on the acceleration-type inventory cycle.

A financial consequence of inventory fluctuations may be noted here. If firms rely heavily on retained profits to finance fixed investment, and if the availability of outside finance is limited, increasing inventories will tie up funds that could otherwise be used for fixed investment; the more fixed investment firms plan to do, the greater the necessity to economize on inventories. Yet the fixed investment may be associated with an upward trend in sales that calls for increased inventory holding; this necessity may therefore restrain firms from ordering as much new plant as they might otherwise do. When sales fall, on the other hand, the liquidation of inventories will replenish their internal finance, permitting them to go ahead with whatever fixed investment they plan under these less promising conditions.

7. Replacement Investment

In the example given at the beginning of section 5 to illustrate the Acceleration Principle, the firm was assumed to be using machines that each lasted ten years, at the end of which they were replaced. With year-to-

---

National Bureau of Economic Research, *Models of Income Determination*, Studies in Income and Wealth, Vol. 28 (Princeton, N.J.: Princeton University Press, 1964). Another good source is Eisner and Strotz, *op. cit.*

[33] See above, p. 145.

year variations in investment, the subsequent replacement pattern became distorted, giving an "echo effect." But the assumption of a precise life was seen to be questionable: a machine does not normally crumble into rust all at once, but may continue to be usable for a considerable time after its customary retirement age. If the firm *could* work its machines longer than ten years, why should it normally replace them at that age? Why, indeed, should it not sometimes replace them sooner?

In section 2, the rate of net yield from a new machine (the MEI) was defined as the rate of discount that equates prospective yields with the machine's price — that is, the ρ of the equation

$$P = \frac{A_1}{(1+\rho)} + \frac{A_2}{(1+\rho)^2} + \cdots \frac{A_n}{(1+\rho)^n}$$

where P is the price, n the life, and A_1, A_2, . . . , etc. the series of net yields expected from the machine. If ρ exceeds the rate of interest r, the machine is worth buying. The alternative formulation is

$$V = \frac{A_1}{(1+r)} + \frac{A_2}{(1+r)^2} + \cdots + \frac{A_n}{(1+r)^n}$$

where V is the sum that, if lent out at the interest rate r over n years, would give the series of yields A_1, A_2, . . . , etc. Here V is the present value of the prospective yields when they are discounted by r. If ρ exceeds r, then V exceeds P; by spending the amount P, the firm can expect to get a series of yields worth more than P.

This calculation can be made at any stage of a machine's life. After, say, three years, there will be a shorter series of yields to look forward to, so that V will be less than it was. But P, which is now the sum the firm could get by selling the machine, will also have fallen. Three years' wear will have reduced its secondhand value — indeed, it may now be worth only what it will bring as scrap metal. So V, though reduced, may still exceed P by a good margin. But P cannot go below the rock bottom represented by its scrap value, whereas when the series of yields is at an end, $V = 0$. At some point, therefore, the difference between V and P will fall below the amount by which the V of a new machine exceeds its P. This is the point at which replacement should occur if the firm wishes to maximize profit.

If the present value of prospective yields is V_1 for the new machine and V_2 for the old, and if the prices of new and old machines are P_1 and P_2 respectively, the gain from replacement will be $(V_1 - P_1) - (V_2 - P_2)$. This is subject to the condition that V_1 must exceed P_1. The firm is not obliged to buy a new machine even if it scraps the old one, and there would be no point in buying a new one if the present value of its expected returns (V_1) were less than its price (P_1). It would pay the firm to go on using the old machine until the passage of time reduces the expected return (V_2) below its scrap value (P_2) and then to sell it without buying a new one. The sale might not realize much money, but if lent at interest this money would still earn more than if it continued to be "locked up" in the old machine.

The fact that a gain is possible from the replacement of a machine implies that there will be a loss from *not* replacing it; to avoid this, the firm must replace when ($V_1 - P_1$) $-$ ($V_2 - P_2$) $= 0$. If the old machine's prospective yields have declined by a given fraction q per year, $V_2 = V_0 - nqV_0$; where V_0 is the erstwhile present value of the yields expected when the machine was new, and n is the number of years since it was installed. If P_2 has reached its minimum scrap metal value before replacement is due, and if this is a fraction s of the original price P_0, it follows that $P_2 = sP_0$ from now onward: $V_2 - P_2 = V_0 - nqV_0 - sP_0$. If the price of a new machine is the same as the original price of the old (*i.e.*, $P_1 = P_0$), and if its prospective yields are the same as those the old machine had to start with (*i.e.*, $V_1 = V_0$), the replacement condition becomes

$$(V_1 - P_1) - (V_1 - nqV_1 - sP_1) = 0,$$

or

$$nqV_1 - P_1(1 - s) = 0.$$

If q and s are constants, the value of n that satisfies this equation will be the number of years after which the machine should be replaced, *i.e.*, its profitable life.

But firms do not normally replace machines with identical new ones; since the old one was bought, technical improvements should have provided something better, so that prospective yields will have increased relative to the price of the machine (*i.e.*, $V_1 - P_1 > V_0 - P_0$); this will hasten replacement. If the *product* of the new machinery is in some way superior to that of the old, this will also cause a sharp decline in V_2. The old machine may still be physically capable of turning out its product, but if this old product cannot compete with its up-to-date counterpart (or can compete only at a much lower price), prospective earnings will decline sharply and may vanish altogether. This, too, will bring about earlier replacement.

Technical advances, however, will not be decisive if the state of expectations deteriorates. Because old machines have a shorter series of yields in prospect, firms may feel more certain of these than of a new machine's longer series – particularly if the new equipment involves the sale of a new product. If pessimism causes firms to make a large allowance for risk in assessing yields, this will depress V_1 more than V_2. In general, gloom about market prospects will depress V_1 more than V_2, simply because V_2 represents a shorter future than V_1. A low level of National Income, downward trends in that level, even the failure of the level to rise as fast as is thought normal – all these things may depress V_1 and thus delay replacement as well as discouraging net investment. Improved expectations, on the other hand, will augment the effect of technical progress in stimulating both net investment and replacement.

Because different firms will take different views of the future, their assessments of V_1 and V_2 will differ, so that even the same sort of equipment will be replaced sooner by one firm than by another. Thus, the "echo effect" will vary not only with general conditions but also from firm to firm; for a given industry, the bunching of new investment in a given year will not necessarily result in a similar concentration of replacement n years later. In any case, the existence of many different kinds of equipment, varying considerably in physical longevity, will cause replacements in the economy as a whole to be spread over many years, even though *all* industries originally installed equipment in the same year. This leaves very little of the "echo effect" mentioned earlier. The considerations now put forward suggest, rather, that equipment installed during one surge of investment demand will tend to be replaced whenever the next surge comes along, rather than after some fixed and predictable time lag.

8. Changes in the Price Level

Decisions about replacement may be complicated by changes in the general level of prices during the life of the equipment. An increase in the price of capital goods relative to that of their products will tend to discourage investment. But even if all prices have been rising together, current equipment prices will now be greater than those paid for similar machines some years ago. If, over those years, a firm has allocated part of a machine's yield to a depreciation fund in such a way as to accumulate the amount originally spent on the machine, the fund will now be too small to buy an identical replacement, and this may discourage replacement if the firm cannot command other internal or external sources of finance.

More important, perhaps, is the effect of rising prices on firms' policies in the future. If they expect the upward trend to continue, they may change their depreciation allowances from an "original cost" to a "replacement cost" basis — that is, they will plan to accumulate a fund sufficient to buy new equipment, however much its price may have risen, rather than merely to replace the money originally spent. This will incline the firm to distribute less dividends than it might otherwise have done. On the other hand, rising prices make it undesirable to accumulate money balances or to retain holdings of fixed interest securities, since these will lose value as prices rise. Firms thus have an incentive to use their depreciation allowances as quickly as possible for purchasing new equipment. The combined effect of these considerations may be to stimulate investment in general.

Rising prices benefit firms with fixed interest debt in the form of debentures or loan stock; the higher prices of their products bring them increased money revenue, but the interest charge does not rise; the burden of debt will become steadily lighter in real terms. This is a variation of the Pigou effect noted in Chapter 5,[34] and it may lead firms to increase investment. Against this tendency, firms may themselves possess money balances and fixed interest securities whose real value decreases as prices rise; here the Pigou effect will cut the other way.

Higher product prices will, of course, be offset by higher input costs. If all prices are rising at the same pace, materials and fuels will be proportionately more expensive, and wage increases will be keeping labor costs in step. If a firm is also charging depreciation on a replacement cost basis, its profits will be rising at exactly the same rate as the general price level, so that they remain the same in real terms (except for the Pigou effect just noted). But the assumption that output and input prices change in exactly the same proportions is a very questionable one. Output prices may be rising because of the pressure of consumers' demand; in the effort to meet this demand, firms may try to obtain more materials, plant, and labor, and so force up input prices. But input prices would rise *after* out-

---

[34] See p. 115.

put prices; sales revenue would thus keep ahead of rising costs, to the benefit of profits. On the other hand, the rise in output prices might be the result of higher costs; if material prices and/or wages are rising, firms may be passing on these cost increases to the consumer by raising product prices. Here, however, input prices would be in the lead, and profits would suffer. Insofar as investment depends on the level of retained profits, it would be stimulated or retarded according to the "phasing" of the change in prices. For reductions in prices, of course, all these considerations apply in reverse.

When the price level changes, there are likely to be expectations of further movements. The prospects of continued price increases may make firms wish to buy as much equipment as possible while prices are still relatively low; there will be some incentive to introduce labor-saving machinery in view of higher wages expected in the future, and firms will build up inventories as promptly as possible. A rise in prices that is thought to be temporary will have the opposite effect; to buy machinery at a time when it is expected soon to be down in price again would appear bad business. Here, then, it is not the change in prices as such, but the state of expectations it brings about, that determines the outcome.[35]

9. Residential Construction

The investment thus far examined is that in fixed business capital and inventories; by acquiring extra plant and stocks of goods, firms hope to be in a better position to supply commodities to the markets where they earn their profits. There remain two further categories of investment — those of government and of residential construction.

Investment in residential construction, which includes houses and apartments, is treated as a separate category for several reasons. First of all, housing units are consumers' durables, and the demand for their services is part of consumption demand. Furthermore, both the long-run and the short-run behavior of residential construction are distinct from the be-

---

[35] The influence of price expectations is discussed more fully in Chapter 13, pp. 319–323.

havior of other categories of investment. In the long run the principal determinant of the demand for new homes is population growth; income change is relatively insignificant. If allowance is made for price changes, the per capita value of residential capital is now only slightly higher than it was in 1890,[36] whereas a real disposable income has increased more than fourfold over the same eight-year period.

In the long run, changes in credit conditions appear similarly unimportant as an influence on investment in residential construction. In recent decades there has been great improvement in the financial institutions serving the housing sector and a consequent increase in the use of mortgage credit to finance home purchase. Yet, over the years, changes in the availability of credit and in the level of interest rates have had little or no influence on the long-run demand for housing. In its ultimate dependence on population, of course, the behavior of residential construction is clearly distinguished from that of most other types of investment.

The short-run characteristics of residential construction also suggest it should be treated as a separate category of investment. Even in the short run, housing is not affected by the level of income or by income changes, but it is highly sensitive to the level of the interest rate and the general availability of credit.[37] Home builders, who construct units for subsequent sale or rental, are heavily dependent on loan finance; from the time when land is purchased and architects are hired, up to the point of sale to a new owner, the builder must borrow a large portion of the investment cost. In general, firms engaged in residential construction are not in a position to finance a significant part of their investment with internal funds, as can industrial and commercial enterprises undertaking the fixed business investment discussed earlier. When interest rates are high, the home builder's cost of operation is increased. Some firms — particularly the many small operators characteristic of the industry, or firms with weak credit ratings — may find difficulty in getting any bank credit at all. As a result, the volume of construction falls.

The burden of high interest rates falls on the potential homeowner as well, of course, and has a retarding effect on the demand for custom-built

---

[36] See L. Grebler and S. L. Maisel, "Determinants of Residential Construction: A Review of Present Knowledge," in Commission on Money and Credit, *Impacts of Monetary Policy* (Englewood Cliffs, N.J.: Prentice-Hall, 1963), p. 487.

[37] For a discussion of recent empirical studies of the short-run determinants of housing investment, see M. K. Evans, *op. cit.*, Chapter 7.

houses just as it does on units built for resale.[38] To the owner-occupier who borrows to buy his house, the monthly mortgage payment is made up partly of interest and partly of repayment of principal; the higher the interest rate, the higher the total monthly payment required. For example, on $20,000 borrowed at 5% and repayable over 20 years, the housebuyer pays $132 per month, or a total of $31,680 over the period of the loan. If the interest rate is 8%, on the other hand, the monthly payments are $167, giving a total payment of $40,640.[39] In addition, under tight credit conditions the potential house purchaser is likely to have to raise a larger down payment than he would under a situation of easier credit and lower interest rates. Thus, high interest rates raise the "cost of operation" for the house-owner, just as they do for the builder.

One interesting aspect of this dependence of the housing industry on interest rates is the peculiar relationship between residential construction and the level of fixed business investment. As mentioned earlier, fixed business investment, though not insensitive to the interest rate, is responsive to other conditions, such as the trends in present and past sales and the general level of business expectations. When the level of business investment is high, perhaps in response to a growing level of economic activity and high sales prospects, the large demand for investable resources tends to drive the interest rate up.[40] In this situation, a high rate of fixed business investment contributes to the financial conditions that bring about contraction in residential construction. By the same token, housing construction tends to expand when the rate of fixed business investment slows down.

This "countercyclical" tendency in housing is further supported by the sensitivity of home building to the level of construction costs. The housing industry competes with other forms of investment for certain resources, such as particular categories of skilled craftsmen and some specialized materials. When the relative costs of these inputs rise, because of the pressure of a high rate of investment in fixed business assets, the overall costs of residential construction are increased. The prices for which new

---

[38] It is interesting to note, however, that the volume of construction of custom units is much less sensitive to financial conditions than is the building of units for resale; see D. A. King, "Housebuilding Activity in 1969," *Survey of Current Business* (October, 1969), pp. 16–22.

[39] The above figures do not take account of tax considerations.

[40] In an investment boom, the actions of monetary authorities may serve to raise interest levels even further. These phenomena are discussed in greater detail in Chapters 11 and 12.

houses can be sold, however, do not respond to movement in the prices of investment goods or inputs to construction. The amount of new housing built and put on the market in any year is a very small fraction of the total housing stock; and thus the general price of housing, new as well as old, is determined to a great extent by the large resale market in used homes. Whether a new house will sell promptly will depend on its price relative to comparable buys among existing units or to the general level of house and apartment rents. The return a builder can expect from a newly constructed unit is thus determined by general housing market conditions. When construction costs rise because of a high rate of business investment, the profit margins of house builders are squeezed, and the volume of residential construction is further reduced. When fixed business investment slackens, construction costs fall and residential construction tends to increase.

These considerations, of course, apply to private expenditure. A small but growing contribution to the volume of residential construction is being made by different levels of government. These programs are based on urban renewal and public housing needs, and they are generally regarded as a social service rather than as a commercial enterprise. The tax-financed portion of such developments is insensitive to the levels of interest rates and construction costs, and these activities are therefore less likely to be affected directly by fluctuations in overall economic activity than housing in general. On the other hand, public housing programs are always susceptible to shifts in federal, state, and municipal budget allocation.

10. Public Investment

Residential construction is not the only area where public funds make a contribution to capital formation. The government is involved in many activities that have the character of investment, ranging from the construction of elementary schools to the purchase of manufacturing and test facilities for the space program. It is not possible, however, to conduct a very precise analysis of these activities, for the United States system of national accounts does not separate out government capital formation.[41]

---

[41] See Chapter 2, pp. 25–27.

All government purchases, be they consumables or capital goods, are lumped into a single expenditure category (*i.e.*, Government Purchases of Goods and Services); the entry for "investment" in the National Income and Product Accounts includes only Gross *Private* Domestic Investment.[42]

The lack of a system of accounting for government investment leads to anomalies in the treatment of certain transactions. If a private electric power utility installs a new generating station, the cost of the facility is recorded as investment in the year in which it is constructed and as a contribution to the nation's capital stock; if the Tennessee Valley Authority builds the same plant, it is not logged as a capital investment but as a current "goods and services" purchase. A new track laid down by a private railroad is an investment; a new runway at a municipal airport is not.

In addition to investment in public facilities such as water systems, roads, and schools, there has at certain times been considerable government outlay for productive plant and equipment not actually utilized by government agencies. For example, many facilities built by the Defense Department, the Atomic Energy Commission, and the National Aeronautics and Space Administration have been acquired for the use of private firms.[43] At the time they were brought into being, these assets were not counted as investments but as government purchases; the distinguishing characteristic of a "private" investment is not who will use the facilities, but who finances the purchase.

In certain defense-related industries these government-owned but privately operated assets have at times constituted a sizable proportion of total productive capital. For example, at the end of World War II, 10 per cent of the steel, half the aluminum, most of the aircraft, and all of the synthetic rubber output of the country was produced by private firms in government plants. Since the late 1940's, many of those facilities have been sold to the firms that operated them, and thereby have been at least partially accounted for as investments. But even today, much of the aircraft and ordnance industries, the atomic energy industry, and the activities supported by the space program are operating on this basis.

---

[42] The National Accounts do include an estimate of public expenditure on "structures." Some of these figures were given at the beginning of this chapter: $25.5 billion was spent on structures in 1967, the major items including $8.5 billion on roads and streets and $6.0 billion on schools. See the *Survey of Current Business* (July, 1968), Tables 3.2, 3.4, and 5.2.

[43] See R. J. Gordon, "$45 Billion of U.S. Private Investment Has Been Mislaid," *American Economic Review*, Vol. 59 (June, 1969), pp. 221–238.

It might appear that these different types of public investments constitute one category of demand whose amount can be fixed entirely at the government's discretion, and which can be varied if necessary to offset an excess or deficiency of demand in the private sector. While it is true that some adjustments can be made on fairly short notice, the flexibility is not as great as it may seem at first. Road construction, for example, must keep up with the needs of a growing economy if transport bottlenecks are to be avoided. Other forms of investment, such as hospital construction, serve social aims that the government may not wish to modify. Defense requirements may make certain projects essential. Educational building by local governments may be difficult to alter, given the communities' aims in this field. Every form of public investment, in fact, is intended to achieve some particular object that may seem too important to be sacrificed even when general economic policy calls for a reduction in aggregate demand.

Because of the difficulty of such decisions, because of the multiplicity of authorities involved, and because of the long-range character of many projects for which contracts are placed some time in advance, the public investment program is difficult to revise on short notice. It may be easier to increase it when economic policy requires expansion; but even then, a good deal of premilinary planning will be necessary, and it would be unreasonable to expect public agencies to invest in projects that do not offer prospects of adequate future benefits. To say that the volume of public investment is the result of government decisions is not to say that it can be changed quickly.[44]

---

[44] These investment outlays constitute only a portion of total government expenditure, of course. The macroeconomic effect of overall government spending and taxation is taken up in Chapter 9.

CHAPTER 8

Foreign Trade and the National Income

1. The Import Function

The demand for a country's exports is an element of aggregate demand; it competes with consumption, investment, and government expenditure for the country's output, and incomes are generated in producing exported commodities in exactly the same way as they are in meeting other demands. The country's own demand for imports, on the other hand, is a *negative* element of aggregate demand; it diverts the expenditure of consumers, business firms, and government away from domestically produced commodities and relieves the pressure on domestic supplies; the incomes generated in meeting it are those of foreign suppliers. If government expenditure and nonfactor charges against output are neglected, the condition of equilibrium is

$$Y = C + I + E - M$$

where E is export demand and M is the demand for imports. If E exceeds M, the equilibrium level of income and output will be higher than it would otherwise have been; if M exceeds E, it will be lower.

Autonomous changes in E and M will set up multiplier effects. Because E is a positive element of aggregate demand, an increase in its value will raise equilibrium income; however, higher import demand will reduce income, since M is negative. In Chapter 6, the working of the Multiplier was seen to depend on the response of consumption (and possibly of investment) to income changes initiated by any autonomous change in demand; if import and export demand are also sensitive to changes in income, this will affect the Multiplier. There seems no obvious reason to expect the demand for exports to be directly affected by changes in the exporting country's income; the buyers of exports are, by definition, residents of other countries. But it would be reasonable to suppose some connection between income and the level of imports. When output rises, the input of materials must increase, and some materials are likely to be imported; the personal incomes generated by higher output may be partly spent on imported consumer goods; and increased investment demand may call for imports of capital equipment. It may be necessary to employ more foreign shipping to bring in the additional goods, and this too adds to imports, since the term "imports" includes purchases of services as well as merchandise from abroad.[1]

---

[1] See p. 27 above.

The general relationship between the level of National Income and the demand for imports is called the *Import Function*. It is a concept analogous to the Consumption and Investment Functions introduced in previous chapters, and it can be represented diagrammatically in similar fashion; if the vertical scale in Figure 5.1 (p. 97) were made to measure imports instead of consumption, the curve $C(Y)$, which could be renamed $M(Y)$ in this context, would show the import demand associated with each income level. The slope of the Import Function at any point shows how the nation's demand for imports changes relative to a given change in income — in symbols, $\dfrac{\triangle M}{\triangle Y}$. This is the *Marginal Propensity to Import* (MPM).[2] The proportion between total import demand and total income, for a given level of income, is the *Average Propensity to Import* (APM).

In 1967, United States imports of goods and services, valued at current market prices, were 5.2% of GNP. The average percentage for the whole period 1958–67 was 4.7%; after 1961, when the figure was 4.4%, the APM gradually increased, and the 1967 value of 5.2% was higher than in any previous year.[3] The MPM, on the other hand, is not so easily estimated by merely comparing recorded changes in income. The $\triangle M$ of the MPM is the change in demand for imports that can be attributed exclusively to the concomitant change in real income $\triangle Y$. At any particular time, however, the actual change in expenditure on imports will be a response not only to the rise or fall of income itself, but also to fluctuations in import prices (in relation to those of domestically produced goods), to changes in the cost and availability of finance, to alterations in import duties and quantitative restrictions, and to many other influences. It is therefore hardly surprising that the ratio of annual import change to income change (as rep-

---

[2] The MPM should not be confused with the "income elasticity of demand for imports," which is the ratio between the *proportionate* change in imports and the proportionate change in income: $\dfrac{\triangle M}{M} \div \dfrac{\triangle Y}{Y}$. The MPM is the ratio between *absolute* changes: $\dfrac{\triangle M}{\triangle Y}$.

[3] The percentages are calculated from Tables 1.1 of *Survey of Current Business*, July, 1968 (for the years 1964–67), and *National Income and Product Accounts of the United States, 1929–65* (for 1958–63). Calculation of the APM in terms of 1958 dollars (Tables 1.2) gives 5.8% for 1967, and an average value of 5.0% for the whole period 1958–67.

resented by the change in GNP, with all magnitudes in 1958 dollars) should have varied considerably over the years: in 1967 it was 20.0%, but in 1963 it was only 5.2%, while in 1960 it was negative — imports actually fell by $0.5 billion although GNP rose by $11.8 billion, giving a value of — 4.2% for the MPM in that year. As shown by the import function below, the average value of the MPM in the period 1958–67 was 7.6%, but this figure should evidently be treated with great caution.

The United States' two "propensities to import" both appear rather low when compared with those of many other countries; for example, Britain's APM over the years 1957–64 was about 29%, while its MPM averaged over 40%; during the period 1951–66, Italy's APM averaged 13% and its MPM 28%.[4] Differences between countries' propensities arise from structural differences in their economies; a country with large agricultural and mineral resources may be much more self-sufficient and thus have a smaller APM than one whose manufacturing sector requires large inputs of imported raw materials. On the other hand, a low APM could be consistent with a high value of the MPM; at high levels of output, domestic supplies of materials may become inadequate and have to be supplemented by imports, or high personal incomes may induce consumers to demand foreign luxuries that they would not have thought of buying when less affluent. The demand for imports may then rise relatively faster than income, even though total imports are still quite a small proportion of income. But it is not possible to lay down any general rules about the value of the MPM; although it will usually be positive (*i.e.*, greater than zero), even this cannot be taken for granted. A country exporting high-quality products may be consuming cheap imported substitutes; a rise in income may make its people feel rich enough to consume their own produce, and they would then import less, not more; the MPM would be negative, even though the APM was still positive and even high. But such cases can be regarded as exceptional.

Like the Consumption Function, the Import Function can be expressed as an equation: $M = M_0 + mY$. Here M_0 is "autonomous imports" — the quantity the country would import even if income were nil; m is the MPM.

---

[4] The British propensities are Brooman's estimates, as given on pp. 182–83 of the British edition of this book (3d ed.; London: Allen and Unwin, 1967); the Italian figures were calculated by Prof. R. Zaneletti of the University of Genoa, and appear in the Italian version of the book, (Milan: Giuffré, 1967).

When quarterly figures for United States imports and GNP for the period 1958–67 are used to estimate values for M_0 and m, the equation becomes

$$M = -14.31 + .076Y$$

where M is imports of goods and services, Y is GNP, and both (as well as the -14.31 value found for M_0) are in billions of 1958 dollars per year.[5] The fact that M_0 has a negative value implies that the United States would import nothing at all if GNP fell as low as \$188 billion (in 1958 dollars). However, this result is merely the consequence of assuming that the Import Function can be represented by a straight line, an assumption that may be reasonable for the values of GNP found in the period 1958–67, but may not be true for much lower values. Another consideration is that, instead of a single Import Function, a more realistic approach might use several; imports could be disaggregated into a number of categories such as raw materials, fuels, and manufactures, and a separate equation estimated for each of them.[6]

Inserting the Import Function, along with a Consumption Function $C = C_0 + cY$, into the equilibrium condition $(Y = C + I + E - M)$ gives

$$Y = C_0 + cY + I + E - M_0 - mY.$$

If an autonomous change in demand occurs, income will move to a new equilibrium. The difference will be

$$Y_2 - Y_1 = C_0 + cY_2 + I_2 + E_2 - M_0 - mY_2$$
$$- C_0 - cY_1 - I_1 - E_1 + M_0 + mY_1.$$

If the autonomous change is in investment $(\triangle I)$, and if the income change induces no further alteration in investment nor any change in exports, the change in equilibrium income will be

$$\triangle Y = c\triangle Y + \triangle I - m\triangle Y$$

---

[5] The quarterly data are from Tables 1.2 of *Survey of Current Business* (July, 1968) and *National Income and Product Accounts of the United States, 1929–65.*

[6] For an example, see L. R. Klein, "A Postwar Quarterly Model: Description and Applications," in *Models of Income Determination*, National Bureau of Economic Research, Studies in Income and Wealth, Vol. 28 (Princeton, N.J.: Princeton University Press, 1964), pp. 11–57. Klein divides imports into (a) crude food and materials and (b) other imports, estimating a different Import Function for each.

(where $\triangle Y$ is put in place of $Y_2 - Y_1$ throughout) from which

$$\triangle Y(1 - c + m) = \triangle I$$

and

$$\frac{\triangle Y}{\triangle I} = \frac{1}{1 - c + m}.$$

This is a static Multiplier, similar to that deduced on p. 138 above, but allowing for the effects of foreign trade by the inclusion of the MPM. It could also, of course, be written

$$\frac{\triangle Y}{\triangle I} = \frac{1}{s + m}$$

if s (the Marginal Propensity to Save) were inserted in place of $1 - c$.

If the MPM is positive (as is normally assumed) it will reduce the value of the Multiplier (k). If c (the MPC) is 0.8 in a "closed" economy (*i.e.*, one with no foreign trade), k will be $\dfrac{1}{1 - 0.8} = 5$. In an "open" economy with $c = 0.8$ and $m = 0.3$, k is $\dfrac{1}{1 - 0.8 + 0.3} = 2$. To the extent that rising demand is channeled off into the purchase of imports, it is not fed back into income to generate fresh demand; it represents a leakage of demand out of the process. To buy imports is to refrain from buying domestic output; in this, the demand for imports is exactly similar to saving, the other leakage by which demand-steam escapes from the multiplier-engine.

2. The Foreign Trade Multiplier

In the preceding argument, it was assumed that the demand for exports remained unaffected by changes in National Income. But this may not be true. One country's imports are other countries' exports; the leakage of demand through the MPM will set up a multiplier process abroad, and the consequent change in other countries' incomes may alter their demand for the home country's exports. Indirectly, then, changes in income may induce changes in exports; how much change depends on the MPMs of the countries whose incomes are affected by the original multiplier leakage and on the size of their own Multipliers.

Suppose there are two countries, A and B. The equilibrium condition requires that any rise in aggregate demand shall be met by an equal rise in income and output:

$$\Delta Y_A = c_A \Delta Y_A + \Delta I_A + \Delta E_A - m_A \Delta Y_A$$

for country A, and

$$\Delta Y_B = c_B \Delta Y_B + \Delta I_B + \Delta E_B - m_B \Delta Y_B$$

for country B. Suppose an autonomous change in investment of $X billions occurs in country A; there is no induced investment in either A or B, so $\Delta I_A = X$ and $\Delta I_B = 0$. If A and B trade only with each other, the demand for A's exports is the same as B's demand for imports, so that $\Delta E_A = m_B \Delta Y_B$, and, conversely, $\Delta E_B = m_A \Delta Y_A$. The above equations may therefore be amended to read

$$\Delta Y_A = c_A \Delta Y_A + X + m_B \Delta Y_B - m_A \Delta Y_A \tag{1}$$

and

$$\Delta Y_B = c_B \Delta Y_B + m_A \Delta Y_A - m_B \Delta Y_B. \tag{2}$$

From the last equation,

$$\Delta Y_B (1 - c_B + m_B) = m_A \Delta Y_A,$$

which may be expressed as

$$\Delta Y_B = \frac{m_A \Delta Y_A}{1 - c_B + m_B}.$$

If this is substituted for ΔY_B in Equation (1) above,

$$\Delta Y_A = c_A \Delta Y_A + X + \frac{m_A m_B \Delta Y_A}{1 - c_B + m_B} - m_A Y_A$$

or, gathering terms,

$$\Delta Y_A \left(1 - c_A + m_A - \frac{m_A m_B}{1 - c_B + m_B} \right) = X.$$

This expression becomes less unwieldy if s_A (country A's Marginal Propensity to Save) is substituted for $1 - c_A$, and s_B for $1 - c_B$. So amended, it is now rearranged as

$$\frac{\Delta Y_A}{X} = \frac{1}{s_A + m_A - \dfrac{m_A m_B}{s_B + m_B}} \tag{3}$$

which is a Multiplier similar to that given on p. 202, except that it includes the extra term $\dfrac{m_A m_B}{s_B + m_B}$, which may be called u_A for short. Because u_A has a negative sign, its effect is to make the Multiplier larger than it would otherwise be; for example, if $s_A = 0.2$, $m_A = 0.3$, $s_B = 0.1$, and $m_B = 0.2$, the Multiplier would be

$$\frac{\triangle Y_A}{X} = \frac{1}{0.2 + 0.3 - \dfrac{0.3 \times 0.2}{0.1 + 0.2}} = \frac{1}{0.3} = 3.3.$$

The omission of the u_A term would have made it only $\dfrac{1}{0.2 + 0.3} = 2.$

In this Foreign Trade Multiplier, u_A represents the feedback of demand from other countries that result from the rise in A's investment. The process involved is like the bouncing of a ball: an investment rise in A raises A's income, and A imports more from B; the rise in B's exports increases B's income so that it imports more from A; A's income is now raised, and it buys more from B; B now sends back the ball as its imports from A rise again; and so on. The collection of propensities given in Equation (3) above shows the final outcome that will be reached when the ball has stopped bouncing. Obviously, the to-and-fro motion will take time; if any significant lags occur, so that the process cannot be completed in a single period, the Multiplier will work dynamically as described in Chapter 6. Also, in real life the ball will be bouncing among more than two countries; A's increased imports from B may lead B to import more from C, which in turn steps up imports from D; if D now responds by importing more from A, the repercussions of A's original income increase will have taken some time to return, and the size of the effect may depend on the route it has taken — for example, if country C's MPM is zero, the ball will never get back to A at all.

If A is a small country and B is the rest of the world, m_B will be small. A rise in income may considerably increase world demand for imports, but A's share of the increased trade will not be great — and m_B is not the world's MPM in general but its marginal propensity to import from A. The smaller m_B is, the smaller will be u_A and country A's Multiplier; for example, if $m_B = 0.01$, and s_A, s_B and m_A have the numerical values given in the example earlier, $u_A = 0.027$ and the Multiplier is 2.11 — not much more than the value of 2.0 that it would have had with $m_B =$ zero.

However, as long as m_B exceeds zero, it will pull more weight in the Multiplier, the smaller the value of s_B. If s_B were zero, the Multiplier of Equation (3) would reduce to

$$\frac{\triangle Y_A}{X} = \frac{1}{s_A + m_A - m_A} = \frac{1}{s_A},$$

i.e., the same as it would be in a "closed" economy; the "overseas feed-back" would exactly compensate for the leakage of demand through the MPM. The greater s_B, the smaller the degree of compensation and the smaller the Multiplier.

Equation (3) gave the Multiplier that operates in response to an autonomous change in country A's investment. That equation will apply equally well when the multiplicand is a change in consumption or in government expenditure; however, when an autonomous change in *exports* starts the process, the results will be different. Country A's exports are B's imports; if A's income is increased through a rise in its exports, B's income must *ipso facto* fall because its imports have increased. While A's experience can still be described by Equation (1), B's Equation (2) must be amended to include a term $-X$, representing the autonomous rise in B's imports, which is the obverse of A's rise in exports. This gives

$$\triangle Y_B = c_B \triangle Y_B + m_A \triangle Y_A - m_B \triangle Y_B - X$$

from which

$$\triangle Y_B(1 - c_B + m_B) = m_A \triangle Y_A - X,$$

so that (with s_B substituted for $1 - c_B$)

$$\triangle Y_B = \frac{m_A \triangle Y_A}{s_B + m_B} - \frac{X}{s_B + m_B}.$$

Substituting this in Equation (1), and proceeding as before, gives

$$\frac{\triangle Y_A}{X} = \frac{1 - \dfrac{m_B}{s_B + m_B}}{s_A + m_A - \dfrac{m_A m_B}{s_B + m_B}} \qquad (4)$$

— a Multiplier that differs from that in Equation (3) by the term

$$\frac{m_B}{s_B + m_B}$$

(which may be called z_A for short) that appears in the numerator of the fraction and, having a negative sign, reduces the value of the Multiplier as a whole. The larger m_B and the smaller s_B, the greater the value of z_A — exactly as with the u_A term. But whereas a high value of m_B increases the Multiplier by making u_A large, it reduces the Multiplier by raising the value of z_A; and $s_B = 0$ actually makes the Multiplier equal zero, whatever the value of m_B. If numerical values $s_A = 0.2$, $s_B = 0.1$, $m_A = 0.3$, and $m_B = 0.1$ are inserted in Equation (4), the value of the Multiplier is

1.43; Equation (3) would give a value of 2.86. So much depends on the nature of the multiplicand that sets the Multiplier to work.

3. The Terms of Trade, the Balance of Trade, and the Exchange Rate

So far, changes in the price level have been ignored; the income changes induced by the Multiplier have been assumed to be in real terms. But an autonomous rise in country A's investment, inducing a multiple rise in aggregate demand, may push up prices as well as "real" output; A's products will become more expensive in relation to those of other countries. Its imports will in any case be increasing because its income is rising; they will increase still more because of their price advantage, unless A's price elasticity of demand for imported goods is zero. A's export customers, on the other hand, may buy less because A's prices are higher; the volume of exports will fall below what it would otherwise have been. The reduction in export volume may, however, be offset by the rise in prices; if the quantity demanded falls 5% in response to a 10% price increase, the *value* of exports will actually rise by 4½%.

If it is desired to show only "real" changes in A's income and aggregate demand, values must be deflated in proportion to the rise in A's price level; the change in exports will then be measured simply by the change in physical quantity. Imports, however, can no longer be measured at their original price level, even though it has not risen; when all other values in the equilibrium equation $Y = C + I + E - M$ are being price-deflated, M must be deflated also. If A's price level has risen 10%, everything must be multiplied by 100/110, which will restore the basis of valuation of C, I, and E to that of A's original price level, but will mean also that imports are now being valued as though their prices had fallen about 10%. The overall effect on the value of imports will then depend on whether the increase in quantity has been greater or less than this percentage; if it was, in fact, only 5%, the value of M will be *less* than before.

To the extent that the volume of exports falls and the volume of imports rises, A's income will tend to fall; but to the extent that the country can now obtain imports more cheaply — more cheaply, that is, relative to its domestic price level — its income will tend to rise. These effects follow not from the rise in A's prices as such, but from the fact that the prices have risen in relation to those of the rest of the world; if world prices had risen 10% and A's 20%, or if world prices had gone down by 10% while A's remained unchanged, the effects would have been much the same. The ratio between world prices and those prevailing in A is called the *terms of trade*. Changes in the terms may be assessed by comparing an index of world prices with an index of A's prices; if both indices are 100 in a given year, and then change so that in the following year world prices are 105 and A's are 115, the "terms-of-trade" ratio will stand at 105/115, or 0.913 as compared with 1.00 previously. For A, imports will now be 8.7% cheaper than before — the terms of trade have moved in A's favor.

A change in the terms of trade will therefore have a threefold effect. The *volume* of export demand will change according to its elasticity with respect to the terms of trade: $\triangle E = +E\epsilon\tau$, where ϵ measures elasticity and τ the proportionate terms-of-trade change. The *volume* of import demand will change similarly, but in the opposite direction, that is, by $-M\eta\tau$, where η is the terms-of-trade elasticity of demand for imports. Finally, the *value* of imports will change in proportion to τ, that is, by $+(M - M\eta\tau)\tau$. The combined effect on aggregate demand will be

$$\triangle E - \triangle M = E\epsilon\tau - [-M\eta\tau + (M - M\eta\tau)\tau].$$

For example, if E and M are each 100, if $\epsilon = 2$, and if $\eta = 1$, a 5% fall in the terms of trade ($\tau = -0.05$) will cause aggregate demand to change by $-10 - [+5 - (100 + 5)\ 0.05]$, or -9.75. Had ϵ been only 0.5, the change in aggregate demand would have been -2.25; if ϵ and η were each 0.5, and if τ were very small, the change would be negligible.[7]

Whatever the change in A's aggregate demand when the terms of trade alter, it will set up multipilier effects of its own, on the lines of Equation (4) (p. 205). If, as was assumed at the beginning of this section, the change in the terms of trade was an incidental consequence of the multiplier effects of a rise in A's investment, there will now be *two* multipliers working simultaneously — *against* one another if the terms-of-trade effect operates to reduce A's aggregate demand, or *with* one another if the effect increases demand. In either case, the outcome of the original rise in investment will

---

[7] This is a particular case of the general rule that τ will not change the balance of $(E - M)$ if $\epsilon + \eta = 1$. See J. Robinson, *Essays in the Theory of Employment*, 2d ed. (Oxford: Basil Blackwell, 1947), p. 143, note 2. In the text above, nothing is said about elasticities of *supply*, though these may play an important part if they are small: on this, see Robinson, *op. cit.*, pp. 138–146.

be modified. Even if A's income and price level are not themselves changing, the terms of trade may rise or fall because of a change in prices in the rest of the world; and a "primary" multiplier effect of the Equation (4) type will be set up in A.

If, before these developments occurred, A's exports and imports were equal to one another, they are likely to finish up out of balance. In the simplest case, in which there is no feedback of demand from overseas — e.g., if $m_B = 0$ in Equation (1), p. 203 — and the terms of trade do not change, there is no change in exports, and imports alter by $m_A \triangle Y_A$. Thus, a country whose income is rising is likely to develop a surplus of imports over exports or to increase the surplus if one already existed; there will be a worsening of its balance of trade. Only if the overseas feedback through $m_B \triangle Y_B$, and the terms-of-trade effect are together of such a nature as to offset $m_A \triangle Y_A$, will the balance of trade not deteriorate. Obversely, a fall in income will eliminate a balance-of-trade deficit and, if it goes far enough, even create a surplus of exports over imports. On the whole, the balance of trade (in the sense of $E - M$) may be expected to vary inversely with the level of National Income.

Suppose, then, that a rise in National Income causes country A's balance of trade to show a deficit. The amount of foreign currency needed for A to buy imports will now exceed the amount that foreigners are prepared to pay for exports from A; A's demand for other currencies will exceed the available supply of them. (Alternatively, it could be said that the supply of A's currency exceeds the demand for it, since A's demand for foreign currency implies readiness to supply its own in exchange, and the supply of foreign currency implies a demand for A's.) It may be that A's excess demand for foreign currency is being met from foreign loans, which supplement A's export earnings; the overall supply will meet A's demand, and A's *balance of payments* (in the sense of *ex ante* receipts minus *ex ante* payments) will be in equilibrium. But if this is not the case, the consequences of disequilibrium will depend on the policy of A's monetary authorities with regard to the exchange rate.

In the foreign exchange market where currencies are traded against each other, the "price" at which a given currency changes hands is its exchange rate; *e.g.*, in the case of the U.S. dollar, the rate is the number of pesos, francs, or any other foreign currency units that is given for one dollar. If, then, there is an excess supply of dollars (implying excess demand for foreign currency by people in the United States), the price of dollars will be forced down, just as it would be in any other market in which supply exceeded demand; in the absence of official intervention, the rate of exchange will fall. But this is tantamount to a change in the terms of trade; it means that foreign-currency prices of exports are reduced while import prices remain the same or, in terms of domestic currency, that import prices rise while export prices stay as before. The terms of trade have moved against the home country; the value of τ, in the formula on page 207, is positive; given suitable values of ϵ and η, the terms-of-trade effect will improve the balance of trade and eliminate the excess supply of the domestic currency.

Unfortunately, there is no guarantee that ϵ and η will be of the right size to bring about this result — at least before the exchange rate has fallen considerably. So the monetary authorities may prefer to keep the rate fixed by meeting excess demand for foreign currency out of a reserve kept for the purpose. The reserve may consist of gold or of any other suitable foreign currency; the authorities will be prepared to trade foreign for domestic currency to any extent at the fixed "official" exchange rate. The success of such a policy naturally depends on the size of the reserve relative to the demands on it; if disequilibrium is persistent, the reserve may eventually be drained away. Fearing this, the authorities may take steps to halt the drain. They may raise interest rates in order to attract foreign lending; they may increase import tariffs so as to reduce the demand for foreign goods; or they may frustrate part of that demand by quantitative restrictions on the inflow of merchandise. If hard pressed, they can even impose exchange control, under which domestic currency cannot be exchanged for foreign currency without their permission; by refusing a suitable number of applications, they may be able to frustrate enough of the demand for foreign currency to minimize the drain on reserves.

Finally, the authorities may try to influence the internal economy in such a way as to reduce aggregate demand and the price level, so that the demand for imports falls and the prices of exports become more competitive in world markets. The following chapter is devoted to this and other aspects of the government's role in the economy.

CHAPTER 9

The State and
the National Income

1. Compensatory Finance and Income Taxation

The government,[1] by its expenditures on goods and services, contributes substantially to aggregate demand; it also augments demand indirectly through transfers, such as pensions, that give the recipients spending power. Taxes, on the other hand, reduce demand by removing funds from the private sector that could otherwise have been used to buy goods and services. By arranging taxes and public spending in an appropriate way, the government can add more to demand than it takes away, or take away more than it adds, or leave aggregate demand unchanged; the aim of "compensatory finance" is to adjust aggregate demand to the level needed to give full employment without inflation.

This adjustment would be a simple matter if each dollar of tax revenue were sure to diminish private demand by exactly one dollar, and if each dollar of public spending made a net one-dollar addition to aggregate demand. If the government estimated demand to be, say, $10 billion above the full-employment level, it could then arrange for a budget surplus of exactly that amount; a deficiency of demand could be offset by an exactly equal budget deficit; and a balanced budget could be provided if the level of demand happened to be at full-employment level to begin with. But the effects of taxes and expenditures are more complicated and less certain than this. Taxpayers may respond to a rise in tax rates by reducing their saving as well as their expenditure, so that each one-dollar increase in tax revenue may represent a cut of only, say, seventy-five cents in aggregate demand. Also, different taxes may have different effects, tax A reducing demand by eighty cents per dollar of revenue, tax B reducing it by only sixty cents.

Public expenditure, too, may to some extent substitute for private spending — for example, the existence of public parks reduces the necessity for private expenditure on recreation facilities. Additional government spending, therefore, may sometimes be offset by a reduction in private demand. A change in the balance of taxation and expenditure, by causing an autonomous change in demand, will induce consequential changes in private spending on consumption, investment, and imports — *i.e.*, it will have mul-

---

[1] The term "government" in this context is meant to include federal, state, and local governmental units.

tiplier effects. And among these effects, indeed, may be the inducement of still further changes in the amounts of revenue and public spending. Thus, though the general principle of compensatory finance is simple, its practical application is likely to be much less so.

With revenue derived from income taxation (T_y) and from indirect taxes (T_g), and with expenditures on goods and services (G) and on transfers (Tr), the government's budget is $(T_y + T_g) - (G + Tr)$. It can alter any single item, leaving the others unchanged, or it can alter two, three, or all of them simultaneously; each of the possible alternatives is likely to affect the economy in a different way, as well as to produce a different effect on the budget itself. The first possibility, which will be examined here, is that of a change only in income taxation, T_y. For the moment, it will be assumed that there are no indirect taxes or transfers, and that goods-and-services expenditure, G, is kept fixed by the government and is not affected by changes in the level of income. Suppose, then, that the current National Income is $10 billion below what the government estimates the full-employment level to be. What change in T_y will close this "deflationary gap"?

If there are no undistributed profits, no nonfactor charges against output, and no transfers, then personal incomes are the sum of factor incomes — *i.e.*, National Income, Y. Income taxation removes part of this, leaving individuals with disposable income of $Y - T_y$. If consumption depends on disposable income, that is, if

$$C = C_0 + c(Y - T_y),$$

the equilibrium income of the economy (which for simplicity is assumed to have no foreign trade) will be

$$Y = C + I + G = C_0 + c(Y - T_y) + I + G.$$

If, C, C_0, I, and G remain the same when income changes, an alteration in tax revenue, $\triangle T_y$, will lead to a change in income

$$\triangle Y = c(\triangle Y - \triangle T_y),$$

so that

$$\triangle Y(1 - c) = - c\triangle T_y$$

and

$$\frac{\triangle Y}{\triangle T_y} = \frac{- c}{1 - c}$$

— which is an "income tax multiplier" whose size depends upon the MPC. For example, if $c = 0.8$, the multiplier is -4, so that the required increase of \$10 billion in the level of income can be brought about by a reduction of \$2.5 billion in tax revenue.

The income tax multiplier is negative for the obvious reason that a fall in taxation leaves more income in the hands of individuals, so that they feel able to spend more on consumption; the less the tax bill, the more they spend. But it also differs from the "simple" Multiplier $\dfrac{1}{1-c}$ in having c as the numerator of the fraction, so that (apart from its negative sign) it is smaller; this is because only a part of the additional disposable income is used for consumption, the remainder being saved. The autonomous rise in demand is not $-\triangle T_y$ but $-c\triangle T_y$. The fact that tax revenue has been reduced while public expenditure has been assumed to remain unchanged means that if the budget was balanced to start with, there will now be a deficit of \$2.5 billion.

The calculations above were in terms of total revenue, not of the *rates* of taxation. If incomes are taxed at a uniform proportional rate t, the revenue T_y will be tY. Let the original rate of tax be denoted as t_1 and the original level of income as Y_1. A change in tax to t_2 and in income to Y_2 will cause revenue to change from t_1Y_1 to t_2Y_2; that is,

$$\triangle T_y = t_2Y_2 - t_1Y_1.$$

Thus

$$\triangle Y = \frac{-c\triangle T_y}{1-c} = \frac{-c(t_2Y_2 - t_1Y_1)}{1-c}.$$

If Y_2 is written $Y_1 + \triangle Y$, this becomes

$$\triangle Y = \frac{-cY_1(t_2 - t_1)}{1-c} - \frac{ct_2\triangle Y}{1-c},$$

so that

$$\frac{\triangle Y(1 - c + ct_2)}{1-c} = \frac{-cY_1(t_2 - t_1)}{1-c}$$

from which

$$\triangle Y = -\frac{cY_1(t_2 - t_1)}{1 - c + ct_2}.$$

Here, the multiplicand is the additional expenditure on consumption that taxpayers wish to make when the cut in the tax rate increases their disposable incomes. For example, if Y_1 is \$350 billion, and the rate of tax is reduced from 11% to 10% of income, the amount of tax revenue will fall by $3.5 billion. If the MPC is 0.8, there will then be a rise of $2.8 billion in consumers' demand, which will be multiplied by

$$\frac{1}{1 - c + ct_2}$$

(whose value in this case is 3.57) to give an eventual rise of $10 billion.

This "rate-of-tax multiplier" applies to *any* autonomous change in demand, not merely to that caused by a change in tax rates. For example, if income rises in response to an increase in investment, the consequential rise in consumption will be

$$\triangle C = c(\triangle Y - \triangle T_y).$$

At a given tax rate, t,

$$\triangle T_y = t\triangle Y$$

so that

$$\triangle C = c\triangle Y(1 - t).$$

The change in income then will be

$$\triangle Y = \triangle C + \triangle I = c\triangle Y(1 - t) + \triangle I,$$

so that

$$\triangle Y(1 - c[1 - t]) = \triangle I$$

and

$$\frac{\triangle Y}{\triangle I} = \frac{1}{1 - c(1 - t)} = \frac{1}{1 - c + ct}.$$

In this case, the government is assumed to remain passive, in the sense that it does not itself initiate any change in demand. The existence of taxation at rate t, however, means that part of the additional factor income is diverted to the public revenue instead of being available for consumption, so that the Multiplier is smaller than it would otherwise have been. Tax revenue will have risen by $t\triangle Y$, so that if there was an exact balance to begin with, there will now be a budget surplus; had income fallen instead of risen, the consequent reduction in tax revenue would have caused a budget deficit.

The assumption made so far, that the tax rate t is a fixed proportion of income, is of course an unrealistic simplification; in fact, income taxation is *progressive* — the larger an individual's income, the higher the proportion of it paid in tax. A rise in National Income will push taxpayers into higher tax brackets so that the average tax rate t will increase; similarly, a fall in income will reduce t. Exactly how much t will change depends not only on the amount of rise or fall in National Income but also on how it is distributed among individuals. Also, because tax rates apply to the money value of income, t will rise or fall when changes in the price level bring about changes in money income even though *real* income may remain the same.

Under a system of progressive taxation, increasing factor incomes will be accompanied by a rise in t, so that a smaller and smaller proportion will be left in private hands as disposable income; the rise in consumption will fall further and further behind the rise in National Income. On the other hand, should factor incomes fall, t will also fall; as tax lightens, disposable income will fall less than proportionately with the decline in National Income, and consumption, though falling, will fall less than it would have if a *proportional* tax — or no tax at all — had been in operation. As already noted, these effects follow changes in money income, whether such changes are due to changes in the volume of output at constant prices, or to changes in prices at a constant level of physical output. Thus, the existence of a system of progressive taxation tends to reduce fluctuations in aggregate demand, thereby making the level of income more stable than it would otherwise be; it acts as a built-in stabilizer of the economy.

Altering the distribution of tax liability between income groups (*e.g.*, by increasing the rate of tax on higher incomes while reducing the rate on lower incomes) will change consumers' demand even though total tax revenue remains the same, if the MPC's of the income groups are different. Though the distribution of factor incomes remains the same (at least initially), the reallocation of tax implies a redistribution of *disposable* incomes; leaving less in the hands of a group whose MPC is low and more with a high-MPC group will lead to greater consumption (as described in Chapter 5, pp. 119–122).

2. Changes in Indirect Taxation

Changes in income taxation are only one of the methods of compensatory finance open to the government. A second alternative is to alter indirect taxes, such as sales taxes and excise taxes on liquor, tobacco, and gasoline. To isolate the effects of such changes, it will be assumed that there are no income taxes or transfers and no nonfactor charges against output, other than indirect taxes, and that government spending on goods and services remains fixed in amount.

Indirect taxes absorb expenditure without directly affecting factor income. When the economy is in equilibrium with indirect taxes yielding a revenue T_g,

$$Y_f + T_g = C_m + I_m + G_m$$

or

$$Y_f = C_m + I_m + G_m - T_g,$$

where Y_f is the sum of factor incomes (*i.e.*, National Income) and spending ($C_m + I_m + G_m$) is at market prices. The initial effect of a rise in T_g will be to increase prices while leaving money incomes unchanged; but this means real incomes have been reduced, and so the quantities of goods and services demanded will fall. This autonomous decrease in real demand will have a multiplier effect, causing a further fall in the equilibrium level of real income. A *cut* in indirect taxation will, of course, have the opposite effect, causing an autonomous increase in real demand, which gives rise to a multiple expansion in real income.

Suppose, as a simplification, that all indirect taxation falls on consumption, so that for I and G market price and factor cost are identical; suppose, also, that I and G are unaffected by changes in the level of income. When indirect taxation is altered, the change in National Income will then be

$$\Delta Y_f = \Delta C_m - \Delta T_g.$$

If consumption at market prices is a fixed proportion of factor incomes (there being no income taxes or transfers and no undistributed profits),

$$C_m = cY_f \quad \text{and} \quad \Delta C_m = c\Delta Y_f;$$

so the eventual change in income will be

$$\Delta Y_f = c\Delta Y_f - \Delta T_g,$$

from which

$$\frac{\Delta Y_f}{\Delta T_g} = \frac{-1}{1 - c}.$$

This "indirect tax multiplier" is larger than the income taxation multiplier $\dfrac{-c}{1 - c}$ given on p. 212, suggesting that the authorities can exert more control over the economy by altering indirect taxes than by changing direct taxation. If it is desired to raise income by \$10 billion, and the MPC is

0.8, a cut in indirect taxes of $2 billion will be sufficient, whereas it would be necessary to reduce income taxation by $2.5 billion to achieve the same result.

This will not hold true, however, if the consumption function is of the form

$$C_m = C_0 + cY_f$$

and the autonomous element C_0 is at market prices, implying that consumers wish to obtain a given quantity of commodities *plus* whatever a proportion c of their money incomes will buy. When market prices go up because of higher indirect taxation, the value of C_0 will rise proportionately; even though factor incomes Y_f have not changed, the amount of money being spent on consumption will rise.[2] The change in consumers' demand at market prices will thus be

$$\triangle C_m = pC_0 + c\triangle Y_f$$

(where p is the proportionate change in prices), giving the eventual change in National Income as

$$\triangle Y_f = pC_0 + c\triangle Y_f - \triangle T_g = \frac{pC_0 - \triangle T_g}{1 - c}.$$

The multiplier in this case is

$$\frac{\triangle Y_f}{\triangle T_g} = \frac{-1}{1 - c}\left(1 - \frac{pC_0}{\triangle T_g}\right).$$

This is smaller than the previous multiplier, the precise difference depending on the size of C_0. If factor costs have not changed, the rise in market prices will be wholly attributable to increases in indirect taxation, so that

$$p = \frac{\triangle T_g}{Y_f + T_g}.$$

When this is substituted for p in the last equation, the multiplier becomes

$$\frac{\triangle Y_f}{\triangle T_g} = \frac{-1}{1 - c}\left(1 - \frac{C_0}{Y_f + T_g}\right),$$

which means that if autonomous consumption C_0 were, for example, one-tenth of the market price value of National Income, the indirect tax multiplier would be only nine-tenths as large as it would have been if C_0 had been zero.

---

[2] It is as though the consumption function $C(Y)$ in Figure 5.1 (p. 97) had been shifted vertically upward.

It may be that consumers are not sensitive to price increases, *i.e.*, they are under "money illusion" in that they continue to spend on autonomous consumption the same amount of *money* as before, instead of spending more in order to obtain the same physical quantity at higher prices. In that case, there will be no rise in the value of C_0, and the indirect tax multiplier will be simply $\dfrac{-1}{1-c}$ as before. The likelihood of this depends on the proportion in which prices are increased by higher taxes; the greater this proportion, the more it will obtrude itself on consumers' attention and destroy their money illusion. On the other hand, if the tax increase is not distributed evenly over all commodities (as with a general sales tax) but is concentrated on a few only (as with a rise in the excise taxes on liquor and tobacco), consumers may feel that the general level of prices is about the same as before and so retain their money illusion. Here, however, consumers may be induced to switch demand away from the taxed products to those whose prices are still the same, and this will complicate the outcome.

Indirect taxes will modify the economy's response to autonomous changes in demand other than those resulting from tax changes. Suppose, for example, that a rise in investment occurs; through the Multiplier, aggregate demand will increase, but indirect taxes will divert a proportion of the additional expenditure into the hands of government authorities, so that it fails to generate further income. If taxation takes the form of a general sales tax, applied at a uniform rate t to all commodities,

$$Y_f + T_g = Y_f(1+t);$$

that is, the market value of aggregate output is its factor cost (Y_f) plus 10% (if $t = 0.1$). The income-equilibrium equation then is

$$Y_f(1+t) = cY_f + I + G.$$

If G remains fixed, and I changes only by the increase in autonomous investment $\triangle I$, the rise in income caused by the latter will be

$$\triangle Y_f(1+t) = c\triangle Y_f + \triangle I,$$

from which

$$\triangle Y_f(1-c+t) = \triangle I$$

so that

$$\frac{\triangle Y_f}{\triangle I} = \frac{1}{1-c+t}$$

— a multiplier that is less than either the simple multiplier $\dfrac{1}{1-c}$ or the

"rate-of-income-tax" multiplier $\dfrac{1}{1-c+ct}$, given on p. 214. Indirect taxation is thus more stabilizing than proportional[3] income taxation when tax rates are kept unchanged.

Attempts to reduce aggregate demand by increasing the rate of tax, however, may be less successful than the preceding arguments may have seemed to suggest. When higher indirect taxes raise market prices, the owners of factors of production may be able to neutralize the effect by procuring higher money incomes for themselves. Labor unions may submit wage claims on the ground that the cost of living has risen and may be strong enough to ensure that the claims are conceded; firms may adjust profit margins appropriately, hoping thereby to keep the real value of profits from falling. If the purpose of increasing indirect taxes is to reduce real incomes and so diminish the inflationary pressure of excessive aggregate demand, the rising prices brought about by the policy may create repercussions that tend to neutralize it; indeed, the eventual result may even be to stimulate inflation instead of checking it.

3. Effects on Investment

So far, changes in taxation have been assumed to affect only consumption, leaving investment unchanged. If investment demand is sensitive to the level of income (*i.e.*, if there is a marginal propensity to invest), the various tax multiplers will have to be amended to allow for this — for ex-

ample, the simple income tax multiplier will become $\dfrac{-c}{1-c-i}$ instead of

$\dfrac{-c}{1-c}$. Changes in the level of aggregate demand may also set up ac-
celeration effects. Finally, tax changes may cause autonomous shifts in the investment schedule that will themselves exert multiplier effects.

If investment depends on profit expectations, taxes will diminish the incentive to invest. Given the prospect of a stream of returns A_1, A_2, A_3, etc., direct taxation at a rate t will reduce the disposable yields to $A_1(1-t)$,

---

[3] But not necessarily more so than *progressive* income taxation.

$A_2(1 - t)$ and so on. Higher indirect taxation, by raising market prices, will reduce the real value of A_1, A_2, A_3, etc.; it may also affect estimates of the revenue to be expected from the sale of the product — if sales are likely to fall because of consumers' reactions to indirect taxes, the amount of prospective yields may be reduced. For maximum effect, tax increases must be expected to be fairly permanent; for example, if a rise in corporate income tax is thought likely to be reversed the following year, it will affect only the first of the series of yields, A_1, A_2, A_3, etc., but investment decisions must consider yields over the whole of an asset's prospective life.

Though estimates of the more distant yields may be very uncertain, a rise in tax alters the odds against the investing firm; for example, if the firm expects that the profit earned in the sixth year from now may be anything between $10,000 and nothing at all, tax at the rate of 40% will reduce the expected upper limit to $6,000 while leaving the lower limit still at zero; the average of possible disposable yields will then be lower for this and every other year in which the capital equipment is to operate. Thus, the MEI schedule of Figure 7.1 (p. 163) will be shifted downward; if the schedule is at all elastic with respect to the cost of funds, the level of investment demand will be reduced. If (as in the "residual funds" theory described in Chapter 7, p. 171) the amount of undistributed profits is an important factor in investment decisions, a rise in the rate of tax that falls on them will check investment by reducing the disposable residue of profit.

This general conclusion may need modification in the light of the detailed operation of the tax system. For example, if a rise in taxation affects only personal incomes, while the corporate tax rate is unchanged, its effect may be to increase the retention of profits, thereby furnishing the means for increased investment. The plowing-back of profits increases the assets of companies and tends to raise the market value of their stock; if capital gains are taxable at a lower rate than personal income, it will benefit wealthy stockholders to have profits retained and reinvested in their corporations rather than distributed in dividends. If indirect taxes are changed in such a way as to divert demand toward commodities whose production requires relatively more capital equipment, there may be a net stimulus to investment. Since tax changes tend to be made piecemeal rather than in the form of equal proportional changes in all taxes, their effects on investment may be much less clear-cut than the preceding general arguments have suggested.

4. Changes in Public Expenditure

Instead of using changes in taxation to adjust the level of income, the government may adopt the policy of altering its own expenditure on goods and services, *i.e.*, raising or lowering the value of G in the equilibrium equation

$$Y + T_g = c(Y - T_y) + I + G.$$

In this equation, both income taxes (T_y) and indirect taxes (T_g) have been included; however, if the revenue from both kinds of tax is assumed to remain unchanged when income alters, and if investment is also unaffected by changes in income, the result of a change in G will be

$$\triangle Y = c\triangle Y + \triangle G$$

so that

$$\frac{\triangle Y}{\triangle G} = \frac{1}{1-c},$$

which is the simple Multiplier introduced in Chapter 6. The effect of a rise in government spending on goods and services is just the same as that of an autonomous rise in investment or exports. If the MPC is 0.8, the Multiplier is 5; to raise National Income by $10 billion, a rise in G of $2 billion is required.

The outcome will be different, however, if the government keeps the *rates* of taxation unchanged. The assumption made earlier, that tax *revenue* stays the same, implies that either the authorities reduce tax rates as income rises (and raise them when income falls) or the revenue arises from a poll tax or other lump-sum imposts. If all revenue is from a proportional income tax at rate t_y, and if this rate is not altered when government expenditure changes, revenue will automatically rise with the level of income, and the multiplier will be

$$\frac{\triangle Y}{\triangle G} = \frac{1}{1-c+ct_y}$$

for the reasons given above on p. 214. If indirect taxation provides the revenue, this too will alter when G is changed, so that if the rate of tax remains fixed at t_g,

$$\frac{\triangle Y}{\triangle G} = \frac{1}{1-c+t_g}$$

— this being the "rate-of-indirect-tax" multiplier given on p. 218 above. With both types of tax in force, the two multipliers combine to give

$$\frac{\Delta Y}{\Delta G} = \frac{1}{1 - c + t_g + ct_y}.$$

If the MPC is 0.8, and if tax rates are $t_g = 0.1$ and $t_y = 0.2$, it will be necessary to raise G by $4.6 billion to produce an increase of $10 billion in National Income. Thus, the Multiplier is only 2.17 when tax *rates* are kept fixed, as against 5.0 when tax *revenue* is maintained unchanged.

In addition to altering goods-and-services expenditure, the government may also change the amount of income transfers, for example by raising social security benefits. The effect will be to increase disposable incomes and thus to stimulate consumers' demand. Transfers may, indeed, be regarded as a form of income taxation in reverse; a rise in transfers has the same effect as a fall in income tax revenue,[4] so that the Multiplier that applies to the latter applies also to the former, except that it works in the opposite direction; that is, its sign is positive instead of negative. If consumption depends on disposable incomes Y_d, which are equal to factor incomes *minus* income taxation *plus* transfers, or

$$C = c(Y - T_y + Tr),$$

a change in the amount of Tr (everything else remaining the same) gives

$$\Delta Y = c(\Delta Y + Tr) = c\Delta Y + c\Delta Tr.$$

In this case,

$$\frac{\Delta Y}{\Delta Tr} = \frac{c}{1 - c},$$

which implies that if the MPC = 0.8, an increase of $2.5 billion in transfers will raise National Income by $10 billion.

Income transfers take the form of money payments to individuals, to be spent at their discretion. Another kind of transfer is the *subsidy*, paid by the government to the sellers of commodities so that they can set market prices below factor cost; instead of receiving cash, consumers obtain the benefit of being able to buy goods more cheaply. As income transfers are income taxes in reverse, so subsidies are negative indirect taxes; an increase in subsidies, therefore, is equivalent to a reduction in indirect taxation and may be expected to have similar multiplier effects.

---

[4] Except where the recipients of transfers have MPC's which differ from those of income tax payers, as discussed on pp. 227–228 below.

With given subsidy rates, the government's total outlay depends on the quantity of subsidized commodities bought, and this will rise and fall along with the level of National Income (though not necessarily in the same proportion). Most kinds of income transfers, on the other hand, will be unaffected when National Income changes: the total amount paid out in military pension, disability, and retirement payments depends on the past and present activities of the armed forces; the total of all payments to Medicare recipients is determined by the number of cases of illness; and so on.

An important exception is unemployment benefits; a reduction in the level of income and output, accompanied by an increase in unemployment, will automatically increase the total amount paid out if the rate of benefit per person is not reduced. This increased transfer payment will prevent disposable incomes from falling as much as factor incomes and will sustain consumers' expenditure at a level above what it would otherwise have been, thus tending to stabilize the economy. Like progressive income taxation,[5] a system of unemployment assistance will act as a built-in stabilizer; even if the government takes no special action to combat recession, the automatic operation of the stabilizers will tend to check the fall in aggregate demand. Unlike income taxes, however, a system of transfers to the unemployed is a stabilizer in one direction only; it helps to defend the economy against recessions, but cannot do anything to check inflationary pressures when full employment has been attained.

5. Alternative Policies and the Budget Balance

Various methods have been examined by which the government can cause the equilibrium level of income to rise or fall. If the income level is $10 billion below that required for full employment, and the MPC is 0.8, a reduction of $2.5 billion in income tax revenue or of $2 billion in indirect tax revenue will be required. Or if tax revenue is kept unchanged, the same effect may be achieved by a rise of $2 billion in subsidies. If the government's budget happened to be balanced to start with ($T_y + T_g = G + Tr$) any of these measures will create a budget deficit; revenue will

---

[5] See p. 215 above.

fall short of expenditure, and the government will finance excess expenditure by borrowing.

If the level of aggregate demand must be reduced so as to eliminate inflationary pressures, things will be the other way around; the government will arrange to have a budget surplus, and the excess of revenue over expenditure will be used to repay debt. Balancing the economy may mean unbalancing the budget.

To argue that a budget deficit may sometimes be desirable conflicts with the traditional principle — regarded until the 1930's as virtually self-evident — that the government must at all costs avoid a budget deficit. It used to be taken for granted that if the state spends more than it obtains by taxation, inflation must inevitably result. An individual who overspends his income risks bankruptcy; similarly, it was argued, a government that finances deficits by borrowing may become insolvent; even if it does not, the increase of the National Debt adds to the burden on the community and on posterity that the debt represents. Indeed, a wise government should make efforts to repay it: the budget, so one nineteenth-century British chancellor said, is "an animal that needs a surplus." The superstitious horror in which deficits were held was pathetically illustrated by the passage of the Federal Revenue Act of 1932. Though more than one-fifth of the working population of the United States was unemployed, the Act revised the tax structure and drastically increased tax rates in an attempt to balance the budget.[6]

The traditional arguments against government deficits are not logically valid if unemployment exists. A budget deficit, by adding to aggregate demand, will expand employment and output; inflationary price increases can occur only if the economy is already in equilibrium at full employment, since output cannot then be expanded rapidly to meet a rise in demand. The "inflation" argument against deficits, therefore, assumes the prior existence of the full employment that deficits are intended to achieve. The objection to increasing debt similarly loses force when the economy is depressed. Internally held public debt represents a transfer between

---

[6] These attitudes about budget policy held sway through most of the depression years. Indeed, E. Carey Brown has argued that government fiscal actions were actually a *contractive* influence over much of the period. Federal expenditures were rising, but their impact was more than offset by reductions in state and local spending and increases in taxation at all governmental levels. See his "Fiscal Policy in the Thirties: A Reappraisal," *American Economic Review,* Vol. 46 (December, 1956), pp. 857–79.

members of the same community; the payment of interest is in effect a transfer from taxpayers to bondholders. The traditional analogy between the state and the spendthrift individual[7] is less reasonable than one between the state and a business firm that may rationally incur debts in order to increase its output.

Whatever the logic of the matter, the authorities may still be constrained to avoid a deficit; if legislators and the public are inexorably convinced of the traditional case for budget balancing, a deficit will not be practical politics. There may be external considerations also — for example, it may be feared that a deficit will alarm foreign creditors, whose efforts to withdraw their loans may then make it hard to maintain the exchange rate; the authorities may fear that an increase of debt may be inconsistent with their current policies of "debt management." In these circumstances, the budget may have to be balanced. But the government is still not left powerless to combat unemployment; even without a deficit, the state can still exert an expansionary influence on aggregate demand.

This possibility exists because of differences between the multiplier effects of taxes and transfers on the one hand and goods-and-services expenditures on the other. Suppose the government (whose budget is assumed to be balanced initially) increases expenditure by $\triangle G$, while simultaneously increasing its revenue from income taxation by $\triangle T_y$. If indirect tax revenue and transfer expenditure do not change, and no induced investment occurs, there will be a change in income

$$\triangle Y = c(\triangle Y - \triangle T_y) + \triangle G,$$

so that

$$\triangle Y(1 - c) = \triangle G - c\triangle T_y.$$

If the budget is to remain balanced, the increase in tax revenue must be equal to the rise in government spending, that is, $\triangle G = \triangle T_y$, so the equation could be written

$$\triangle Y(1 - c) = \triangle G(1 - c),$$

giving

$$\triangle Y = \triangle G.$$

The rise in income is exactly equal to the increase in government expenditure.

---

[7] This analogy has been well named the "anthropomorphic fallacy" by S. S. Alexander, in his "Opposition to Deficit Spending for the Prevention of Unemployment," in *Income, Employment and Public Policy, Essays in Honor of Alvin H. Hansen* (New York: Norton, 1948).

Here, two multipliers have been set to work in opposite directions. Had tax revenue been unchanged, $\triangle G$ would have increased income by $\dfrac{\triangle G}{1-c}$; if $\triangle G = 100$ and $c = 0.8$, the rise in income would have been 500. The rise in tax revenue, if left to work on its own, would have reduced income by $- \dfrac{c \triangle T_y}{1-c}$; with $\triangle T_y$ equal to 100, this would have meant a fall in income of $- 400$. Put together, the two multipliers give a change in income of $500 - 400$, or 100. This result is independent of the value of the MPC;[8] it does not matter whether c is 0.9 or 0.2 — the change in income must be

$$\triangle Y = \frac{\triangle G}{1-c} - \frac{c \triangle T_y}{1-c}.$$

Or, since $\triangle G = \triangle T_y$,

$$\triangle Y = \triangle G \frac{1-c}{1-c} = \triangle G.$$

This is the simplest case of the so-called "balanced-budget theorem."[9]

A budget that includes only goods-and-services expenditure and income tax revenue will always, if balanced, impart a stimulus to the economy; it means the authorities are collecting in taxes income that would otherwise have been partly saved and are using it all to finance expenditure. If the authorities wish to exert no *net* effect on aggregate demand, *i.e.*, to contribute to it no more than the amount of demand eliminated by taxation, they should budget for a surplus. Thus, given the nineteenth-century view that the state should be as self-effacing as possible in its role as the "night watchman" of the economy, the traditional preoccupation with debt repayment makes *political* sense, even though it is not *economically* rational unless a state of continuous full employment is assumed to exist.

However, the budget may include transfers and subsidies on the expenditure side, while the revenue may come from indirect taxes as well as from income taxation. If it is these items that change, the results may be very different from the simple case examined above. For example, if an increase in goods-and-services spending, $\triangle G$, is financed by an increase

----

8 In the extreme case in which the MPC $= 1$, the change in income is undefined.

9 T. Haavelmo, "Multiplier Effects of a Balanced Budget," *Econometrica*, Vol. 13 (October, 1945), pp. 311–318. See also R. A. Musgrave, *The Theory of Public Finance* (New York: McGraw-Hill, 1959), Chap. 18, for this and other budgetary multipliers, and for further references.

in indirect taxation, $\triangle T_g$, the effect on income will be nil; the additional expenditure will raise income by $\dfrac{\triangle G}{1-c}$, and the additional indirect taxation will reduce it by $-\dfrac{\triangle T_g}{1-c}$. Since the budget balance requires the additional expenditure ($\triangle G = \triangle T_g$), the two multiplier effects cancel out exactly, leaving income the same as before.

Similarly, an increase in transfer expenditures, financed by extra income taxation, may fail to change the level of income. It was seen on p. 222 that a rise in transfers will increase income by $\dfrac{c\triangle Tr}{1-c}$; additional taxation will reduce it by $-\dfrac{c\triangle T_y}{1-c}$. If $\triangle Tr = \triangle T_y$, the two effects will exactly neutralize each other, leaving income unchanged. If a rise in transfers were combined with additional *indirect* taxation, the net effect could even be a *fall* in the level of income.

It may be, however, that the MPC of the recipients of transfers is different from that of the taxpayers who pay the additional taxes. For example, if the taxes are collected on the incomes of rich people who continue their consumption almost unchanged, while the transfers are small pensions given to old people with no other resources, the net effect will obviously be an increase in aggregate demand. If the rich taxpayers' MPC is denoted by c_1, the pensioners' MPC by c_2, and the MPC of the rest of the community[10] by c_3, the effect of an equal increase X in taxes and transfers will be

$$\triangle Y = \frac{c_2 \triangle Tr}{1-c_3} - \frac{c_1 \triangle T_y}{1-c_3} = \frac{X(c_2 - c_1)}{1-c_3}.$$

---

[10] The assumption here is that though taxpayers and pensioners have different MPC's, their expenditure travels through the same "circuit" of income recipients each of whom has the same MPC, c_3. The expenditure by pensioners of $c_2 X$ gives rise to a series of further payments such that the final effect on aggregate demand and income is

$$c_2 X + c_3 c_2 X + c_3{}^2 c_2 X + \ldots + c_3{}^n c_2 X$$
$$= c_2 X(1 + c_3 + c_3{}^2 + c_3{}^3 + \ldots + c_3{}^n)$$
$$= c_2 X \frac{1}{1-c_3}.$$

Similarly, the taxpayers' reduction of expenditure by $-c_1 X$ will give rise to $-c_1 X \dfrac{1}{1-c_3}$ as the change in income.

If $c_1 = 0.6$, $c_2 = 0.9$, and $c_3 = 0.8$, an X of \$6.7 billion will raise income by \$10 billion, even though the budget is still balanced and there is no additional public goods-and-services spending.

Transfers were described earlier as an income tax in reverse; a reduction in tax liability, therefore, is akin to a transfer payment, and the argument of the previous paragraph may be applied to a redistribution of tax incidence among income groups. If, without any change in the level of government spending or in total tax revenue, tax liability is reshuffled so that people whose MPC is high are left with more disposable income and those with a low MPC with correspondingly less, there will be a net increase in aggregate consumption, which through the Multiplier will increase the equilibrium level of income. In the equation above, substituting for $\triangle Tr$ the amount of tax reduction enjoyed by lower MPC groups will show the results of such redistribution.

By these methods, then, it may be possible to expand income and employment without incurring a budget deficit. The same logic applies, of course, where it is necessary to *reduce* aggregate demand without a budget *surplus*. Public goods-and-services spending may be diminished and tax reliefs of an equal amount given; transfers to high MPC groups may be cut and taxes on low MPC groups reduced; or tax liability may be redistributed from high to low MPC groups. But it should be observed that the degree of disturbance to the budget will be greater if it must be kept balanced than if a surplus or deficit is allowed. To raise income by \$10 billion by increasing equally both taxes and goods-and-services spending, the latter must rise \$10 billion; but in the example on p. 221, where taxes were not increased, only \$2 billion in extra expenditure was required. In the "tax and transfers" example above, \$6.7 billion of additional transfers were needed to raise income \$10 billion; had taxes been left unchanged, only \$2.2 billion would have been necessary. If a deficit were to be incurred by reducing taxes without changing expenditure, and if the MPC were 0.8, a \$2.5 billion income tax cut would achieve the same result as a \$10 billion increase in goods-and-services expenditure that was financed by an equal *increase* in income tax revenue under a balanced budget.

This last difference may be the best reason for preferring deficit finance. When the economy is depressed, tax reductions are likely to improve the atmosphere of enterprise in the private sector, while increases in taxation (even though accompanied by higher government spending) may do further damage to the state of expectations that (as was seen in Chapter 7) is important in the determination of investment. The government's choice must depend on which they think will damage business confidence more — higher taxes or the mystic dread inspired by the spectacle of a deficit.

Naturally, the public's attitudes and expectations about government budget policy are heavily influenced by the nature of the information they are given, and in the United States, until recent years, discussion of this question has been clouded by the existence of three alternative versions of the federal budget. The *administrative* budget, which was made up by the President and submitted to Congress, omitted several fiscal flows — the most important being the transactions of the federal trust funds, such as those of the social security system. In order to keep better account of the total flows of cash between the federal treasury and the private sector, a consolidated cash budget was created. Since the cash budget included the activities of the trust funds, it was quite possible for the two budgets to present different estimates of the size of the federal deficit — even for one to be in the black while the other was in the red. Finally, neither the administrative nor the cash budget used the same definitions of revenue and expenditure as are applied in estimating the National Income Accounts; specifically, the administrative and cash budgets showed Federal loans as expenditures, and the budgets were on a "cash" rather than an "accrual" basis. And so a third, *National Income Accounts*, budget was provided in order to reconcile these differences in definition. Given these three different budgets, it sometimes required careful analysis to determine whether the federal government was incurring a deficit or not, and if so, how large it was.

Following the recommendations of a 1967 report by a President's Commission on Budget Concepts, however, a single *unified comprehensive budget* was adopted. Beginning with the 1969 fiscal year, the new unified budget replaces the former administrative and cash budgets;[11] the improved accounting and budgeting framework should help clear up unnecessary confusion about the economic significance of federal taxation, transfers, and expenditure.

The federal budget does not tell the whole story, of course. Estimates of the overall effect of the government on the level of economic activity

---

[11] See "Comparison of New and Old Budget Concepts," in *The Budget of the United States Government, 1969* (Washington, D. C.: U. S. Government Printing Office, 1968), pp. 464–472. The unified budget still differs slightly from the national income accounting definitions; see *Survey of Current Business* (February, 1968), pp. 11–16.

are incomplete without consideration of the budgetary policies of state
and local units. Of the $178.4 billion in government purchases of goods
and services shown in Table 2.2 (p. 24), $87.8 billion represents state and
local spending. Depending on the year, these units may be in surplus or in
deficit; in 1967, for example, they contributed $1.4 billion to a combined
government deficit of $13.8 billion in the National Income and Product
Accounts. In practice, state and local governments do not decide their individual revenue and expenditure programs with an eye to their influence
on the national economy — that is, no state or municipality engages in
compensatory fiscal policy in the sense that the federal government does.
But they have an influence nonetheless, and their activities must be taken
into account in any attempt to plan a certain degree of imbalance, be it
surplus or deficit, in the budget of the government as a whole.[12]

6. Limitations and Alternatives

With improved accounting systems and growing public understanding
of the potential influence of federal deficits on a sagging economy, it may
not be so difficult to budget for a deficit when necessary. The real obstacles
to compensatory finance may in fact be encountered when a surplus is
needed to check inflationary pressures. The government's room for maneu-
vering may be much less here than the foregoing equations have seemed to
suggest. Reductions in goods-and-services spending may be impractica-
ble — the scale of defense expenditure, for example, is presumably the
minimum needed in view of the political situation, and cannot be diminished without endangering the nation; cuts in certain public services, such
as police and justice, could impair the working of the economy; reductions
in some other forms of public spending, for example, health services, would
be offset by higher private expenditures. Attempts to reduce transfers, such
as pensions, might be so unpopular that a democratically elected government could not be expected to make them. In short, the level of government
spending, though high, may be the minimum needed for national security,
economic efficiency, and the satisfaction of public opinion.

---

[12] For an analysis of these activities, see D. A. King and M. Lefkowitz, "The
Finances of State and Local Governments," in *Survey of Current Business* (October,
1967), pp. 20–32.

If expenditures are irreducible, the government must turn to tax increases as a means of anti-inflationary policy. Yet if taxes are already high, it may fear to raise them further. Apart from the political disadvantages of such action, higher income taxation may be expected to damage incentives and to stimulate tax evasion; raising indirect taxes may merely lead to claims for higher money incomes.

Finally, the time factor must be considered. The authorities need time to analyze the situation and to assess the prospects, time to devise appropriate policies, and time to carry them out. Even after Congress has approved the necessary changes in taxation and expenditure, there will be a lag before these measures begin to exert their effects on the economy.[13] By that time, however, conditions may have worsened so much that the remedies are no longer adequate; alternatively, a cyclical movement may have already begun to reverse itself, and by the time they come into force, the government's measures may turn out to be the opposite of what is required. A strong argument for having "built-in" stabilizers, such as progressive taxation and a scheme of unemployment compensation, is that they will work without delay to correct an imbalance. The government's *ad hoc* policy decisions, on the other hand, need to be framed to allow for time lags, and this requirement is likely to make the problem of compensatory finance perplexingly difficult.

If it is found impossible to reduce expenditure or increase taxes, and if such measures would in any case take too long to improve the situation, there is little possibility of reducing excessive aggregate demand by means of budgetary policy; the government must therefore find some other method of achieving its objective. It can turn to *monetary policy*, which works through control of the quantity of money and the cost and availability of credit. To explore the possibilities of monetary policy, it is necessary to examine the part played by money in the economy, and this will be done in Chapters 11 and 12.

---

[13] These policy lags will be additional to those already present in the working of the economy, *i.e.*, the various lags discussed in Chapter 6. The multipliers given in the present chapter have all been set out in static form; realism would require them to be dynamized by the inclusion of time lags, and the task of stabilization policy would then appear even more difficult. See A. Ando and E. C. Brown, "Lags in Fiscal Policy: A Summary," reprinted in W. L. Smith and R. L. Teigen (eds.), *Readings in Money, National Income and Stabilization Policy* (Homewood, Ill.: Irwin, 1965).

CHAPTER 10

Prices, Wages, and
Aggregate Supply

1. The Aggregate Supply Curve

In the last five chapters, the various components of aggregate demand — consumption, investment, government spending, exports, and (negatively) imports — have been examined in detail, especially with regard to their relationship with current real income. It was found that consumption depends partly on income and partly on such other factors as consumers' assets and liabilities; that investment may be influenced to a small extent by current income but depends much more on firms' expectations of future profit, on past changes in income, and on the cost of financing new projects; that government spending, being largely determined by political decisions about such matters as the necessary scale of defense expenditure, is essentially autonomous of current income; and that, while imports can be expected to vary with income to some degree, exports are affected only indirectly through the feedback described in Chapter 8. In the light of all these findings, the original "equilibrium equation"

$$Y = C + I + G + E - M$$

has been amplified and extended in various ways so as to bring in the marginal propensities to consume, import, and invest; to allow for the effects of taxation; to introduce additional variables such as income from previous periods, and so on.

Obviously the equation could be expanded and elaborated still further along these lines. However, the fact remains that, as it stands, the "equilibrium condition" is subject to a serious limitation — namely, that because all quantities are stated in real terms, it throws no light on the determination of the general price level. Yet the behavior of prices is of great interest and importance to individuals, business firms, and governments. Large and sudden changes can be highly disruptive — impoverishing or enriching people according to whether they happen to be debtors or creditors, upsetting normal economic calculations, and creating uncertainties that inhibit the rational use of resources. Even where governments aim at minimum interference with the working of the economy, they usually attempt to maintain reasonable price stability through monetary policy. No theory of the working of the economy as a whole can be complete, therefore, unless it explains the determination of the general price level as well as the volume of "real" output. A full explanation will not be possible until *money* has been introduced into the analysis, but first it is necessary to relax certain assumptions on which the argument up to this point has been based.

The assumptions in question are those made at the end of Chapter 4. The first was that because of the strength of labor unions, money wages can be regarded as "inflexible downward" in the face of unemployment — that is, they will not be forced down by the existence of excess supply in the market for labor. The second was that the employment-output relationship is not such as to involve diminishing returns to labor over the range of outputs that the economy is likely to be required to produce. The combined effect of these two assumptions has been to ensure that the price level would remain constant at all levels of employment and output, except when aggregate demand became so high that it could not be satisfied by the volume of full-employment output; on this basis, it has been possible to analyze the determination of real income and output without having to deal at the same time with the effects of variations in prices.

It can be claimed that neither assumption is wholly unrealistic: unemployment in the United States has not, in fact, been accompanied by significant reductions in money wages during the 1950's and 1960's, and the marginal product of labor can for practical purposes be regarded as constant over a certain range of levels of output, if much capital equipment is designed to rigid labor requirements of the "one man, one machine" variety.[1] But conditions may change over time, and assumptions that are reasonably realistic in one decade may cease to be so in the next; it may happen, too, that both of these particular assumptions do not hold true simultaneously over a wide range of outputs.[2] To increase the generality of the analysis, it is necessary to consider the effects of relaxing them. To begin with, only the assumption of constant returns to labor will be

---

[1] Provided, too, that there are "constant returns to scale" whereby a given proportionate increase in all productive factors always yields the same proportionate increase in output. Then the employment of an additional man, using a machine that would otherwise have stood idle, will always raise output by the same amount, up to the point at which all available machines are in operation.

[2] When output and employment are fairly high, the fact that labor input is large relative to the capital stock makes it probable that labor's marginal product will be diminishing markedly — yet in this situation, labor unions will have no difficulty preventing reductions in money wages, even though there is not quite full employment. At low levels of employment, things may be just the other way around, with the marginal product of labor virtually constant but with money wages falling under the pressure of mass unemployment despite the unions' efforts. The two assumptions will then be valid only in the middle ground between these extremes — yet the middle ground may not be very wide.

dropped; for the time being, it will be convenient to go on treating the level of money wages as constant at all levels of employment and output.

From now on, then, the marginal product of labor will be assumed to diminish as the level of employment increases. The employment-output relationship is once more of the kind exemplified by the $Q(N, \bar{K})$ curve of Figure 4.1 (p. 68), whose slope becomes less and less steep as the number of man-hours employed rises beyond N_2. It will be remembered from Chapter 4[3] that firms will not wish to hire more than the number of man-hours at which the marginal product of labor (MPL) equals the real wage (W or, alternatively, w/p — the money wage divided by the price level), since any additional labor would then cost more to hire than it would contribute to output. This condition, MPL $= w/p$, can easily be rearranged as $p = w/\text{MPL}$; in this form, it defines the minimum price at which firms will be prepared to sell the output of a given quantity of labor. Thus, if the money wage w is \$2 an hour, and at the current level of employment the MPL is 10 units of output, the lowest price at which firms will be willing to supply their products is 20 cents per unit; this is just enough to cover the wage cost of the marginal unit of output. Firms will not, of course, be loath to receive a higher price, but if p were to rise to, say, 25 cents, it would pay them to expand output and employment until the MPL had fallen to 8 units — as long as the money wage remained at \$2 per man-hour. Since it has already been assumed that w is constant, this means that price will vary inversely with the MPL, which itself varies inversely with employment and output. The greater the volume of output, the higher the price level at which firms will find it just worth their while to produce it.[4]

It must be emphasized that these calculations take no account of the demand side of the market. The value of p given by w/MPL at any given level of output is a *supply price* that indicates the terms on which firms would be willing to produce and sell that particular quantity of commodities, regardless of whether it happens to be the quantity that buyers are currently demanding. Looked at in another way, there is a minimum total revenue from supplying goods and services, $s = pQ$, that firms must re-

---

[3] See p. 76.

[4] The simple numerical examples in this paragraph would be literally applicable only in an economy producing a single homogeneous commodity under competitive conditions. In the multiproduct economy of real life, p must be taken as an *average* of the prices at which the $p = w/\text{MPL}$ condition would be satisfied in the markets for all the separate commodities.

ceive (or at any rate expect to receive) if they are to be induced to supply a quantity of real output Q. For a given production function (and accompanying values of the MPL) the supply price p is determined by the level of money wages; therefore the minimum expected revenue to suppliers may also be expressed as a function of the level of real output and the money wage rate, *i.e.*, $s = s(Q, w)$.

The relationship between Q and s for a given $\bar{w}$ (the bar over the symbol indicates that the wage rate is held constant) is shown by the "aggregate supply curve," $s = s(Q, \bar{w})$, in Figure 10.1.[5] At any point along $s(Q, \bar{w})$, the supply price is shown by the slope of the straight line joining that point to the origin of the diagram; thus the slope of the line p_1 is the

---

[5] This curve should not be confused with the "aggregate supply function" developed by Keynes (*General Theory*, p. 25) and used by some later writers, notably S. Weintraub — *e.g.*, in his *An Approach to the Theory of Income Distribution* (Philadelphia: Chilton, 1958). Keynes relates "the expectation of proceeds which will just make it worth the while of the entrepreneurs to give [a particular level of] employment" directly to the level of employment itself; *i.e.*, instead of s and Q, his function relates s and N. However, this relationship has the disadvantage of not explicitly indicating the price level implied in any given value of s; for the purposes of the analysis presented here, therefore, the aggregate supply curve of Figure 10.1 is more convenient.

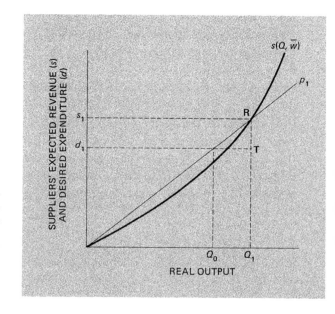

Fig. 10.1

The aggregate supply curve, indicating the expected revenue required to induce firms to produce different levels of real output

price at which firms are willing to provide a real output of Q_1, receiving the sum of money s_1 in return. The curve $s(Q, \bar{w})$ slopes upward from left to right, climbing more and more steeply to indicate that as output increases the level of the supply price rises. Since w is constant by assumption, the fact that the MPL falls as output and employment increase means that $\bar{w}/\text{MPL}$ must rise in value as output expands. The more gradual the decline in the MPL, the more closely will $s(Q, \bar{w})$ approach a straight line through the origin;[6] the faster the MPL falls, the greater the convexity of $s(Q, \bar{w})$ toward the right. If a change in the technique of production were to alter the MPL at every level of output, the whole curve would shift upward or downward; a change in the money wage w from one constant level to another would have the same effect — for example, a rise from \$2 to \$3 per man-hour, applying at all levels of employment, would shift $s(Q, \bar{w})$ upward by a distance equal to half its original height at each point.

Introducing aggregate supply into the analysis in this way stresses the role of the price level in determining the equilibrium of the economy. Not only must aggregate demand be exactly sufficient to purchase the whole volume of current output; but the price level must also be such (given the value of the constant w) that firms are willing to produce precisely that output. The same point was made in Chapter 4, but in somewhat different terms.[7] In the labor market depicted in Figure 4.3 (p. 77), the curve $N_d(W)$ indicates, for any given level of real wages, the number of man-hours that profit-maximizing competitive firms will wish to employ. The volume of output produced by this number of man-hours is the physical quantity of aggregate supply forthcoming at the given real wage, though, of course, it may not be the quantity required to satisfy the current level of aggregate demand. Since the real wage measured on the vertical axis in Figure 4.3 is the money wage divided by the price level ($W = w/p$), a movement along $N_d(W)$ can be caused either by a change in w or a change in p. In the context of the labor market, it is natural to focus attention on changes in w rather than p, and for certain purposes to assume p fixed; in the present analysis the emphasis is reversed — it is w that is

---

[6] Thus, the original assumption of a constant MPL would make the curve $s(Q, \bar{w})$ *perfectly* straight; given $p = \$1$, so that the axes of Figure 10.1 are graduated in identical units, the curve $s(Q, \bar{w})$ would then be equivalent to the $Y = D$ line of Figure 6.1 (p. 136).

[7] See p. 78.

assumed constant, leaving variations in p as the cause of changes in the volume of aggregate supply.

So far, nothing has been said that was not implicit in the argument of Chapter 4; but it will be recalled that further developments there had to be postponed for lack of information about the behavior of aggregate demand.[8] The lack having been dealt with in the last five chapters, it is now possible to carry the analysis further by bringing demand into the picture.

2. Aggregate Demand and the Price Level

To find the equilibrium level of output and the price level consistent with it, it is necessary to introduce an aggregate demand curve into Figure 10.1. However, the "aggregate demand function" defined at the beginning of Chapter 6 (p. 136), and drawn as the curve $C(Y) + Z$ in Figure 6.1, is not appropriate here, because both income and demand were specified in real terms. To bring aggregate demand into Figure 10.1, it is necessary to know not only the physical quantities that buyers wish to purchase at each level of real income, but also the prices at which their purchases are being made. When these physical quantities are multiplied by the appropriate prices, the amounts of money that result can be measured along the vertical axis of Figure 10.1 to show how much buyers wish to spend at each level of real income — the latter, of course, being measured on the horizontal Q axis, since real income and output are identical for the economy as a whole. The prices required for this purpose are those already indicated by the aggregate supply curve, if it can be assumed that sellers always offer their products at the supply prices given by the value of $\bar{w}/\text{MPL}$; the possibilities that arise if they do otherwise will be examined later, but for the time being this is a useful simplifying assumption. It will also be assumed, as a way of keeping the analysis clear of needless complication, that the economy has neither foreign trade nor a government, so that aggregate demand is merely the sum of intended consumption and investment expenditures.

Suppose, then, that firms are producing the volume of output Q_1 and are offering it for sale at prices whose average equals the slope of the line

---

[8] See p. 80.

p_1. Suppose, also, that at this level of real income the quantity of commodities needed to satisfy aggregate demand is Q_0; at the price level p_1, this physical quantity can be bought with a money expenditure of d_1. The physical output Q_1 is thus associated with aggregate demand of d_1 in money terms; and a curve showing the general relationship between output and desired money expenditure must pass through point T, which lies vertically above Q_1 and is at the same height as d_1. Here the money value of aggregate supply, s_1, exceeds that of aggregate demand by $s_1 - d_1$, an amount also represented by the length of the line RT. Firms are unable to sell a part of their output and so are not receiving the revenue needed to induce them to produce the output Q_1. Accordingly, they will reduce production; as they do so, output becomes less than Q_1, point R moves to the left down the aggregate supply curve, and, because of the curve's convex shape, the price level falls.

Meanwhile, the money value of aggregate demand will also be reduced, partly because of the fall in the price level and partly because of the fall in real income that is occurring as output shrinks; point T will be moving both leftward and downward. The process will continue as long as any excess supply exists — that is, as long as there is a vertical gap between R and T. The volume of output will continue to decrease and the level of prices will fall until R and T coincide, and aggregate demand and supply are equal. As T moves in response to these changes in output, it will trace out the "aggregate demand curve" appropriate to Figure 10.1. It will show the amount of money buyers wish to spend at each possible level of real output when goods are offered at the appropriate "supply price" p; in symbols, the curve traced out will be $d = d(Q, p)$.

Notice, however, that such a curve has not in fact been drawn in the diagram. This is because it is not yet possible to say what its general shape is likely to be, apart from the fact that it can be expected to slope upward from left to right. The difficulty is to know how much the physical quantities demanded will be affected by changes in the price level as well as by alterations in real income. It may be, of course, that they will not be affected at all; a 1% rise in prices will then raise both income and demand by exactly 1% in money terms, leaving the underlying "real" relationship unchanged. Figure 10.1's aggregate demand curve could then be drawn by the simple procedure of (a) ascertaining the "real" demand associated with each level of real income, $D(Q)$; and (b) multiplying this demand by the price level indicated by the aggregate supply curve for each level of real income, yielding an aggregate demand relationship of the form $d = p \, D(Q)$. If the "real" aggregate demand function happens to be an upward-sloping straight line similar to the curve $C(Y) + Z$ in Figure 6.1 (p. 136), this procedure will result in a curve with the general shape of $d(Q, p)$ in Figure 10.2. It should be noted that d is influenced by the supply price, p, which in turn is dependent upon the money wage rate w. Thus, implicit in the drawing of the curve $d(Q, p)$ (as in Figure 10.2) is the assumption of the same constant money wage rate, $\bar{w}$, that was used in constructing the corresponding aggregate supply curve.

A numerical example may help to clarify the derivation of the demand curve. Suppose consumers always wish to consume four-fifths of their income and that firms plan a fixed amount of investment, in real terms, equal to 20 units of output. At a price level of $1 per unit of output, the aggregate demand function is $D = 0.8(Q) + 20$. If the price level were the same at all levels of output, aggregate demand at selected levels of Q would be as follows:

Q (units)	90	95	100	105	110
D ($)	92	96	100	104	108.

These figures show a "straight-line" relationship between real income and demand of the kind illustrated in Figure 6.1. Now suppose that supply prices ($ per unit of Q) at the various levels of Q are as follows:

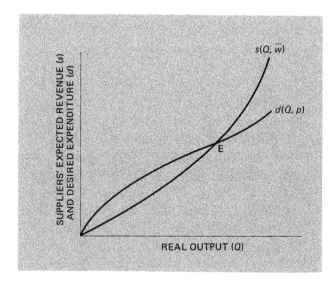

Fig. 10.2

Aggregate supply and demand curves. The demand curve indicates the total desired expenditure at each level of real output if goods are offered at the appropriate "supply price."

Q (units)	90	95	100	105	110
p ($/unit)	0.85	0.9	1.00	1.15	1.35.

When both Q and D are multiplied by these prices, the resulting pQ's are the values of aggregate supply for the different values of Q, and the pD's are aggregate demand in money terms:

Q (units)	90	95	100	105	110
$pQ = s$	76.5	85.5	100	120.7	148.5
$pD = d$	78.2	86.4	100	119.6	145.8.

When these figures are plotted in a graph, they are consistent with curves similar to those shown in Figure 10.2.

Over most of its length, $d(Q, p)$ has a curvature similar to that of the aggregate supply curve. To the right of the intersection of the two curves at E, expected revenue is greater than desired expenditure, while to the left of the intersection the reverse is true, indicating that E is a point of stable equilibrium with respect to both real output and the price level. It corresponds to the point E in Figure 6.1, where income and aggregate demand are equal; just as aggregate demand in real terms exceeds output to the left of E and falls short of it to the right, so in Figure 10.2 the amount of money that buyers wish to spend is greater than the value of aggregate supply to the left of E and smaller to the right of it.

The curve $d(Q, p)$ of Figure 10.2, then, is merely a translation into money terms of a "real" aggregate demand function that is not itself affected by the fact that prices change when the level of real income alters. However, variations in the price level may very well exert an influence of their own on the volume of "real" demand, and to the extent that they do so they will cause the shape of the demand curve to be different from that shown in Figure 10.2.

This possibility arises from the fact that price changes may bring about alterations in the distribution of income. When the aggregate supply curve was first introduced, it was assumed that money wages were constant at all levels of output and employment. As long as this is the case, changes in prices will bring about changes in real wages in the opposite direction. When the volume of output increases, and prices rise because of the consequent fall in the MPL, workers will find that the purchasing power of their money wages is reduced, so that they have lower real incomes than before. This does not necessarily mean that the total earnings of labor have fallen in real terms, since the lower real wage per man-hour may be more than offset by the fact that more man-hours are being employed to produce the increased volume of output. What is likely, however, is that the total of real wages will be a smaller *proportion* of total real income, because of diminishing returns to labor.[9]

If wage earners have a higher marginal propensity to consume than the recipients of profits do, the reduction in their share of total income will cause consumption to fall below the level it would otherwise have attained. This "redistribution effect" on consumption will become stronger and stronger as the price level climbs with further increases in output. The "real" aggregate demand function of Figure 6.1 will be shifting downward as real income increases; when it is transformed into the curve $d(Q, p)$ of Figure 10.2 by multiplying "real" demand by the price level appropriate to each volume of output, it will no longer have the curvature shown in the diagram. At the very least, the convexity of the right-hand section of the curve will be diminished — that is, its slope will increase less rapidly as it climbs toward the right. A strong redistribution effect may actually flatten it into a straight line or even reverse the curvature so that it resembles the demand curves of Figure 10.3. But since there is no *a priori* reason for the effect's being either strong or weak, it is not possible to assign a characteristic shape to the curve; those shown in Figures 10.2, 10.3 and 10.4 have been drawn as they appear solely for reasons of visual clarity.

It is worth noting that the redistribution effect operates equally well when, instead of prices rising with money wages constant, prices remain constant while money wages fall; it is not necessary for prices to rise in absolute money terms, but only to rise *relative* to money wages so that the value of p/w increases. A change in "absolute" prices (*i.e.*, in p alone) may affect aggregate real demand in a number of other ways, which have already been noted in previous chapters;[10] but the strength of these influences is uncertain, and in any case they cut both ways. Some cause real demand to fall when prices rise; others cause it to increase, so that their

---

[9] Total real wages are the real wage per man-hour multiplied by the number of man-hours employed, *i.e.*, NW. Their share in total real income is NW/Q. Since N/Q is the inverse of the average product of labor (APL), and W equals the MPL at any point on the aggregate supply curve, the "wage share" can also be written MPL/APL. As output rises, the MPL falls; the "wage share" will be reduced if the APL does not fall as fast as the MPL. Marginal quantities fall more slowly than their corresponding average quantities only when the latter are falling at a decreasing rate (for example, when a firm's average production cost is approaching its minimum). This situation seems unlikely in the case of labor productivity, so the "wage share" may be presumed to diminish as output and employment increase.

[10] See Chapter 5, pp. 114–116, for effects on consumption, and Chapter 7, pp. 189–191, for effects on investment.

combined effect will not necessarily change the shape of the aggregate demand curve in one way rather than another. Changes in p can also have certain monetary consequences that may affect real demand; for example, the financing of real investment will require larger amounts of money when prices rise. If firms' efforts to obtain money drive up the cost of borrowing, some firms may decide to curtail or postpone capital projects, and investment will then be reduced in real terms. For the present, however, these financial effects will be left out of account until money has been brought into the analysis — as it will be in the next chapter.

3. Variations in Prices and Money Wages

The intersection of the aggregate supply and demand curves indicates both the equilibrium level of physical output and (given the constant money wage $\bar{w}$) the equilibrium level of prices. If an autonomous change in "real" demand occurs, it will shift the aggregate demand curve to intersect the aggregate supply curve at a new equilibrium position. Thus, in Figure 10.3, an increase in real investment will raise the aggregate demand curve from $d_1(Q,p)$ to $d_2(Q,p)$; equilibrium moves from E_1 to E_2, output rises from Q_1 to Q_2, and prices increase from the level indicated by the slope of p_1 to that indicated by the slope of p_2. As long as firms continue to offer their output at its supply price (*i.e.*, $\bar{w}/$MPL), their response to the increase in demand will be to attempt to produce more commodities and to raise their selling prices only when the expansion of output and employment reduces the marginal product of labor, making price increases necessary to meet the rising value of $\bar{w}/$MPL. The transition from the old equilibrium at E_1 to the new one at E_2 will then take the form of an upward movement along the aggregate supply curve.

However, firms may react in a different way. Faced with excess demand equal to E_1T in money terms, they may begin by raising prices to the level that buyers seem willing to pay — namely, the price level p_3. The price rise will immediately create an incentive for firms to increase production, since the excess of price over marginal labor cost $\bar{w}/$MPL shows that they will add to their profits if they hire more labor and expand output; but before the expansion can get under way, the situation may be made more complicated by the effects of the price increase on aggregate demand. If the "real" relationship between income and demand remains unchanged, the amount of money that buyers wish to spend will rise in the same proportion as the price level, and in money terms the excess demand will be still larger than before.[11] On the other hand, the price increase will have set the redistribution effect to work, because with money wages constant, real wages have fallen; at the original level of output Q_1, both total real wages and the "wage share" in income will be reduced in proportion to the rise in prices, causing a fall in real consumption to the extent that the wage earners' MPC exceeds the MPC of profit recipients.[12]

---

[11] This demand shift is not shown in Figure 10.3. Recall that $d(Q, p)$ was drawn on the assumption that suppliers always charge the "supply price" (p) appropriate to any level output. If they charge more than this amount, the demand curve shifts upward accordingly.

[12] Suppose that total income is 100, wages 60, and profits (assumed for simplicity to be the only other form of income) 40. Prices rise 10%; income is for the moment unchanged in real terms, but rises to 110 in money terms; wages remain 60; and

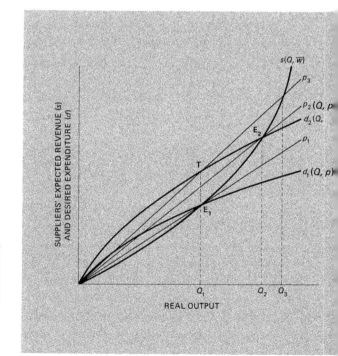

Fig. 10.3

Change in the equilibrium levels of real output and prices resulting from an upward shift in real demand.

Conceivably the two effects may exactly offset one another, if the redistribution effect happens to be just strong enough to eliminate the excess demand and no more; but there is no necessary reason why it should be, and if it is not, aggregate demand will now be higher than T in money terms, and firms may increase prices still more. Even if they do not do so, the price level p_3 is an inducement to expand output well beyond the new equilibrium level Q_2. If firms now increase output to the point at which $p_3 = \bar{w}/\text{MPL}$ — that is, Q_3, where p_3 meets the aggregate supply curve — they will have created an excess of supply over demand, because output level Q_3 is considerably larger than the equilibrium level Q_2. Now they will be obliged to reduce prices and production again. Eventually, by a sequence of overshootings and overcorrections, output and the price level will reach the new equilibirium position at E_2, but the path of convergence will have been much less smooth than the movement along $s(Q, \bar{w})$ that occurred when firms kept prices continuously at the $\bar{w}/\text{MPL}$ level.

For the new equilibrium at E_2 to be attainable, it is of course necessary that the output Q_2 not be greater than the quantity of goods and services that the economy can produce at full employment. If full employment had already been reached at the original level of output Q_1, no convergence toward E_2 would have been possible. In such a situation, efforts to increase total production will be unavailing, and firms will be much more likely to raise their selling prices in response to the pressure of excess demand. This price rise, as has already been seen, will shift the aggregate demand curve upward, except insofar as its movement is restrained by the redistribution effect.

At this point, however, the aggregate supply curve is also likely to shift, because the original assumption that money wages are constant is breaking down. To the extent that firms *try* to increase output to meet increased real demand (since even at full employment an individual firm can increase output by drawing resources away from others), their attempts to hire more labor for the purpose will create an excess of demand over supply in the labor market, and this will cause the money wage w to rise. Alternatively, if firms' initial reaction to the rise in real demand is to raise

---

profits rise to 50. If the wage earners' MPC is 0.8 and the profit recipients' MPC is 0.2, consumption will now be 58 in money terms and 52.7 at the original price level. Before prices rose, consumption was 56; thus, it has fallen in real terms by almost 6% because of the fall in the "wage share" from 60% to 54.5% of income.

prices rather than output, the consequent fall in real wages may cause the supply of labor to fall[13] below the level needed to sustain the current level of output, so that money wages must be increased to restore real wages to their original level. In addition, labor unions can be expected to react to the rise in prices by insisting on compensating increases in money wages to maintain their members' living standards. Since the supply curve $s(Q, \bar{w})$ shows the money value of each level of output (Q) when it is multiplied by its supply price $\bar{w}/\text{MPL}$, the rise in w will now increase the value of s associated with each level of Q; the curve $s(Q, \bar{w})$ will therefore move vertically upward in proportion to the increase in w, continuing to move as long as w goes on rising.

With money wages and prices rising at the same rate, there will be no reduction in real wages and therefore no redistribution effect to restrain the upward movement of the aggregate demand curve. *Both* curves will be shifting upward simultaneously, as shown in Figure 10.4. It will be recalled that when the demand curve $d(Q, p)$ was introduced (p. 239), it was defined for a particular fixed level of the money wage rate $\bar{w}$, as was the supply curve. As the money wage rate rises, however, the supply curve shifts upward, and the "supply price" associated with each level of output increases. But this same "supply price" enters the functional relationship for demand — i.e., the p in $d(Q, p)$ — and therefore the demand curve must be redrawn for each change in w. In symbols, the influence of changes in money wages may be reflected by amending the former demand relationship to read $d = d(Q, p, \bar{w})$.[14]

Initially the aggregate supply curve is $s(Q, \bar{w}_1)$. An autonomous increase in real demand has just shifted the aggregate demand curve up to $d(Q, p, \bar{w}_1)$; this curve intersects the supply curve at E_1 — but this equilibrium cannot be attained, because it is not possible for output to expand beyond the full-employment level Q_f. For the moment, then, the money value of aggregate demand is d_1, while that of aggregate supply is s_1, so that there is an "inflationary gap" of excess demand equal to $d_1 - s_1$. Both prices and money wages now rise in response to this situation, with the result that the aggregate demand curve shifts to $d(Q, p, \bar{w}_2)$ and the aggregate

---

[13] Provided that the labor supply slopes upward from left to right, as in Figure 4.3 on p. 77.

[14] In words, this functional relationship may be stated as follows: "demand (*d*) is a function of the level of output (*Q*) and the price level (*p*), which in turn is dependent on the money wage rate (*w*) due to the pricing policy assumed to be followed by suppliers."

supply curve to $s(Q, \bar{w}_2)$. Once again, their intersection shows that equilibrium is unattainable, since E_2 also lies to the right of Q_f; the "inflationary gap" therefore persists and is now equal to $d_2 - s_2$. This imbalance will bring about further increases in prices and money wages, causing the aggregate supply and demand curves to move still further upward; the process will continue indefinitely, unless for some reason the aggregate demand curve fails to keep pace with the movement of the aggregate supply curve. If, when the supply curve reaches the position $s(Q, \bar{w}_3)$, the demand curve has risen only as far as $d(Q, p, \bar{w}_3)$, an equilibrium will at last be attainable at E_3; the inflationary gap has been eliminated, and the upward movement of the two curves will now cease.

A similar sequence, but with the curves shifting downward instead of upward, can be expected to occur when the initial position is below the full-employment level of output — provided that money wages are free to fall as well as to rise. Up to this point, it has been assumed that money wages were "inflexible downward," being prevented from falling by the

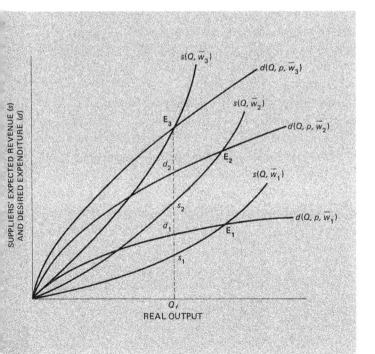

Fig. 10.4

Full-employment equilibrium under flexible wages and prices

existence of strong labor unions. If this assumption is now abandoned, it follows that whenever there is an excess of supply over demand in the labor market (*i.e.*, whenever employment is less than full), the competition of workers for jobs will force down the level of money wages. But when the wage level falls, the aggregate supply curve necessarily shifts downward; at any level of output, the supply price w/MPL will fall as w diminishes, thus reducing the minimum revenue s that will be sufficient to induce firms to produce that level of Q. At the lower price level, the money value of the "real" demand associated with any given real income will be less than before, and so the aggregate demand curve will shift downward also. Suppose that the aggregate demand and supply curves happen to be those shown as $d(Q, p, \bar{w}_2)$ and $s(Q, \bar{w}_2)$ in Figure 10.4, giving an equilibrium of E_2; but suppose also that the output indicated on the Q axis vertically below E_2 is less than the output available at full employment — as it would be if the point Q_f were moved some distance to the right. The shortfall of output below the full-employment level means that an excess supply of labor exists; this causes money wages to fall, and the aggregate supply curve consequently shifts down to the position $s(Q, \bar{w}_1)$.

If the aggregate demand curve remained at its former level, the new intersection would give a new equilibrium at a higher level of employment and output — indeed, if the intersection were far enough to the right to reach the full-employment level of output, the excess supply of labor would be eliminated and money wages would fall no further. But aggregate demand cannot, in fact, remain at $d(Q, p, \bar{w}_2)$ because the downward shift of the aggregate supply curve will cause prices to fall[15] to a level compatible with the new wage rate w_1. As a result, the demand curve will move downward also. If it reaches the $d(Q, p, \bar{w}_1)$ position at the same time as the aggregate supply curve reaches $s(Q, \bar{w}_1)$, their new intersection at E_1 will still be at a less-than-full-employment level of output. The excess supply of labor will persist, money wages and prices will continue to fall, and the downward movement of the supply and demand curves will go on. For the movement to stop, the demand curve must fall more slowly

---

[15] When the two curves intersect at E_2, prices will equal the slope of a straight line from the origin through the point E_2. (This line has not been drawn in the diagram, but it can easily be imagined from similar price lines in preceding diagrams.) Even if aggregate demand remains at its former level, any intersection with $s(Q, \bar{w}_1)$ to the right of E_2 will give a lower price level — so prices must necessarily fall as soon as the aggregate supply curve moves down.

than the supply curve, so that their intersection gradually moves to the right; when they at last intersect above the full-employment level of output, labor will no longer be in excess supply, money wages and prices will cease to fall, and the two curves will move no further downward.

The general conclusion of this analysis is that if money wages and prices are free to rise or fall to any necessary extent (*i.e.*, "flexible" both upward and downward), a full equilibrium will be reached only when both of two conditions are satisfied. First, the aggregate demand for commodities must equal their aggregate supply, in the sense that the volume of output and the price level must be those indicated by an intersection of the demand and supply curves. Second, the demand and supply of labor must be equal — that is, the intersection of $s(Q, \bar{w})$ and $d(Q,p, \bar{w})$ must occur at the full-employment level of output. If money wages are "inflexible downward," so that they do not fall when there is an excess supply of labor, the second condition is no longer necessary for equilibrium at less-than-full-employment levels of output; with w constant, the intersections E_1 and E_2 in Figure 10.3 are perfectly stable equilibrium positions, even though full employment is not reached in either case.

However, to specify the conditions for equilibrium is not to imply that they will be fulfilled. To say that, with money wages and prices flexible, equilibrium exists only when aggregate demand and supply are equal at full-employment output is not to say that the economy will necessarily find its way to such an equilibrium — it means only that it will not find an equilibrium anywhere else. In the particular situations discussed in connection with Figure 10.4, it appears that once the demand and supply curves are shifting upward or downward together, their movement will be halted (*i.e.*, equilibrium will be reached) only if demand lags behind supply so as to shift their intersection to correspond with the full-employment level of output. Thus, when prices are falling, real demand will increase relative to real income until it is sufficient to absorb all the output produced at full employment; when prices are rising, real demand will fall until full-employment output is enough to satisfy it. Without such a convergence on the point of full-employment output, the curves will continue to move, and prices will go on rising or falling.

The outcome will then depend on the speed with which the movement is taking place. If all adjustments (*e.g.*, the revision of expenditure plans in money terms, firms' decisions to alter their selling prices, and so on) are made almost instantaneously, the curves will move very quickly, and the price level will collapse towards zero or zoom towards infinity, depending on the direction of the movement. The economy will break down unless the government steps in with measures to restore price stability. A slow rate of adjustment, on the other hand, will change the movement of the price level into a relatively gentle upward or downward trend, which may not have time to proceed very far before it is reversed by an autonomous change in real demand or by some other external influence. It is possible, in fact, to imagine an economy that never attains short-period equilibrium at all, yet never experiences great fluctuations in prices and output either. In such an economy, it would not be disastrous if the movement of the demand and supply curves was not accompanied by any tendency for them to intersect at the level of full-employment output.

Nevertheless, such a tendency might exist. It could result from the operation of the Pigou effect described on pp. 114–116 above. As prices fall, the purchasing power of money balances continuously increases; their owners, feeling themselves more affluent, increase their real consumption relative to their real incomes. Eventually this effect will raise total real demand to equality with full-employment output, so that there is no longer any excess supply of labor to push down money wages and keep the demand and supply curves falling. When prices are rising, the effect is reversed; the falling real consumption of the holders of money balances will eventually reduce real demand to the level required for full-employment equilibrium, thus eliminating the excess demand for commodities that has been pushing the demand and supply curves upward. But it has been suggested that the Pigou effect is likely to be weak and that it may be offset by expectational influences working in the opposite direction. In an economy where the adjustment process goes forward rapidly, prices may have to rise or fall a long way before the Pigou effect becomes strong enough to halt their movement.

If the economy is no longer assumed to be closed, the foreign sector can be brought in as a stabilizing influence; as prices rise, reductions in exports and increases in imports will diminish total real demand, while the reverse effects will expand real demand when prices are falling. The inclusion of government in the model will have similar consequences; as money incomes rise in line with the price level, the proportion available for private expenditure will be reduced by progressive income taxation, while government spending programs that are fixed in money terms will represent decreasing real expenditure as the price level rises.

One possible source of stabilizing effects, however, still remains to be considered — namely, the monetary system. When prices are increasing, larger and larger quantities of money are needed to transact all the economy's sales and purchases; when prices are falling, money requirements are correspondingly reduced. In order to consider the implications of this relationship between money and prices, and to see what other influences may be exerted from the monetary side, it is necessary to examine in detail the role of money in the economy.

CHAPTER 11

Money and Output

1. The Supply of Money

The essential characteristic of money is its general acceptability in exchange for other things. A dollar bill cannot be eaten or worn or used in any other way to satisfy wants directly, yet there is no doubt that any wage earner would rather be paid in dollar bills than be given a part of the physical output he has helped to produce. He is prepared to take payment in this form because he knows that storekeepers will accept the bills from him in return for the goods he buys; and they, in turn, accept his payment because they are sure the bills will be accepted by the people from whom *they* buy. It is this mutual confidence that enables paper currency and coins of negligible intrinsic worth to be used as a medium of exchange.

By the test of general acceptability, however, currency and coin are far from being the most important form of money. The major part of the United States' stock of money consists of the demand deposits of commercial banks, which in mid-1968 amounted to $144.5 billion, against only $42 billion of paper currency and $5 billion of coin.[1] There are many small transactions, such as the purchase of a newspaper on the street, for which payment by means of a bank deposit would obviously be unsuitable; but the dealings of business firms with one another, as well as many payments between firms, governments, and individuals, are carried out much more conveniently and safely by the handing over of checks than by the exchange of currency. Checks are merely a means of transferring deposits from one owner to another. For example, when firm A pays firm B for a consignment of materials, it normally sends a check, as a result of which A's deposit at the bank is reduced and B's correspondingly increased. Because such transfers of deposits are regarded by the recipients as complete and final settlement, the banks' demand deposits must be classified as money.

Deposits are debts that banks owe to their customers. Against these

---

[1] Figures from the *Federal Reserve Bulletin* (July, 1968), p. A-17. In addition to demand deposits, there were $188 billion of "time deposits," *i.e.*, accounts not transferable by check and not subject to withdrawal on demand; unlike demand deposits (which have both these attributes) time deposits bear interest. It may also be noted that only $42 billion of the $47 billion of currency and coin was in circulation among the general public, the remainder being held by banks as part of their reserves.

liabilities, the banks hold assets such as government bonds and the obligations of business firms to which they have made loans; if banks are to remain in business, the interest they earn on these assets must be enough to cover their operating costs, to meet the interest payable on time deposits, and to make a profit for their proprietors. However, each bank must also hold sufficient reserves of "cash" (consisting of both currency and deposits with the Federal Reserve System) to allow it to meet the claims of depositors who wish to withdraw currency, or of other banks whose customers have deposited checks drawn on it. The proportion of reserves to deposits is not left to the banks' own discretion, but is laid down for them by the Federal Reserve System (or by state law) in the form of "reserve requirements." But even without the legal obligation to do so, any bank would maintain some sort of cash reserve as protection against the possibility that withdrawals might from time to time exceed the inflow of newly deposited cash.

The ratio of cash to deposits would depend, first, on the banker's judgment of the probable amount and timing of such net withdrawals and, second, on the interest he would forgo by not using the cash to acquire more remunerative assets. The greater the yield obtainable from holding securities and making loans, the greater the cost of holding reserves; when interest rates are high, bankers might well reduce their reserve ratios, so that a given amount of reserves would then be compatible with a larger total of deposits. If the banks were able to find enough borrowers wanting loans at these high rates, they would open new accounts in their favor, thereby expanding loans and deposits simultaneously; the total of deposits (and therefore of the whole money supply) would have risen in response to the level of the interest rate. By preventing banks from reducing their reserve ratios in this way, legal requirements cause the supply of money to be inelastic with respect to the rate of interest.

The *amount* of reserves, as distinct from their *ratio* to deposits, depends partly on the public's preferences between bank deposits and currency and partly on the activity of the Federal Reserve. People are at liberty to deposit with the banks any part of their currency holdings that they feel exceed their requirements and to draw on deposits whenever they want more currency. The banks are left passively holding whatever currency the public does not wish to hold; and if the total stock of currency never changed, a change in public preferences could have a considerable effect on reserves. However, given the willingness of the Federal Reserve to offset such changes by altering the amount of currency in existence, they need not cause more than temporary disturbances. As a determinant of the banks' cash reserves, the public's demand for currency is much less important than official action directed to altering the banks' holdings of the other form of "cash," *i.e.*, deposits with the Federal Reserve System.

When the Federal Reserve buys securities in the market, the sellers pay its checks into their accounts at the commercial banks; when the banks present the checks to "the Fed," they are credited with larger deposits there. Similarly, a sale of securities by the Federal Reserve will cause a fall in the commercial banks' Federal Reserve deposits; in this case, "open market operations" have reduced the banks' reserves. Should the banks attempt to restore their reserves by making use of their right to borrow from the Federal Reserve, it can raise the rate of interest (the "discount rate") on such loans so as to make them too expensive to be more than a temporary expedient.

Suppose, then, that the banks' reserves have been increased by $10 million as a result of the Federal Reserve System's open market operations; they are now in a position to expand their own deposits. The limit of the expansion will be determined by the reserve ratio. If this happens to be, say, 15% on demand deposits, the maximum possible increase in such deposits would be $67 million, since the $10 million additional reserves are 15% of this amount.[2] There are, however, several reasons why the expansion may stop short of the limit. To increase their lending, the banks must find borrowers; but there may be no unsatisfied demand for bank loans at current interest rates, while the rates at which more loans *would* be demanded are so low as to be unprofitable to the banks. The original open market operations will, in any case, have depressed interest rates to some extent; as rates fall, the holding of reserves becomes less expensive in terms of the interest forgone, and banks may be content to leave part of

---

[2] An *individual* bank will not, in fact, immediately increase its deposits up to this limit. It will begin by offering new loans up to only 85% of the additional reserves, because it knows that the borrowers (to whose accounts new deposits have been credited) are likely to write checks in favor of the customers of other banks, which will then claim settlement via a transfer of reserves. But the other banks, on obtaining the transfer from the first bank, will themselves be able to expand deposits. Since many of them will, in any case, have started with additional reserves as a result of the Federal Reserve's open market operations, the first bank's own customers will soon be depositing checks drawn on new deposits at the other banks. A further expansion of lending will then be justified; and so the process of increasing deposits will continue. As long as the $10 million extra cash stays in the banking system as a whole, the banks can, if they wish, collectively go up to the $67 million limit.

their additional cash as "free reserves" over and above the legal requirement.

Also, as total deposits increase, there may be a change in the public's
preference for currency, and its effect may be to drain off some of the
banks' increased reserves. If the rise in bank loans has stimulated business
activity and employment, more currency will be needed to meet enlarged
payrolls, much of which may go to increase the currency circulation in
retail trade instead of being immediately redeposited. Thus, the increase
in demand deposits might very well stop short of the $67 million limit;
it is difficult to guess even approximately how far it would go in any particular set of circumstances.

It seems, then, that though the Federal Reserve can be confident of adjusting the commercial banks' reserves to whatever level it desires, it cannot predict with any accuracy the subsequent effect on total bank
deposits. Nevertheless, it will be convenient for the purposes of later
analysis to assume that the Federal Reserve can control the banking system sufficiently well to be able to set the total quantity of money at whatever level it thinks desirable.[3]

Because demand deposits and currency are generally acceptable as
means of exchange, they have a particular convenience as *assets*; anyone
who holds them possesses a command over goods and services that he can
exercise at any time in the future. In the traditional phrase, money acts
as a "store of value." However, value can be stored in the form of any
durable asset; the distinctive feature of money is its *liquidity*. If the
owner of a house wishes to exchange it for something else, he must first
sell it for money. However, when he tries to sell the house, he may find
that buyers are few and prices low. The disadvantage of such an asset is
obvious — its holder cannot be sure of realizing its full value quickly at
any time in the future. Money is free of this risk; as an asset, it is perfectly
liquid and in that respect superior to other "stores of value."

But it would be misleading to draw a very sharp distinction between
the liquidity of money and the nonliquidity of other assets. Among the
latter, there are considerable differences in the degree of liquidity. The
banks' time deposits, for example, are so liquid that they are often called

---

[3] The foregoing is, of course, the merest thumbnail sketch of the working of the
U. S. banking system; for further details the reader is referred to Shapiro, Soloman,
and White, *Money and Banking*, 5th ed. (New York: Holt, Rinehart and Winston,
1968), and to J. Tobin, "Commercial Banks as Creators of 'Money'," in D. Carson
(ed.), *Banking and Monetary Studies* (Howewood, Ill.: Irwin, 1963).

"near money" or "quasi money"; though they cannot be withdrawn until a certain period has elapsed, the period is usually a fairly short one,[4] and at the end of it the owners of such deposits are certain to receive the amounts originally deposited, so that there is no risk of loss. By contrast, the owner of common stock in a corporation can exchange it for money with no delay at all — he need only telephone his broker, who will sell it for him on the stock market; in this respect, common stock is a very liquid asset. But the price obtained for the stock may be considerably less than the price at which the owner originally bought it; he can never be sure that a quick sale will not involve a capital loss, and so the asset is less liquid than, say, a time deposit at a bank.

At the extreme of illiquidity come physical assets such as real estate, which may take quite a time to find buyers and may fail altogether to find them at prices that will cause no loss to the sellers. It may happen, of course, that at the moment of sale the price of a particular asset of this type is actually higher than that at which the owner bought it, so that he gets a capital gain; the essential point, however, is that he cannot know in advance whether he will make a gain or a loss if he has to sell the asset at any particular time in the future.

Thus, assets can be ranged in order of liquidity: currency and demand deposits at the top end of the scale, certain physical assets at the bottom, and the remainder at various points in between. Very near the top, in addition to the banks' time deposits, come certain other forms of near money, such as savings bank deposits and the shares of savings and loan associations, that are close competitors with money in its role as a liquid asset. The institutions that supply them have a strong family resemblance to the commercial banks, inasmuch as they hold "paper" assets — securities and the obligations of individual borrowers to whom they have made loans — the revenue from which provides them with profits after they have met their operating costs and paid interest on their own liabilities. Like the commercial banks, they aim to maximize profit, subject to the requirement that they must always be able to meet their obligations to their creditors. Consequently, many factors that influence the behavior of the banks — for example, changes in interest rates — can be expected to have similar ef-

---

[4] It may, in fact, be anything from 30 days to more than twelve months, depending on the agreement between banker and customer at the time a given deposit is made. The rate of interest payable often depends on the length of notice, the "longer" deposits earning the higher rates. See p. A-11 of any issue of the *Federal Reserve Bulletin.*

fects on that of the "nonbank financial intermediaries" (or NBFI's, as these institutions may be called for short). They are not, however, subject to the same legal reserve requirements as the banks,[5] so that on occasions when the banks themselves are restrained from expanding deposits by the need to maintain their reserve ratios, the NBFI's may still be able to increase the supply of their own liabilities, with the result that liquid assets as a whole will increase even though the quantity of money remains constant.

For the time being, these complications will be by-passed by assuming that currency and demand deposits are the only liquid assets as well as the only means of exchange in the economy, and that their supply is effectively controlled by the monetary authorities (*i.e.*, the Federal Reserve System). As long as this supply is exactly sufficient to satisfy the demand for it, the behavior of the monetary side of the economy will be compatible with the equilibrium of aggregate supply and demand described in Chapter 10. However, an excess or shortfall of the demand for money against the supply of it is likely to upset any previously existing equilibrium in the rest of the economy, while disturbances in the markets for commodities and labor will themselves upset the balance on the monetary side. What, then, determines the demand for money? To answer this question, it will be convenient to distinguish between the demand for it as a means of payment and the demand for it as a liquid asset (this is, of course, a highly artificial distinction, extremely difficult if not impossible to apply in practice, but it is adopted here merely as an expository device).

2. The Transactions Demand for Money

Until the period between World Wars I and II, most economists paid little attention to the demand for money as an asset on the ground that rational individuals would hold only the amounts they needed to make

---

[5] Many of them must, however, conform to legal requirements in other ways. For example, mutual savings banks and savings and loan associations are permitted to hold only certain types of assets such as home and other mortgages, U. S. government obligations, and corporate bonds. For more details on NBFI's, see R. W. Goldsmith, *Financial Institutions* (New York: Random House, 1968).

current payments. Since money does not yield interest, an individual who found himself with more of it than he needed for payments purposes would use the surplus to acquire income-yielding assets such as bonds, stocks or real estate; he might even increase his consumption rather than continue to hold a "barren" asset. Consequently, it was argued, the usual effect of an increase in the supply of money would be to raise the level of prices, since the additional money would be financing an increase in the demand for goods and services. Conversely, a reduction in the money supply would cause people's holdings to fall below the level needed for payments, and their efforts to restore their money balances by selling other things would force the price level down. This view, emphasizing money's means-of-payment function to the exclusion of its liquid-asset role, was formalized as the "Quantity Theory of Money."[6]

This theory may be stated in terms of Irving Fisher's[7] "equation of exchange" or "quantity equation," $M_sV = PT$. Here, M_s is the existing supply of money and V its rate of turnover per unit, or "velocity of circulation"; T is the number of transactions occurring within a given period, and P is the average amount of money exchanged at each transaction, *i.e.*, an average of prices.[8] So defined, M_sV and PT are two ways of describing the same thing: each is a measure of the turnover of money in the economy, so that the equation necessarily holds true under all circumstances — it is an identity. Thus, the quantity equation does not itself prove anything; it is not a theory in the sense of a testable hypothesis that can be either true or false. The Quantity *Theory*, however, is the proposition that when M_s changes, the principal effect will be on P rather than

---

[6] What now follows in the text is a simple version of the theory as it seems to have been understood by the majority of economists up to the 1920's. Some writers amended and developed it in various ways, but no attempt is made here to take account of their individual contributions. It is also necessary to distinguish between the very simple theory described above, and the "Modern Quantity Theory" for which the University of Chicago is well known. In the hands of Professor Milton Friedman and others, it is a much more sophisticated formulation — though it does arrive at many of the same conclusions as the older "quantity theorists." See "The Quantity Theory of Money — A Restatement," Professor Friedman's introductory essay in *Studies in the Quantity Theory of Money* (Chicago: University of Chicago Press, 1956), which he also edited.

[7] Irving Fisher, *The Purchasing Power of Money* (New York: Macmillan, 1911), Chap. VIII.

[8] Note that P is not an *index* of prices. An index would give the proportionate change in prices since some base year; it would not be appropriate here, since M and T are both "absolute" magnitudes.

V or T. In its most extreme form, the theory holds that V and T will not normally alter at all when M_s changes, but that P will change in the same proportion as M_s. Doubling the quantity of money, for example, would double the general price level.

But P is not the price level in the ordinary sense; it is the average amount of money exchanged *per transaction*, and since transactions include the payment of wages and dealings in bonds and shares as well as the purchase of commodities, P is very far from being merely an average of retail or wholesale prices. Unless a special assumption is made concerning the behavior of noncommodity prices, the Fisher version of the Quantity Theory is ambiguous. If a rise in M_s were to produce an increase in bond prices and nothing else, it would be true that P had risen, but it would not be what is usually meant by "a rise in the price level." In this respect, the Fisher equation is less clear than the Cambridge[9] version, which instead of all transactions includes only those "final" purchases that are counted in National Expenditure. Instead of PT, the Cambridge equation has pQ, where Q is the physical quantity of "final" commodities (consumer goods, investment goods, and so on) and p is an average of their prices. By definition, p excludes the prices of securities and of "intermediate" goods and services. It is, therefore, much closer to being an indication of the price level as the term is usually understood, though it still includes the prices of investment goods and exports and the imputed prices of government services, along with the prices of consumers' commodities.

The substitution of pQ for PT means that the Cambridge equation cannot include Fisher's "transactions velocity" V; instead, it introduces "income velocity" — the rate of turnover of money, not in *all* transactions, but only in the purchase of "final" commodities. With V' as the symbol for income velocity, the equation becomes $M_sV' = pQ$, or $M_sV' = y$, since National Expenditure at current prices pQ is identical with National Income at current prices y.[10] Usually the equation is written $M_s = ky$, where k is $1/V'$, *i.e.*, the inverse of income velocity; if money turns over four

---

[9] So called because it originated at Cambridge, England, was taught there for many years, and appears in the writings of the great Cambridge economists: *e.g.*, Alfred Marshall, *Money, Credit and Commerce* (London: Macmillan, 1923), pp. 44 *et seq.*; Pigou, "The Value of Money," *Quarterly Journal of Economics*, Vol. 32 (1917–1918), pp. 38–65; J. M. Keynes, *A Tract on Monetary Reform* (London: Macmillan, 1923), Chap. III.

[10] The lower case y indicates income at current prices or "money income"; income at constant prices or "real income" is denoted by an upper case Y.

times a year, each unit must "rest" for a quarter of that time. This inversion is more than a mere manipulation of the velocity concept: when money is "at rest," it must be in the hands of someone who wishes to hold it instead of spending it immediately; k is the average fraction of income that people desire to keep in money form, and ky measures the community's demand for money, M_d. Thus, the equation $M_s = ky$ brings together the supply of money (M_s) and the demand for it $(M_d = ky)$ in an equilibrium condition. If M_s should increase, equilibrium can be restored by changes in k or y. But if k is fixed and physical output Q is not affected by the change in M_s, income can rise only through an increase in the price level — that is, since $y = pQ$, a rise in y occurs through a rise in p. Thus changes in the quantity of money will bring about equal proportionate changes in the price level.

The vital assumption here is not that k and Q cannot change at all, but that they do not change merely because of changes in M_s. Obviously, increasing population and productivity are likely to increase Q as time goes by, whatever is happening to money and prices. In the short run, however, output can be stimulated by a rise in M_s if it occurs in a situation of less than full employment. If $M_s = ky$ to begin with, balances are already high enough to meet holding requirements, so the additional M_s will be spent. But additional spending in these circumstances will have the effect of drawing unemployed resources into activity, raising output rather than the price level; only when full employment is reached will the effects of further spending show themselves wholly in price increases. As an explanation of the general price level, under which changes in p are attributable solely to changes in M_s, the Quantity Theory cannot hold true except in conditions of full employment — if, indeed, it is true even then.

The Cambridge version is more useful, however, if it is regarded not as a theory of the general price level but as a theory of the demand for money. The equation $M_d = ky = kpQ$ can then be taken to mean simply that the desired quantity of money is a function of the level of money income. Whether money income increases because of a rise in Q or because of a rise in p, the effect is the same: the demand for money will rise by k times the amount of the increase in pQ. If k is constant, the relationship between money income and the desired quantity of money will hold true at every level of output and employment, so that this approach is not subject to the limitation noted at the end of the last paragraph. But can k be assumed constant? It certainly cannot if there exists an asset-demand for money that is determined by influences other than money income; the desired quantity of money could then rise or fall independently of any change in pQ, necessarily altering the value of k whenever it happened. For the time being, this possibility will be ruled out by assuming that no one wishes to hold money as an asset and that the demand for it arises only in connection with the need to make current payments; even then, however, the assumption of a constant k is open to an important qualification, as will be shown presently.

The need to hold money for payments purposes (*transactions balances*) arises from the fact that the receipts and expenditures of individuals and firms (and every other economic entity) are never perfectly synchronized. For example, a man who is paid a salary at the end of each month will have to keep a certain part of it in hand to cover the next month's day-by-day expenditures; as the month goes by, the balance he started with will become smaller and smaller until it disappears and is replaced out of the next salary check. If the man spends the same amount each day, his *average* balance will be equal to half his total monthly expenditure. If he were paid his salary by the week instead of by the month, his average transactions balance would be reduced to an amount equal to half his *weekly* expenditure — only a quarter of the average balance he required when he was being paid monthly. Even if his salary cannot be paid more frequently than once a month, he can still reduce his average balance by arranging to buy as much as possible on credit during the month, settling his accounts at the end of it when he receives his salary check. In either case, he will have improved the synchronization of his receipts and payments by bringing them closer together, with the result that he can manage with a smaller average holding of money.

Often, of course, an improvement in the synchronization of one person's (or firm's) transactions can be achieved only at the cost of worsening someone else's. When a business allows its customers to buy on credit, the reduction in the customers' transactions balances may be offset by the firm's need to hold a larger balance than would be necessary if all its sales were for cash.[11] The transactions requirements of the community as a whole are therefore likely to be much less compressible than those of any single individual or firm. Given the relative timing of all receipts and pay-

---

[11] It may also work the other way, depending on the timing of the firm's own expenditures. If it pays for its supplies at the end of each month, it will be accumulating a balance in the course of the month if cash sales bring in fairly regular daily receipts; the average balance will be larger than if the firm could "clear" receipts against expenditures on the same day at the month's end.

ments and the way they interlock among the various entities that make up
the economy (that is, given the "payments habits" of the community), the
total transactions balances required will depend on the level of money
income. If prices rise, more money will be needed to buy and sell the same
physical quantity of goods and services; if there is no change in payments
habits, the level of transactions balances will rise in proportion to the increase in prices. If the volume of real output goes up, with equal increases
in real incomes and expenditure, the fact that larger quantities of goods
and services are now being bought and sold means that a proportionate
increase in transactions balances will be required.[12] In the assumed absence of an asset demand for money, the proportion between desired
transactions balances and money income is the k of the Cambridge equation; it seems, then, as though it ought to be reasonable to regard k as a
constant.

This conclusion, however, rests on the assumption that payments habits
are fixed — *i.e.*, that individuals, business firms, and other "transactors"
either cannot or do not wish to change the existing degree of synchronization between their receipts and expenditures. But most of them do, in fact,
have some control over the timing of their transactions: individuals can
choose between running charge accounts and paying cash for everything
at the time of purchase; business firms can postpone their payments by
taking up commercial credit; by careful planning, transactors may be able
to reduce their balances quite considerably. How much they will try to do
so depends on a number of things. Holding on to a sum of money involves
a sacrifice of interest: the holder either forfeits the interest he could have
earned by lending his money to somebody else, or, if he has borrowed
the money he is holding, he must pay interest on it. The higher the rate of
interest, the greater the cost of maintaining transactions balances and the
greater the incentive to keep them as low as possible. On the other hand,
it also costs something to economize on them; for example, if a firm delays
settlement of suppliers' accounts until they can be met from expected sales
revenue, it will lose whatever discount the suppliers give for prompt payment, and this loss must be counted against the saving of interest from the
reduction in the firm's transactions balance.

---

[12] It may also happen that changes in the distribution of income (*e.g.*, in favor
of people who have more opportunities to buy on credit) and in the commodity composition of output (in favor of goods whose producers are more willing to sell on
credit) may alter the need for transactions balances when money income varies. To
keep the analysis simple, these possibilities are ignored here.

Minimizing transactions requirements, therefore, involves some effort in arranging the most economical timing of receipts and expenditures. It may also involve other inconveniences, such as that incurred by a consumer who finds himself obliged to buy from stores that give credit, when he would have preferred to make cash purchases elsewhere if his transactions balance had been big enough to allow it. If the interest rate to be paid or forgone on transactions balances is high, it will be worth incurring these costs in order to keep balances low; but if interest rates fall, the convenience of running higher balances will cost less, and a general increase in them can be expected.

Transactors can hardly ever be sure in advance of the precise numbers and amounts of the payments they will have to make in the future, and many of them will also be uncertain about their expected receipts over a given period. So, in addition to a basic amount that is thought to be sufficient to finance all "normal" transactions (*i.e.*, those that can be foreseen with a fair degree of certainty), an individual or firm will find it advisable to hold a "precautionary balance"[13] to provide against possible emergencies. The greater this is, the greater the assurance that its holder will not be caught without sufficient funds to meet some urgent and unexpected need for cash. However, precautionary balances are subject to diminishing returns in terms of the convenience they afford, since the larger they are, the more remote the contingencies that further increases will provide against. It is a good idea to have a few extra dollars on hand in case one's automobile breaks down on a long journey, but few people would think it worthwhile to provide against the possibility of having to take a transatlantic air flight at a moment's notice. The desired amount of precautionary balances will be that whose "marginal convenience" is just equal to its marginal interest cost. If interest rates rise, it will become too expensive to insure against some of the less likely contingencies, and so the demand

---

[13] This term has become conventional since Keynes first used it in the *General Theory* (p. 195). But it may be questioned whether it is really very useful to distinguish between transactions and precautionary balances. The latter could be described as the part of transactions balances intended to insure the holders against uncertainty; but since *all* future transactions are to some extent uncertain, the two kinds of balances shade imperceptibly into one another.

It should also be noted that holding money is not the only way to provide for emergencies; even in a sudden crisis, there may still be time to arrange a bank loan or a mortgage or to sell a nonmonetary asset of some kind. A precautionary *money* balance is needed only to cover situations in which cash payment must be made on the spot.

for precautionary balances will fall; conversely, when interest rates fall, larger balances will be desired. Demand will, of course, also vary with the level of money income, just as in the case of basic transactions balances; if prices rise, the amounts of money that may have to be spent in sudden emergencies will be correspondingly increased, while a rise in the volume of output will create greater possibilities of such emergencies occurring.[14]

The demand for money for transactions and precautionary purposes (which from now on will be lumped together and called simply "transactions demand") thus depends on (a) the volume of output (or real income, which is identical with it); (b) the general price level; and (c)

---

[14] The reasons for holding transactions and precautionary balances are similar to those for holding inventories of input materials and finished products in a manufacturing business. Just as a business firm must decide what inventory to hold in view of the level of its output and the costs of maintaining inventory, so must transactors decide what balances they need in relation to their financial turnover and the costs involved. See W. J. Baumol, "The Transactions Demand for Cash: An Inventory Theoretic Approach," *Quarterly Journal of Economics*, Vol. 66 (November, 1952), pp. 545–556; also Miles Fleming, "The Timing of Payments and the Demand for Money," *Economica*, Vol. 31 (May, 1964), pp. 132–157.

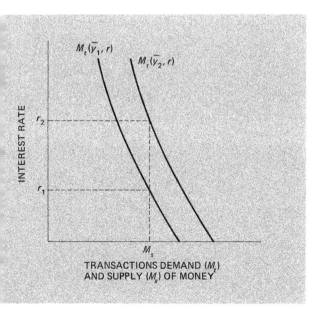

Fig. 11.1

The transactions demand for money and the interest rate at which demand is in equilibrium with the money supply. The two demand curves are for different levels of money income.

the level of interest rates. Demand can be expected to rise and fall in direct proportion to (a) and (b), and inversely with (c). In terms of the Cambridge equation, k will be a constant only so long as interest rates do not change; when they do, transactors' views will change concerning the fraction of money income over which it is desirable to keep command in money form, because the cost of doing so will have altered.[15]

Algebraically, the transactions demand can be written

$$M_t = M_t(pQ, r) = M_t(y, r)$$

where the $M_t(. . .)$ on the right-hand side is the functional relationship between money income, pQ or y, the interest rate, r, and the demand for transactions balances, M_t. A curve showing the relationship between transactions demand and interest rates will have the general shape of $M_t(\bar{y}_1, r)$ in Figure 11.1 (the bar over the y indicates that money income is held constant at level y_1). When prices rise and/or the volume of output increases (that is, when money income, y, goes up for one reason or another), the curve will be shifted to the right, say to position $M_t(\bar{y}_2, r)$. A further rise in money income will shift it still more to the right, while a

---

[15] Also, since $k = 1/V'$, the income velocity of money will vary according to the level of interest rates; but where k varies inversely, V' will vary directly with interest.

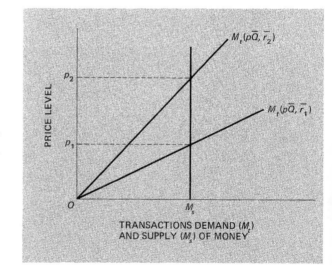

Fig. 11.2

The transactions demand for money and the price level at which demand is in equilibrium with supply under different interest rates. Real output is held fixed.

fall will move it to the left. In fact, there will be a family of M_t curves, each one corresponding to a different level of money income. If the supply of money available for transactions purposes is fixed at M_s, the intersection of the various M_t curves with the vertical line above M_s will show the interest rates at which the demand and supply of money are in equilibrium at each level of money income. Thus, when the demand for transactions balances is that shown by $M_t(\bar{y}_1, r)$, interest must be r_1 to equate demand and supply; while at a higher level of money income the demand curve will have moved to $M_t(\bar{y}_2, r)$ and the equilibrium interest rate will be r_2.

This way of putting things stresses the role of interest rates in balancing transactions demand against the available supply of money. It would be easy to change the emphasis in favor of, say, the price level by drawing a curve such as $M_t(p\bar{Q}, \bar{r}_1)$ in Figure 11.2, which shows the different amounts of money needed for transactions purposes at the price levels shown on the vertical axis (p), given a fixed volume of output $(\bar{Q})$ and the interest rate. Because transactions demand is assumed to vary proportionately with the price level, the function is a straight line through the origin, sloping upwards from left to right. Given the supply of money M_s, demand and supply will be in equilibrium when the price level is at p_1. If the rate of interest were to rise, the M_t curve would shift to a steeper slope such as $M_t(p\bar{Q}, \bar{r}_2)$, showing that transactors are demanding lower balances than before at each price level; to maintain equilibrium, prices must now rise to p_2.

A similar construction can be used to show how transactions demand varies with the volume of output when the price level and the interest rate are fixed. When the vertical axis of Figure 11.2 measures output (Q) instead of prices, transactions requirements will rise proportionately with Q, giving a demand curve similar to those shown in the figure; its intersection with the line above M_s will indicate the level of Q at which equilibrium exists.

All these relationships have, of course, been put forward on the assumption that transactions demand (in the broad sense that includes precautionary requirements) is the *only* kind of demand for money. It is now time to relax this assumption and to consider the possibility that transactors may wish to hold balances that exceed their payments requirements — in other words, the asset demand for money must now be brought into the analysis.

3. The Demand for Money as an Asset

Money has the distinctive feature of being the only asset that is perfectly liquid, but it also has the disadvantage of yielding no income. If the owner of a money balance exchanges it for bonds, he will receive a return in the form of interest; the purchase of stock will give him the prospect of dividends; and the acquisition of physical assets to be employed in production can bring him a flow of profits. In the case of transactions balances, it was seen that it is worth sacrificing these yields for the convenience of being able to make payments at times when receipts are not coming in to finance them. But why should anyone be willing to sacrifice income in order to hold "idle" balances in addition to the "active" ones needed for transactions purposes?

The reason is that the ownership of illiquid assets involves the risk of loss as well as the prospect of gain, so that it sometimes seems worth giving up the latter in order to avoid the former. If money is lent out at interest, so that the asset the creditor now holds is someone else's promise to pay, there is a chance that the debtor may default on his obligation. If the money is used to buy stock in a corporation, it may happen that no dividends are distributed or even that the corporation goes out of business with consequent loss to the stockholders. If physical assets are bought for use in production, it may turn out that there is little demand for the resulting output, and no profits are made; moreover, not all assets can be sold again when the owner regrets having acquired them and wants to get his money back. Even if all these risks are avoided by the purchase of an asset free of default risk, yielding a return that is fixed and certain, and easily resalable in a well-organized market, there still remains the possibility that a subsequent fall in its price may cause the owner to incur a capital loss.

Examples of assets with the characteristics just mentioned are the long-term bonds of the government and of large corporations. The holder of a $1000 bond bearing interest at the fixed rate of 4% is certain to receive $40 a year as long as he holds it. However, the $1000 is merely a nominal value;[16] the price at which such bonds are currently changing hands in

---

[16] See p. 117. The "nominal" value is often – though by no means always – the price at which the bond was first issued by the original borrower (*i.e.*, the government or a corporation). It is usually (but again, not always) equal to the redemption

the market may be either higher or lower according to the continuously changing pressures of demand and supply. Thus, if a man buys one for $900, and the market price then falls to $700, he will have sustained a loss roughly equivalent to five years' interest. The rate of yield when he bought the bond was $40 ÷ $900, or 4.4%. Now, at a price of $700, it is $40 ÷ $700 or 5.7%; if he had waited for the price to fall before buying it, he would have had a higher return on his money.

If, then, a potential bond buyer thinks there is a strong possibility of a fall in price, and therefore of a rise in the rate of yield, he will prefer to hold on to his money for the time being. It should be noted that it is not the prospective price decline in itself, but his lack of certainty about it, that makes him wait. If he knew in advance exactly when the price would fall, he could buy the bond now for $900, sell it just before it drops to $700, and then buy it back afterwards. But since, in the nature of things, he cannot be sure just when and by how much the price will go down, he will refrain from buying for the moment; the $900 that he has decided not to spend on the bond will stay in his hands as a *speculative balance* over and above any amount he is holding for transactions purposes.

In deciding whether or not the price of the bond is likely to fall, the potential buyer will have compared the current price with what he considers to be the normal level in the light of past experience. If the price is much higher than it has ever been in the past, he is likely to feel that it cannot possibly go higher still; since the odds are all on the side of a fall in the near future, he would be sure to incur a capital loss if he were to buy now, so he will hold on to his speculative balance for the time being. At the other extreme, when the bond price is unprecedentedly low and the chances of a further fall seem negligible, he will exchange his whole speculative balance for bonds in order to obtain the capital gain that is in prospect. If the current price happens to be somewhere in between these upper and lower limits, he will have to weigh the chances of a future rise against those of a fall, and divide his "portfolio" (*i.e.*, his total assets, however composed) between money and bonds according to his estimate of the probabilities. In general, it can be said that the higher the current bond price, the greater the likelihood of a future fall and the smaller the number of bonds he will hold; while the lower the price, the

---

price, *i.e.*, the number of dollars that will be paid to the holder of the bond when the repayment date (the maturity) is reached.

better the chances of a subsequent rise and the larger the proportion of bonds in his total portfolio.

In practice, of course, holding a money balance is by no means the only alternative to holding bonds. If an individual wishes to reduce the number of bonds in his portfolio, he can do it by substituting some nonmoney liquid asset for them, for example, by acquiring savings-and-loan shares, which carry no risk of capital loss but at the same time — unlike money — yield an income. For the time being, however, it will greatly simplify the analysis if it is assumed that the only available asset other than money is a certain type of irredeemable fixed-interest bond. This implies that there are no other "paper" assets in existence and that physical assets, such as the machinery operated by business firms, are never offered for resale; their owners are assumed to acquire them as soon as they are produced, with the intention of retaining them as long as they last. On this basis, the only relevant rate of interest is the yield on bonds, which is inversely related to their market price; that is, a high bond price implies a low rate of interest, and a low price a high rate.[17] New borrowing will take the form of the issue of new bonds exactly like those already in existence,[18] but it is assumed that the number of bonds is already very large, so that the new ones likely to be issued during any short period will not be enough to increase the existing total by more than a negligibly small proportion. This means that new bonds must be sold at the price already ruling in the market for "old" bonds; the rate of yield — that is, the market rate of interest — will not be affected by decisions to borrow, but will be determined by the preferences of the community between the two types of assets — bonds and money — that are available to them.

If these preferences are the same as those of the individual bond buyer

---

[17] This relationship can be expressed as $r = iN/P$, where r is the rate of yield, i is the "nominal" interest rate on the bond (the "coupon rate," as it is often called), N is the nominal value of the bond, and P is its market price. Thus, a $1000 bond bearing a nominal 4% will yield 3.3% when the market price is $1200, 5% when the price is $800, and so on.

[18] If the bonds were issued by the government, this would imply that only the government could borrow; business firms could then acquire additional capital only by plowing back undistributed profits. A less restrictive alternative is to suppose that any firm can borrow, but is obliged by law to do so by issuing irredeemable fixed-interest bonds with the same nominal value and coupon rate as the bonds already in existence. Combined with some sort of legal provision to eliminate the risk of default, this requirement would ensure that all bonds are homogeneous even though they do not all emanate from the same borrower.

described a little earlier, the proportions in which the community wishes to hold bonds and money will depend on the market price of bonds. The higher the market price, the smaller the number of bonds and the larger the money balances everyone will wish to hold; the lower the bond price, the greater the desire to hold bonds and the smaller the demand for money. Since the price of bonds is inversely related to the interest rate, the demand for speculative balances, denoted here as M_a, will be greatest when the interest rate is low and will decline as the rate rises; the relationship will be as shown by the curve $M_a(r)$ of Figure 11.3, sloping downward from left to right. Like the typical demand curve for an ordinary commodity, $M_a(r)$ shows the quantity demanded increasing as the price falls, except that in this case the "quantity" refers to speculative balances and the "price" is the interest forfeited by holding them.

The position and shape of $M_a(r)$ depend on the attitudes of the various individuals and organizations whose separate demands are aggregated in it. Some of them — the "pure speculators," as they may be called — are interested only in the prospects of capital gains and losses, because they have very definite expectations about future interest rates. Anyone who is convinced that a certain bond price is "normal" and that temporary deviations from it will quickly be corrected will not wish to hold any bonds at all when the interest rate is even fractionally below the level corresponding to the "normal" bond price, since he would, he believes, be cer-

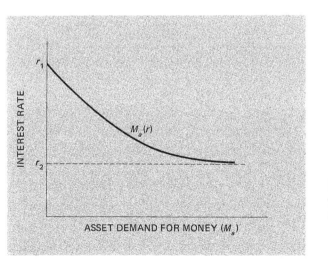

Fig. 11.3
The demand for money
as an asset

tain to sustain a capital loss. On the other hand, when the interest rate is above "normal" (*i.e.*, when the bond price is below its "normal" level), he will be sure of a capital gain if he converts his whole portfolio into bonds, and he will then hold no speculative balance at all. If everyone else took exactly the same view, the curve $M_a(r)$ would be a horizontal line lying infinitesimally below the level of the "normal" interest rate.

However, other speculators may not agree with him as to which rate is normal. Those who think it is lower will be holding bonds when he is holding money, while those who think it is higher will still be prepared to retain their speculative balances when he himself has exchanged the whole of his for bonds. This will give $M_a(r)$ a downward slope, starting at the level of interest (r_1 in Figure 11.3) that is high enough to make everyone hold bonds and reaching horizontal at some lower level (r_2), at which no one wishes to hold anything but money. The extent and steepness of the downward-sloping section will depend on the diversity of opinion among the pure speculators, and the degree of diversity may, like the opinions themselves, change in the course of time and thereby alter the shape and position of the curve.[19]

The term "pure speculator" perhaps suggests the smart operator of popular myth, who constantly plays the market in the hope of making a killing. But the aim of the speculator may very well be the more modest one of avoiding loss — as he switches from money into bonds and back again, he may be less concerned about securing capital gains than about preventing the total value of his portfolio from being reduced. However, whether they are motivated by hope or by fear, pure speculators have the common characteristic of holding firm views about the future behavior of the interest rate. Other people, by contrast, may feel much less sure of the prospects. Instead of focusing on a single interest rate, they may regard any rate as "normal" as long as it lies between certain upper and lower limits; within this range, they will be undecided as to whether the rate is more likely to fall or to rise. Because their expectations are so uncertain, they will hold money and bonds simultaneously, in proportions that will depend partly on their willingness to take risks and partly on the yield to be obtained from bond holdings.

This can be seen by considering the case of an individual whose expectations are neutral in the sense that he thinks the chances of a fall in the

---

[19] Keynes attached a good deal of importance to this diversity of opinion; see the *General Theory*, p. 172.

interest rate are just the same as those of a rise; for example, if the rate is 4% at present, he may regard a change to 5% as neither more nor less likely than a change to 3.3%. In terms of the market price of a $1000 bond paying a nominal 4%, this means that the probability of a rise to $1200 is exactly equal, in his view, to the probability of a fall to $800. The chances are not affected by the number of bonds he buys — with a holding of ten bonds he stands to gain or lose $2000, with a hundred bonds $20,000, and so on. No matter what the size of his holding, the risk of loss is always balanced by an equal chance of gain.

As a proportion of his total assets, his possible gains and losses depend on the way he distributes his resources between bonds and money. Suppose his total portfolio is worth $100,000. If he retains $90,000 in cash and buys ten $1000 bonds with the remainder, a fall of $200 in the bond price will cause the total value of his assets to rise or fall by 2%; if he holds a hundred bonds and no cash, the possible gain and loss are each 20% of his portfolio; on a half-and-half distribution he could gain or lose 10%. His problem, then, is to decide how much of his portfolio he is prepared to risk. The answer will depend on the relative values he puts on the prospects (equally probable) of gain and loss, and on the way those values change as his stake increases; the greater his stake, the more the risk of loss is likely to weigh in comparison with the chance of gain. Depending on how cautious or adventurous[20] he is, there will be some level of bond holding beyond which he will feel that the unpleasantness of losing another dollar would more than outweigh the satisfaction of gaining one, and this is the level he would choose if the only inducement to hold bonds were the chance of capital gains.

However, bonds offer the additional attraction of yielding interest; against the risk of losing $200 on each bond he holds, the individual must set not only the chance of gaining $200 but also the certainty of a $40 interest receipt per annum — and this will induce him to hold more bonds than he would otherwise have done. Just how many more he will hold depends on a number of things. If he thinks the chances of the bond price changing either way are fairly low, the fact that interest is certain will give it a good deal of weight relative to the risk of loss. If he thinks that

---

[20] But not on how optimistic or pessimistic, since he has already been assumed to regard the probabilities of loss and gain as equal. He is in the position of a race-goer who has decided that a certain horse has a fifty-fifty chance of winning and must now make up his mind whether to bet $5, $50, or $5,000 on it — or whether not to place a bet at all.

the price, though sure to change, is unlikely to do so by more than the amount of the interest paid, he will again be encouraged to hold bonds, because the risk of loss will be almost completely offset by the prospect of interest, leaving him with a net chance of gain. On the other hand, if he is thinking in terms of price changes only during the next week or month, the amount of interest accruing will probably not be enough to make much difference — 4% per annum is only 0.33% per month and 0.077% per week. Within this "context of expectations," his bond holding will be determined by the current level of the interest rate; the higher the rate, the greater the compensation it provides for the risk of loss, and the greater the inducement to hold bonds instead of money. The individual's asset demand for money will therefore be a decreasing function of the interest rate, of the kind represented by the curve $M_a(r)$ in Figure 11.3. There may be no level of interest high enough to induce him to give up holding money altogether, in which case his demand curve will not meet the vertical axis at r_1, but will become vertical somewhere to the right of it; at the other extreme, there will be some low level of interest (r_2) at which the compensation for risk taking is so inadequate that he holds all his assets in the form of money, and his demand curve, $M_a(r)$, becomes horizontal.

Those whose asset demand for money is determined in this way can be called "risk averters"[21] to distinguish them from the pure speculators considered earlier. Most people, however, are likely to combine the characteristics of both groups; for example, a man who thinks there is an 80% chance of the interest rate falling will be a speculator to the extent that he buys bonds in the expectation of a price increase, and a risk averter to the extent that he retains a holding of money to offset the 20% chance of a price reduction. The higher or lower the level of interest, the less likely it becomes that anyone will keep an open mind as to whether it will subsequently rise or fall; risk averters will become speculators holding portfolios that consist exclusively of either money or bonds depending on whether the current interest rate is very low or very high. At intermediate rates, increasing uncertainty will convert speculators into risk averters, and their portfolios also will contain a mixture of bonds and money. Since both speculation and risk aversion separately give rise to asset demands

---

[21] The concept of "risk aversion" is especially associated with the name of Professor J. Tobin; see his "Liquidity Preference As Behavior Towards Risk," *Review of Economic Studies*, Vol. 25 (February, 1958), pp. 65–86.

for money that vary inversely with interest, a combination of the two will do the same, giving a demand curve with the downward-sloping characteristic of $M_a(r)$ in Figure 11.3.

The stability of the combined curve will, of course, depend on how volatile or stable its constituent elements happen to be. It seems reasonable to suppose that the risk aversion element will be the less changeable of the two; people's willingness to face a given risk of loss depends on how cautious or adventurous they are by nature, and though these psychological characteristics may change over time, it is unlikely that they will alter drastically overnight. The greater the influence of risk aversion in the combined asset demand for money, then, the less the likelihood of sudden shifts in $M_a(r)$. The speculation element, by contrast, can change quickly and sharply if expectations about future interest rates are suddenly revised. For this part of the demand for money to be completely stable, every speculator must be convinced that a certain "normal" interest rate will continue to rule in the future; moreover, any departure of the current rate from this level must take him by surprise, and he must expect it to move back to normal fairly quickly rather than move still further away from it.

The necessity for this last condition can be seen by considering the case of a speculator who believes 4% to be the normal rate, but interprets a change to 4½% as the beginning of a swing that may go as high as 6% before returning to normal. At the 4½% level, the market price of a $1000 bond with a 4% "coupon rate" is $890; if he were to exchange his money holding for bonds at this price, he would gain $110 per bond when the normal 4% level was regained. But since he believes the interest rate will go higher still, he will prefer to wait until the 6% limit is reached; he will then be able to buy at $670, gaining $330 per bond when interest returns to 4% and the bond price is once again $1000. If he had initially been holding bonds, his expectation of a rise to 6% would have induced him to sell at the beginning of the movement, with the intention of buying back when the price reached $670. Similarly, a *fall* in the current rate might cause him to expect a further fall, inducing him to buy bonds in order to sell them again when the rate reaches rock bottom.

If all other speculators react in this way to changes in the current interest rate, the demand curve for speculative money balances will shift upward whenever the current rate rises and downward when it falls; when the rate reaches either of the limits beyond which no further divergence from normal is expected, the curve will immediately return to its original position. Since speculators may also change their views from time to time regarding the "normal" level of the interest rate and the upper and lower limits within which it can vary, it would be surprising if their demand curve were to retain a given position for any length of time.[22] The larger the speculative element in the combined asset demand for money, therefore, the greater the likelihood of instability in the overall curve $M_a(r)$.

So far, it has been assumed implicitly that bonds can be exchanged for money, and money for bonds, without expense. But if the ownership of bonds is fairly widespread, there will have to be some sort of market for them in which intermediaries such as brokers bring buyers and sellers together and charge fees or commissions for so doing. If they make a standard charge of x cents per bond handled, the effectiveness of any given interest rate in compensating risk averters for the possibility of capital loss will be reduced, so that the demand for bonds will be less (and that for money greater) than it would have been in the absence of dealing expenses. The importance of this factor depends on the length of time that buyers expect to hold the bonds they acquire; if they are sure they will have no need to sell the bonds for at least two years, the dealer's charge will be relatively small when set against the interest accruing over such a long period. But when a buyer thinks he may need to sell again within a month or two, his prospective interest earnings over that time may be more than wiped out by dealing expense, and he will therefore continue to hold money. Also, dealers are unlikely to charge precisely x cents per bond regardless of the number involved in any given transaction, since their operating costs will be much the same whether five, fifty, or even five hundred bonds are being bought and sold. If they make a higher charge per bond in the case of small transactions, the owners of small money balances will be discouraged from buying bonds even at

---

22 It is conceivable that it might be in constant movement between the upper and lower limits, if speculators have no particular views about the existence of a long-term "normal" rate but merely expect future rates to be anywhere between, say, 3% and 7%. Within these extremes, they will wish to hold money whenever the rate is rising and bonds when it is falling, irrespective of the absolute level of the interest rate at any given moment. Their demands will cause the movement of the rate to continue until it reaches one of the limits, at which the cessation of movement will cause the demand to be reversed (*e.g.*, so that instead of wishing to hold money, speculators demand bonds when the upper limit is reached) and to begin a fresh movement back to the opposite extreme. In this case, the demand curve for speculative balances would be continually rising and falling.

high interest rates, and their holdings will swell the asset demand for money beyond what it would otherwise have been. In general, the higher the scale of dealers' charges, and the greater the differential in favor of large transactions, the more the demand curve $M_a(r)$ will be pushed upward and to the right.

When the transactions demand for money was examined earlier, it was seen that payments requirements vary directly with the level of money income: the higher the general price level and the greater the volume of output, the larger the money balances needed to effect the economy's sales and purchases. In the case of *asset* demand, on the other hand, the connection with money income is less obvious and more complex. It might, indeed, seem that on the assumptions so far made there ought to be no connection at all. Suppose, for example, the price level increases. It is true that the real value of money balances will fall proportionately — but so, too, will the real value of bonds whose yield is fixed in money terms, so that as long as asset holders are assumed to be choosing only between money and bonds, there is no reason why they should alter their holdings. The rise in prices will not cause the demand for money to change, except insofar as it may have modified speculators' views about future interest rates.

However, the very fact that the price level is rising makes it impossible to leave physical assets out of consideration. It was originally assumed that these were acquired solely for use in some productive activity, with no thought of the possibility of resale. On this basis, even a house would be bought only for the owner to live in himself or obtain income by renting it out; he would not regard it as a marketable asset to be held for a limited period as an alternative to money and bonds. As long as everyone believes that the prices and yields of houses, machines, and all other physical assets will remain unchanged in the future, there can be no speculation with regard to them such as there is in the case of bonds, and their existence will not affect the choice between bonds and money. Even if the range of assets is broadened to include stock (as representing indirect ownership of corporations' physical assets), it can be treated as merely another species of bonds. But when the general price level rises, physical assets and stock will retain their real value while that of money and bonds is falling; if the price trend is expected to continue, there will be a "substitution effect" by which the demand for physical assets and stock increases at the expense of the demand for both bonds and money.

In this way, rising prices may be expected to cause the asset demand for money to fall.

This effect, however, is not the consequence of the increase in prices itself but of the general expectation that they will *continue* to rise. Once they have been stabilized at a new, higher level, and everyone is persuaded that no further increases are to be expected, the substitution effect will no longer operate, and the asset demand for money will revive. In fact, it is likely to be larger than it was before. The rise in the price level will have increased the money values of all physical assets and equities; if there has been no change in the total quantity of money, existing balances will now form a smaller proportion than before of the nominal value of all assets taken together. However, the original proportion can be seen as the result of a deliberate choice on the part of owners of wealth; given the cost of holding money (in terms of yields forgone on alternative assets), they chose to hold $x\%$ of their total wealth in the form of money rather than commit all their resources to holdings of less liquid assets. If they now attempt to restore their money balances to the original $x\%$ of total assets, their asset demand for money will have risen in proportion to the increase in the general price level.

The same considerations apply when total assets increase in real terms through additions to the volume of physical capital; if owners of wealth do not wish to find their overall holdings becoming steadily less liquid, they will try to increase their money balances more or less in proportion[23] to the growth of their total assets. The accumulation of real assets is, of course, a relatively slow process for the economy as a whole and is closely connected with the long-run growth of real income — as physical capital increases, it yields greater real output, out of which more can be invested in further additions to the capital stock. But short-run variations in real income cause little change in the total of real assets, so that they have a negligible "wealth effect" on the asset demand for money. As long as the

---

[23] The aggregate proportion may very well change to some extent, since the growth of total assets may be accompanied by changes in the *distribution* of wealth. For example, a tendency for physical assets to be more heavily concentrated in the hands of large firms would reduce the overall proportion of money to total assets, if such firms habitually maintain lower money balances (relative to their total assets) than smaller ones. Among individuals, too, the distribution of wealth might change in favor of people whose risk aversion was less than average and who therefore desired smaller money ratios — this, too, would pull down the average proportion. A change in the price level will also redistribute wealth away from money holders to the owners of "real" assets, with the possible consequence of a change in the desired ratio of money to total assets.

analysis is confined to the short period, then, changes in money income will raise or lower the asset demand for money only to the extent that they involve increases or reductions in the general price level.[24]

The effects can be illustrated diagrammatically with the aid of a construction similar to Figure 11.3. Only now the expression for the asset demand for money, $M_a(r)$, must be modified to take real assets and the price level into account:

$$M_a = M_a(p, r, \bar{A}),$$

where $\bar{A}$ represents the stock of real assets and is constant in the short run. The demand curve actually drawn in Figure 11.3 shows the response of the asset demand for money to different levels of interest rate at a *given* price level. When prices rise, the curve — which should be relabeled $M_a(\bar{p}, r, \bar{A})$ — will shift outward to the right, indicating that the asset demand for money at a given interest rate will be greater the higher the general price level.

If prices rather than interest rate were measured on the vertical axis, a diagram similar to Figure 11.2 would result, except that the curves of $M_t(p\bar{Q}, \bar{r})$ would be replaced by curves showing the asset demand for money, $M_a(p, \bar{r}, \bar{A})$. At a given interest rate the curve would show the asset demand varying proportionately with the price level; it would be a straight line starting at the origin. A higher rate of interest would cause the curve to slope more steeply, while a lower rate would be shown by a more gently sloping curve.

On the other hand, if the volume of output rather than the price level were measured on the vertical axis, a curve showing the asset demand for money at different levels of real income (given the interest rate and the general level of prices) would be a vertical line similar to that shown above M_s, indicating that changes in real income make no difference to asset demand in the short run. The position of the line will depend on the interest rate and the price level: the higher the interest rate, the closer it will be to the vertical axis, while the higher the price level, the further right it will lie.

It must be emphasized that the expectational effects of price changes are ignored in these constructions. For example, if the curve shown in Figure 11.3 were labeled $M_a(\bar{p}_1, r, \bar{A})$, it would indicate the demand curve that exists when the price level is p_1 and is expected to remain so; another

---

[24] See J. Tobin, *op. cit.*, and D. Patinkin, *Money, Interest and Prices*, 2d ed. (New York: Harper and Row, 1965), pp. 278–279.

curve (not shown) would be relevant when prices are, and are expected to remain, at the level p_2. They are alternative possibilities that exist at the same moment of time, rather than successive stages in a process of price change.

4. Monetary Equilibrium and the Level of Output

Now that the transactions and asset demands for money have been examined in detail, they can be put together into a single "demand for money" (or in Keynes' term, "liquidity preference"[25]) function, to be ready for confrontation with supply. The transactions demand, M_t (with precautionary demand included in it), was denoted as

$$M_t = M_t(pQ, r),$$

that is, as a function of money income, pQ, and the interest rate, r. Similarly, the asset demand was expressed as

$$M_a = M_a(p, r, \bar{A}).$$

Since the total stock of real assets, A, is constant in the short run, the expression for M_a may be simplified to

$$M_a = M_a(p, r).$$

Adding the two demands together gives the total demand for money M_d:

$$M_d = M_t(pQ, r) + M_a(p, r)$$

or

$$M_d = M_d(p, Q, r).$$

---

[25] See the *General Theory*, pp. 166–174 and Chapter 15. Keynes' "incentives to liquidity," namely the transactions, precautionary, and speculative "motives," correspond to the subdivisions of the demand for money made in the present text. He regarded the first two as depending on the level of money income — in symbols, $M_t = M_t(y)$ — and the third as depending on the interest rate — *i.e.*, $M_a = M_a(r)$ — so that the liquidity-preference function as a whole was

$$M_d = M_t(y) + M_a(r).$$

He thus excluded the interest rate as an influence on transactions and precautionary demand (M_t), and prices as an influence on speculative demand (M_a). Moreover, the latter is the asset demand only of the "pure speculators" described above; that of "risk averters" does not appear. In diagrammatic terms, $M_t = M_t(y)$ gives a vertical line parallel to the r axis in Figure 11.1, while $M_a = M_a(r)$ is shown in Figure 11.3.

For equilibrium, demand must equal supply. It was suggested earlier that the supply of money can be treated as a constant determined by the monetary authorities; when this is denoted M_s, the condition of monetary equilibrium may be written

$$M_s = M_t(pQ, r) + M_a(p, r) = M_d(p, Q, r).$$

This means that, for any given level of real assets, a given money supply, M_s, will satisfy demand only if prices, output, and the interest rate are at appropriate levels in relation to one another. If all three variables were completely free to change, a great many combinations of their possible values would be consistent with equilibrium. In fact, the number of possible combinations is limited by the existence of other relationships between them — for example, by the fact that the level of Q depends partly on that of r through the latter's influence on investment. If monetary equilibrium is to coexist with a balance of aggregate demand and supply of commodities, p, Q and r must satisfy not one but several sets of equilibrium conditions. To illustrate, it will be convenient to begin by making the simplifying assumption (which will be relaxed later) that both A and p are constant, so that only Q and r are capable of variation. It will then be seen that, although many different pairs of values of Q and r would be consistent with monetary equilibrium, only one pair will be capable of giving a balance of aggregate demand and supply of commodities as well.[26]

In Figure 11.4, the curves $M_d(\bar{p}, \bar{Q}, r)$ show how the total demand for money varies with the interest rate at different levels of income. For example, $M_d(\bar{p}, \bar{Q}_1, r)$ is the sum of the transactions and asset demands that exist when income is Y_1, or $\bar{p}Q_1$ (where $\bar{p}$ is the price level that has been assumed constant). When output increases from Q_1 to Q_2, income rises from Y_1 (or $\bar{p}Q_1$) to Y_2 (or $\bar{p}Q_2$). Because a larger volume of goods and services is now being bought and sold, transactions demand will be greater at all levels of interest, and the curve that represents it — $M_t(\bar{y}_1, r)$ in Figure 11.1 — will be pushed to the right — to $M_t(\bar{y}_2, r)$. When this de-

[26] The analysis that follows is based on J. R. Hicks, "Mr. Keynes and the Classics: A Suggested Interpretation," *Econometrica*, Vol. 5 (April, 1937), pp. 147–159 (reprinted in his *Critical Essays in Monetary Theory* [Oxford: Clarendon Press, 1967], and in W. Fellner and B. F. Haley, eds. for the American Economic Association, *Readings in the Theory of Income Distribution* [Homewood, Ill.: Irwin, 1946].) See also his *A Contribution to the Theory of the Trade Cycle* (Oxford: Clarendon Press, 1950), Chapter XI; and "The Classics Again" in *Critical Essays*.

mand is added to the asset demand (which remains unchanged in the position shown in Figure 11.3, since short-run changes in output have no effect on it), the combined curve will show a rightward movement to the position $M_d(\bar{p}, \bar{Q}_2, r)$. A further rise in output to Q_3, making income Y_3 (*i.e.*, $\bar{p}Q_3$), will push the curve still further to the right to the position $M_d(\bar{p}, \bar{Q}_3, r)$. The higher the level of output, the further the demand curve will lie to the right.

It will be noticed that all the curves converge to the horizontal at a minimum level of interest r_0. This may be the rate that, in the opinion of pure speculators, is the lowest to which interest can ever fall. Since the only possible change from r_0 is a future rise in the rate, bond holding would entail a certainty of capital loss — so speculators will now have zero demand for bonds and an infinitely elastic demand for money. Alternatively, if there are no speculators with firm views of this kind, r_0 may be the rate at which interest is no longer sufficient to compensate risk averters for the danger of capital loss — so that they will not wish to hold any

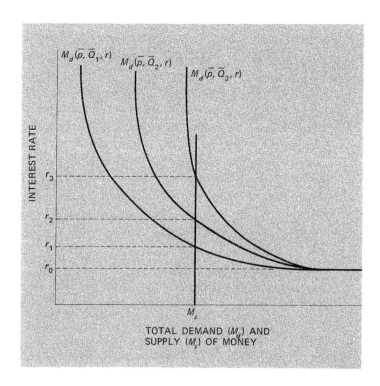

Fig. 11.4

The total demand for money and the interest rate at which demand is in equilibrium with the money supply. The three demand curves are for different levels of real output, prices being held constant.

bonds at all and will be prepared to hold indefinitely large amounts of money. Alternatively again, if risk aversion is very weak (that is, if there are plenty of people willing to take the chance of loss even when the off-set provided by interest is very small), the minimum rate will depend on the level of dealers' charges. The lower the interest rate, the longer the period over which interest receipts will be canceled out by the initial deal-ing expense; when this period is so long that no one is prepared to hold bonds for the time needed to begin to obtain a net yield, the minimum rate will have been reached. Whatever the reason for the existence of such a minimum at r_0, it means that the whole of any increase in the stock of money will now be willingly added to the balances everyone is content to hold; it will be absorbed into the "liquidity trap" — as Dennis Robertson has called the elastic part of the demand-for-money curve.

At very high interest rates, the curves become vertical; here the asset demand for money has disappeared altogether, while transactions (in-cluding precautionary) demand has been pared down to the absolute minimum required to effect purchases and sales at the given level of in-come. The greater the volume of output, the larger this minimum re-quirement will be, as shown in Figure 11.4.

If the supply of money is as indicated by the vertical line at M_s — which implies that supply is inelastic with respect to the interest rate — the inter-sections of the various demand curves and the M_s line will show the levels of interest needed to give monetary equilibrium at each level of income. Thus, if income happens to be Y_1 (or $\bar{p}Q_1$) so that the relevant demand curve for money is $M_d(\bar{p}, \bar{Q}_1, r)$, supply and demand will be equal when the interest rate is r_1. When income is Y_2 (or $\bar{p}Q_2$), the relevant demand curve is $M_d(\bar{p}, \bar{Q}_2, r)$, and the equilibrium interest rate is r_2. At income Y_3 (or $\bar{p}Q_3$), the rate will be r_3 — and so on. The larger the value of Y (which in this case means the greater the volume of output, Q, since the price level p is constant throughout), the higher the level of r at which the demand and supply of money are balanced.

This relationship can be shown more directly than it is in Figure 11.4. In Figure 11.5, the vertical axis measures the interest rate as before, but the horizontal scale shows levels of income instead of quantities of money; the curve LM_1 connects all the pairs of values of Y and r (Y_1 and r_1, Y_2 and r_2, and so on), which in Figure 11.4 were found to be associated with one another when the demand and supply of money were in equilibrium. It can be seen that LM_1 is horizontal at its left-hand extreme, where very low levels of income are involved; the transactions demand is very small here, so that the quantity of money M_s is capable of satisfying a large asset demand as well. Indeed, to induce wealth owners to hold the amount of money available for this purpose, the interest rate must be at its minimum level r_0. On the far right, LM_1 becomes vertical at a high level of income; this is where M_s is only just sufficient to meet minimum transactions requirements, and the rate of interest has risen to the level needed to extinguish asset demand altogether. Between these extremes, the curve steadily increases in slope as the level of income rises.

Thus LM_1 shows, for each income level, the interest rate at which monetary equilibrium exists when the supply of money is fixed at a particular level, say M_s^1. If the latter were to be increased to M_s^2, the equilibrium value of r would be lower at each level of Y, except where the minimum interest rate r_0 has already been reached. The corresponding LM curve will now lie to the right of LM_1 in the position indicated by the LM_2 curve in the diagram. Further increases in the quantity of money will shift the curve still further to the right, while reductions will shift it to the left; the LM_1 and LM_2 shown in Figure 11.5 are merely two members of a numerous family of possible LM curves, each drawn on the assumption of a different quantity of money.

The curve LM_1 is a pictorial representation of the equilibrium condition $M_s^1 = M_d(\bar{p}, Q, r)$, which is the same as that given earlier except that the money supply is specified as M_s^1 and the price level is constant

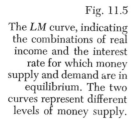

Fig. 11.5

The *LM* curve, indicating the combinations of real income and the interest rate for which money supply and demand are in equilibrium. The two curves represent different levels of money supply.

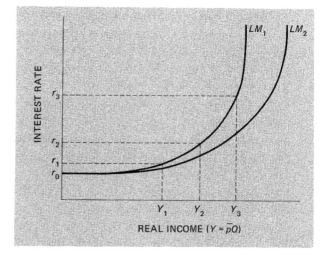

at $\bar{p}$. If Q were also given a fixed value, it would determine r in the sense of indicating which level of interest is compatible with monetary equilibrium. Alternatively, if r were fixed, it would determine Q. But since both of them are free to vary, the equation and its corresponding LM_1 curve merely show which *pairs* of values (such as Q_1, r_1) satisfy the equilibrium condition. To decide which of these pairs is also compatible with equilibrium between the aggregate demand and supply of commodities, it is now necessary to recall the relationship between Q and r in the saving-investment relationship.

It was shown in Chapter 3[27] that when aggregate demand and supply are in equilibrium, saving must equal investment when both terms are taken in the *ex ante* sense; in symbols, the condition for equilibrium in the market for commodities can be written $I = S$. If the demand for investment is assumed to be elastic with respect to the current interest rate, while all other investment-determining forces (such as the availability of finance, as distinct from its interest cost) are constant, the level of I will depend on r; that is, $I = I(r)$ where the $I(. . .)$ on the right-hand side of the equation represents the functional relationship between the other two terms. Saving, on the other hand, is more likely to depend on current real income than on the interest rate; if the consumption function is taken to be $C = C(Y) = C(\bar{p}Q)$ (implying that influences other than real income are either absent or constant), then the fact that saving equals income minus consumption means that it, too, is a function of real income — in symbols, $S = S(\bar{p}Q)$. The $I = S$ condition can therefore be rewritten

$$I(r) = S(\bar{p}Q),$$

meaning that the aggregate demand and supply of commodities will be in equilibrium only when the values of r and Q are such as to satisfy the equation ($\bar{p}$, of course, remaining constant throughout). For a given Q, the equation shows the equilibrium value of r, while for a given r it shows that of Q. But (just as with the condition of monetary equilibrium discussed earlier) the fact that both Q and r are variables means that the equation can do no more than indicate which *pairs* of values of Q and r are compatible with an equilibrium of aggregate demand and supply.

This is shown diagrammatically in Figure 11.6. The top half is identical with the Marginal Efficiency of Investment curve shown in Figure 7.1 on

---

[27] See pp. 54–59.

p. 163; the function $I(r)$ shows the various amounts of investment demand (measured on the upper side of the horizontal axis) that will be
forthcoming at the interest rates indicated on the vertical scale, on the
assumption that firms push investment to the point where the expected
rate of return is equal to the interest cost of financing it. Thus, r_1 calls
forth investment I_1, r_2 calls forth investment I_2, and so on. The lower
half of the diagram shows the relationship between real income (measured downward from the origin on the vertical scale) and saving
(measured along the underside of the horizontal axis); this part is similar
to Figure 7.2 on p. 174, except that it has been turned through 90 degrees
and contains only a "saving function" $S(\bar{p}Q)$ that shows how the amount
of desired saving varies with the level of income.[28] When real income

---

[28] In the diagram, $S(\bar{p}Q)$ has been drawn as a straight line through the origin,
implying that the community wishes to save the same proportion of income, however
large or small the latter happens to be. However, it is not necessary to the analysis
that this should be so; the same conclusions would follow if $S(\bar{p}Q)$ were drawn so
as to cut the vertical axis below the zero point, or if it were curvilinear.

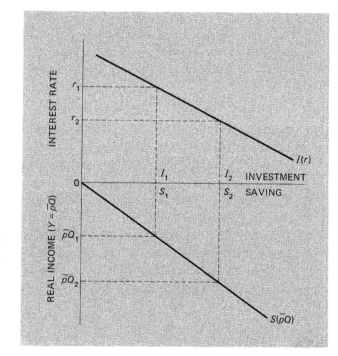

Fig. 11.6

Combinations of real
income and the interest
rate that are consistent
with saving-investment
equilibrium

happens to be $\bar{p}Q_1$, savings is S_1; when it is $\bar{p}Q_2$, saving is S_2 — and so on for other possible values of $\bar{p}Q$.

The two halves of the diagram are linked by the equilibrium condition $I = S$. Thus, aggregate demand equals aggregate supply when $I_1 = S_1$, that is, when interest is r_1 and real income is $\bar{p}Q_1$. Similarly, $I_2 = S_2$ requires that the interest rate be r_2 and real income $\bar{p}Q_2$. Every other point along the horizontal axis will represent a saving-investment equilibrium for which the appropriate values of r and $\bar{p}Q$ are given by the MEI and $S(\bar{p}Q)$ curves respectively. It is not difficult to see that the lower the level of r, the higher that of $\bar{p}Q$; the greater the demand for investment, the larger the real income needed to generate an equal amount of saving.

When this relationship is shown directly, as in Figure 11.7, it takes the form of a downward-sloping curve, labeled *IS*. Since Figure 11.7 has the same axes as Figure 11.5, it can also include *LM* curves. Suppose, then, that the quantity of money happens to be M_s^1, so that the various pairs of interest rates and real income levels consistent with monetary equilibrium are those indicated along LM_1. (The curves LM_2 and LM_3 should be ignored for the moment.) Where *IS* and LM_1 intersect at A, the interest rate is r_2 and real income is $\bar{p}Q_1$. At this point, there is an equilibrium of *both* the demand and supply of commodities, $I = S$ or $I(r) = S(\bar{p}Q)$, and the demand and supply of money, $M_s^1 = M_d(\bar{p}, Q, r)$. As long as

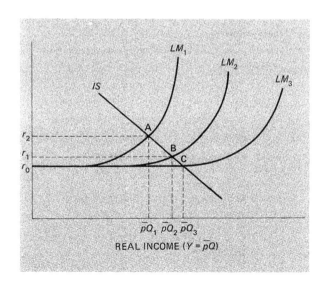

Fig. 11.7

The *IS* and *LM* curves and the equilibrium levels of real income and the interest rate

the supply of money continues to be M_s^1 there is no other point at which the two equilibrium conditions can be satisfied simultaneously.

If, for example, interest were r_1 and real income $\bar{p}Q_2$, saving-investment equilibrium would exist since B is a point on *IS*. But the level of interest needed for monetary equilibrium at $\bar{p}Q_2$ would be that indicated by a point on LM_1 vertically above B, which is obviously a good deal higher than r_1. At B, then, there would be an excess of demand for money, with the result that the interest rate would be driven upwards. This rise in the interest rate would reduce investment demand, creating an excess of saving over investment at $\bar{p}Q_2$ and thereby causing real income to fall. These movements will cease only when interest has settled at the r_2 level and real income has reached $\bar{p}Q_1$ — that is, when point A has been attained.[29]

For equilibrium to exist at point B, it would be necessary for the quantity of money to rise from M_s^1 to M_s^2 causing LM_2 to replace LM_1. Still another increase, this time to M_s^3 would push the *LM* curve out to the LM_3 position, giving equilibrium at C where the interest rate is r_0 and real income is $\bar{p}Q_3$. But now that the minimum interest rate r_0 has been reached, *IS* will continue to intersect the *LM* curve at C no matter how far to the right *LM* is pushed by further increases in the quantity of money; the horizontal stretch passing through C is common to all *LM* curves lying to the right of LM_3. Thus, $\bar{p}Q_3$ is the highest level of real income that can be reached by expanding the money supply.

Further increases in real income can now occur only if the *IS* curve itself shifts to the right, either because of an autonomous rise in investment demand (*i.e.*, a rightward shift of the $I(r)$ curve of Figure 11.6) or because of a fall in the propentity to save (*i.e.*, a movement of the $S(\bar{p}Q)$ curve closer to the vertical axis in Figure 11.6, so that less is saved at any given income level). This means that, if $\bar{p}Q_3$ is less than the full-employment level of real income, it will not be possible to eliminate unemployment merely by adopting an appropriate monetary policy; the authorities must also try to manipulate the "real" variables of saving and investment. This situation is conventionally referred to as the "Keynesian case," since it was Keynes who first suggested it as a theoretical possibility.[30]

---

[29] The adjustment process is likely to involve a good deal of "over-shooting," as the reader will discover if he traces out the sequence in Figures 11.4 and 11.6; moreover, it may be complicated by time lags that prevent equilibrium being reached and set up oscillations instead. See J. R. Hicks, *A Contribution to the Theory of the Trade Cycle* (Oxford: Clarendon Press, 1950), Chapter XI.

[30] See the *General Theory*, pp. 201–202. He added that "whilst this limiting case

Leaving aside the "Keynesian case," it is conceivable that monetary policy may be ineffective for another reason. In Figure 11.7, the IS curve has been drawn with a fairly gentle slope, so that it cuts LM_1, LM_2, and LM_3 at successively higher levels of real income. But now suppose Figure 11.6's MEI curve, $I(r)$, slopes very steeply, implying that investment demand is inelastic with respect to the interest rate; and that the $S(\bar{p}Q)$ curve has a more gentle slope, meaning that the Marginal Propensity to Save is high and that only a small increase in income is needed to provide the extra saving to balance a substantial rise in investment.[31] These conditions will cause the IS curve to slope very steeply, and shifts in the LM curve will then change the equilibrium level of real income very little. In the extreme case in which the IS curve is completely vertical (so that points A, B, and C are one above the other), real income cannot change at all from the level indicated by the position of the IS curve, no matter how far LM may be pushed to the right by changes in the quantity of money. Just as in the "Keynesian case," the only way of raising the level of $\bar{p}Q$ (if it is below the full-employment level) is to act on the determinants of saving and investment.

It may be, however, that the IS curve is actually more elastic than the slopes of the MEI and $S(\bar{p}Q)$ curves (Figure 11.6) seem to imply. As well as responding to changes in the interest rate, investment demand may be influenced to some extent by the level of real income,[32] rising as income increases and falling when it diminishes. The investment function will then be $I = I(r, \bar{p}Q)$ instead of the $I = I(r)$ assumed earlier; in Figure 11.6, an increase in real income will shift the MEI curve to the right. As long as the curve is not completely vertical, a fall in the interest rate will have more far-reaching effects than those already described. When the initial increase in investment has brought about a rise in real income via the curve $S(\bar{p}Q)$, the very fact that income has risen will cause a further investment increase through a movement to the right of the MEI curve. This movement will produce a further income rise, inducing another shift of MEI – and so on. The eventual change in $\bar{p}Q$ in response

---

might become practically important in [the] future, I know of no example of it hitherto" (p. 207).

[31] In other words, the Multiplier (1/MPS) will have a low value. To the extent that a fall in r causes a rise in investment, the consequent rise in income will be smaller, the higher the MPS.

[32] This possibility was considered on pp. 172–178 in Chapter 7.

to the original fall in r will consequently be greater than it would have been if MEI had stayed put; the IS curve in Figure 11.7 will reflect this by sloping less steeply than it would otherwise have done.[33]

Another possibility arises if saving varies with the rate of interest as well as with real income. The higher the rate of return on bonds, the greater the incentive to save in order to buy them; it may be doubted whether such an incentive has very much effect on saving behavior in practice, but to the extent that it does, the saving function must be amended to read $S = S(r, \bar{p}Q)$ instead of merely $S = S(\bar{p}Q)$ as before. A reduction in interest will therefore not only generate additional investment demand but will also cause $S(\bar{p}Q)$ in Figure 11.6 to move closer to the vertical $\bar{p}Q$ axis, indicating that the desire to save has diminished at all possible levels of real income. The ensuing rise in real income will consequently be greater than if $S(\bar{p}Q)$ had retained its original position; the slope of the IS curve in Figure 11.7 will be gentler than it would have been if saving depended only on $\bar{p}Q$. If, in addition, investment demand responds to changes in real income in the way described in the previous paragraph, the IS curve may be much more elastic with respect to the interest rate than is suggested by the slopes of the original MEI and $S(\bar{p}Q)$ curves. The power of monetary policy to raise the level of real income and employment will be correspondingly greater, as long as the economy is not pushed into the position described in the "Keynesian case."

It must be remembered, however, that the analysis has so far proceeded on the simplifying assumption that the price level remains constant throughout — so it would be unwise at this stage to begin drawing firm conclusions regarding policy. All that can be said at present is that the intersection of IS and LM_1 in Figure 11.7 shows the interest rate and income level at which two equilibrium conditions are simultaneously fulfilled. First, the supply of money equals the demand for it — in symbols,

$$M_s = M_d(p, Q, r);$$

and second, the aggregate demand for commodities equals aggregate supply:

$$S(pQ) = I(r),$$

or

$$S(pQ, r) = I(r, pQ)$$

---

[33] This is an example of the working of the "compound" Multiplier described on p. 139.

if the modifications suggested in the last two paragraphs are introduced. As long as the price level is constant, no other conditions are necessary for a complete equilibrium of the economy. The assumption of constant prices implies (as explained at the end of Chapter 4) that labor's marginal product is the same at all levels of employment and that money wages are inflexible; if unemployment exists because $\bar{p}Q_1$ is less than the full-employment level of output, it will not push down money wages, and nothing will happen to disturb the equilibrium situation given by the intersection of IS and LM_1. When these extreme assumptions regarding the labor market are abandoned, so that the price level is free to change, further equilibrium conditions must be specified, as will be done in the next chapter.

CHAPTER 12
Money and Prices

1. Interest, Output, and the Price Level

The condition of monetary equilibrium was originally expressed (p. 281) as

$$M_s = M_d(p, Q, r) = M_t(pQ, r) + M_a(p, r)$$

where M_s represents a fixed supply of money.[1] A rise in the price level p will cause the demand for money to increase; to restore equilibrium, r must rise, or Q fall, or both. Alternatively, the increase in prices can be regarded as reducing the real value of the money supply. If the equation is divided through by p, giving

$$\frac{M_s}{p} = M_d(Q, r) = M_t(Q, r) + M_a(r),$$

the effect is to express both supply and demand in real terms. Instead of a given number of dollars (or "nominal" money), the money supply is now a given volume of purchasing power (or "real" money); a rise in p reduces the quantity of goods and services over which M_s gives command and thereby diminishes the quantity of "real" money M_s/p. On the demand side, $M_t(Q, r)$ and $M_a(r)$ are the amounts of purchasing power needed to satisfy transactions and asset holding requirements. If the supply of nominal money is M_s^1 and the price level is p_1, the equilibrium condition will be satisfied by any of the pairs of values of Q and r indicated by the curve marked $L(M_s^1/p_1)$ in the top right-hand quadrant (I) of Figure 12.1.[2]

This part of Figure 12.1 is very similar to Figure 11.7 (p. 287), with the difference that its horizontal axis is marked Q instead of pQ: that is, it measures volumes of physical output instead of the money values found my multiplying output by a constant price level $\bar{p}$.[3] In Figure 12.1, the

---

[1] As in the preceding section, the symbol for assets (A) has been left out, on the ground that the analysis is at present concerned only with the short period.

[2] The diagram and the ensuing discussion are based on W. L. Smith, "A Graphical Exposition of the Complete Keynesian System," *Southern Economic Journal*, Vol. 23 (October, 1956), pp. 115–125; and on M. Blaug, *Economic Theory in Retrospect* (Homewood, Ill.: Irwin, 1962), p. 579.

[3] This raises the obvious difficulty that a heterogeneous collection of goods and services cannot be summed in quantity terms. There would, of course, be no problem if only one commodity were produced — but this would be a highly unrealistic assumption to make about the output of a whole economy. Accordingly, it is necessary to regard each value of Q as representing a set of quantities of the various commodities

position of the $L(M_s/p)$ curves depends on the price level as well; thus, a rise in prices from p_1 to p_2 will cause $L(M_s^1/p_1)$ to shift to the left to the position $L(M_s^1/p_2)$, even though the stock of nominal money is unchanged at M_s^1. A *fall* in the price level, on the other hand, will shift the $L(M_s/p)$ curve to the right. A change in M_s will have the same effect as in Figure 11.7, an increase pushing the curve to the right and a decrease pushing it to the left. It is quite possible, therefore, that a simultaneous change in both M_s and p could leave the $L(M_s/p)$ curve in exactly the same position as before.

The *IS* curve has much the same significance as it did earlier: it shows all the pairs of values of Q and r (rather than $\bar{p}Q$ and r as in Figure 11.7) at which saving-investment equilibrium can be achieved. As long as the demand for investment and the willingness to save are independent of the price level, the *IS* curve will not be affected (that is, it will not change its position or shape) when a rise in p reduces the supply of "real" money and causes the monetary equilibrium curve to shift from $L(M_s^1/p_1)$ to $L(M_s^1/p_2)$. The curve will now intersect *IS* at T instead of R, indicating that a lower volume of physical output (Q_2 instead of Q_1) and a higher interest rate (r_2 instead of r_1) are needed if monetary equilibrium is to coexist with an equilibrium of saving and investment. Had p fallen instead of rising, the $L(M_s/p)$ curve would have shifted to the right, intersecting the *IS* curve at a higher level of Q and a lower value of r. In fact, every new level of p will give a different $L(M_s/p)$ curve and thus necessitate a different combination of values of Q and r to satisfy the equilibrium conditions → except in the extreme case (analogous to the "Keynesian case" discussed earlier) when the $L(M_s/p)$ curve has shifted so far to the right that *IS* intersects it along its horizontal section.

What this part of Figure 12.1 does not show is why prices should be at one level rather than another. Given p_1 and the nominal money supply M_s^1 output will be Q_1 and interest r_1; given p_2, they will be respectively Q_2 and r_2 — but why should either p_1 or p_2 prevail? To answer this question, it is necessary to consider the other parts of the diagram. The lower left-hand quadrant (III) represents the labor market; it is exactly the same as Figure 4.3 in Chapter 4, except that it has been turned around and rotated through 90 degrees to the left. Man-hours (N) are now meas-

---

the economy produces; when Q rises by, say, 5%, it implies that the output of each individual commodity has risen by exactly 5% as well. To avoid index-number problems, it is also necessary to assume that the pattern of relative prices remains the same at all levels of output, whatever happens to the general price level.

ured downward from the origin on the vertical axis, while real wages
(w/p) are measured leftward from the origin along the horizontal scale.
The curve $N_d(W)$, which shows the marginal product of labor at each
possible level of employment, is derived from the production function
$Q(N, \bar{K})$ shown in the lower right-hand quadrant (II); this is Figure 4.1
(from Chapter 4) turned upside-down. The supply of labor is shown by
the curve $N_s(W)$, whose intersection with $N_d(W)$ shows that full employment exists when N_1 man-hours are being worked and real wages are
$(w/p)_1$.

If the labor market is perfectly competitive (*i.e.*, if there are no labor
unions, minimum wage laws, or other limitations on the adjustment of
money wages), any imbalance between demand and supply will cause
w to fall or rise until real wages are $(w/p)_1$ and employment is N_1. The
$Q(N, \bar{K})$ curve of Quadrant II shows that output will then be Q_1. For

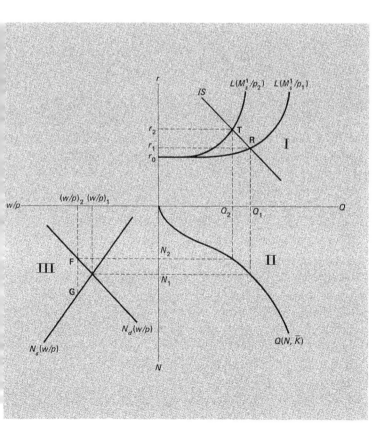

Fig. 12.1

The conditions for
macroeconomic
equilibrium.

savings-investment equilibrium at this volume of output, interest must be r_1; for monetary equilibrium at Q_1 and r_1, prices must be p_1 as long as the quantity of nominal money is M_s^1. With prices at p_1, money wages will also be determined; though many pairs of values of w and p would be consistent with the ratio $(w/p)_1$, there is only one w — which will be denoted w_1 — capable of giving this ratio when the price level is p_1

When money wages are w_1, prices p_1, employment and output N_1 and Q_1, and the interest rate r_1, a complete equilibrium exists in the economy as a whole. The equilibrium conditions in any single part of it depend on those prevailing in every other part. Suppose, for example, that the price level is p_2 instead of p_1. With a nominal money supply of M_s^1, the monetary equilibrium curve will now be $L(M_s^1/p_2)$, which intersects the IS curve at T. Here, investment balances saving, and the demand for money equals the supply; output is Q_2, and interest is r_2. As far as the forces at work in Quadrant I are concerned, equilibrium exists. But an output of Q_2 calls for the employment of only N_2 man-hours. If real wages are $(w/p)_2$, they will be equal to labor's marginal product at this level of labor input, and firms will be content to supply the output Q_2. But at this wage rate the demand for labor will fall short of supply by FG, and if money wages are flexible downwards, the pressure of the excess supply of labor will cause them to fall.

As long as the price level remains p_2, the fall in w will mean a reduction in real wages (w/p); firms will now increase output up to the point where the marginal product of labor equals the real wage. Aggregate supply will exceed the aggregate demand indicated by the Q_2 below point T in Quadrant I. Prices, then, will fall below the p_2 level, thereby increasing the quantity of "real" money, pushing the monetary equilibrium curve to the right, reducing the interest rate, and increasing the volume of output needed to satisfy aggregate demand. The fall in prices will tend to offset the effects on (w/p) of the decline in money wages, necessitating further reductions in w. But both p and w will continue to fall until the real wage $(w/p)_1$ has been reached — at which point there will be an overall equilibrium, with aggregate demand and supply balanced at Q_1 and the demand and supply of labor balanced at N_1.

A complete equilibrium, then, requires that all of the following conditions shall be simultaneously fulfilled:

(a) Saving must equal investment. Since $I = I(r)$ and $S = S(Q)$, the condition $I = S$ means that

$$I(r) = S(Q).$$

If investment is also influenced by Q and saving by r, the equation becomes

$$I(r, Q) = S(Q, r). \tag{1}$$

(b) The supply of money must equal the demand for it. When both are expressed in real terms, this means that

$$\frac{M_s}{p} = M_d(Q, r) = M_t(Q, r) + M_a(r), \tag{2}$$

where M_s is a fixed quantity of nominal money.

(c) The demand and supply of labor must balance. Supply is a function of the real wage, *i.e.*,

$$N_s = N_s\left(\frac{w}{p}\right). \tag{3}$$

Demand is derived from the aggregate demand for commodities through the production function

$$Q = Q(N, \bar{K}), \tag{4}$$

but it also depends on the real wage, since the level of employment most profitable to firms is found where labor's marginal product equals the real wage, *i.e.*, where

$$\frac{dQ}{dN} = \frac{w}{p} \tag{5}$$

— the marginal product of labor, dQ/dN, being derived from the production function defined in (4).

Given the various functional relationships — namely, the investment and savings functions in (1), the "liquidity" functions in (2), the labor supply function in (3), and the production function in (4) — and given, too, the supply of nominal money as fixed by the monetary authorities, there will be a single set of values for r, Q, p, w and N (the "unknowns" of the system) that will satisfy the whole set of equations simultaneously. When these values obtain, the economy will be in full equilibrium.

Under the conditions set out above, it appears that the economy can reach equilibrium only at full employment and that the forces of supply and demand will, in fact, ensure that equilibrium is attained.[4] But this is not to say that the best way of achieving full employment is merely to

---

[4] Provided, however, that there are no time lags long enough to prevent the adjustment process being completed before the parameters of the system (*e.g.*, the stock of capital) have altered or before some exogenous change has produced a fresh disequilibrium; and that the adjustment is not itself complicated by expectational fac-

leave p and w to vary as necessary to give Q_1 and N_1. Such changes are likely to take time and to entail awkward readjustments of the pattern of relative prices and wages; falling prices, too, tend to reduce business optimism and so diminish investment demand. Suppose output is initially at Q_2. Instead of waiting for prices to fall from p_2 to p_1, the monetary authority can expand the supply of nominal money, pushing the monetary equilibrium curve to the right. An increase from M_s^1 to M_s^2 giving a curve that would be labeled $L(M_s^2/p_2)$ in place of the $L(M_s^1/p_1)$ shown in Figure 12.1, would move aggregate demand from Q_2 to Q_1 just as effectively as a fall in prices would. Money wages must still fall to the level at which real wages are $(w/p)_1$, but with prices unchanged at p_2 the reduction in w will be less than would have been needed if prices had simultaneously fallen to p_1. It would even be possible to avoid reducing money wages if the monetary authority is willing to expand the nominal supply beyond M_s^2. Initially this would push the monetary equilibrium curve far enough to the right to intersect the IS curve beyond the level of full-employment output Q_1, with the result that prices would begin to rise. With w unchanged, this rise would automatically reduce real wages towards the $(w/p)_1$ level, while it would also cause the quantity of real money to fall until equilibrium was attained, with a new monetary equilibrium curve $L(M_s^3/p_3)$ taking the place of $L(M_s^1/p_1)$ and intersecting the IS curve at R.

A policy of this kind might be called for if it was known that labor unions would effectively resist any reduction in money wages, though they would take no action (because of money illusion) if rising prices caused real wages to fall. In this case, the labor supply function given in (3) above will no longer be sufficient to describe market behavior; in addition to $N_s = N_s(w/p)$, an extra condition

$$w \geq w_0 \tag{3a}$$

will be needed to indicate that money wages will remain at the minimum level w_0 except when market conditions call for higher values of w — when the original function (3) will once more apply. The rise of prices to p_3 will be a once-for-all adjustment in order to reduce real wages to $(w/p)_1$ (equal to w_0/p_3); no further change will be needed when full-employment equilibrium has been reached.

If, however, the original situation came about because unions forced a rise in money wages with the express purpose of keeping *real* wages

---

tors — for example, the possibility that buyers, thinking that price reductions will continue, respond to a fall in p by cutting expenditures.

at $(w/p)_2$, every subsequent increase in p will give rise to a claim for a compensating increase in w, and a "wage-price spiral" will develop. Here, instead of equation (3a) above,

$$w/p \geqq (w/p)_0 \qquad (3b)$$

is needed to indicate that *real* wages will not be allowed to fall below a minimum level. Under these circumstances, if the monetary authority were to stabilize the quantity of nominal money in order to halt the increase in prices, the real wage would remain at $(w/p)_2$, unemployment equal to FG would persist, the interest rate would be r_2, and output and employment would be Q_2 and N_2 respectively. The prevailing unemployment would be prevented from forcing a reduction in money wages, and the economy would now settle into a position of "underemployment equilibrium."[5]

This is not, however, the only possible situation in which the economy might be unable to reach full-employment equilibrium. Even if wages and prices were completely flexible, the IS curve might be inelastic to the rate of interest and lie wholly to the left of Q_1 in Quadrant I of Figure 12.1; or, no matter how much the quantity of nominal money was increased, the intersection of the IS curve with the $L(M_s/p)$ curve might still lie to the left of Q_1 along the part of $L(M_s/p)$ corresponding to the minimum interest rate of r_0. These, of course, are the two possibilities already discussed in the previous chapter[6] in connection with Figure 11.7. Either of them will give rise to a downward wage-price spiral. As unemployment causes money wages to fall, real wages will be pushed down and firms will be induced to increase supply — but because aggregate demand cannot increase, the excess supply will merely force the price level down; real wages will rise again, only to be further reduced when the pressure of unemployment causes another reduction in money wages. In these conditions, downward inflexibility of money wages could be positively advantageous; the economy would still suffer from unemployment, of course, but it would at least avoid continuous price deflation.

Against this, it might be argued that if prices only fall far enough, the Pigou effect is certain sooner or later to shift the IS curve sufficiently to the right to intersect $L(M_s/p)$ above the full-employment level of output Q_1. As

---

[5] The diagrammatic equivalent of condition (3b) above is the suppression of the part of $N_s(w/p)$ to the right of G in Figure 12.1's Quadrant III, and its replacement by the vertical broken line between G and the (w/p) axis. This assumes that labor unions are strong enough to insist on *prompt* increases in w whenever p rises.

[6] See pp. 288–289.

the real value of cash balances grows, their owners will feel more and more disposed to increase the proportion of income they spend on consumption; the curve $S(\bar{p}Q)$ of Figure 11.6 will move gradually closer to the vertical axis, so that each level of r will be associated with a higher real income, and the *IS* curve of Figure 12.1 will consequently shift to the right. If the price level were prevented from falling by the downward inflexibility of wages, the Pigou effect would be unable to work, and the economy would be left with chronic unemployment; so any policy measures that break down the rigidity of money wages are, after all, to be welcomed.

However, prices may have to fall a long way before the Pigou effect becomes strong enough to eliminate unemployment, and in the meantime certain other effects will be at work in the opposite direction. If everyone assumes that price reductions are going to continue, the prospective rise in the real value of cash holdings may induce people to try to increase their present holdings by saving more – so Figure 11.6's curve of $S(\bar{p}Q)$ will swing further away from the vertical axis, and Figure 12.1's *IS* curve will shift to the left. Aggregate demand will fall, and output and employment will be reduced. Business firms contemplating investment projects will expect future yields to decline in money terms because of the downward trend of prices, and their estimates of the rate of return on the capital assets they can buy at present prices will be depressed;[7] the MEI curve will move to the left, Figure 12.1's *IS* curve will also shift leftward, and output and employment will fall. The eventual outcome will depend on whether the Pigou effect, which will be getting stronger and stronger as the price level falls, at last becomes so strong that it more than offsets the expectational effects just described. If it does, aggregate demand will expand to the full-employment level, and money wages and prices will have no further reason to fall.

The very fact that prices have been stabilized, however, is likely to cause expectations to be revised. If no one thinks any longer that prices will fall in the future, then investment demand will revive, the proportion of income saved will fall even further than the level to which the

---

[7] In terms of the MEI formula

$$P = \frac{A_1}{1+\rho} + \frac{A_2}{(1+\rho)^2} + \frac{A_3}{(1+\rho)^3} + \cdots + \frac{A_n}{(1+\rho)^n}$$

given on p. 160, this means that the A's will all be reduced in money terms in proportion to their distance ahead in the future; but since P is expressed at current prices, the equation can only be satisfied by a lower value of ρ (where ρ is the MEI) than would have emerged if prices were expected to remain unchanged.

Pigou effect has brought it, and aggregate demand will expand *beyond* the full-employment level. Prices and money wages will then rise again, setting the expectational and Pigou effects into reverse, and continuing until the reduction in the stock of real money moves the $L(M_s/p)$ curve far enough to the left to intersect the *IS* curve at the full-employment level of Q. Thus, even if wage flexibility does not lead to continuous deflation, it is still likely to cause considerable instability in the price level.

Additional complications may be introduced by the redistribution effect described in Chapter 10.[8] If the share of wages in total income falls when real wages are reduced, the proportion of income saved will increase if the MPC of wage earners exceeds that of profit recipients; the *IS* curve will shift to the left. Accordingly, the fall in real wages from $(w/p)_2$ to $(w/p)_1$, which was seen to be necessary to bring about full employment, will involve a greater reduction in money wages and prices than would otherwise have been needed. The price level must not only fall from p_2 to p_1 — that is, enough to make the monetary equilibrium curve cut the original *IS* curve at R — but it must fall still further, so as to push the $L(M_s/p)$ curve far enough to the right to compensate for the fact that *IS* has been shifted to the left by the redistribution effect. Provided it is still possible for the *IS* and $L(M_s/p)$ curves to intersect Q_1, full-employment equilibrium will still be reached, though at a rate of interest lower than the r_1 that would have prevailed if *IS* had not been displaced. If, on the other hand, the shift of *IS* has carried it so far to the left that it cuts $L(M_s/p)$ at a point to the left of Q_1 even at the minimum interest rate r_0, only through the Pigou effect — if at all — will full-employment equilibrium be reached.

In this last situation, as in earlier ones, the essential reason for the economy's difficulties in reaching full employment lay in the inadequacy of investment demand relative to the desire to save; because of this relationship, the *IS* curve was positioned so far to the left that neither price reductions nor the expansion of the supply of nominal money was able to make the $L(M_s/p)$ curve cut it above Q_1. The implication for government policy is obvious: it should take action to shift *IS* to the right. If public-goods-and-services expenditures are regarded as "collective consumption"[9] (C_g) financed by the taxation of factor incomes (T_y), saving may be redefined as

$$S = Y - C_p - C_g = (1 - c)Y + cT_y - C_g$$

---

[8] See p. 244.   [9] See pp. 44–45.

where C_p is private consumption – equal to $c(Y - T_y)$ – and c is the MPC. If $(1 - c)$ is replaced by s (the Marginal Propensity to Save), the expression becomes

$$S = sY + (1 - s)T_y - C_g,$$

so that saving now consists of an "induced" element, sY, and an "autonomous" one $(1 - s)T_y - C_g$, which will, of course, be zero if the amount of collective consumption C_g is exactly equal to the reduction in private consumption $(1 - s)T_y$ brought about by taxation. By increasing C_g or reducing T_y or by a mixture of both,[10] the government could reduce the autonomous element, thereby pushing the curve $S(\bar{p}Q)$ of Figure 11.6 vertically downward and linking each level of r with a higher level of real income. The IS curve of Figure 12.1 would then shift to the right.

This is, of course, merely another way of expressing the possibilities of budgetary policy already outlined in Chapter 9. However, the analysis of the present chapter shows that there is one case in which budgetary policy of this kind might turn out to be inappropriate and ineffective – namely, when labor unions' policy is to maintain a minimum *real* wage higher than the level consistent with full employment. Just as the expansion of the supply of nominal money would then bring about a wage-price spiral, so also would the rightward shift of the IS curve create an excess of aggregate demand over supply, tending to force the price level upward while failing to secure full employment.

2. Liquid Assets, Financial Intermediaries, and Monetary Policy

In Figure 12.1, a number of separate equilibrium conditions were brought together into a system in which the supply and demand of commodities, labor, and money are mutually interdependent; a change in any one of the variables is likely to affect each of the others. However,

---

[10] A further possibility would be to introduce, or increase, income transfers such as social security benefits. The definition of saving would then become

$$S = sY + (1 - s)(T_y - Tr) - C_g$$

where Tr represents such transfers. An increase in Tr has the same effect as a reduction in T_y, subect to the qualifications noted on p. 223.

the model is still highly simplified. Its most obvious limitation, perhaps, is that it is *static*: it shows the balance of forces in the economy at a given moment of time, without regard to what has happened in the past or what is to come. If the system were to move forward through time, it would be necessary to allow for the fact that investment will be gradually increasing the stock of capital, so that the production function of Quadrant II will be moved steadily upward and to the right; any given level of employment will yield a larger and larger output of goods and services. The movement will be quickened by technical progress — *i.e.*, by improvements in production methods, in the design of capital equipment, and in the degree and diffusion of labor skills. Population growth will cause a gradual shift of the labor supply curve in Quadrant III, while any change in the slope of the production function will cause the MPL curve to move; between them, these changes will alter the equilibrium of the labor market. These effects will be examined in a later chapter.

The second limitation of the analysis centering on Figure 12.1 is the result of the assumption (made on p. 270 above) that the only "paper" asset available as an alternative to money is a single type of irredeemable fixed-interest bond. In reality, of course, there are many different kinds of non-money paper assets. There are, for example, time deposits at banks; bonds redeemable within a number of years, as well as irredeemable ones; deposits in mutual savings banks; and corporation stock.

In the model specified earlier, the bonds were illiquid, since owning them entailed the risk of capital loss; the only way to avoid this risk was to hold money, so that "liquidity preference" could be taken to be synonymous with the demand for money. But where there is a wide range of assets to choose from, the illiquidity of one asset can be avoided by holding a more liquid one — which need not, however, be as liquid as money. A wealth holder can obtain a given degree of liquidity in his portfolio of assets by making an appropriate selection from *all* the available kinds of assets — $x of money, plus $y worth of short-term bonds, plus $z worth of stock, and so on. If he comes to desire a higher degree of liquidity, he can get it by selling some of his bonds and acquiring, say, savings bank deposits in their place, without altering his holding of money at all. Though money is still the only means of effecting transactions, it is far from being the only means of satisfying liquidity preference.

One way of allowing for this liquidity demand would be to change the meaning assigned to the $M_a(r)$ curve in Figure 11.3. Instead of representing only the asset demand for money, the curve could be made to represent the demand for *all* liquid assets. Instead of measuring money, the horizontal scale would measure quantities of liquid assets; the interest rate measured on the vertical scale would be an average of the yields on illiquid assets (*e.g.*, long-term bonds), the interest on near money itself being ignored. The curve $M_a(r)$ would then imply that the "long rate" (as the interest on illiquid long-term assets may be called for brevity) depends on the quantity of liquid assets available, which may, of course, change without the quantity of money itself changing. An increase in the supply of Treasury Bills, for example, will create more liquid assets than the community wishes to hold at the currently prevailing long rate; to restore equilibrium, the long rate must fall until increasing fear of future capital loss causes the demand for liquid assets to rise to equality with the supply of them.

From the original interpretation of Figure 11.3 (that is, with $M_a(r)$ representing the asset demand for money only) it appeared that control of the money supply gave the authorities the power to set the interest rate at any desired level above the minimum r_0; with this power, they could determine real income and the price level, subject to various limitations regarding the interest elasticity of investment, the state of the labor market, and the flexibility of money wages and prices. Now, however, it seems that control of the money supply may not be enough. A reduction in the quantity of money, intended to raise the long-term interest rate, could be offset by an increase in the quantity of other liquid assets; while a fall in the latter could raise the long rate even when the money supply is being increased. The authorities have to think in terms of influencing the supply of liquid assets in general, not just of controlling the supply of money. In this, they are helped by the fact that some important non-money liquid assets are obligations of the federal government – chiefly three-month Treasury Bills. By replacing Treasury Bills with long-term bonds (*i.e.*, by the procedure known as "funding," which lengthens the average maturity of the National Debt), the authorities can reduce the outstanding volume of liquid assets; they can increase it by the reverse procedure. Debt management, in fact, is a vital aspect of monetary policy.

However, merely changing the meaning attached to the $M_a(r)$ curve of Figure 11.3, in the way suggested above, is an unsatisfactory way of handling the liquidity preference of an economy with many types of "paper" assets other than money. It implies that a hard-and-fast line separates assets that are liquid from those that are not, though the least liquid of the former may actually differ very little from the most liquid of the latter; and it furnishes only one interest rate, which is an average of those of the arbitrarily selected "illiquid assets." In fact, there will exist a *system* of interest rates, which will be in equilibrium when the quantity demanded of each type of asset is exactly equal to the quantity in existence. Rates will vary according to the relative liquidity of the assets; when two of them differ only in degree of liquidity, higher interest will be needed to persuade the owners of the less liquid one to go on holding it instead of exchanging it for the other.

When the quantity of a particular asset increases, the initial effect will be to reduce its price and raise its rate of yield; these changes will attract an inflow of demand at the expense of other assets, and their prices will fall in consequence, while the price of the first is made to rise part of the way back toward its original level. The eventual outcome will be a realignment of the whole interest rate structure. How widespread these repercussions will be depends on the readiness of wealth holders to switch from one asset to another. The extent of the repercussions also depends on certain institutional factors, such as the fact that some assets, such as Treasury Bills, are in such high denominations (the cheapest is $1000) that individuals do not normally hold them. In addition, the commercial banks need to maintain their reserve ratios, which reduces their ability to exchange short-term for long-term assets in response to favorable long-term interest rates. For many assets there probably exists a solid core of holdings that their owners will not relinquish even when alternatives become more attractive, and these owners' reluctance will limit the overspill of demand from one asset market to another.

In such realignments of interest rates, those for illiquid assets change less than those for the more liquid ones. For an irredeemable bond yielding $40 per annum, a fall in the market rate of interest from 4% to 3% means a rise in price from $1000 to $1333; an increase in interest from 4% to 5% will reduce the market price from $1000 to $800. By contrast, a bond that is redeemable in one year's time[11] will rise in price from $1000

---

[11] The relationship of bond prices and yields is given approximately by the formula

$$r = \frac{iN + \dfrac{N - P}{n}}{P}$$

where r is the yield (*i.e.*, the "market rate" of interest), i is the "nominal" interest rate, N is the nominal value of the bond, P is the market price, and n is the number of years from now to the redemption date. The $(N - P)/n$ term in the formula is a rough measure of the annual capital gain or loss that results from buying a bond at

to just under $1010 when market interest falls from 4% to 3%, while an increase in the interest rate from 4% to 5% will cause the price to fall from $1000 to only $990. For the "short" bond, interest changes must be great to alter its capital value very much, whereas the value of "long" bonds swings widely in response to quite small movements in interest. What the market regards as the highest and lowest possible long-term bond prices will thus mark out a fairly narrow band of interest rates — say 2½% to 8%. If the long-term rate were 8% (implying a price of $500 for the irredeemable bond just mentioned), a subsequent rise in price might seem so certain that holders of short bonds would try to switch into "longs," and the diversion of demand from the short bond market would send the prices of "shorts" down. But the latter need only reach $960 for the rate on one-year bonds to become 8.3%, at which it would be higher than the long rate — though the more liquid asset would normally be expected to yield a lower rate of interest than the less liquid one. At the other extreme, a high price for "longs" would switch demand into the short bond market, forcing the price of short bonds up; but a price of $1030, for a one-year bond yielding $4 per annum, would mean that the interest rate was below 1%. Thus, given the state of expectations about the normal level of long-term rates, the interest rate structure for illiquid assets will be tethered between fairly narrow limits, while rates for the more liquid assets will show wider variations.

This has important implications for monetary policy. If the authorities wish to bring about a rise in long-term rates, they must be ready to let short rates increase substantially. But high short rates have certain disadvantages. They raise the interest cost of the government's short-term borrowing, which is substantial. In mid-1968, 47% of federal marketable securities ($232 billion in total) were redeemable within one year, so that a rise in the short rate from 5% to 6% would increase the federal government's interest payments by approximately $1 billion a year. Also, the fact that many short-term interest-bearing obligations of the United States are in the hands of foreign residents (roughly $7 billion [12] in mid-1968)

---

less or more than its nominal value, when the nominal value is the amount for which it will be redeemed at maturity. The smaller the value of n, the larger the value of $(N - P)/n$ and the greater its importance relative to the "flat yield" iN/P. In the case of an irredeemable bond, n equals infinity so that the $(N - P)/n$ term vanishes; the formula then reduces to that given in footnote 17 of Chapter 11.

[12] See *Federal Reserve Bulletin*, p. A-77, Table 9. The main short-term liability to foreigners was the amount of demand deposits in U.S. banks owned by foreigners; but this is not included here, since it does not bear interest.

means that a rise in short rates will increase the flow of interest to the rest of the world, thereby worsening the United States' balance of payments. These considerations may weaken the authorities' resolution in attempting to raise the level of long-term interest rates; on the other hand, if they can create the conviction that the "normal" level of long-term rates will be higher in the future than it has been in the past, the displacement of short-term rates resulting from the intermarket movements described above will be less.

The authorities' task may be made easier by another factor. Once long-term interest rates begin to rise, the market prices of long-term bonds and other illiquid assets will be falling; if they are sold at that time, their owners will sustain capital losses. The only way the owners can avoid loss is to retain the assets until interest rates fall again and bond prices recover; in the meantime, they are "locked in" to their asset holdings. Business firms will be unwilling to finance new investment by the sale of bonds; individuals, too, are likely to postpone expenditures that they would have to finance by the sale of securities. The most important "lock-in" effect, however, may be that on financial intermediaries such as banks, which will find that the liquidity of their balance sheet position has been reduced, as a result of which they will be less willing to lend. This "Roosa effect," as it has been called, [13] will cause a reduction in the availability of credit as a result of a rise in interest rates; even if higher rates do not themselves discourage borrowers, the unwillingness of lenders to lend will frustrate the demand for loans.

But business firms and individuals do not usually hold large enough quantities of financial assets for this "lock-in" effect to work on them very strongly; and the financial intermediaries that may be affected by the Roosa effect can only be those that are already established and in possession of long-term bonds whose capital value can be reduced.[14] If an excess of demand over supply of credit were to persist at high interest rates, there would be an incentive for *new* lending institutions to enter the field. By offering high borrowing rates, they would attract idle money balances and proceed to lend this money at still higher rates to borrowers who had

---

[13] After Robert V. Roosa, who first described it in his "Interest Rates and the Central Bank," in *Money, Trade and Economic Growth: Essays in Honor of John H. Williams* (New York: Macmillan, 1951).

[14] For criticisms of the "Roosa effect," see W. L. Smith, "On the Effectiveness of Monetary Policy," *American Economic Review*, Vol. 46 (September, 1956), pp. 588–606.

been unable to obtain credit through the usual channels. To the extent that they were successful in doing this, they would be thwarting the monetary authorities' intention of making credit scarcer as well as dearer. Admittedly, such institutions are unlikely to be created overnight in response to a temporary increase in the level of interest rates; but insofar as there is already a tendency for nonbank financial intermediaries to grow faster than the commercial banks through which monetary policy works, the NBFI's frequently are in a position to reduce the effectiveness of monetary control.[15]

When fiscal policy was considered earlier (Chapter 9), it was noted[16] that changes in taxation and expenditure take time to affect the working of the economy, and that measures that would be perfectly appropriate in the absence of lags may actually turn out to be destabilizing. The same can be said of monetary policy. The authorities are continuously reviewing and analyzing the situation of the economy, but there will inevitably be some interval between the emergence of a need for policy changes and their recognition of that need. A further lag will ensue between the Federal Reserve's "pulling the levers" (*e.g.*, undertaking open market operations and adjusting the discount rate) and the consequential changes in commercial bank deposits and interest rates. The economy's response to these changes — for example, the modification of investment plans in the light of increased interest rates and reduced availability of credit — will take still more time. Meanwhile, many other things may be happening: expectations about future interest rates and prices may be changing, investment intentions may be revised, and so on. The greater the lapse of time involved, the more complicated and unforeseeable will be the outcome of the initial policy measures.

Some economists, indeed, consider that because the overall lag is likely to be long, attempts to control the economy by monetary measures can be dangerously destabilizing and should therefore not be undertaken.[17]

---

[15] The argument that the expansion of NBFI's has impaired the effectiveness of traditional monetary control has been particularly associated with the names of J. G. Gurley and E. S. Shaw; see their "Financial Aspects of Economic Development," *American Economic Review*, Vol. 45 (September, 1955), pp. 515–538.

[16] See pp. 230–231.

[17] The best-known proponent of this view is Professor Milton Friedman; see, for example, his "The Lag in Effect of Monetary Policy," *Journal of Political Economy*, Vol. 69 (October, 1961), pp. 447–466. He argues that the lag may be as long as eighteen months, so that when current policy measures finally come to exert their effect on the economy, they will have the character of random disturbances. His conclusion

This view is at the opposite extreme from the more traditional conception of monetary policy, which pays little attention to lags and assumes that the weapons at the authorities' disposal will produce an almost instantaneous effect on the level of activity. But while it is right to reject this oversanguine view, the majority of economists would probably agree that time lags are not so long as to make the weapons too dangerous to use. The existence of lags does, however, mean that great skill is required in the exercise of monetary policy.

The arguments put forward in this chapter suggest that there is a good deal of scope for the use of monetary policy in controlling the economy, but that it is unwise to expect too much of it. Control of the supply of money, debt management, and the application of direct controls over lending may be highly efficacious in some situations but relatively useless in others, depending on the interest elasticity of investment, the policies of employers and unions in determining prices and wages, the state of opinion as to "normal" interest rates, expectations of further increases in the general price level, and the rate at which output is growing. With a favorable conjunction of all these factors, monetary policy will be effective in checking excessive demand or in preventing unemployment; the occasions when all of the necessary conditions are satisfied are likely to be few, but so also will be the occasions when none of them are. Since the usual situation is likely to be between these extremes, monetary measures will at most times exert a relatively mild influence.

This may seem a disappointing — perhaps even alarming — conclusion when it is put beside that reached at the end of the previous chapter, namely that fiscal measures may sometimes be unable to control the economy. If neither monetary nor fiscal weapons can be surely relied on, it is possible that in certain situations the authorities will be unable to

---

is that the monetary authorities should not be allowed to operate a "discretionary" policy (*i.e.*, a policy of trying to manage the economy by the frequent adjustment of monetary variables) but should be instructed merely to maintain a prescribed rate of growth of the money supply, the rate being chosen to match the long-run growth rate of the economy. For a criticism of Friedman's argument, see J. Kareken and R. M. Solow, "Lags in Monetary Policy," in *Stabilization Policies*, edited by E. Cary Brown for the Commission on Money and Credit (Englewood Cliffs, N.J.: Prentice-Hall, 1963). Kareken and Solow provide alternative estimates of the relevant lags, showing how they are distributed over time. For example, they find that a little less than half of the overall response of investment demand to interest changes can be expected to occur within three months, another quarter of the response within the next three months, another sixth within the next half year, and so on.

manage the economy at all — it will be like a disobedient dog that has slipped its leash and refuses to answer the whistle. But it is perhaps salutary to recognize that governments may occasionally be powerless and to reflect that this may be part of the price of certain freedoms that the community thinks valuable; in any case, since the "conjuncture" of the economy is constantly changing, the authorities may need only to wait a little for control to become possible again.

CHAPTER 13
Inflation

1. Definition and Measurement

When the conditions of full-employment equilibrium were presented in Chapter 12, much attention was given to the possibility that the economy might underfulfill them, with the result that output would fall short of the full-employment level, while prices and money wages, if flexible downward, would fall. But this is not the kind of disequilibrium that has been typical of the years since World War II. In most countries, the problems facing fiscal and monetary policy makers have not been large-scale "demand-deficiency" unemployment and falling money values, but, on the contrary, a continuous and seemingly irresistible upward movement of prices. In the United States, the rate of increase has been fairly slow by international standards,[1] and there have been periods when the price level hardly rose at all. Even so, consumer prices increased by approximately one-fifth between 1958 and 1968, and the advance registered in 1968 alone was 4.3% — a rate that, if continued unchanged into the future, would raise the price level by 50% in just under ten years and double it in seventeen.

A sustained rise in prices of this magnitude can be called "creeping" inflation, to distinguish it from "galloping" (or "hyper") inflation, which occurs when annual increases are 20% or 30% or more, and from "trotting" inflation, which proceeds at intermediate rates. It is often assumed that creeping inflation must eventually accelerate through the trotting stage until it is galloping at ever faster rates, culminating in the collapse of the currency and the disruption of economic life. But although this sequence has certainly happened in some cases (the most spectacular being those of Germany in 1923, Hungary in 1947, and China in 1949), there are enough counter-examples of strong but nonaccelerating inflations (such as those of Brazil, Argentina, and certain other Latin American countries in

---

[1] For some comparative figures, see the table "Changes in Cost of Living," in *International Financial Statistics* (published monthly by the International Monetary Fund). Over the period 1958–1966, 30 out of 59 countries registered increases in consumer prices between 20% and 50%, implying average annual rises between 2½% and 6%. In nine countries, prices rose between 50% and 200%, *i.e.*, at average annual rates between 7% and 25%; while four had still faster rates of increase, the top place going to Brazil, which had a thirty-fold rise in price level over all eight years.

the 1950's and 1960's) to show that acceleration and collapse are by no means inevitable.[2]

The word *inflation* has so far been used in its everyday sense of "rising prices," but it should be noted that this is by no means the only meaning which has been given it in the past. To old-fashioned Quantity Theorists, for instance, inflation was synonymous with an increase in the quantity of money; on the extreme assumptions of fixed velocity and transactions, such an increase would necessarily raise the price level, but the rising prices would be the *effect* of inflation, not the thing itself. A similar distinction has often been made by Keynesian writers, who have defined inflation as an excess of aggregate demand over supply when there is full employment. In a closed economy with low inventories and no institutional barriers to price increases, this situation would certainly cause prices to rise — but it is the excess demand that would be the inflation, the increase in prices being merely the symptom indicating its existence. However, excess demand *need* not lead to increases in price level; in an open economy, it can be met by expanding imports, so that as long as the economy is able to finance a balance-of-trade deficit, the price level will remain unchanged. Also, as will be argued later, a sustained upward movement of prices can be brought about by causes other than excess demand at full employment, and it would surely be anomalous to refuse to call it inflation on the ground that there is no excess demand. For these reasons, it is desirable to have a definition that refers directly to the phenomenon to be explained — *i.e.*, the rise in prices — rather than to any of its possible causes; so, in what follows, the word *inflation* will, much as in everyday speech, be used to mean no more than a continuing increase in the general price level.

This is not to say that *every* rise in prices is to be regarded as inflationary. A current increase may be merely one of a series of slight up-and-down movements around a constant level, or it may accompany a short-run expansion of output as the level of capacity utilization is increased.[3] Again,

---

[2] In Brazil, for example, prices increased at the following annual rates during the 1950's: 1952, 25%; 1953, 20%; 1954, 19%; 1955, 20%; 1956, 21.7%; 1957, 19.2%; 1958, 14%.

[3] In Figure 10.3 (p. 244) an increase in aggregate demand from $d_1(Q, p)$ to $d_2(Q, p)$ caused the intersection with the aggregate supply curve to move from E_1 to E_2, so that the price level rose from p_1 to p_2. Given constant money wages and appropriate changes in the money supply, this price increase would merely reflect the transition

it may be a once-for-all adjustment to some change in the economy's external situation — for example, perhaps it has become necessary to switch to a new source of imports whose prices are higher than those of the country whose supplies are no longer available. In each of these cases, the rise in prices will lack the chronic, self-sustaining character of inflation, though it may, of course, be difficult in practice to be sure that it is merely a short-run adjustment and not the beginning of an inflationary trend.

A very different situation would be one in which inflationary price increases are prevented (for the time being, anyway) by government controls; this is "suppressed" inflation, as distinct from the "open" inflation that would have existed in the absence of government intervention. Here, too, the definition of inflation in terms of rising prices will no longer be satisfactory. But these are exceptional cases; in all others, the common usage will be perfectly applicable.

To determine the rate at which inflation is proceeding, it is necessary to decide which of the available index numbers of prices is the most appropriate indicator. Should it be the index of consumer prices or of wholesale prices? Should it be an "implicit GNP deflator" that includes the prices of all "final" commodities entering GNP? The trouble is that each index may give a different measure of the rate of inflation; there may even be times when one index rises while others show no change, so that the diagnosis of inflation will depend on which one is being used as the criterion.[4] Moreover, even if all the various index numbers are moving exactly in step with one another, they may overstate the rate of price increase because of bias due to their construction. For example, when a cheap new commodity replaces an old one in consumers' expenditure, an index of consumer prices may nevertheless continue to include that of the old commodity at its "base year" weight, while excluding the price of the new one because it was not available in the base year. If the old commodity has gone up in price because it is now bought in quantities too small to justify large-scale production, the index will show a rise in the general price-level that is out of line with reality.[5] Consequently there

---

from one short-run equilibrium situation to another; once prices reached p_2 there would be no reason for them to rise further.

[4] For example, the Department of Labor's Consumer Price Index rose 2.7% between May, 1966, and May, 1967, while the index of wholesale prices rose only 0.2% over the same period.

[5] G. J. Stigler and others, Price Statistics Review Committee of the NBER, *The*

may be some doubt at times not only about the speed at which inflation is going forward, but even as to whether it is occurring at all. However, when *all* price indexes continue to rise month by month and year by year at annual rates of 4% or more, it will be beyond dispute that inflation is under way; the faster it goes, the less noticeable will be the discrepancies between the different indexes and the less important the effect of bias.[6]

The fact that price movements are measured in terms of percentage changes per month or per year underlines a most important characteristic of inflation — it is a process that unfolds itself over *time*. For people who are living in an inflationary economy, it makes a great deal of difference whether the price level is rising at 5%, 15%, or 50% per annum; a pensioner, for example, will suffer hardship if the real value of his income is falling at 5% a year, but it will be tolerable compared with his suffering if the rate is 50%. During mild inflation, economic behavior will not be very different from what it would have been with a constant price level; but when prices are rising fast, much effort will be diverted to finding ways of avoiding loss and if possible profiting from the situation, with the result that re-sources are likely to be allocated less efficiently than they would otherwise have been — for example, through attempts to accumulate inventories (as an alternative to holding cash) well above the level that would have been aimed at under normal circumstances.

The analysis must therefore explain not only what caused the inflationary process to get under way in the first place, but also why it is going forward at, say, 10% per year rather than 5% or 25%; it must take account of the time lags that occur in it and allow for the effects of concomitant changes such as the expansion of productive capacity through investment and technological improvements. In other words, it must be dynamic. However, the static analysis centering on Figure 12.1 (p. 295) will still be relevant and useful in showing the various ways in which the inflationary process can be set in motion.

Price Statistics of the Federal Government (New York: National Bureau of Economic Research, 1961), found that the average annual 2% rise in the Consumer Price Index during the 1950's might have been due entirely to upward bias on this and other kinds.

[6] On the question of the definition and measurement of inflation — and indeed on all other aspects of it — see M. Bronfenbrenner and F. D. Holtzman, "A Survey of Inflation Theory," *American Economic Review*, Vol. 53 (September, 1963), pp. 593–661; and H. G. Johnson, *Essays in Monetary Economics* (Cambridge, Mass.: Harvard University Press, 1967), Chapter III.

2. Demand Inflation

The first of these ways has already been briefly described in Chapter 10 (pp. 245–247) and even more briefly in Chapter 3 (pp. 48–50). An autonomous increase in aggregate demand will at first cause physical output to rise, if it was initially below full-employment level; given fixed money wages and diminishing returns to labor, some increase in prices will occur as output expands. If aggregate demand is still excessive when output reaches its full-employment limit, an "inflationary gap" will exist and the price level will continue to rise. Some offset to the excess demand may be provided by increasing imports, but it may be supposed that the government will sooner or later take action to limit this; and although excess demand in one sector may be met for the time being by drawing on inventories and switching supplies from other sectors (for example, by diverting to the domestic market goods that had been intended for export), this action will merely generalize the excess demand by diffusing it among all branches of the economy. By causing a proportionate increase in the money value of full-employment output, the rise in prices will automatically generate an equivalent expansion in the total of money incomes. Far from choking off demand, it will provide the community with the means to spend more — though much will depend, of course, on the way in which the additional money income is allocated between the different groups of income recipients. As the newly generated money income is spent, it will cause prices to rise yet again, generating still more money income, and so on.

The process resembles the working of the Multiplier described in Chapter 6, except that where the Multiplier involves the expansion of output in real terms, the inflationary process increases the value of output only in money terms. Given the shape usually attributed to the short-run consumption function, the "real" Multiplier is *convergent*, in the sense that the successive increases in real demand become smaller and smaller until they are negligible and a new equilibrium is attained. Under inflation, on the other hand, aggregate demand can increase in money terms as fast or even faster than the money value of output, and so the analogy with the "real" Multiplier breaks down. Nonetheless, it prompts the question, may the inflationary process be similarly convergent, even though it may be so for different reasons?

The analysis in section 1 of Chapter 12 (p. 293 ff.) suggests that the answer is "yes" — provided that the quantity of "nominal" money is not allowed to increase. This can be shown with the aid of Figure 13.1, which is the same kind of three-quadrant diagram as Figure 12.1 on p. 295. To begin with, full-employment equilibrium exists, with output at Q_1, employment at N_1, and interest, prices, money wages, and the money supply at r_1, p_1, w_1, and M_s^1 respectively. This situation is now upset by an autonomous increase in aggregate demand, which shifts the IS curve to the right[7] to a new position IS_2; this intersects the original monetary-equilibrium curve, $L(M_s^1/p_1)$, above point Q_2 on the output axis, so that aggregate demand can be satisfied only by a level of output higher than the Q_1 available at full employment. This excess demand in the market for goods and services will cause the general price level to rise, thus reducing the purchasing power of the original stock of nominal money (M_s^1) and causing the $L(M/p)$ curve to shift to the left. When prices have risen as far as p_2, the monetary-equilibrium curve will have moved to the new position $L(M_s^1/p_2)$, intersecting the IS_2 curve vertically above Q_1. At this point, aggregate demand is once again equal to the output forthcoming at full employment, the gap has been eliminated, and prices will rise no further — the inflationary process has "converged" on a new equilibrium.

What happened was this: As the price level rose, the demand for money for transactions purposes increased, leaving less of the existing quantity M_s^1 available to satisfy asset demand. The interest rate increased in order to eliminate enough of the asset demand (and of the transactions demand also, since it too is interest-elastic) to bring the total demand for money back into balance with the supply. The rise in the interest rate choked off some of the investment demand (and some consumers' demand too, if saving is at all responsive to the increase in interest) to the point where aggregate demand was once more equal to Q_1.

As long as the quantity of nominal money remains M_s^1, then, equilibrium will be restored in Quadrant I with prices at p_2 and the interest rate at r_2. However, the increase in the price level will now have thrown Quadrant III's labor market out of equilibrium. The original level of real wages —

---

[7] If the initial change was an autonomous rise in consumers' demand, this will have reduced the propensity to save. In Figure 11.6 (p. 286) it will have shifted the curve $S(\bar{p},Q)$ closer to the vertical income axis. If the original increase was in investment demand, it will have pushed the curve $I(r)$ further to the right. Either of these effects will in turn cause the IS curve to shift to the right.

(w_1/p_1), or $(w/p)_1$ — was such that the demand and supply of labor were exactly in balance; but as the price level rises, the real wage rate will fall and excess demand for labor will develop. To the extent that rising prices gradually eliminate the inflationary "goods gap" in Quadrant I, they simultaneously create a "labor gap"[8] in Quadrant III. If the price level were to increase from p_1 to p_2 in a single jump, so that money wages re-

---

[8] These terms are similar to those introduced by Bent Hansen in his *A Study in the Theory of Inflation* (New York: Kelley, 1951). He, however, speaks of a "factor gap" rather than "labor gap"; the latter term is preferred in the present text because labor is the only factor of production whose supply and demand are specified. Insofar as the diffi-culty of obtaining extra labor may lead firms to demand more capital equipment, this will shift the *IS* curve in Figure 13.1 further to the right; the "capital gap" will give rise to a new "goods gap." See also R. Turvey and H. Brems, "The Factor and Goods Markets," *Economica*, Vol. 18 (February, 1951), pp. 57–68.

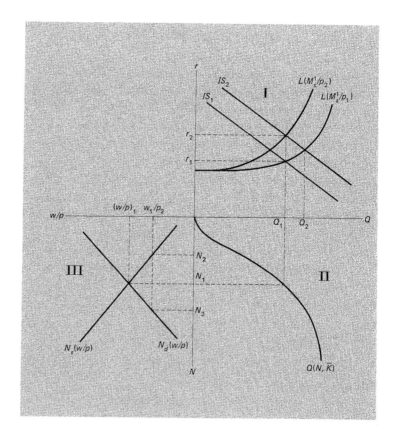

Fig. 13.1

The mechanism of inflation viewed in a static general equilibrium framework

mained at the w_1 level for the time being, the real wage rate would at once fall to w_1/p_2, and a maximum "labor gap" of $N_3 - N_2$ would be opened up. The pressure of this excess demand would then force the money wage rate rapidly upward in an attempt to offset the rise in prices and restore equilibrium at the original real wage $(w/p)_1$ — which would be reached when the money wage had risen to a level w_2 such that $w_2/p_2 = w_1/p_1 = (w/p)_1$. However, if prices go from p_1 to p_2 in a series of small steps, real wages will fall a little below $(w/p)_1$ at each step, creating enough excess demand for labor to cause money wages to rise; in this sequence, the maximum labor gap $N_3 - N_2$ will never be reached, because increases in money wages are following hard on the heels of increases in the price level. In either case, however, money wages must rise sufficiently to restore the level of real wages at which labor market equilibrium is achieved.

An appreciable lag of money wages behind prices will mean that the real wage rate is constantly below $(w/p)_1$ as long as the price level is rising. If the labor supply curve has the slope of $N_s(w/p)$ in Quadrant III, the number of man-hours the labor force is willing to work will be reduced below N_1, and the volume of output will consequently fall below Q_1; this fall will widen the goods gap of Quadrant I and put additional upward pressure on the price level. On the other hand, the wage lag will also mean that labor's share of total income is reduced; if wage earners have a higher MPC than other income recipients, aggregate real saving will be increased,[9] and the IS curve will be shifted leftward from its original position IS_2, causing the goods gap to narrow and offsetting to some extent (perhaps even more than offsetting) the widening that resulted from the fall in the labor supply. Both effects will, of course, disappear when equilibrium has at last been regained in the labor and goods market.

If the level at which prices eventually converge is considerably higher than that from which they started, and if it takes some time for the new equilibrium level to be reached, the process of getting there is likely to be complicated by expectational effects. Having been accustomed to price stability at the p_1 level, individuals and firms may at first assume that the rise in prices will soon be reversed or, at any rate, that it will not be followed by further increases. When the upward movement does in fact continue, they will come to count on an upward trend in the future, and their behavior will be altered in a number of ways.

One effect will be to reduce the demand for money in real terms (*i.e.*, for

---

[9] This is the "redistribution effect" described in Chapter 10, pp. 241–242.

M/p). The expectation of future reductions in its purchasing power will create an incentive to economize on the holding of money balances. If prices are going to rise 5% a year, $100 will be worth only $95.24 (*i.e.*, $100 × 100/105) in terms of what it will buy a year hence, and the holder will have incurred a real cost of $4.76 in addition to the yield forgone by not exchanging the money for some remunerative asset. It is true that the return on fixed-interest loans will also be reduced by the prospective price increase. For example, if interest is currently 5%, the $5 accruing on a $100 loan will be sufficient only to offset the fall in the real value of the principal and interest; the "real" interest rate will be zero, and the cost of holding the $100 will be no more than the reduction in its purchasing power. But (as noted earlier, on pp. 277–278) the relevant alternative to holding cash will now be the acquisition of stock and physical assets, which keep their real value when prices are rising. When the real yields obtainable from such assets are added to the expected fall in the purchasing power of money, the cost of retaining money balances will appear to be higher than if prices had been expected to remain unchanged. Consequently, the demand for them will be reduced. Thus, the current fall in the quantity of "real" money, which is occurring as a result of *actual* price increases and is causing Figure 13.1's $L(M_s/p)$ curve to shift to the left, will be matched to some extent by a reduction in demand due to the expectation of future price increases — so that the leftward movement of the $L(M_s/p)$ curve will be less than it would otherwise have been. To bring about a new equilibrium in Quadrant I, the *actual* price level will have to rise further than it would have had to in the absence of these expectations.

However, while a given rate of increase in actual prices will be causing the quantity of "real" money (M_s/p) to fall continuously over time, the demand for money will go on falling only if the *expected* rate of increase is itself continually increasing. A given rise in the expected rate (say from 0 to 5%) will cause a once-for-all reduction in the amount of "real" money everyone wishes to hold. When firms and individuals have adjusted their balances to the level that seems desirable in view of the increased real cost of holding them, there is no reason for them to wish to reduce these balances any further; they will seek to do so only if they come to expect that prices are going to rise still faster than had seemed probable earlier — say, by 8% instead of 5%. For the demand for "real" money to go on falling, then, the rate of expected price increases must be continually increasing.

Moreover, demand will not continue to fall in exact proportion to the rise in the rate of expected price increases. As the increasing real cost of retaining balances causes them to be reduced, the inconvenience of further reductions will become greater and greater. As long as money continues to be used at all, there will be some minimum real quantity below which demand cannot fall, since a complete synchronization of receipts and payments can never, in the nature of things, be achieved throughout the whole economy. Thus, the fall in the supply of "real" money must eventually overtake the fall in demand, with the result that the price level will at last be stabilized — though at a higher level than would have been reached if price expectations had remained passive (in the sense that the price level attained at each stage was expected to remain in force indefinitely). When this position is achieved, and the actual price level at last ceases to rise, there will be a downward revision of expectations, which will cause the demand for "real" money to increase. The $L(M_s/p)$ curve will be shifted to the left, the interest rate will rise above the level consistent with full-employment equilibrium, and the economy will move into a recession unless the monetary authorities (having up to this point refrained from increasing the quantity of nominal money) now provide whatever increase is needed in the nominal money supply to satisfy the revived demand for it.

Expectational effects on the IS curve through changes in investment demand and in the willingness to save have already been briefly indicated in Chapter 12 (p. 300) — though the analysis there was concerned not with rising but with falling prices. If business firms believe that prices are going to rise continuously in the foreseeable future, they will expect the stream of prospective net returns from current investment to increase steadily in money terms, compared with what returns would be if prices remained unchanged. If, in their view, the selling prices of their products will be going up at the same rate as the prices of their inputs (including the money wages they will be paying their labor), and if both input and output prices are expected to keep step with the rising general price level, then the prospective *rate* of return on current investment (*i.e.*, the MEI) will increase in money terms by exactly enough to offset the expected upward movement of prices, so that in real terms it will be unchanged. However, the expected price increases will reduce the real cost of financing investment projects through fixed-interest loans. If the current interest rate happens to be 6%, and if prices are thought likely to rise continuously at 4% per annum, the cost of borrowing will be (on the firms' reckoning) only 2% in real terms, so that projects that would not have been considered on the assumption of constant future prices will now appear worth undertaking. This inflationary expectation will cause the IS curve in Figure 13.1 to shift to the right of the IS_2 position (to which it moved as a result of the initial increase in aggregate demand), so that prices will have to rise further than would otherwise have been necessary in order to make the $L(M_s/p)$ curve intersect the IS curve above Q_1 in Quadrant I and thereby restore a noninflationary full-employment equilibrium.

From the point of view of investing business firms, the prospective rise in prices means that they can look forward to a continuous fall in the real value of the interest payments they will be making; but from the point of view of lenders (if they have price expectations similar to those of the firms) it means a fall in the real value of their future *receipts*. Insofar as interest rates influence saving, it follows that the expectation of rising prices will cause a reduction in the propensity to save, reinforcing the movement of the IS curve to the right. But making loans at fixed interest is not the only way of employing savings; other ways, such as the purchase of corporation stock or real estate, yield returns whose money value rises along with the price level. To the extent that savers are able to take advantage of these possibilities, they may very well go on saving as high a proportion of income as before – perhaps even increasing saving, if they believe that rising prices will enhance the real yield on these assets, for example, by bringing them large capital gains as stock prices go up.

Acquiring such "inflation-proof" assets may not, however, be possible for people with low incomes: these assets may not be purchasable in small quantities; dealing expenses may be high on modest transactions; and they may carry risks that cannot be offset by diversification when portfolios are small.[10] Instead of venturing into the stock or real estate markets, therefore, lower income groups are likely to hedge against inflation by accelerating their purchases of consumer durables; this will increase their consumption relative to income and represent a fall in the propensity to save.[11] If they can count on future increases in their money incomes (for

---

[10] Even when the average yield on stock of all kinds is rising in line with the price level, there will be some stock whose yields lag behind and others that race ahead. With ample funds, a buyer can hold a large enough selection to ensure that his overall return is about average; but if he could not afford more than a small holding of the stock of one corporation, which through bad luck or bad management failed to make a profit, he would be worse off than if he had lent at fixed interest.

[11] If it is thought preferable to regard as consumption only the part of the durables' value which is used up during the current year, the remainder will still count as saving

example, because their money wages are subject to escalation, or because past experience has made them expect that their wages will rise), it will even pay them to go into debt for this purpose, if finance companies are still prepared to give installment credit — since the future repayments will fall steadily as a proportion of their incomes.

Thus the expectation that prices will go on rising will cause the *IS* curve to lie further to the right than it would have done if expectations had been "passive," and it will make the goods gap wider than it would otherwise have been. It should be noted that a given rate of expected price increase will be associated with a given *position* of the *IS* curve; for the curve to go on moving further and further to the right, the rate of expected price increase must be continuously increasing, causing the "real" interest rate to go on falling so that it induces more and more investment demand and less and less saving. In this respect, the response of the *IS* curve to price expectations resembles that already observed with regard to the real demand for money as it affects the $L(M_s/p)$ curve. Thus, if prices are rising at a steady 5% per annum, and if everyone expects this rate of increase to be maintained in the future, the position of the *IS* curve will be fixed, and the real demand for money will be of a given size relative to real income and the nominal interest rate. The only continuing change, in these circumstances, will be the steady fall in the real money supply, M_s/p, brought about by the actual rise in the price level, and this will eventually bring the inflation to an end — always provided, of course, that the quantity of nominal money is not allowed to increase.

3. Inflation, the Money Supply, and Budgetary Policy

If, then, inflation can be made to "converge" by holding the nominal money supply constant, what is to prevent the monetary authorities from doing just that? Indeed, why should they not prevent inflation from developing in the first place, by actually *reducing* the quantity of nominal money? If, when the initial increase in aggregate demand takes place, the

---

(see pp. 15 and 112) but it will also count as investment in "consumers' capital" — as, indeed, it does in the case of the purchase of a house. Either way, it has the effect of helping to push the *IS* curve further to the right.

authorities reduced M_s^1 to a lower level M_s^0 such that $M_s^0/p_1 = M_s^1/p_2$, the monetary-equilibrium curve would immediately move to a new position coinciding with the $L(M_s^1/p_2)$ curve shown in Figure 13.1. Aggregate demand would balance aggregate supply at the level of output Q_1, there would be no goods gap, the labor market would remain in equilibrium at the N_1 level of employment, and the price level would continue unchanged at p_1. Why not, then, leave it to the monetary authorities to prevent inflation or, at any rate, to check it once it has begun?

Unfortunately, such a policy would be much more difficult to apply in practice than it appears in the simplified model of Figure 13.1, and it could easily be incompatible with the maintenance of full employment. Suppose the authorities were to adopt the simple rule of reducing the nominal money supply whenever prices begin to rise, continuing to do so until price stability is regained; and suppose that the labor market is not the "competitive" one of Figure 13.1's Quadrant III, but a more realistic one in which labor unions are strong enough to enforce a minimum level of money wages. An autonomous increase in aggregate demand, occurring when output happens to be below the full-employment level Q_1, will not only cause output to expand but will also cause prices to begin rising well before Q_1 is reached.[12] If the authorities react by immediately reducing the nominal money supply, so that the interest rate rises sufficiently to choke back aggregate demand to its original level, prices and output will both remain the same as before;[13] price stability will have been maintained at the cost of preventing any reduction in unemployment.

On the other hand, a policy of permitting prices to rise as long as employment is less than full, and of reducing the nominal money supply only when excess demand at Q_1 is forcing up the price level in an unambiguously inflationary manner, would require the authorities to know precisely what level of employment is "full" — and this, as has already been argued in Chapter 4,[14] may be very difficult when there is a large amount of

---

[12] Provided, of course, that there are diminishing returns to labor, as implied by the shape of Quadrant II's production function $Q(N, \bar{K})$. With money wages fixed, the existence of diminishing returns means that the "aggregate supply curve" introduced in Chapter 10 will have the upward curving shape of the curve $s(Q, \bar{w})$ in Figure 10.2, so that higher levels of output are associated with higher price levels; see pp. 235–237.

[13] That is, by reducing M_s, the authorities will have caused the $L(M_s/p)$ curve to shift to the left so that it exactly offsets the original rightward shift of the *IS* curve, which it will now intersect at a point vertically above the original level of Q.

[14] See pp. 82–91.

frictional unemployment due to current changes in the structure of the economy. Moreover, the authorities' task is one that continues endlessly; as the stock of capital grows and technology gradually improves, the full-employment level of output will be increasing and the real demand for money associated with it at any given interest rate will be growing. External disturbances, changes in payments habits, and variations in the pattern of relative prices will also be altering the amount of nominal money needed to satisfy the demand at any given price level. Not only will the authorities be making constant adjustments from day to day and week to week, but they will also have to consider the rate of growth in the money supply likely to be needed over the next twelve months or more. For these purposes, no simple rule can be laid down; the authorities must run a continuing analysis of the situation as it develops and alter the nominal money supply whenever and to whatever extent they think necessary. All the problems of timing noted in Chapter 12 (pp. 308–310) can arise, and there is also the possibility of errors in judgment, so that monetary restriction may either be so severe as to "overkill" the inflation and cause recession or be so late that the price level goes on rising after all.

However, these difficulties are not peculiar to monetary policy as such; if the government instead tried to check inflation by means of budgetary policy — which would exert its effects via the IS curve instead of the $L(M_s/p)$ curve — it too would be faced with the problem of time lags and might over- or underestimate the amount of pressure required. What *is* special about monetary policy is that reductions in the nominal money supply will cause the interest rate to rise. If the original movement from IS_1 to IS_2 in Figure 13.1 had been precisely offset by a rise in the monetary equilibrium curve from $L(M_s^1/p_1)$ to $L(M_s^0/p_1)$ — which coincides with the $L(M_s^1/p_2)$ curve shown in the diagram, since $M_s^0/p_1 = M_s^1/p_2$ by assumption — the price level and the volume of output would have remained unchanged at p_1 and Q_1 respectively, but the interest rate would have risen from r_1 to r_2. If further rightward movements of the IS curve were similarly offset by leftward shifts in the $L(M_s/p)$ curve, r would climb still higher.

But increases in the interest rate create a problem with regard to the government's borrowing requirements. If the budget is currently in balance, with revenue exactly sufficient to finance expenditure, the total public debt will be neither increasing nor diminishing; the "net borrowing requirement" will be zero. However, unless the outstanding debt was originally financed entirely by the sale of irredeemable bonds, at any given time some part of it will be coming due for repayment, and the government will need to sell new securities in order to redeem the maturing old ones. Thus there will still be a "gross borrowing requirement" even when no net borrowing is taking place. The amount of this gross requirement depends on (a) the average length of the outstanding debt — if it consists mainly of long-term bonds, the proportion maturing in any week or month will be small, while if it is made up wholly of three-month Treasury Bills, it must be refinanced in its entirety four times a year; (b) the way in which past borrowing has been done, since this may cause a "bunching" up of maturities at a given time; and (c) the total amount of debt in existence. If a large proportion of the debt happens to fall due for refinancing just after the interest rate has been forced up by the monetary authorities' efforts to prevent inflation, the government will find that the interest cost of the public debt has sharply increased; the longer the period for which interest stays high, the greater the proportion of the debt that will have to be renewed on unfavorable terms. If refinancing is done by the issue of long-term bonds, the higher interest cost will persist until they reach maturity some years later. On the other hand, if maturing bonds are replaced by short-term borrowing, in the hope that this debt can later be refinanced by long-term bond issues when the interest rate has fallen again, the average length of the total debt will be reduced,[15] and the gross borrowing requirement will increase in the future. The prices of existing government bonds will fall, with the likelihood that speculation on further falls will drive them lower still; the public credit will be eroded, and the government may begin to fear that it will soon be unable to raise fresh loans on any terms at all.

If the government could run a budget surplus large enough to permit all maturing debt to be redeemed out of current revenue, the need for new borrowing would be eliminated and the problem would be solved. It is difficult to increase rates of taxation quickly, however, and it may be impossible to reduce expenditure sufficiently to yield a big enough surplus, since the surplus would have to be very large indeed if the total debt is high in proportion to revenue and the average length of the debt

---

[15] This is the reverse of the "funding" described on p. 304. When bonds are replaced by Treasury Bills or other short-term obligations, the government may be said to be "un-funding" its debt.

fairly short.[16] If this solution is ruled out, and the government is unwilling to see bond prices fall below some minimum level, it will have to instruct the monetary authorities to intervene in the market and absorb any excess supply of bonds, which would otherwise have pushed the price below the designated "support level." But in this case the authorities have been compelled to abandon their earlier policy of restricting the nominal money supply and actually to reverse their policy by creating new money through the purchase of bonds.[17]

Preventing the price of bonds from falling is equivalent to preventing the interest rate from rising. Suppose the aim is to keep interest at the r_1 level in Figure 13.1, even though the IS curve has just moved from IS_1 to IS_2. It was seen earlier (p. 317) that the excess demand will generate a rise in prices that will carry the $L(M_s/p)$ curve from $L(M_s^1/p_1)$ to $L(M_s^1/p_2)$ and cause interest to rise to r_2, as long as the nominal money supply remain M_s^1. To maintain the interest rate at r_1, the authorities must *increase* the money supply so as to push the $L(M_s/p)$ curve to the right of $L(M_s^1/p_1)$ until it intersects IS_2 at the level of r_1. This increase will make it impossible to close the "inflationary gap," which in fact will now be larger than the original Q_1Q_2. Prices will rise and go on rising; the authorities will be obliged to continue increasing the money supply indefinitely (or until the IS curve moves back to the left, either autonomously or under the pressure

---

[16] The surplus will be sufficient to redeem all maturing debt if $sR = kD$, where R is tax revenue, s is the proportion of it not required to meet current expenditure, D is total marketable interest-bearing debt, and k is the fraction of D maturing in the period over which R is measured. Dividing both sides by R gives

$$s = k\frac{D}{R}.$$

If the ratio of debt to annual expenditure, D/R, is 4, and if the average maturity is four years, so that $k = 0.25$, new borrowing can be avoided only if $s = 1$, i.e., if government spending is stopped altogether and all tax revenue is used to retire debt. In the United States, D/R was roughly 1.4 in mid-1968, while k was about 0.2, so that s would have had to be 0.28 to satisfy the equation. It need hardly be pointed out that a budget surplus of more than one-quarter of current revenue is much too large to be a practical possibility. Still, if even a small surplus can be achieved, it will ease the situation in another way: a cut in public spending (or a rise in taxes that cuts private spending) will reduce aggregate demand, shifting the IS curve to the left; this will lower the interest rate again, even if only by a little.

[17] The authorities' purchases are open market operations of the expansionary kind (See chapter 11, pp. 255–256); they increase the commercial banks' reserves and thereby enable the banks to increase their own deposits, so that the total money supply is increased.

of fiscal measures) in order to offset the rising trend of prices and keep the $L(M_s/p)$ curve in the desired position. Interest rate stability will be achieved at the cost of continuing inflation.

The government may, of course, take the view that it is more important to prevent inflation than to stabilize the interest rate and allow the monetary authorities to contract the money supply while it grapples as best it can with the problem of debt refinancing. Unfortunately, this is not the only problem it will have to face. Government securities are important assets in the portfolios of banks and other financial institutions, and a substantial fall in their market values will put a severe strain on the monetary system. There will be widespread discontent among individual bondholders whose assets fall in value and among home buyers faced with higher mortgage rates; this will be politically embarrassing to a government that depends on their votes. To the extent that higher interest rates discourage investment more than other elements of aggregate demand, the economy's growth rate will be reduced because of the slower rate of expansion of the capital stock; if public opinion sets a higher value on growth than on price stability, this too may inhibit the government's anti-inflationary policy. Foreign countries, forced to raise their own interest rates to check outflows of capital funds attracted by higher yields in the domestic economy, will protest that they are being pushed into recession and will urge the government to relax the pressure on interest rates.

Though these additional difficulties need not cause the policy of monetary restriction to be abandoned altogether, they may very well cause it to be applied less rigorously: the $L(M_s/p)$ curve can be made to rise, but not by enough to carry the interest rate to the r_2 level; the "inflationary gap" will be reduced but not wholly eliminated; and the price level will therefore increase. If the rate at which prices rise depends on the size of the gap,[18] the inflation will proceed more slowly than it would have done if interest had been prevented from rising above r_1; but as long as the government is not willing to allow interest to go all the way to r_2, the nominal money supply will have to be continually increased to offset the tendency of rising prices to shift the $L(M_s/p)$ curve to the left, and the inflation will not be brought to a halt by monetary restriction.

---

[18] This assumption is "external" to the static model presented in Figure 13.1. The latter merely indicates the condition of short-run equilibrium and the changes that can be expected if these conditions are not fulfilled; it does not show whether the changes will occur quickly or slowly, because it has no time dimension. See above, p. 315.

In these circumstances, the only possibility of convergence will be through a leftward movement of the *IS* curve — that is, through a fall in the real demand for goods and services. Various reasons why this should happen have already been briefly indicated in earlier chapters.[19] If there is a persistent tendency for money wages to lag behind prices, real consumption will be reduced by the redistribution effect if wage earners happen to have a higher MPC than other groups. However, unless the lag is continually lengthening (so that real wages w/p fall steadily lower), this shift in consumption will merely push the *IS* curve a certain distance to the left at the moment when the inflation begins and thereafter cause no further shift — it will be a once-for-all effect, which could indeed be reversed if the lag were to shorten, in which case the *IS* curve would move back to the right. The Pigou effect, by contrast, will push the curve further and further to the left as long as prices go on rising, since the real value of cash assets will then be continuously falling; though unless the influence of asset holdings on consumers' behavior is strong, the push will not be very forceful.

Another continuing reduction in real consumption will be brought about by the effect of rising prices on certain money incomes (such as pensions, interest payments on bonds, and certain salaries and professional fees) which are fixed by law, contract, and custom for long periods. They will be adjusted from time to time (for example, by new legislation to increase social security payments), but the consequent revival of their recipients' real consumption will be only temporary, falling away again as prices continue to climb. However, when inflation has gone on long enough to make everyone expect it to continue in the future, fixed-income recipients will try to get these payments adjusted more and more frequently, for instance, by tying social security benefits to an appropriate price index so that they increase automatically when prices rise. The more successful these efforts, the less will the recipients' real consumption be reduced, and the smaller, therefore, will be the leftward movement of the *IS* curve.

If other countries' prices remain unchanged, inflation will make exports dearer and dearer in foreign markets, while imports will become relatively cheaper in the domestic market, as long as the exchange rate is unaltered. Given appropriate price elasticities of demand,[20] the volume of imports

---

[19] See pp. 242 and 250.
[20] See pp. 206–209.

demanded will rise and that of exports will fall, thereby diminishing aggregate demand in the domestic market and shifting the *IS* curve to the left. But the concomitant balance-of-payments deficit, which will be increasing continually as inflation proceeds, will sooner or later cause the exchange rate to fall, reviving the demand for exports and reducing that for imports — with the result that the *IS* curve will move to the right again.

When all these considerations are taken together, it seems that the original rightward shift of the *IS* curve to IS_2 will be followed by a movement back towards the left during the early stages of inflation. Then, as prices continue to rise — as they will, if the second movement has not completely canceled out the first — the curve will begin to drift back toward the right. At some point, everyone will begin to expect prices to go on rising in the future, and this expectation (for the various reasons given earlier) will cause an additional rightward shift, carrying the curve to the right of the IS_2 position. If the government tries to push it back by reducing its own demand for goods and services and/or by raising taxes (and cutting transfers) in order to diminish the private sector's demand, its task will be easier the more quickly it acts; the further the inflation has progressed, the larger the budget surplus (measured in real terms) that will be needed to eliminate the inflationary gap. But it was argued in Chapter 9 [21] that public expenditure is hard to contract without major policy changes; that it is difficult to increase taxes if they are already at high rates; and that it takes time to do either. The government may find that whatever surplus it can arrange immediately will not shift the *IS* curve far enough to the left to halt the inflation, and that during the time it takes to budget for a larger one, the curve will have moved further to the right, making it necessary to increase the surplus yet again. When (and if) [22] the surplus eventually becomes large enough to halt the inflation, prices will have risen to a level appreciably higher than that from which they started.

Even if the government makes no deliberate effort to shift the *IS* curve by means of budgetary policy, the effects of inflation on its real expenditure and revenue may nevertheless cause the curve to move. As prices rise, spending programs drawn up in money terms will become inadequate to achieve their objectives; if the legislature refuses further appropriations,

---

[21] See pp. 230–231.

[22] It may be that even the largest attainable surplus is not enough to wipe out the inflationary gap — or that a surplus is not possible at all. In wartime, for example, no government is likely to reduce military spending merely to avoid inflation.

the amount of government expenditure must fall in real terms, causing the
IS curve to shift to the left. Normally, however, governments are expected
to provide a given physical volume of services (such as defense, law enforcement, and diplomatic representation), increasing their money outlays appropriately when rising prices make such provision more costly;
real expenditure will then remain unchanged and the *IS* curve will be
unaffected.

On the other hand, if the tax system is progressive, revenue will be
increasing in real terms. When prices and money incomes rise simultaneously in the same proportion, real income remains unchanged; but the
increased money incomes are subject to higher rates of tax, so that a
smaller proportion of real income is left in the hands of the taxpayers,
causing them to reduce their real consumption. Provided the government
does not increase its own real expenditure, this reduction will shift the
IS curve to the left.[23] The effect will be less, the longer the time lag between the receipt of income and the payment of tax on it, since the inter-
vening rise in prices will have reduced the real value of the tax by the
time it is paid. Even so, prices would have to rise faster and faster, accelerating at the same rate as the average rate of taxation, in order to
prevent tax payments from taking a larger proportion of real income.[24]

---

[23] The taxpayers themselves will, of course, be saving less than before in real terms,
as well as consuming less; the increase in saving that shifts *IS* to the left will be that
done by the government — that is, the budget surplus due to rise in revenue in excess
of expenditure.

[24] With a one-period lag, the proportion of current income paid in tax period 2
will be $t_1 Y_1/Y_2$, where t_1 is the average rate of tax applicable in period 1; similarly
the proportion in period 3 will be $t_2 Y_2/Y_3$, where t_2 is higher than t_1 because higher
money incomes have moved all taxpayers further up a progressive tax scale. If money
incomes have risen in exactly the same proportion as the price level, then $Y_1/Y_2 = p_1/p_2$
and $Y_2/Y_3 = p_2/p_3$; and the condition for tax payments to be a constant fraction of
income can be written

$$t_1 \frac{p_1}{p_2} = t_2 \frac{p_2}{p_3},$$

which can be rearranged as

$$\frac{t_2}{t_1} = \frac{p_3}{p_2} \Big/ \frac{p_2}{p_1}.$$

— so that if t_2 were 12% and t_1 10%, the rise in prices between periods 2 and 3 would
have to be 20% faster than that between periods 1 and 2 if the proportion of total income taken in tax were not to increase. It follows that if prices are rising at a constant
rate, a progressive tax system *must* reduce taxpayers' disposable real income in spite
of the existence of the lag.

If, in addition, the government is slow to adjust social security benefits and other transfer incomes to offset the effects of price increases, the real consumption of the recipients will fall, assisting the leftward movement of the *IS* curve. The larger the part the government plays in the economy — *i.e.*, the greater the proportion of public to private goods-and-services spending, the bigger the share of transfers in the total of private incomes, and the higher the general level (as distinct from the progression) of taxes — the more strongly these effects will operate, and the more the system of public finance will act as an automatic stabilizer to reduce inflationary pressure even when the government takes no special measures to that end. If the government does adopt a positive budgetary policy, the effects just mentioned will make its task easier.

4. "Cost-Push" and "Demand-Shift"

At the beginning of Section 2 it was assumed that influation was started by an autonomous increase in aggregate demand occurring at a time when output was already at its full-employment level: the excess demand "pulled" the price level of goods and services upward, and though the level of money wages also rose, it was a consequence and not a cause of the inflationary pressure. By contrast, in the "cost-push" theory of inflation, the causal sequence is reversed: the initial impulse is given by an autonomous rise in money wages or other input prices, in response to which the prices of "final" goods and services are raised to cover the increase in costs. The rise in prices, however, causes real wages to fall back to their previous level, and the forces that brought about the original rise in money wages then cause them to increase yet again, with the result that prices will be raised once more — and so on. At each stage, it is the rise in costs that pushes up prices; there does not have to be any excess demand for goods and services — indeed, the process could go forward even if aggregate demand were somewhat below the level needed for full-employment output.

A basic assumption of the "cost-push" theory is the existence of strong labor unions that insist on compensating increases in money wages whenever the price level rises, so as to prevent any reduction in real wages; the labor market consequently has a "floor" of the kind described earlier in Chapter 4 (p. 93). From time to time, when the unions feel strong enough, they will try to increase the real wage by claiming money wage adjustments in excess of those needed merely to offset rising prices, and when they succeed, the increases will give the initial push that sets the wage-price spiral in motion. Alternatively, an autonomous rise in the cost of imported inputs may provide the push; as long as the unions respond to the consequent increase in output prices by forcing a rise in money wages, a cost-inflationary spiral will ensue. It is also assumed that business enterprises fix the selling prices of their products by calculating "direct" costs per unit of output (*i.e.*, wages and materials) and adding a conventional percentage markup to cover overhead and provide a margin of profit. When prices are "cost determined" (or administered) in this way, an increase in money wages will automatically be followed by compensatory price increases, which will reduce the level of real wages again and lead to further wage claims.

The timing of the process will, of course, vary from one industry to another, depending on differences in the strength and leadership of unions, on the amount of resistance that employers put up against wage claims, and on the rapidity with which firms raise their products' prices when higher wages have increased their production costs. It will also be complicated by unions' attempts to maintain "differentials" between their own members' earnings and those in other occupations, as, for example, when locomotive engineers demand higher wages on the ground that a recent rise in porters' pay has narrowed the gap between them. If there is an appreciable lag in the adjustment of selling prices when money wages have risen, real wages will be increased for the time being at the expense of profits, and aggregate demand may be stimulated through the redistribution effect — with the result that some demand inflation will be injected into the original "cost-push" sequence if the economy is already near full employment.

It was seen earlier that demand inflation must eventually be halted if the supply of nominal money is not allowed to increase; the same thing is true of cost inflation. Suppose the economy is initially in the equilibrium situation given in Figure 13.1 by the intersection of IS_1 and $L(M_s^1/p_1)$ with output and employment at Q_1 and N_1 respectively; but with the difference that the supply curve of labor is no longer the $N_s(w/p)$ of Quadrant III, but the vertical broken line below $(w/p)_1$ as far as its intersection with $N_d(w/p)$ — this is the "wage floor" established by the labor unions. If the unions try to raise the floor by insisting on increases in money wages, the supply curve will tend to move to the left; but if business firms im-

mediately raise their selling prices when higher money wages increase
their production costs, the labor supply curve will be held back in its
original position, and real wages will remain $(w/p)_1$. However, the rise
in prices and money wages means that more and more money will be
needed for transactions purposes. If the nominal money supply is not increased, less money will be available to satisfy asset demand, and the
rate of interest will be forced up; in Quadrant I, the $L(M_s/p)$ curve will
move to the left as the real quantity of money falls, and will now cut IS_1
to the left of Q_1 so that aggregate demand is no longer sufficient to absorb
the whole of full-employment output. As demand falls, firms will be more
cautious about raising prices and will begin to cut output instead; with
employment somewhat reduced, the marginal productivity of labor will
rise, and firms will be willing to pay higher real wages than before. Further
increases in money wages will no longer be offset by price rises, and the
vertical wage floor will at last move to the left, intersecting the $N_d(w/p)$
curve at a level of employment less than N_1. When real wages have reached
the level aimed at by the unions, no further wage claims will be presented,
and prices will cease to rise. The cost inflation will have converged on
a new equilibrium.

This outcome, however, will be possible only if the government and
monetary authorities are prepared to allow the interest rate to rise and
the level of employment to fall to whatever extent is necessary to halt the
inflation. If they are unwilling (for any of the reasons put forward in the
previous section) to let the interest rate go above a certain level, it will
be necessary to increase the quantity of nominal money whenever rising
prices threaten to push the $L(M_s/p)$ curve too far to the left. If the government is politically committed to maintaining full employment, the
money supply must be expanded to prevent price increases from pushing
$L(M_s/p)$ away from its original intersection with IS_1. As long as aggregate
demand is prevented from falling, firms need not hesitate to raise their
prices whenever increases in money pages push up production costs, nor
need the unions moderate their wage claims for fear of creating unemployment among their members; thus, the wage-price spiral will continue indefinitely — or rather, it will not be halted by any obstacle on the monetary
side of the economy. If, in these circumstances, the inflation does converge
after all, it will be because progressive taxation is reducing real consumption through its effect on disposable incomes, or because government expenditure is declining in real terms, or because fixed-income recipients'

real demand is falling, or because of the Pigou effect — that is, for the various reasons that have already been noted as likely to operate under demand inflation. Expectational effects, too, will be generated in the way observed earlier; if they are so strong as to outweigh the forces making for convergence and so cause a net increase in aggregate demand, they will inject an element of "demand-pull" into the cost inflation already under way.

The fact that money wages are being raised through collective bargaining between labor unions and employers is not in itself evidence that inflation is of the cost-push type; given the institutional structure of the labor market, the negotiating procedure will be the same whether wage claims are prompted by rises in the cost of living, or by unions' feeling that a labor shortage has improved their bargaining power, or by the unions' determination to increase real wages. Similarly, the fact that business firms are raising prices in response to increases in wage costs is not an infallible indicator of cost inflation; the rise in money wages may have been due to their own attempts to expand output to meet an autonomous increase in demand,[25] as an alternative to raising their prices in the first instance. Even if prices and wages are spiraling upwards against a background of excess capacity and unemployment, it is still not safe to assume that no demand-pull is present. Recent changes in the composition of demand may have created a good deal of frictional unemployment, so that the full-employment level of output [26] is actually less than the current level of aggregate demand, low though that may appear to be.

Thus, a process that seems at first sight to be one of cost inflation may in reality be due to the pressure of excess demand or, at any rate, may combine both demand-pull and cost-push elements. The problem is to determine the comparative strength of the two. In his well-known study of the relationship between unemployment and money wage changes in

---

[25] In a perfectly competitive labor market, firms' efforts to outbid one another for labor will push up money wages directly; but where they belong to employers' organizations that negotiate collectively with unions, individual firms will be inhibited from offering higher wage rates. The increase will come about through unions realizing that the demand for labor has risen and that employers are now likely to offer less resistance to a wage claim. If, pending the negotiation of new standard rates, firms try to attract more labor by offering bonuses and other above-standard inducements that are not counted as part of the wage rate proper, there will be a tendency for earnings to rise faster than wage rates. This "wage-drift," as it is called, is usually regarded as a symptom of demand inflation.

[26] See the definitions given above on pp. 85–89.

Britain during the last hundred years,[27] A. W. Phillips found that wage rates rose rapidly when unemployment was low, fell when it was high, and remained unchanged when about 5½% of the labor force was out of work. Plotting in a diagram the points relating wage changes to unemployment in the various years, he found that the best "fit" was given by the curve shown as AA in Figure 13.2. He took this to mean that when unemployment was below 5½% the number of vacancies exceeded the numbers seeking work, *i.e.*, that there was an excess of demand for labor, and that this excess demand caused wage rates to climb; while a level of unemployment greater than 5½% meant an excess supply of labor, which caused wages to fall.

If it is assumed that the demand for labor was a reflection of the aggregate demand for goods and services, and that changes in money wages caused the general price level to alter (though not to the same extent, because of year-to-year increases in labor productivity, which in themselves reduce wage costs per unit of output), the shape of AA — the "Phillips curve" — is consistent with the hypothesis that price increases, when they occurred, were caused mainly by the pressure of excess aggregate

---

[27] A. W. Phillips, "The Relationship Between Unemployment and the Rate of Change of Money Wage Rates in the United Kingdom, 1861–1957," *Economica*, Vol. 25 (November, 1958), pp. 283–299.

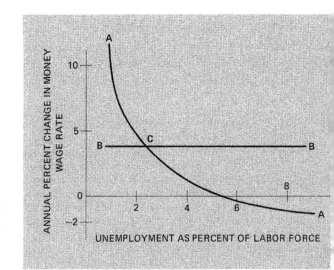

Fig. 13.2

The Phillips Curve

demand. Had money wages risen only in response to unions' efforts to maintain or increase real wages regardless of the supply-and-demand balance in the labor market, there would have been a scatter of points indicating changes in money wages in the different years, with the height of each point depending only on the magnitude of recent price changes and on the unions' success in obtaining equivalent (or more than equivalent) money wage adjustments. A line showing the *average* annual change in money wages could then have been horizontal like Figure 13.2's BB, implying that wage and price increases were not determined by demand and supply pressures in the labor and goods markets – which would, of course, be consistent with the hypothesis of pure cost inflation. The shape of AA thus appears to suggest that demand-pull was stronger than cost-push during the period covered by the figures. Phillips also found that *changes* in the level of unemployment, as well as the absolute level, affected the rate at which money wages rose or fell – presumably because firms interpreted a fall in unemployment as a sign that demand was increasing and therefore tried to hire more labor in anticipation of it; while rising prices did, in fact, induce *some* cost-inflationary wage increases in a few particular years when unusually large rises in import prices caused unprecedented jumps in the cost of living.

R. G. Lipsey, reworking Phillips' data, calculated[28] that over four-fifths of the variance in money wage rates could be associated with the level of unemployment and its rate of change. However, he also found that the relationship was much weaker in the later part of the period than in the years before 1913, and that price changes were much more important as an explanatory variable after 1920. A "Phillips curve" fitted to British data for 1923–1939 and 1948–1957 resembles neither AA nor BB in Figure 13.2 but a combination of the two such as ACB, with the CB section nearly horizontal at a level of money wage increase rather less than 1%, and with the point C vertically above the 4% level of unemployment – suggesting that while excess demand for labor would still cause wages to rise, cost-inflationary pressures would take over in times of excess supply, preventing the latter from forcing wage rates down.[29]

---

[28] R. G. Lipsey, "The Relation Between Unemployment and the Rate of Change of Money Wage Rates in the United Kingdom, 1862–1957: A Further Analysis," *Economica*, Vol. 28 (February, 1960), pp. 1–31.

[29] It should be emphasized that the evidence here is "suggestive" rather than conclusive; see Lipsey's own caution on the point, *op. cit.*, p. 31.

Applying a similar analysis to the U. S. economy in the period 1900–1958, R. J. Bhattia[30] found much less evidence of a Phillips-type relationship; the effect of cost-of-living changes on changes in earnings appeared to be greater than that of the level of unemployment in the period as a whole, while in the post-1948 years it was "not possible to determine whether changes in prices are the causal variable, or whether prices rise because the unions are able to extract large wage concessions independently of price changes." Other studies[31] have found a connection between changes in money wages and the level of profits in the United States since World War II, but it is not clear whether the relationship ought to be attributed to demand-pull or to cost-push pressures. If it resulted from business firms autonomously increasing their profit margins, it would be the latter: "markup inflation," or "profit-push," is simply another possible species of cost inflation. If, on the other hand, profits rose because excess demand was forcing up prices ahead of money wages, the observed relationship would be consistent with a diagnosis of demand inflation.

Another relationship, this time clearly indicative of cost-push, is that found between increases in money wages and the strength of labor unions. In a study of the United States for 1963–1966, for example, Gail Pierson classified industries as weakly unionized or strongly unionized according to the percentage of the industry's workers who were in establishments where a majority of the work force was under some form of collective bargaining agreement.[32] She found that when there was low unemployment, workers in the two groups of industries received almost equal wage gains. When considerable unemployment existed, however, the strongly unionized workers received wage increases between 0.6 and 1.7% greater than those in the weakly unionized group. Miss Pierson concluded from these results that unions can affect the rate of change of wages independent of the demand for labor and, therefore, that "union strength does make a

---

[30] R. J. Bhattia, "Unemployment and the Rate of Change of Money Earnings in the United States, 1900–1958," *Economica*, Vol. 28 (August, 1961), pp. 286–296.

[31] For example, a further one by Bhattia, "Profits and the Rate of Change in Money Earnings in the United States, 1935–1959," *Economica*, Vol. 29 (August, 1962), pp. 255–262; or G. L. Perry, *Unemployment, Money Wage Rates, and Inflation* (Cambridge, Mass.: M.I.T. Press, 1966).

[32] G. Pierson, "The Effect of Union Strength on the U.S. 'Phillips Curve'," *American Economic Review*, Vol. 58 (June, 1968), pp. 456–467. The initial investigation of this relationship was carried out in the context of the British economy; see A. G. Hines, "Trade Unions and Wage Inflation in the United Kingdom, 1893–1961," *Review of Economic Studies*, Vol. 31 (October, 1964), pp. 221–252.

difference; it significantly worsens the terms of the tradeoff between un-employment and inflation."

All these considerations suggest that, whatever may have been the case before 1917 or even before 1941, the possibility of cost inflation is a real one in present-day conditions; and this possibility, as will be seen presently, is of some importance from the point of view of public policy. Meanwhile, it is necessary to take note of one more theory of inflation, namely the "intersectoral demand shift" hypothesis of Charles Schultze.[33] This theory was put forward as an attempt to explain the price increases of 1955–1957, in view of the fact that neither demand-pull nor cost-push appeared to be operating at that time. Schultze argued that if prices and money wages are assumed to be rigid downward but flexible upward, a change in the *pattern* of demand will cause prices to rise in those sectors of the economy where demand has risen, but will not cause them to fall in the sectors where demand has been reduced, with the result that the average of all prices will necessarily rise even though aggregate demand has neither risen nor fallen. As the demand-gaining sectors attempt to increase output, they will bid up money wages and the prices of the material inputs they use; to the extent that labor and materials cannot simply be reallocated from the demand-losing industries (*i.e.*, if these factors of production are neither homogeneous nor perfectly mobile), the general level of money wages and other input prices will rise. The disturbance of wage differentials between industries and occupations will also cause some upward readjustment of money wages in sectors that have not themselves gained demand. In some of the demand-losing sectors, prices may actually be raised; with diminished sales and output, overhead costs per unit may have risen sufficiently to cause firms to feel that an increase in markup is needed to cover them.

On the other hand, there are sectors in which the assumption of downward price rigidity is not valid, and if they happen to be the demand losers, they will register a fall in prices that could offset the rises in the demand-gaining sectors, leaving the general price level unchanged. Moreover, when demand shifts back to a sector that lost it earlier, but which still has unemployed labor and excess capacity, that sector will be able to reexpand output to meet the revived demand without raising prices.

---

[33] C. L. Schultze, "Recent Inflation in the United States," Study Paper No. 1 for Joint Economic Committee, *Study of Employment, Growth and Price Levels* (Washington: U.S. Government Printing Office, 1959).

Conceivably, demand shift to an excess capacity sector from one whose prices are flexible downward could cause prices to fall in the latter without rising in the former — thus causing the general price level to move *downward* in a "demand-shift *deflation.*" Much will depend, too, on the amount and the speed of the change in the composition of demand. If the demand for each sector's output is rising at the same pace as its productive capacity is growing through investment and technological progress, or is falling at a rate that just matches the rundown of its capacity through depreciation and the "wastage" of its labor force, all prices could remain unchanged. The mere fact that the pattern of demand is changing is not in itself sufficient to cause inflation; and Schultze's claim that demand changes must be regarded as a continuing source of upward pressure on the general price level does not, therefore, seem well founded. But it is certainly possible to agree that there will be times when the large-scale introduction of new commodities or sudden changes in preferences or in income distribution, will produce a sufficiently large dislocation of the demand pattern to start the price level rising in the way he describes.

Like demand-pull and cost-push, "demand-shift" inflation will eventually bring itself to an end if the quantity of nominal money is not increased. Rising prices will reduce the real quantity of money, increase the rate of interest, and cause aggregate demand to fall. When not a single sector remains in which demand exceeds supply — or, alternatively, when excess supply in some sectors has become great enough to break through the downward rigidity of prices, so that price reductions offset such price increases as still occur in demand-gaining sectors — then the general price level will at last have been stabilized, though at the cost of considerable unemployment in the sectors with excess supply.

5. The Pace of Inflation

So far, attention has been focused mainly on the possible *causes* of inflation. But (as noted on p. 315) it is particularly important to account for the *speed* at which inflation goes forward, whatever may have been the impulse which originally started it off; for this purpose, a dynamic analysis is needed. The reader may already have noticed that the "Phillips curve" introduced in the last section does, in fact, embody a dynamic hypothesis: not only do money wages rise in response to excess demand in the labor market, but they also rise at an *annual* rate that depends on the amount of excess demand relative to the full-employment labor supply. A similar hypothesis with respect to the market for goods and services would make the annual rate of increase in the price level ($\dot{p}$) a function of the proportion by which aggregate demand (D) exceeds supply (S). In symbols:

$$\dot{p} = f\left(\frac{D - S}{S}\right)$$

— so that if $(D - S)/S$ happens to be 2%, $\dot{p}$ will be, say, 4%, while a 5% value of $(D - S)/S$ will give a $\dot{p}$ of, say, 10%, and so on. The essential point is that the movement of the price level is expressed as a rate of increase over *time*. In the case of a convergent demand inflation, the proportion by which prices must rise to restore equilibrium will depend on the size of the initial goods gap. In symbols,

$$\frac{\triangle p}{p} = \phi\left(\frac{D - S}{S}\right).$$

However, the left-hand side of the equation has no time dimension; unlike $\dot{p}$, which is a rate of increase per year, the price rise $\triangle p/p$ could be accomplished in a few hours or days or be stretched out over many months without ceasing to satisfy the equation. To explain why the price level should rise at a particular rate over time, it is necessary to examine the various lags that operate in the economy and to allow for concomitant changes — such as the expansion of productive capacity through investment and technical improvements — that will take place as time elapses.

First of all, there will be a *price-adjustment* lag in markets for goods and services: the length of time between the emergence of excess demand and/or increases in production costs, and the consequential rise in prices. When a "goods gap" suddenly opens up, there will be some delay, even if only a very short one, before firms become aware that the pressure of demand has risen and decide on their response to it. In some markets, the response will be merely a passive acceptance of the increased prices offered by buyers who are trying to outbid one another for limited supplies, and the price-adjustment lag will then depend on the rate at which buyers escalate their bids. When the sellers take the initiative in setting prices (that is, when firms are "price makers" rather than "price takers"), some of them may be held back for a time by the fear of losing sales to competitors who may refrain from increasing their own prices; others may wait to see whether the expansion of demand will be maintained or turn out to be merely a temporary fluctuation, raising prices only when they are sure it is the former. In certain cases, indeed, the act of raising prices will itself involve costs, such as those of printing and issuing new catalogs, which may cause firms to postpone price increases for a time. Thus, even where prices are "demand determined" in the sense that they respond directly to the emergence of excess demand, their increase will be subject to a time lag varying from market to market.

In sectors where prices are "cost determined" (or administered), firms fix their selling prices by the conventional procedure of adding a given markup to their direct costs of production; the existence of excess demand will not *directly* affect these prices, though it may do so indirectly if firms' efforts to increase output cause their costs to rise as a result of pressure on supplies of inputs. Except in the case of "final" products, any given sector's output is also an input from the point of view of other sectors, so that a rise in the price of any intermediate commodity will set up a chain reaction of price increases elsewhere. With a price-adjustment lag at each stage, the repercussions of an initial price increase in the market for a basic commodity may take a long time to work themselves out.

For the economy as a whole, the ultimate direct costs, after the canceling out of intersectoral transactions, are those of labor and imported inputs. If all prices were cost determined, the rate of increase of the general price level ($\dot{p}$) would depend on (a) the rate at which money wages are rising ($\dot{w}$); (b) the rate ($\dot{x}$) at which productivity, in the sense of output per unit of labor, is increasing; (c) the rate of increase in import prices ($\dot{m}$); and (d) the time lag between changes in wage and import costs and the consequent changes in prices. Over a period of time, increases in output per unit of labor will reduce the effect of rising money wages on the wage cost per unit of output; if there is an overall one-period lag, the relationship can be written

$$\dot{p}_t = a(\dot{w} - \dot{x})_{t-1} + (1 - a)\dot{m}_{t-1}$$

where a is the share of wage costs in total direct cost. Thus, if money wages were to rise 6% and productivity 3% in a given period, if import prices were unchanged, and if wage costs were two-thirds of the total (*i.e.*, $a = \frac{2}{3}$), the price level would rise 2% in the following period. There is, of course, no reason why the time lags should necessarily be the same for all the variables; for example, firms may know that import prices fluctuate rapidly and so may refrain from adjusting their selling prices until they are sure a given rise in import costs will not soon be reversed, whereas an increase in money wages, coming at the end of a period of negotiations with labor unions, is likely to be reflected in higher prices almost immediately because firms have had notice of it and know that it will remain in force for some time.[34]

Increases in money wages are themselves subject to a *wage-adjustment* lag. When excess demand in product markets causes firms to try to expand output, their efforts to hire more workers will create excess demand in the labor market if employment is near full to begin with. If excess demand (D) is the excess of job vacancies (V) over unemployment (U), stated as a proportion of the labor force (N), then a one-period lag between the emergence of the excess demand and the adjustment of money wages will mean that

$$\dot{w}_t = f(D_{t-1}) = f\left(\frac{V-U}{N}\right)_{t-1}.$$

Phillips found that the lag was negligible over most of the period he studied, but in the years 1948–1957 he obtained the best "fit" for his relationship by assuming a wage-adjustment lag of seven months; L. A. Dicks-Mireaux, on the other hand, found a shorter lag — something less than six months, with an average length of three.[35]

When money wages are being pushed up solely by unions' efforts to offset increases in the cost of living, their rate of increase will depend partly on the rate at which prices are rising and partly on the unions' success in obtaining their demands. But the processes of collective bargaining will take time; thus, $\dot{w}_t = a\dot{p}_{t-1}$ where negotiations impose a one-period time lag and a measures the extent to which wage claims succeed (complete success being indicated by $a = 1$). If unions are strong and aggressive enough to

---

[34] L. A. Dicks-Mireaux found (for Britain, 1946–1959) that the lag between wage increases and price adjustments was three months or less and was about half that between changes in import prices and changes in the domestic price level. See his "The Interrelationship Between Cost and Price Changes, 1946–59: A Study of Inflation in Post-War Britain," *Oxford Economic Papers*, Vol. 13 (October, 1961), pp. 267–292.

[35] Dicks-Mireaux, *op. cit.*, p. 275; Phillips, *op. cit.*, p. 297. It should be noted that their results are not quite comparable, since Phillips' $\dot{w}$ is the annual change in an index of wage rates, while that of Dicks-Mireaux is the annual change in total wage and salary payments divided by the number of employees — *i.e.*, an index of earnings, which implicitly includes a "wage-drift" element absent from Phillips' measure.

obtain wage increases over and above those needed to compensate for the effects of cost-of-living increases, so that money wages would be rising even if $\dot{p}_{t-1} = 0$, the equation would become

$$\dot{w}_t = \dot{p}_{t-1} + \beta_{t-1}$$

where β represents this additional "push," and a has been omitted since it must be equal to one if β is positive. The term β may itself be dependent on other variables, such as increasing unionization or increases in profits and productivity if these are made the basis for unions' wage claims.

The various lagged relationships described in the last few paragraphs can be combined in a number of ways to show the development of an inflation through time. For example, a one-period price-adjustment lag, in a closed economy where prices are cost determined, will mean that $\dot{p}_t = \dot{w}_{t-1} - \dot{x}_{t-1}$. If there is a wage-adjustment lag of one period, and wage increases are due solely to union pressure that more than offsets past price rises, $\dot{w}_{t-1} = \dot{p}_{t-2} + \beta_{t-2}$ as in the last paragraph. Combining the two equations gives

$$\dot{p}_t = \dot{p}_{t-2} + \beta_{t-2} - \dot{x}_{t-1}$$

which means that the current period's rate of price increase will be equal to that registered two periods previously, plus an additional percentage if unions were successful in raising real wages in the previous period, but minus a percentage due to that period's increase in labor productivity. If prices were stable in $t - 2$, so that $\dot{p}_{t-2}$ was zero, but if unions were at that time putting forward wage claims that were greater than could be met by increasing productivity in $t - 1$, the result would be a pure cost inflation beginning in period t. If, from $t - 1$ onward, each period's β is exactly equal to the $\dot{x}$ of the succeeding one, prices will rise every second period by the same proportion as in t, i.e., by $\beta_{t-2} - \dot{x}_{t-1}$.

This highly simplified model is, of course, only one of many that could be set up by combining excess demand and cost determination assumptions in different ways and by varying the length and pattern of the time lags. More detailed and realistic models would have to include additional variables; for example, by disaggregating demand into its component elements so as to allow for differences between consumers' behavior and that of government expenditure, and by bringing in the supply of money. With each new variable, another time lag would be added to the model. The possibilities raised by lags in the collection of taxes and in the appropriation of additional funds for government expenditure have already been noted.[36] On the monetary side, too, there will be lags in the adjustment of supply and demand in financial markets and in the response of aggregate demand to higher interest rates.[37]

Instead of the simple one-period lags assumed so far, a more complicated pattern may exist; for example, the price-adjustment lag may be distributed over several periods because of differences in the various industries' speed of response to excess demand and rising costs, so that, say, food prices rise immediately, clothing prices one period later, durables' prices in the period after that, and so on. The lags themselves are likely to vary with the proportionate amount of demand-pull or cost-push; where firms would hesitate to raise prices immediately on the strength of a 1% increase in costs or a fairly small excess of demand over capacity, they will lose no time in raising them when costs have risen 10% or when they are swamped with orders they cannot fill. A particularly important lag — though extremely difficult, if not impossible, to measure — is that between changes in the current rate of price increase and changes in the rate of expected *future* price increases. It may be that once people have revised their expectations about future price changes, the very fact of their having already done so will dispose them to adjust their expectations more quickly, so that the lag will shorten and cause inflationary pressure to rise as described earlier (pp. 319–323).

Obviously, the possible combinations of lags are so numerous that an enormous variety of dynamic models of inflation could be constructed. The essential point, however, is that the existence of lags ensures that prices will rise at some given rate over time, instead of shooting up instantaneously either to some new equilibrium level (in the case of a convergent inflation) or to infinity. With the lapse of time, investment will be gradually augmenting the economy's capital stock, technical progress will be increasing its productivity, and the growth of the labor force will be expanding potential total output. Where prices are being pulled up by excess demand, the continuing increase in supply will eventually remove the source of inflationary pressure — unless aggregate demand is

---

[36] See pp. 330–331 above. An interesting theoretical model in which, after an initial inflationary shock, prices continue to rise indefinitely solely because of a one-period lag in tax collection, is presented by Julio H. G. Olivera in "Money, Prices and Fiscal Lags: A Note on the Dynamics of Inflation," *Quarterly Review*, Banca Nazionale del Lavoro, Rome (September, 1967), pp. 258–267.

[37] See above, pp. 308–309.

itself growing at the same rate or faster. In the case of cost inflation, it has been seen that rising productivity offsets the effect of money wage increases on labor costs; while demand-shift inflation will be mitigated to the extent that the growth of resources makes it possible for demand-gaining sectors to expand without having to offer higher remuneration to attract factors of production from demand-losing sectors. Thus, an important aspect of official policy against inflation, supplementing the fiscal and monetary measures described earlier, is to encourage the growth of output and productivity; for example, by tax provisions favoring investment at the expense of consumption and by helping resources move into markets where demand is growing and away from those where it is declining.[38]

6. Incomes Policy

The anti-inflationary policies that have so far been considered were concerned wholly with eliminating or offsetting excess demand: either fiscal policy would shift Figure 13.1's *IS* curve back toward the left, or monetary policy would do the same to the $L(M_s/p)$ curve. Whichever method was chosen, the object was to cause the two curves to intersect vertically above the full-employment level of output, instead of the right of it as they did initially because of the autonomous increase in demand that started the inflation. However, these measures will no longer be appropriate if prices are rising in response to cost-push, which (as was argued on p. 332) can cause inflation to occur when there is no excess of aggregate demand over supply, and to continue indefinitely as long as the authorities are prepared to expand the quantity of nominal money sufficiently to prevent rising prices from shifting $L(M_s/p)$ curve to the left. If the government stabilizes the price level by refusing to allow the money supply to be increased any further or by reducing its own expenditure and/or raising taxes, the result will be unemployment; and if the amount of unemployment needed to stop the inflation turns out to be a large percentage of the labor force, the remedy will seem worse than the disease.

In these circumstances, the government may attempt to check inflation

---

[38] This side of government policy has been called "supply management," as distinct from the "demand management" that seeks to manipulate consumption, investment, etc.

in another way — by an *incomes policy*, the object of which is to keep the prices of factors of production (which are incomes to their owners and costs to their hirers) from rising at rates that are too fast to be compatible with price stability. If, for example, prices are rising only because wage costs are increasing, and if higher money wages are being asked and given only because prices are going up, an incomes policy would try to halt the spiral by directly restraining price increases and by preventing money wages from rising faster than productivity and so raising wage costs. Since cost inflation can come about through "profit-push" as well as "wage-push," it is necessary for an incomes policy to restrain profit margins as well as money wages; moreover, labor's willingness to accept wage restraint is likely to depend on the placing of some kind of limitation on dividends and other kinds of personal income from property. A full-fledged incomes policy thus applies over a wider field than a "wage-price" policy of the kind attempted in the United States in 1962–1967.

In their 1962 report, the Council of Economic Advisors set up "guideposts" for the fixing of wages and prices. They recommended (a) that "the rate of increase of wages rates (including fringe benefits) in each industry [should] be equal to the trend rate of overall productivity increase" (a rate later quantified, in the Council's 1964 report, as 3.2%), with certain exceptions for special circumstances; and (b) that prices should "fall in an industry whose rate of productivity increase exceeds the overall rate, rise in the opposite case, and remain stable if the two rates of productivity increase are equal." Nothing was prescribed with regard to nonwage incomes and profit margins, apart from the limitation tacitly implied in the price guidepost;[39] no special institutions were set up to supervise the application of the policy and promote its acceptance; the Administration assumed no powers of legal enforcement, but relied on general exhortation and the public stigmatizing of wage and price changes that went beyond the established limits.

The virtual abandonment of the guideposts in 1967 came after objections that prices had risen more than wages, that profits had risen more

---

[39] If, in a particular industry, wages are increasing at the overall average rate of productivity increase (say, 3%), while productivity in that industry is rising at a faster-than-average rate (say, 6%), wage costs per unit of output will actually be decreasing (by about 3%); if the product price is unchanged, profit per unit of output will therefore have risen. By proposing that prices should be reduced in such cases, the Council was implying that profit margins should be held constant.

than both, and that the Council's figure of 3.2% was lower than the true rate of annual productivity increase up to 1966. However, it can be claimed that the guidepost policy was successful to the extent that the price level was more stable in the United States during 1962–1967 than in countries that applied more elaborate incomes policies,[40] and that things might not have been very different even if something more far-reaching had been attempted. This is because even the most carefully administered incomes policy is liable to get into difficulties over the conflicts of interest that are bound to arise once cost inflation is under way.

The essential problem is that although labor as a whole will gain nothing in real terms if money-wage increases are countered by equal proportionate rises in the general price level, matters do not appear in this way to any *single* labor union. Suppose that industry X produces commodities making up 5% of the GNP and that wages are half its total production costs. A 10% increase in its workers' money wages will raise X's prices by 5%, and put up the *general* price level by only 5% of that, *i.e.*, by 0.25%. Provided no other industry's workers obtain wage increases leading to rises in the prices of their products, the workers in industry X will enjoy an increase of 9.75% in their *real* wages at the expense of a 0.25% reduction in everyone else's. Some of the gain will be at the expense of profits if firms in X are slow to raise product prices; there will also be some transfer of real income from the recipients of social security benefits and other fixed incomes.

Only when prices are fully adjusted, when social security benefits have been revised, and, above all, when labor unions in other industries have obtained offsetting increases in money wages financed by raising their products' prices, will real wages in X be back to their original level. By that time, X's unions may have submitted demands for a fresh increase in money wages. Thus there is a distinct advantage in being the first in the field with wage claims; and as this becomes more widely appreciated, a competitive scramble is likely to develop. To end it, there must be general agreement not only on the division of National Income between

---

[40] For some international comparisons, see C. T. Saunders, "Macro-Economic Aspects of Incomes Policy," in *The Labour Market and Inflation*, ed. by A. D. Smith for the International Institute for Labour Studies (New York: St. Martin's Press, 1968); also H. A. Turner and H. Zoeteweij, *Prices, Wages and Incomes Policies* (Geneva: International Labor Office, 1966). Analysis of the U.S. experience in the sixties is provided by G. L. Perry, "Wages and the Guideposts," *American Economic Review*, Vol. 57 (September, 1967), pp. 897–904.

wages, profits, and other forms of income, but also on the division of the wage share itself between workers in different industries and occupations. This however, implies some kind of interunion agreement regarding the pattern of relative wages, in addition to the more traditional processes of collective bargaining between unions and employers regarding absolute wages; or alternatively, a general acceptance of the pattern of relative wages as it happens to be at the moment when the incomes policy is first introduced.

If "guidepost" norms could be adopted when relative wages were considered generally satisfactory, they would have a fair chance of halting cost-inflation — at any rate, for a time, since the growth of the economy would eventually make a different relative wage pattern necessary in view of the changed composition of output and its implications for labor requirements. But it is precisely in the opening stages of a cost inflation, when the previously existing wage pattern has been upset, that the necessity for an incomes policy will be most felt. If new rules of the "guidepost" type are then introduced, unions that have so far been lagging in the race to claim higher money wages will feel that their position of temporary inferiority in the wage structure is now being made permanent, and their resentment may be enough to make the policy unworkable.

However, this does not mean that nothing can be hoped for from an incomes policy. It certainly means that the policy must be applied with political skill as well as economic expertise, that very full consultation with all interested parties should be undertaken at every stage, and that the rules should not be too rigid — it should be possible, for example, to approve above-norm wage increases that are coupled with prospective productivity increases accruing from the abandonment of restrictive practices. It must be remembered, too, that experience of this form of economic management is still very limited. Considering that the alternatives may be either to let the inflation proceed unhindered or to check it by monetary and fiscal policies that produce unemployment, it would be unwise to dismiss it as unworthy of further trial.

CHAPTER 14

Business Cycles

1. The Problem

In the preceding five chapters, various methods have been described by which the government may attempt to maintain full employment and avoid inflation. Each of them was seen to have its difficulties and weaknesses. How important those weaknesses are depends on the nature and size of the disturbances the economy is likely to encounter. Some of them may be of a far-reaching, long-term character; for example, the invention of a cheap synthetic substitute for a raw material of which a country has previously been the sole supplier may depress its economy for decades. A more frequent type of disturbance, however, is the periodic rise and fall in the level of activity and employment that has come to be known as the business cycle or the trade cycle, which has been experienced by all industrial countries since the nineteenth century. While governments may have the greatest difficulty in overcoming the effects of major structural changes in the economy, they should be able at least to mitigate cyclical fluctuations by means of suitable monetary and fiscal policies.

This would be a simple matter if fluctuations occurred in truly cyclical fashion, so that they were as foreseeable as the ebb and flow of the tides. A perfectly regular cycle would carry the economy from "peak" to "trough" and back again with uniform *frequency* and *amplitude*. That is, the time taken to move from one peak level of output to the next would always be the same, and the level of output and employment would always vary in the same proportion between the upper and lower turning points. But such cycles have never occurred. Even if the economy, left to itself, would have generated them, their regular sequence would have been upset by external happenings. Wars and political changes, sudden advances in technical knowledge, discoveries of oil and gold, spontaneous changes in consumers' preferences, good and bad harvests — any of these and countless other possibilities can alter the underlying pattern. A single country, moreover, will be influenced by fluctuations in other countries, since these will affect its trade with the rest of the world. Not surprisingly, then, the historical record shows considerable variations in the frequency and amplitude of cyclical movement. For example, between the Civil War and the late 1950's the United States experienced cycles whose trough-to-trough duration varied from three to eight years. Britain, on the other hand, experienced cycles between 1870 and 1914 whose duration ranged from seven to ten years.[1]

To complicate matters still further, there have been marked differences between individual industries with respect to both the timing and the severity of cycles. For example, the output of capital goods industries has always varied much more than that of others, while residential construction has pursued a rhythm of its own, with cycles of 20–25 years proceeding independently of the fluctuations taking place in the economy as a whole. Finally, the behavior of indexes other than those of output and employment — such as stock prices, inventories, and the general price level — has often been at odds with the pattern of fluctuations in output and employment.

It is hardly to be expected, then, that anything like a perfectly uniform and symmetrical cyclical movement is to be discerned in the historical record. Nonetheless, past fluctuations have not been so irregular as to make the use of the word "cycle" entirely inappropriate. Some of the apparent irregularity, indeed, can be attributed to the fact that not one but several cycles seem to have been operating concurrently. J. A. Schumpeter distinguished three: the short *Kitchin* cycle of approximately 40 months' duration, the longer *Juglar* averaging 9½ years' length, and the very long *Kondratieff wave* taking more than 50 years to run its course.[2] To these may be added the *Kuznets* cycle, or "secular swing," of 16–22 years,[3] which has been described as "so pronounced that it dwarfs the 7 to 11 year cycle into relative insignificance."[4] With cycles of different lengths superimposed on one another, it is not surprising that the shorter ones should have been somewhat distorted in frequency and amplitude; for example, the effect of the Kuznets cycle has been to make successive Juglars mild and severe by turns.

The rhythm, then, is complex; but it has been sufficiently regular to sug-

---

[1] For details, see R. C. O. Matthews, *The Business Cycle* (Chicago: The University of Chicago Press, 1959), pp. 205–226, and the references given there.

[2] J. A. Schumpeter, *Business Cycles* (New York: McGraw-Hill, 1939), pp. 169 ff. The names given to the various cycles are those of the economists who first suggested them. Kitchin and Kondratieff wrote in the early 1920's; Juglar's work was published as early as 1862.

[3] S. Kuznets, *National Product Since 1869* (New York: National Bureau of Economic Research, 1946). The suggestion that it should be called the "Kuznets cycle" was first made by P. J. O'Leary and W. A. Lewis, "Secular Swings in Production and Trade, 1870–1913," *The Manchester School*, Vol. 23 (May, 1955), pp. 113–152.

[4] O'Leary and Lewis, *op. cit.*, p. 113.

gest that past fluctuations may have been due to certain recurring causes that it should be possible to identify and perhaps to control. The attempt to find them has brought forth a large number of theories, some attributing cycles to wholly *exogenous* causes (*i.e.*, arising from outside the economy) such as periodical variations in climatic conditions affecting crop yields;[5] others asserting them to be generated *endogenously* through the inner nature and motion of the economic system itself. An extreme example of the former group is the theory that cycles are entirely the result of random "shocks" that, in a completely haphazard and uncoordinated fashion, disturb the economy's component parts. It has been shown that the application of such shocks to models constructed so that no endogenous fluctuations are possible can generate fairly regular cycles that closely resemble those actually recorded in the past.[6] If a *stochastic* hypothesis of this sort is correct, it would be pointless to look for a single causal factor recurring at regular intervals, since each fluctuation must have been the result of a unique set of circumstances; the fact that cycles run similar courses need not (according to this view) be taken to imply similarity of causation.

However, the ability of stochastic models to produce lifelike cycles does not rule out the possibility that past fluctuations may, in fact, have been generated endogenously. If there are good reasons for supposing that there are certain functional relationships within the economy (such as that between personal incomes and consumers' demand) whose interaction seems likely to give rise to systematic fluctuations, no cycle theory can be acceptable that does not take account of them — if only negatively, by showing that their influence is negligible compared with that of outside disturbances. The particular interaction on which several "endogenous"

---

[5] This was the essence of the celebrated "sunspot theory," advanced by Jevons in 1875. The periodicity of sunspots, it was claimed, caused an equivalent periodicity in weather and thus in harvests; the resulting fluctuations in agricultural prices, through their effects on the industrial sector, brought about variations in output as a whole.

[6] Irma Adelman, "Business Cycles — Endogenous or Stochastic?" *Economic Journal*, Vol. 70 (December, 1960), pp. 783–796. Mrs. Adelman set up a "naive model" in which consumption, investment, etc., were assumed to grow at steady rates over time and to be independent of one another, so that in the absence of external influences the system would have traced a straight-line growth path without fluctuations. When "erratic shocks" were applied to the variables in the form of random departures from their trend values, systematic cycles were generated. See also G. H. Fisher, "Some Comments on Stochastic Macroeconomic Models," *American Economic Review*, Vol. 42 (September, 1952), pp. 528–539.

theories[7] have been based is that between the Multiplier and the Accelerator, which will now be considered in detail.

2. The Multiplier-Accelerator Interaction

In the dynamic Multiplier sequence worked out in Chapter 6 (p. 142) it was shown that, given a one-period consumption lag, an autonomous rise in demand will give rise to a succession of income changes in subsequent periods; these changes become smaller and smaller as a new equilibrium is approached. In Chapter 7 (p. 179) it was shown that, on certain assumptions, changes in income will induce investment demand through the Accelerator (v). Thus each stage of the original Multiplier process gives rise to fresh investment demand that will set another Multiplier going; this process, in its turn, will give rise to additional investment demand that will set up fresh multiplier effects — and so on. By this interaction, income will be made to rise by more than it would have if the Multiplier had been acting alone. It might appear that the combined effects of the Multiplier and Accelerator must cause income to rise continuously; and if the Accelerator is of the form

$$I_t = v(Y_t - Y_{t-1}),$$

so that no time lags are involved, this will indeed be the case.[8] The intro-

---

[7] See J. R. Hicks, *A Contribution to the Theory of the Trade Cycle* (Oxford: Clarendon Press, 1950); R. M. Goodwin, "A Model of Cyclical Growth," reproduced in R. A. Gordon and L. R. Klein, eds. for the American Economic Association, *Readings in Business Cycles* (Homewood, Ill.: Irwin, 1965); M. Kalecki, *Theory of Economic Dynamics* (London: Allen and Unwin, 1954); and N. Kaldor, "A Model of the Trade Cycle," *Economic Journal*, Vol. 50 (March, 1940), pp. 78–92.

[8] With $C_t = cY_{t-1}$ and $I_t = v(Y_t - Y_{t-1})$, then

$$Y_t = cY_{t-1} + v(Y_t - Y_{t-1}).$$

This, in turn, can be rearranged to give

$$\frac{Y_t}{Y_{t-1}} = \frac{v - c}{v - 1},$$

which means that the income of any period must exceed that of the previous period by a fixed proportion, as long as c is less than 1.0. For example, if $v = 2$ and $c = 0.5$, Y_t will be 50% greater than Y_{t-1}; Y_{t+1} will be 50% greater than Y_t, and so on. If the consumption function were unlagged, so that $C_t = cY_t$, the proportion Y_t/Y_{t-1}

duction of a one-period lag, however, creates the possibility of a cyclical movement, as the following analysis will show.

Assuming no government, no foreign trade, and no output lag, income in period t will be

$$Y_t = C_t + I_t.$$

Consumers' demand depends on the last period's income, but has an autonomous element:

$$C_t = C_0 + cY_{t-1}.$$

The one-period lag in the Accelerator means that

$$I_t = v(Y_{t-1} - Y_{t-2});$$

when aggregate demand changes, firms try to adjust their capacity to it in the following period. There is no autonomous investment, so the equilibrium condition can be written

$$Y_t = C_0 + cY_{t-1} + v(Y_{t-1} - Y_{t-2}).$$

If there has been no change in income during previous periods, so that Y_{t-1} and Y_{t-2} are both equal to, say, 100, there will be no investment in period t, and Y_t will be equal to consumption expenditure. If C_0 equals 20 and c equals 0.8, it can be seen that Y_t will be 100 — exactly the same as the income of the two preceding periods. As long as no autonomous investment occurs and the value of C_0 remains unchanged, income will continue to be 100 in the future.

But now suppose there is an upward shift in the consumption function at time $t = \hat{t}$,[9] so that the value of C_0 rises permanently from 20 to 30; $Y_{\hat{t}}$ will now be equal to 110 instead of 100. When the next period is reached, consumption will be $30 + 0.8(110) = 118$; the Multiplier has been set in motion, and if left to itself would cause income to converge on a new equilibrium value of 150. But it will not be left to itself, since the rise in income in period $\hat{t}$ will have induced some investment through the Accelerator. For example, assume that v equals 1.2 for the particular time unit being employed in this "period analysis." Investment in period $\hat{t} + 1$ will be $1.2(110 - 100) = 12$; when added to the consumption demand

would be equal to $v/(v-s)$ (where s is written in place of $1-c$). With $v = 2$ and $c = 0.5$, Y_t would be one-third larger than Y_{t-1}; Y_{t+1} one-third larger than Y_t, and so on indefinitely.

[9] The hat over the time index t indicates the particular period in which the cycle begins.

of 118, this makes $Y_{\hat{t}+1}$ equal to 130. Similarly, income in the next period will be

$$Y_{\hat{t}+2} = 30 + 0.8(130) + 1.2(130 - 110) = 158$$

— it has already been carried above the value toward which the Multiplier alone would have moved it.

When the value of income is calculated for succeeding periods, it is found that $Y_{\hat{t}+3}$ is 190, $Y_{\hat{t}+4}$ is 220.4, $Y_{\hat{t}+5}$ is 242.8, and $Y_{\hat{t}+6}$ is 251.1. Although income is still rising in period $\hat{t} + 6$, it can be seen that the *rate* of increase has declined considerably; the next period's income actually falls below the level reached in $\hat{t} + 6$, since

$$Y_{\hat{t}+7} = 30 + 0.8(251.1) + 1.2(251.1 - 242.8) = 240.8.$$

From this point onward, income continues to fall because the Accelerator has been thrown into reverse; successive reductions in the level of income induce *dis*investment, which has the effect of making income shrink still further. Thus, investment in $\hat{t} + 8$ is equal to $1.2(240.8 - 251.1) = -12.3$; and $Y_{\hat{t}+8}$ is consequently 210.4. By the time period $\hat{t} + 11$ is reached, income has returned approximately to its original level; but it continues to fall and is subsequently carried to still lower levels until the rate of fall at last slackens, another turning point is reached,[10] and it begins to rise once again.

The effect of introducing the lagged Accelerator, therefore, is to change the original sequence into a cycle. At first, income rises faster than it would have if the Multiplier alone had been at work; "accelerator-induced" investment demand is added to the consumption demand induced by successive increases in income. But there is now no question of a gradual convergence toward a new equilibrium income level at which the system can settle down once the adjustment process is completed.

The essence of the Acceleration Principle, it will be recalled, is that once investment has risen in response to an initial increase in income, no further rise is called for if income goes on growing by successive amounts equal to its original increase, while a subsequent diminution in the rate of income growth will cause the amount of investment actually to fall. Thus, unless the values of v and c are so high that income grows at a progres-

---

[10] If the numerical calculation had been continued to this stage, it would have been seen that there is something very odd about this part of the cycle. To avoid undue complication, the point is ignored for the moment; but it will be taken up again later, on p. 361.

sively increasing rate, investment cannot go on rising as fast as it did in the early stages of the sequence. But since investment demand is itself one of the determinants of income, a slackening of the rate of growth of investment will cause a decline in the rate of income, which in turn will cause the *amount* of investment to fall; [11] the rate at which income is growing will diminish still more, until at last it stops rising altogether. At this peak level of income, however, investment will still be positive; because of the lag in the Accelerator, investment demand is still being generated by the rise in income that occurred in the period just before the peak was reached. This makes it inevitable that income will fall again as soon as the peak has been reached; since at the peak itself, income has ceased to rise, investment demand will fall to zero immediately afterward, and aggregate demand will be reduced below what it was at the peak.

Since income is now falling, the capital stock built up earlier is larger than is required to produce current output, and firms will attempt to reduce their capacity by disinvestment, *i.e.*, by not replacing equipment as it wears out. The faster the rate at which income falls, the greater the desired disinvestment. The considerations that now apply are the same as when income was rising, except that everything is moving in the opposite direction, with income falling and investment negative instead of positive. Eventually the decline of income will slow up and halt, disinvestment will cease, and that very fact will cause aggregate demand and, therefore, income to revive again; the system will rise once more into the positive phase of another cycle.

In this sequence, the values of v and c are of great importance. If they are high, income will rise continuously at an ever-increasing rate, and there will be no downturn and therefore no cycle. Thus if the value of v is changed from 1.2 to 3 in the numerical example given earlier (all other values remaining the same), income will reach a value slightly above 10,000 in period $\hat{t} + 6$ (instead of the 251 that was attained with $v = 1.2$) and it will still be increasing. Its path will be similar to curve A in Figure 14.1. At the opposite extreme, low values of v will also fail to generate a cycle; income will merely converge to the new equilibrium level that would have been achieved by the operation of the Multiplier alone and

---

[11] In the numerical example already given, investment reaches a peak of 38.4 in period $\hat{t} + 4$; in the following three periods, it is successively 36.5, 26.9, and 10.0, after which it becomes negative, with a value of -12.3 in $\hat{t} + 8$. Thus, the level of investment begins to fall two periods before the decline of income starts.

will stay there. The Accelerator will cause income to grow faster during
the initial stages of the expansion process, but it will not be strong enough
to alter the eventual outcome. Such a convergence would occur if, for example, the Accelerator were 0.25 instead of 1.2 in the sequence worked
out above; it is exemplified by curve B in Figure 14.1. For cycles to occur,
then, the values of v and c must lie between certain upper and lower extremes: provided they do so, income will oscillate about a central value
equal to the equilibrium income that would eventually have been reached
by the Multiplier had v been zero.

Three distinct types of cycle may be generated, according to the values
of v and c. If v is small relative to c (which itself is assumed to be less
than 1.0) the oscillations will be "damped" — that is, they will become

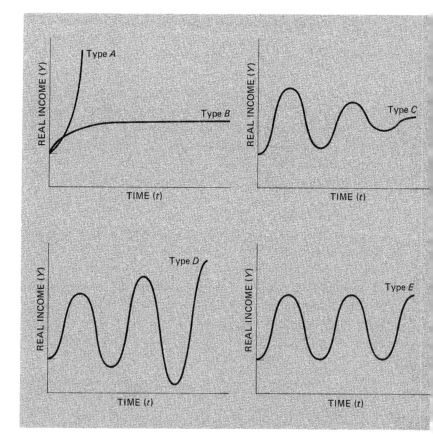

Fig. 14.1
Different Types of
Business Cycles

weaker and weaker and eventually die away altogether, leaving income constant at its central value. Curve C in Figure 14.1 illustrates this kind of fluctuation. High values of v, on the other hand, give rise to "antidamped" cycles that, in the manner of curve D, become stronger as time passes, with the vertical distance between turning points increasing at every revolution. The third type of cycle is the perfectly regular one exemplified by curve E, which once started continues indefinitely at a constant amplitude and is neither damped nor antidamped. It can be shown[12] that the present model will generate E-type cycles only when v is exactly equal to 1.0; since this is only one among many possible values of v, the chances that such a stringent condition will be fulfilled for any length of time must be considered very small. For the United States, empirical evidence suggests that when v is calculated on an annual basis[13] its value is about 3.0. If this were assumed in the present model, the cycle would be either the antidamped D-type or the explosive A-type. The implications of this result will be considered presently.

Meanwhile, it must be emphasized that the Multiplier-Accelerator interaction illustrated above is by no means the only possible one. It would no doubt be more realistic to suppose that the consumption lag is shorter than the investment lag — say, three months as against one year. Both lags might be distributed over several periods, so that investment, for example, would depend on the changes in income that had occurred during the past two or three years. The values of v and c may very well change in the

---

[12] See J. R. Hicks, *A Contribution to the Theory of the Trade Cycle, op. cit.*, pp. 69–72 and Mathematical Appendix, pp. 184–186. P. A. Samuelson, in "Interactions Between the Multiplier Analysis and the Principle of Acceleration," *Review of Economic Statistics*, Vol. 21 (May, 1939), pp. 75–78, used a model in which consumption is lagged one period and investment is induced by the current change in consumption, so that

$$Y_t = 1 + cY_{t-1} + vc(Y_{t-1} - Y_{t-2})$$

— the "1" being a dollar of government spending that acts as a multiplicand. He found that the condition for E-type cycles was $c = 1/v$. In the model given in the text, v does the work of vc in Samuelson's; replacing his vc by v turns the condition into $v = 1$. See also R. G. D. Allen, *Mathematical Economics, op. cit.*, Chap. 7.

[13] This would assume that the "investment period" defined on p. 180 is one year in length. In fact, it is difficult to estimate the true investment period for the whole economy; for some industries it will be short and for others long, so that an aggregation problem would exist even if each individual industry's investment period were known (which it is not). If new evidence were to show that six months was a more realistic figure than a year, it would be necessary to think of the Multiplier-Accelerator interaction as running in terms of half-year periods with a v of 6.0.

course of the cycle, perhaps for exogenous reasons or perhaps in response to the cyclical movement itself; for example, the onset of a depression, causing a sudden worsening of expectations, would no doubt increase firms' desire to disinvest and thereby cause v to increase during the downturn. If an output lag (hitherto excluded by assumption) is brought into the model, things will be complicated still further. Finally, there is the possibility, not so far considered, that autonomous investment may occur in addition to the investment induced through the Accelerator.

If, in the sequence traced earlier, the rise in autonomous demand in period $\hat{t}$ had been for investment goods instead of for consumption, the satisfaction of this demand (which, in the absence of an output lag, may be assumed to have taken place within period $\hat{t}$ itself) would have raised productive capacity as well as setting off a multiplier process. The output-capital ratio is the inverse of the Accelerator v (*i.e.*, $1/1.2$), so autonomous investment of 10 units will raise output by 8.33, that is, by slightly more than the amount of additional production needed to satisfy the multiplier-induced increase in consumers' demand in $\hat{t} + 1$. Alternatively, it will meet a good part of the demand for investment goods induced in $\hat{t} + 1$ through the Accelerator.[14] If autonomous investment now remains at 10, it will have the effect of partially damping down the cycle, as well as ensuring that fluctuations take place about a rising trend instead of the constant income level that has so far been assumed.

The original Multiplier-Accelerator interaction can thus be modified in various ways to achieve greater realism, albeit at the cost of increased complexity. Its chief offense against realism, however, may require modifications of a kind not so far suggested. It has already been noted that the simple model is very unlikely to generate E-cycles (because this would require v to be precisely 1.0) and will most probably (since v is judged to be typically greater than 1.0) produce either antidamped D-type or explosive A-type movements. Yet the historical record shows that actual

---

[14] The argument here assumes that capital installed in period t becomes productive in $t + 1$; that is, that the periods t, $t + 1$, etc. are so chosen as to be equal in length to the "investment period," which is taken to be uniform throughout the economy. This may, of course, be untrue in particular cases. For example, the autonomous investment of a given period may be part of a long-range project (such as the digging of a new Panama Canal), which will take many years to complete and which can produce nothing until it is finished. In the meantime, its contribution to productive capacity will be nil, and its current effects will be precisely similar to those of the autonomous increase in consumption assumed in the original sequence.

fluctuations have not continually increased in amplitude in the manner of a D-cycle nor has there been an "explosion." If the economy really has a tendency to generate such movements, they must somehow have been prevented from developing their full effect. One obvious limit on upward movements is the economy's productive capacity at full employment; if there is a lower limit also, the amplitude of fluctuations will be less than the value of v by itself would have caused it to be.

3. Floors, Ceilings, and Shocks

The possibility of such a lower limit is easily seen by considering the downswing phase of the cycle in the numerical example given earlier. When income reached its peak, the halt in growth caused investment to fall; this decine reduced income in the following period, the fall in income induced disinvestment, income fell further, and so on. If the arithmetical calculations of pp. 355–356 are continued, it will be found that income reaches $-$ 15 in period $\hat{t} +$ 12, with investment at the very low figure of $-$ 76 (both figures having been rounded to the nearest whole number). In the next period, consumption is at its minimum[15] level of 30, investment is $-$ 64, and income is therefore $-$ 34. This, it turns out, is the "trough" of the cycle, since income recovers to a positive value of 7.6 in $\hat{t} +$ 14 and to 86 in $\hat{t} +$ 15, after which it goes on rising toward a new peak.

That both income and investment should become negative during the downswing is, of course, highly unrealistic, but it is not impossible as long as both are defined as net of depreciation. Negative net investment implies that all or part of current depreciation is not being made good, so that the capital stock is shrinking as more and more units reach the end of their productive lives without being replaced; but disinvestment can hardly exceed the amount of depreciation, since that would mean that capital was being destroyed before it had ceased to be productive. If the disinvestment *desired* in any period is greater than current depre-

---

[15] It is assumed that C_0, the autonomous element in consumption, is a minimum level (here equal to 30) below which consumers will not reduce their expenditure; the consumption function $C_t = C_0 + cY_{t-1}$ is not valid for negative values of Y_{t-1}. Without this condition, consumption would itself become negative in $\hat{t} +$ 14, which would be nonsensical.

ciation, the excess will have to be carried forward and added to the desired disinvestment of the following period. In the numerical example,
the capital stock has an average value of 180, *i.e.*, v times the "central
value" of income (150) about which the cycle rotates; if the average life
of capital is ten periods, depreciation in any single period will average
18.0, so that the large amounts of disinvestment called for in $\hat{t} + 12$ and
$\hat{t} + 13$ could not have been realized.[16]

Since disinvestment cannot exceed depreciation, then income cannot
fall below a minimum value, or "floor," equal to autonomous consumption
minus current depreciation — in symbols, $Y_{min} = C_0 - D$, where D is
depreciation.[17] If C_0 exceeds D, the "floor" value of income will be positive, and the economy will be prevented from plunging into the depths
into which the numerical example originally carried it in periods $\hat{t} + 12$
to $\hat{t} + 16$. When income has been at its minimum level for two consecu-
tive periods, the fact that it is no longer falling means that no further disinvestment will be required — except, of course, for the backlog already
accumulated in the past. When the backlog has been worked off, the term
$- D$ will disappear from the income-determining equation, and income
will rise once more, setting the Accelerator in motion and starting the upswing of a fresh cycle. However, the new cycle will not be the next phase
of the original one. Even if the value of v is such that it would generate
antidamped cycles in the absence of constraints, the fact that income
has been stationary at its "floor" value for several periods means that the
cycle must start again at the beginning.[18] Instead of a succession of fluc-

---

[16] The figure of 18.0 is merely an average over the whole cycle: it takes no account of possible "echo effects" (see p. 181). If all equipment is assumed to fall due
for replacement precisely ten periods after installation, depreciation will depend on
the amount of gross investment ten periods earlier; *e.g.*, depreciation in $\hat{t} + 14$
will be 38.4 (the net investment of $\hat{t} + 4$) plus the depreciation made good in
$\hat{t} + 4$ which is now again due for replacement. On this basis, the amount of depreciation will vary from period to period and will greatly complicate the working
of the numerical example. However, except in the very special case in which the life
of capital is equal to exactly half the duration of a complete E-cycle, it will not
change the fact that some desired disinvestment will fail to be achieved during the
downswing —which is the essential point in the text above.

[17] Since Y is *net* income, gross income is $Y + D$; and gross income cannot be less
than minimum consumption C_0. The value of D will, of course, be smaller, the
longer the average life of capital assets.

[18] At the point where recovery begins, the situation will be the same as it was
in period $\hat{t}$, except that the multiplicand is now D instead of the original increase
in C_0.

tuations of increasing amplitude, there will be an endless repetition of the first revolution of a D-cycle; in this way, the occurrence of fairly regular fluctuations can be consistent with a high value of v.

The "floor" just described is a very low one. Autonomous investment, due to technological innovations and long-range planning, may be a substantial amount in each period and may indeed be increasing through all the phases of the cycle in response to a long-term growth trend in the economy. If population is growing, the amount of minimum consumption C_0 is likely to increase from period to period. These factors will not only raise the height of the floor, so that income reaches its minimum value while net investment is still positive; but they may also give it an upward tilt, so that recovery begins earlier than it would otherwise have. Each time the economy rises from the floor to begin a new revolution of the cycle, it will do so from a higher level of income than on the previous occasion. Instead of revolving around a stationary central value, as it was assumed to do in the numerical example, the cycle will now be moving around a rising trend of income.

Just as the downswing of the cycle may be stopped by a floor, the upswing may be halted by coming into contact with a "ceiling." The ultimate limit on the rise of real income is the economy's productive capacity at full employment; if it happens to lie below the maximum level of income that the cycle would have reached had it been free to run its course, investment demand will be in excess of saving when the system runs up against the ceiling, and a backlog of demand will have to be carried forward to the next period. Meanwhile, the cessation of income growth will reduce the amount of accelerator-induced investment to zero, so that as soon as the backlog of investment demand has been satisfied, income will fall again and the downswing phase of a new cycle will have begun. The sequence is, it appears, much the same as that which occurred when the downswing encountered the floor, except that the algebraic signs are all reversed; instead of the desire to *dis*invest, it is now the desire to *invest* that is frustrated.

It may be objected, however, that the analysis fails to allow for the effects of the inflationary pressures that will be set up when the economy draws close to the full-employment ceiling.[19] As the growing shortage of

---

[19] It should be remembered that the income-determining equation is in real terms. If Y_t and Y_{t+1} are both equal to full employment real income, their real investment de-

labor forces wages up, a wage-price spiral is likely to develop and inflation may become chronic. Instead of being reduced to zero, the amount of induced investment demand may actually increase; the shortage of labor and the rise in wages give firms an incentive to substitute capital for labor in production. Conscious that there is excess demand for their products, and wishing to expand production to meet it, firms will try to invest more than before. If prices are expected to go on rising, capital goods may be sought also as a hedge against inflation. The excess of investment demand over saving may actually increase, so that it is no longer a question of merely working off a backlog. But the historical record does not show regular bursts of strong price inflation; price changes certainly occurred during past cycles, but not in such a way as to suggest that upswings normally gave rise to inflationary gaps at full-employment income. The "ceiling" hypothesis must therefore be regarded as doubtful.

It may also be unnecessary. If downswings are stopped by a floor as described earlier, each cycle starts afresh from the beginning; instead of following the D curve along its full length, the system repeats part of the first revolution over and over again. If the upper turning point of the first revolution happens to lie below the ceiling, each upswing will come to an end of its own accord before full employment has been reached. If there were no floor, of course, the cycle would be able to proceed unhindered to its second, third, and subsequent revolutions, eventually coming up against the ceiling. When, in due course, income fell below the ceiling and the cycle was resumed, it would begin again at the downswing phase of the first revolution; and a series of apparently regular fluctuations would then follow in spite of the antidamped value of v. Thus it is not necessary for the cycle to encounter *both* the floor and the ceiling.[20] Either one of them will be sufficient to prevent the cycle's getting beyond the first revolution; consequently, if the role assigned to one of them appears to be unrealistic, it may be discarded as long as the other is retained.

The choice need not be irrevocable; conceivably, the cycle might proceed for quite a long time as a series of fairly even "bounces" along the

---

mand in $t + 2$, *i.e.*, $v(Y_{t+1} - Y_t)$, will be zero even though the money value of Y_{t+1} exceeds that of Y_t because of rising prices.

[20] There is, however, one case in which both floor and ceiling would be required: where the value of v is so high as to cause an "explosion" in the manner of curve A in Figure 13.1. The ceiling will then break the rise of income, which in due course will "explode" downwards until checked by the floor; the next movement will be an upward explosion that proceeds until checked by the ceiling — and so on.

floor and then be propelled towards the ceiling by an unusually rapid growth of autonomous demand. On reaching the ceiling, it would bounce back, but it would reach a lower turning point well above the floor, at which the Accelerator would go into reverse and cause income to rise again for another collision with the ceiling; subsequent fluctuations would then be a series of bounces off the ceiling.[21] However, as long as the value of v in the simple Multiplier-Accelerator interaction is too high to be consistent with regular E-type fluctuations, either a floor or a ceiling must be brought into the model; it is not possible to dispense with both of them.

Nevertheless, it is extremely difficult to argue from empirical evidence that either the floor or the ceiling has ever actually played the part assigned to it in the model. From the record, it seems extremely doubtful whether the ceiling was ever reached during the nineteenth century; certainly the ceiling was not touched in the period between World Wars I and II. It would be equally certain that the floor has never been reached either, if the criterion were assumed to be the occurrence of negative net investment, since net investment seems to have been positive even in the worst depression years.[22] But it was suggested earlier that accelerator-induced disinvestment is likely to be offset by some amount of autonomous investment. The difficulty is to distinguish one category from the other and to decide whether a given year's net investment was positive only because autonomous investment demand was present or because the cycle had come to its lower turning point before reaching the floor. It is therefore possible to argue that past fluctuations should not be interpreted as antidamped cycles whose movement was interrupted by collisions with the floor and/or the ceiling, but that, on the contrary, they may actually have been C-type damped cycles that were continually strengthened by exogenous "shocks" of one kind or another.

This argument need not involve unrealistic assumptions about the value of v. Though the condition for damped fluctuations in the simple model is that v should be less than 1.0 (a value dismissed earlier as unreasonably low), this "critical value" can be raised by altering the model in various ways; for example, distributing the consumption lag over several past pe-

---

[21] Thus, it would not be inconsistent to regard pre-1939 cycles as "floor-based" fluctuations, while considering the milder fluctuations of the post-1945 period to have been a series of "bounces off the ceiling" — the ceiling itself, of course, being upward-sloping because of the long-run growth trend.

[22] Investment did drop very close to zero, however, during the worst years of the depression of the 1930's.

riods will allow damped cycles to occur with v greater than 1.0.[23] Another possibility is that the price of capital goods (relative to other commodities) may vary directly with the amount of investment demand, thus changing the value of v in the following period. For example, when investment is high during the upswing of the cycle, the consequent rise in the relative prices of capital goods will make firms seek less capital-intensive methods of production; the variation in v will then have a damping effect, even if its average value over the whole cycle happens to be quite high.[24]

Suitably modified, then, the model could be made to give damped oscillations that, if permitted to run their course without disturbance, would allow the system to settle down to an even tenor. The appearance of regular fluctuations would be due to the occurrence of erratic shocks that set fresh cycles going or reinforce existing ones so that they are prevented from dying away. A model of this sort[25] might be claimed to accord better with the observed course of events than do antidamped models, since the cycles it generates are necessarily somewhat irregular and therefore lifelike, and since it makes provision from the outset for the external happenings that are constantly affecting the economy. On the other hand, since it allows the internal functional relationships to play a part in producing cycles (in other words, since it contains an endogenous as well as a stochastic element), the model is not open to the objection raised earlier against the *purely* stochastic hypothesis — namely, that it explains too little.

It cannot yet be claimed that any single theory of cycles commands universal assent, though in recent decades there has undoubtedly been a

---

[23] For example, if the income-determining equation were changed to
$$Y_t = c_1 Y_{t-1} + c_2 Y_{t-2} + v(Y_{t-1} - Y_{t-2}),$$
where $c_1 + c_2 = c$, the condition for damped cycles would be $v = 1 + c_2$, so that if c_2 were 0.5 the "critical value" would be 1.5. See R. G. D. Allen, *Mathematical Economics, op. cit.,* Chap. 7.

[24] The investment function $I_t = v(Y_{t-1} - Y_{t-2})$ would then become
$$I_t = v_1 Y_{t-1} - v_2 Y_{t-2},$$
where $v_1 < v_2$ if $Y_{t-1} > Y_{t-2}$ and $v_1 > v_2$ if $Y_{t-1} < Y_{t-2}$. The term $v_2 Y_{t-2}$ would represent actual capital existing at the beginning of period t, while $v_1 Y_{t-1}$ would represent desired capital.

[25] This type of theory is particularly associated with the name of Ragnar Frisch; see his "Propagation Problems and Impulse Problems in Dynamic Economics" in *Economic Essays in Honour of Gustav Cassel* (London: Allen and Unwin, 1933).

marked narrowing of the area of disagreement; for example, very few economists now accept a purely monetary explanation, though such a theory was strongly held as late as the 1930's.[26] On one important point, however, it may be said that there is now fairly general agreement, namely, that fluctuations are to be regarded as a part of the process of long-term economic growth. Such a view was put forward as early as 1912 by J. A. Schumpeter,[27] who argued that fluctuations were an integral part of long-run development, in the sense that they were both a consequence and a cause of it. Since then, and especially within the last twenty years, the theory of long-run growth has received increasing attention; and it will be considered at length in the next chapter.

---

[26] Notably by R. G. Hawtrey and F. A. von Hayek.

[27] In his *Theory of Economic Development* (Cambridge, Mass.: Harvard University Press, 1934); first published as *Theorie der Wirtschaftlichen Entwicklung* in 1912.

CHAPTER 15

The Theory
of Growth

1. Investment and the Growth of Income

From one year to another, output may remain the same or even fall, but in the long run it can be expected to follow an upward trend. This presumption accords with historical experience; the United States, for example, produced in 1967 over three times the volume of goods and services that it did in 1929. In the rest of the world, some countries have grown faster, others more slowly, but the universal tendency has been for output to expand considerably from decade to decade. One obvious reason for this expansion is the growth of population, which has more than doubled since the turn of the century.[1] Even if the stock of capital and methods of production had remained unchanged, a steady increase in the number of workers would have caused output to grow, though more slowly than the labor force itself because of diminishing returns.[2] But capital has, in fact, increased substantially. In most economies investment is normally greater than the amount required to provide for capital consumption, so that each year's flow of output includes the means of increasing the flow in the following year; in the United States the stock of capital in manufacturing alone has doubled since 1948.[3] Methods of production, too, have been continually improving, though it is impossible to say at exactly what rate;[4] many technological advances have to be "embodied" in new equipment, so that their effects on output cannot be separated unambiguously from those of the investment that "carries" them. The dissemination of technical knowledge, the expansion of education, public health improvements that enhance workers' longevity and vigor, and other kinds of "investment in human resources" have also helped to bring about a long-run growth in output.

All these growth-inducing factors — population increase, technological

---

[1] For a useful discussion of long-term growth in population and output in different countries, see S. Kuznets, *Modern Economic Growth* (New Haven, Conn.: Yale University Press, 1966).

[2] See pp. 66–70. In Figure 4.1 on p. 68, a steady increase in employment beyond N_2 brings progressively smaller additions to output.

[3] See *Survey of Current Business* (December, 1967).

[4] Attempts to estimate the contribution of technical progress to United States growth have come up with conflicting results. For a discussion of recent efforts and an indication of the theoretical and empirical problems involved in research on this question, see E. F. Denison, "Some Major Issues in Productivity Analysis," in *Survey of Current Business*, Part II (May, 1969).

progress, and investment in both material capital and human resources —
may be expected to continue operating in the future. Accordingly, the
working of the economy should be examined in a context of secular expansion of resources and output. Some questions that have to be answered
are these: What determines the rate of growth in a given economy? Is the
growth of output likely to exceed that of population, so that income per
head and living standards rise in the long run? Under what conditions
does the growth rate accelerate, decelerate, or stay constant over the
years? Is growth inherently stable or unstable? As productive capacity
increases, will it all be utilized or will an increasing proportion of labor
and capital be unemployed? Alternatively, is growth likely to be inflationary?

Because of its short-run character, the theory of income determination
presented in earlier chapters does not attempt to provide direct answers
to questions of this sort. Diagrams such as Figure 6.1 (p. 136) and Figure
7.2 (p. 174) are drawn on the assumption that population, the stock of
capital, and the techniques of production are all fixed for the time being.
Even though net investment is continually adding to the stock of capital,
the time perspective is too short for this to make any difference to the
situation — investment is merely one element of aggregate demand, and
changes in it are of interest only because of their effects on the equilibrium
of the economy. But when the analysis is no longer confined to the short
run, it is necessary to allow for the facts that investment does add to productive capacity and that if all the additional capital is brought into use,
income and output will rise as a consequence. In symbols, $\Delta Y = \sigma I$,
where σ is a measure of the productivity of capital[5] (and, it will be noticed, the inverse of v, the "capital-output ratio" defined on p. 179).

The question then arises whether aggregate demand will increase sufficiently to absorb the whole of the additional output. The rise in income
generated by additional output will certainly induce an increase in consumption, provided the MPC is greater than zero. But unless the MPC is
equal to 1.0, consumption will take up only a part of the additional production, leaving a remainder ($s\Delta Y$, where s is the Marginal Propensity
to Save) that will have to be absorbed by an increase in investment if it

---

[5] More precisely, σ is the *marginal* productivity of capital; it may not be the same
as *average* productivity, *i.e.*, that of the capital stock as a whole (symbolized as
Y/K). However, it is a convenient simplification to assume that marginal and average
productivities are equal, so that $\Delta Y/I = Y/K$.

is to be absorbed at all. The likelihood of such an increase occurring depends on the extent to which the demand for investment responds to the rise of income; for the moment, it is sufficient to note that the condition for continuing growth without the development of excess capacity is that there must be an increase in investment demand, $\triangle I$, equal to $s\triangle Y$. Since $\triangle Y = \sigma I$, this condition may be restated as $\triangle I = s\sigma I$, or

$$\frac{\triangle I}{I} = s\sigma.$$

Thus, if s is 0.1 (*i.e.*, if one-tenth of income is saved), and if σ is 0.5 (*i.e.*, $1 worth of output requires $2 worth of capital to produce it), investment demand must grow at the rate of 0.05, or 5% per annum, if the economy's productive capacity is to continue to be fully used. If the s in $\triangle I = s\triangle Y$ is a constant (in other words, if the community always saves a fixed proportion of income, whatever its income may be), the proportionate increase in investment $\triangle I/I$ will be the same as the proportionate growth of income $\triangle Y/Y$; the term $s\sigma$ will then define the rate of growth of income as well as that of investment.

This relationship is illustrated in Figure 15.1 (which is similar to Figure

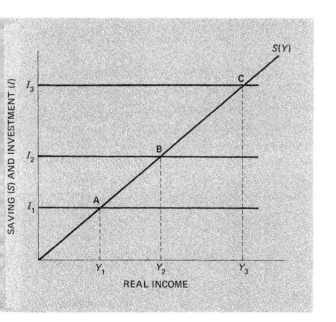

Fig. 15.1

Investment levels consistent with growing income. The MPS is constant.

7.2 on p. 174): income is measured on the horizontal axis, and saving and net investment on the vertical; all quantities are in real terms. The savings function $S(Y)$ is a straight line starting at the origin; its slope is equal to both the MPS and the APS, and it is assumed to remain unchanged for a considerable period of time. The initial level of investment demand is shown by I_1, which intersects $S(Y)$ at A to give an equilibrium income of Y_1; here, it is assumed, full employment exists. As soon as the new capital equipment represented by investment I_1 comes into service, income will rise to Y_2 — the proportion between the rise in income, $Y_2 - Y_1$, and investment I_1 being the output-capital ratio σ. For Y_2 to be the new equilibrium level of income, investment must rise to I_2; the new investment line will then intersect $S(Y)$ at B, vertically above Y_2. In due course this investment will cause output and income to rise by σ times I_2, giving a new income level Y_3; for this to be balanced by aggregate demand, investment must rise yet again to I_3 so that I_3 intersects $S(Y)$ at C. As long as investment rises appropriately in each period, the process will continue indefinitely, with income rising by σ times the last period's investment and investment rising by s times the increase in income, so that income grows steadily at a rate equal to $s\sigma$.

2. The Harrod Model of Growth

The formulation presented above, which in its essentials is that of E. D. Domar,[6] is not a complete theory of growth, because the demand for investment is left undetermined. Given the values of s and σ, it shows how large that demand must be in successive periods if output is to go on rising, but it makes no attempt to explain what the amount of investment will actually be. In this respect, it differs markedly from Roy Harrod's well-known "dynamic theory," to which it otherwise bears a strong resemblance. Harrod uses a "fundamental equation"[7]

$$GC = s,$$

---

[6] E. D. Domar, *Essays in the Theory of Economic Growth* (New York: Oxford University Press, 1957), p. 91.

[7] R. F. Harrod, *Towards a Dynamic Economics* (New York: St. Martin's Press, 1948), pp. 77 *et seq.*; see also his "Second Essay in Dynamic Theory," *Economic Journal*, Vol. 70 (June, 1960), pp. 277–293.

where G is the rate of growth of income ($\triangle Y/Y$), C is the ratio of investment to the change in output ($I/\triangle Y$), and s is the fraction of income saved (S/Y). The equation could thus be written

$$\frac{\triangle Y}{Y} \cdot \frac{I}{\triangle Y} = \frac{S}{Y}$$

which, when the Y's and $\triangle Y$'s are canceled out, reduces to the familiar *ex post* identity of saving and investment. If I and S are taken in the *ex ante* sense, however, the equation defines an equilibrium condition in which $\triangle Y/Y$ is what Harrod calls the "warranted rate of growth," denoted G_w to distinguish it from the actual growth rate G.

In static equilibrium, producers are satisfied with the level of current output if they are neither accumulating unwanted stock nor conscious of excess demand for their products. Similarly, growth is proceeding at an equilibrium (or "warranted") rate if producers find that the increase in output they have planned[8] is exactly balanced by a concomitant increase in aggregate demand. They are then, in Harrod's words, "content with what they are doing" and "in a state of mind in which they are prepared to carry on a similar advance" in the future. If growth is to proceed at this "warranted" rate, saving must continue to be matched by *ex ante* investment, the amount of which is assumed to depend on the current increase in income and output. In symbols,

$$I = C_r\triangle Y,$$

where C_r is a "coefficient of capital requirements" showing the amount of new capital[9] needed to produce an additional unit of output. At a given rate of interest,[10] and with technical progress that is "neutral" in the sense that it does not change the capital intensity of production as time goes

---

[8] It is not, of course, necessary that each individual firm find that its planned output is equal to demand. The condition described above applies to planned output as a whole and could be consistent with surpluses and shortages in particular industries.

[9] In his definition of capital, Harrod emphasizes that he is including all inventories and work-in-progress, as well as fixed capital. "Required" investment, therefore, consists not only of new machinery, buildings, etc., but of additions to inventories in proportion to the increase in output. At a later stage of his argument, Harrod puts some weight on this point (*Towards a Dynamic Economics*, p. 90). His fixed investment is, of course, net of depreciation.

[10] Changes in the cost of financing new investment may alter firms' views as to the most remunerative proportions in which to combine capital goods with other productive factors, thus changing the value of C_r. The same considerations apply to changes in real wages.

by,[11] C_r will be constant; it is, in effect, the capital-output ratio v of the Acceleration Principle as defined on p. 179. If an equilibrium of *ex ante* saving and investment existed to start with, it will be preserved as output increases if $C_r \triangle Y = sY$. This condition can be rearranged to read $\triangle Y/Y = s/C_r$; the value of $\triangle Y/Y$ that satisfies the equation is the "warranted" rate of growth G_w, and the "fundamental equation" can accordingly be rewritten

$$G_w C_r = s.$$

If the economy continues to grow at this rate, it will be following an "equilibrium path."

A graphical illustration of the theory is given in Figure 15.2, whose axes measure income horizontally and saving and investment vertically.[12] The savings function is the same as in Figure 15.1; its slope is the s of the "fundamental equation." The straight lines $I(\triangle Y)$ represent Harrod's investment function $I = C_r \triangle Y$, which may also be written

$$I_t = C_r (Y_t - Y_{t-1}).$$

Investment is zero if current income is the same as that of the previous period (*i.e.*, if $Y_t = Y_{t-1}$), and so $I_1(\triangle Y)$ cuts the income axis at a point Y_0 representing the income of the last period. The slope of $I_1(\triangle Y)$ is equal to C_r and is steeper than 45° on the assumption that $C_r > 1$.

Saving-investment equilibrium exists when income is Y_1; this exceeds the previous period's income by $Y_1 - Y_0$, so that the warranted rate of growth, defined as $(Y_t - Y_{t-1})/Y_t$, is equal to $(Y_1 - Y_0)/Y_1$. When the next period $(t + 1)$ is reached, Y_1 will have become the preceding period's income, and the investment function will have shifted to $I_2(\triangle Y)$; if the value of C_r has not changed, $I_2(\triangle Y)$ will be parallel to $I_1(\triangle Y)$. The intersection of $I_2(\triangle Y)$ with $S(Y)$ now gives an equilibrium income of Y_2, so that the warranted rate of growth in period $t + 1$ equals $(Y_2 - Y_1)/Y_2$. Similarly, $t + 2$'s investment function will be $I_3(\triangle Y)$, giving an equilibrium income of Y_3 and a warranted growth rate of $(Y_3 - Y_2)/Y_3$. By the properties of similar triangles, it can be seen that the warranted

---

[11] Harrod's usage of "neutral" differs from that of other writers, especially J. R. Hicks; see F. H. Hahn and R. C. O. Matthews, "The Theory of Economic Growth: A Survey," *Economic Journal*, Vol. 74 (December, 1964), pp. 779–902.

[12] For a diagrammatic treatment in terms of growth rates rather than absolute levels of income, see C. S. Soper, "Jorgenson on Stability in the Sense of Harrod," *Economica*, Vol. 31 (November, 1964), pp. 408–411.

growth rates in each of the periods are all equal to each other; warranted growth thus proceeds at a constant proportionate rate as long as the values of s and C_r remain unchanged. As time goes by, the investment function will shift further and further to the right, so that income will continue to increase at the warranted rate, provided saving-investment equilibrium is maintained from period to period.

Since investment demand here depends on the growth of income, Harrod's model appears to be an example of the Multiplier-Accelerator interaction described in the previous chapter — but with the special feature that the Accelerator is unlagged. The implied assumption is that firms compare the existing state of demand for their products (which they are assumed to know precisely) with that of the previous period and *simultaneously* carry out whatever investment is needed to bring their capital up to current requirements. This assumption, it may be argued, is not very realistic: firms take time to become aware of the state of their markets, and by the time they make the appropriate investment decisions the next period will already have arrived. Even if such decisions *are* made simultaneously with the growth of demand, time is needed to put them into effect, so that the investment actually being carried out at a given moment will not be related to current changes in demand.

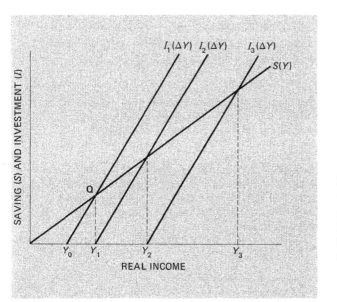

Fig. 15.2

The "warranted" growth rate is determined by the level of investment as a function of changing income and the MPS.

The insertion of a lag into Harrod's investment function, however, changes the model almost beyond recognition. If, instead of $C_r(Y_t - Y_{t-1})$, I_t is made equal to $C_r(Y_{t-1} - Y_{t-2})$, it immediately becomes autonomous of current income, since both Y_{t-1} and Y_{t-2} become unchangeable historical facts once period t has been reached. Instead of $I_1(\triangle Y)$ in Figure 15.2, period t's investment function will be a horizontal straight line whose distance above the income axis depends on the amount of income growth that occurred in the previous period. If both saving and investment are lagged one period, the model is identical with the Multiplier-Accelerator interaction presented in Chapter 14, in which income did not grow but merely fluctuated about a constant level.[13] The inclusion of lags, with the object of increasing the realism of the Harrod model, may therefore disqualify it altogether as a theory of growth.[14]

Autonomous investment does not appear in the "fundamental equation," but Harrod is prepared to bring it in if necessary as an additional variable k. The equation then becomes

$$G_w C_r = s - k$$

where k is the proportion between autonomous investment and current income.[15] Since C_r and s are assumed constant, the presence of k has the seemingly paradoxical effect of reducing the warranted rate of growth G_w. In Figure 15.2, the introduction of autonomous investment demand will shift $I_1(\triangle Y)$ vertically upward, and since it slopes more steeply than $S(Y)$ (because C_r exceeds s), it will now intersect the latter to the left of Q; the equilibrium output of period $t = 1$ will be reduced below Y_1, and the warranted rate of growth will be less than $(Y_1 - Y_0)/Y_1$. It

---

[13] It will be remembered, however, that given a sufficiently large value of v (in Harrod's terminology, C_r) the model will produce an uninterrupted rise in income; in this case, the system continues to be a "growth model" even when lagged.

[14] See J. R. Hicks, "Mr. Harrod's Dynamic Theory," *Economica*, Vol. 16 (May, 1949), pp. 106–121.

[15] *Towards a Dynamic Economics*, p. 79. Harrod argues that "in the long run k must disappear, for in the long run all capital outlay is justified by the use to which it is put," though "it may be very important to separate it out in the short period." When k is thus specified, the alternative expression for the "fundamental equation," as given on page 373 above, now becomes

$$\frac{\triangle Y}{Y} \bullet \frac{I_i}{\triangle Y} = \frac{S}{Y} - \frac{I_a}{Y},$$

where I_i is induced and I_a is autonomous investment. This simplifies to $S = I_i + I_a$, a slightly more elaborate version of the saving-investment equilibrium condition.

may fall to zero or even become negative if the amount of autonomous investment is sufficiently large. This result brings out the fact that the role of growth in Harrod's model is to induce sufficient investment to offset current saving; the appearance of an additional offset, in the shape of autonomous investment, means that less induced investment is required for the purpose, and so the growth rate must fall if equilibrium is to be maintained.

Another consequence of the fact that C_r exceeds s is that the short-run equilibrium positions shown in Figure 15.2 are *unstable*. A slight divergence from Q, for example, will produce a tendency toward further divergence. If output in period $t = 1$ turns out to be slightly greater than Y_1 because firms have overestimated the demand for their products, the demand for investment will exceed saving, and firms will be under pressure to expand output still more. Conversely, a slight shortfall of production below Y_1 will create a surplus of saving over investment demand, which will tend to depress output to still lower levels; the further output moves from equilibrium, the greater the pressure forcing it still further away. Such a movement will mean that the excess of current income over the last period's income is no longer equal to $Y_1 - Y_0$, so that the actual growth rate now differs from the warranted rate ($Y_1 - Y_0)/Y_1$.

A change in the value of C_r or s will have similar consequences. An increase in s, for example, will cause $S(Y)$ to slope more steeply so that it cuts $I_1(\triangle Y)$ at a point above and to the right of Q. The equilibrium level of income will be higher than before, but because the initial effect of the movement of $S(Y)$ is to create an excess of saving over investment at the existing income level Y_1, income will tend to fall instead of rising towards its new equilibrium value. In this case, the fact that the equilibrium level of income has increased means that the warranted growth rate has risen — yet the very increase in G_w will have set up pressures causing the *actual* growth rate G to fall below its original value.

Harrod's own demonstration of this instability begins by comparing the *ex post* and *ex ante* versions of the "fundamental equation." Since GC and G_wC_r are both equal to s, they are equal to one another; [16] consequently,

---

[16] This, it may be noted, implies the assumption that *ex ante* saving always equals *ex post* saving. The s of $GC = s$ is merely the proportion of income *actually* saved, while that of $G_wC_r = s$ is the proportion that income recipients *wish* to save. The two could very well be different as, for example, when shortages frustrate consumers' buying plans.

any difference between G and G_w entails an equal but opposite difference between C and C_r. Thus, if G exceeds G_w, then C_r exceeds C, which means that the amount of investment required to produce the current increase of output is greater than the amount actually being made; firms will be demanding more equipment and materials than are currently available, and the effort to supply them will cause output to rise faster than before. But this will make the excess of G over G_w still greater, so that the actual growth rate, far from returning to equality with the warranted rate, will run away from it. In the same way, an initial shortfall of G below G_w will cause C to exceed C_r, with the result that G will be reduced still further.

This argument has done no more than put the analysis of the preceding two paragraphs into Harrodian terms. The symbols C_r and C represent $I/\triangle Y$ in the *ex ante* and *ex post* senses respectively; *ex post* investment is identical with saving, so C could equally well be written $S/\triangle Y$. A difference between C_r and C, therefore, is a difference between investment demand and saving.[17] Similarly, since G is defined as the actual value of $(Y_t - Y_{t-1})/Y_t$, and G_w as the value that would be consistent with saving-investment equilibrium, a difference between G and G_w means that Y_t is not at its equilibrium value.[18] To say that $C_r > C$ when $G > G_w$ is thus the same thing as saying that investment demand exceeds saving when income is above its equilibrium level. The instability of the warranted growth rate is the instability of saving-investment equilibrium, at a given moment of time, when the slope of the investment function exceeds that of the saving function.

With equilibrium thus unstable, the consequences of a departure from it depend on the rapidity with which the level of production can respond to such a disturbance. If the reaction is instantaneous, output will immediately fall to zero or rise to the limit of productive capacity, according to the direction of the displacement. With a one-period lag, on the other hand, output will remain unchanged for the time being; an excess of investment demand over saving will be carried forward as unsatisfied demand, while a deficiency of investment will cause an accumulation of unsold goods to be carried over. When the next period is reached and firms

---

[17] $C_r \neq C$ implies $I/\triangle Y \neq S/\triangle Y$; multiplying both sides by $\triangle Y$ gives $I \neq S$. It is assumed (as has already been noted) that saving plans are always realized, *i.e.*, that *ex post* equals *ex ante* saving.

[18] Since the value of Y_{t-1} is fixed (being a matter of past history by the time period t is reached), Y_t is the only term that can vary in the expression $(Y_t - Y_{t-1})/Y_t$; consequently, G and G_w, if different in value, imply different values of Y_t.

take fresh production decisions, they will presumably try to work off the backlog of demand (or the accumulation of inventories) by making output higher (or lower) than it would otherwise have been. Income will once again differ from its equilibrium value, and a fresh backlog of demand (or accumulation of inventories) will have to be carried forward, creating similar situations in the next and subsequent periods.

Since Harrod does not include any lags in his model (and indeed seems to rule them out by insisting that its instability "has nothing to do with the effect of lags"), it might be supposed that he is assuming the first of these possibilities, *i.e.*, an immediate runaway of output to one extreme or the other. But when he speaks of "centrifugal forces . . . causing the system to depart further and further from the required *line of advance*,"[19] he seems to be thinking of the more gradual divergence that would occur if an output lag were present, with output tracing a path that over a succession of time periods deviates more and more from the course it would have taken if warranted growth had continued. Given appropriate values of s and C_r as well as a one-period output lag, the system will certainly be unstable in this second sense.[20] Harrod, however, implies that its instability over time is unconditional, *i.e.*, that the system will never under any circumstances return to the warranted growth path once it has deviated from it. In view of the ambiguity of his concept of instability, arising from his failure to specify the lags involved, it is not surprising that he has been criticized on this point by a number of writers.[21]

---

[19] *Towards an Economic Dynamics*, p. 86. Italics added.

[20] If in Figure 15.2, $I_1(\Delta Y)$ slopes much more steeply than $S(Y)$, an excess of output in the initial period (*i.e.*, at time $t=1$) over the equilibrium level Y_1 will create an even greater excess of investment demand over saving. With a one-period output lag, this excess will be carried forward to period 2; if firms try to clear the whole backlog by adding an equivalent amount to period 2's equilibrium output, the difference (D) between actual and equilibrium output will be greater in period 2 than in period 1 (in symbols, $D_2 > D_1$). But period 2's equilibrium output (Y_2) will itself be larger than that of period 1, since the investment function will have shifted to the right — and will, in fact, lie somewhat to the right of $I_2(\Delta Y)$. If D_2, as a proportion of Y_2, is greater than D_1 as a proportion of Y_1, the system will be unstable in the sense that Harrod seems to have in mind. This condition will be fulfilled if, for example, $C_r = 4$ and $s = 0.2$, but not if, say, $C_r = 1.5$ and $s = 0.5$.

[21] See, for example, H. Rose, "The Possibility of Warranted Growth," *Economic Journal*, Vol. 69 (June, 1959), pp. 313–332; and Dale W. Jorgenson, "On Stability in the Sense of Harrod," *Economica*, Vol. 27 (August, 1960), pp. 243–248. Jorgenson argues as follows: Actual growth equals G_w plus the growth of a "disequilibrium variable," D, which at the outset was equal to $\Delta Y(C_r - C)$ and which goes on increasing at a rate k. If, however, k is less than G_w, the "disequilibrium variable"

If warranted growth *is* unstable over time, an upward deviation will carry the actual growth rate progressively further above it; but there is an ultimate limit to this divergence, namely, the "natural rate of growth" G_n, which Harrod defines as "the rate of advance which the increase of population and technical improvements allow." Actual growth G may exceed G_n for a time — for example, when the economy is emerging from a recession and re-employing labor and equipment previously idle. But once full employment has been regained, it will be impossible for output to grow faster than G_n. There is no similar limit, however, to the possible value of G_w; a high propensity to save, for example, might cause the warranted growth rate to exceed the "natural" rate — in which case G, even if it is at first equal to G_w, will soon fall away from it because of its inability to exceed G_n for very long. The initial divergence will then increase, pulling G below G_n and dragging the economy into a recession. If, on the other hand, G_w is below G_n, it is no longer inevitable that G must deviate from it, though it may still do so because of some chance disturbance. With G and G_w equal but less than G_n, there will be an increasing gap between actual output and the output that the economy is capable of producing when all its resources are employed.

Only if G_w equals G_n will it be possible to combine steady growth with full employment; yet there is no reason to suppose that this equality will be achieved except by accident, since the magnitudes that determine the two growth rates (s and C_r in the case of G_w; the rates of population increase and technical progress in the case of G_n) are all assumed to be determined independently of one another and of the actual rate of growth G. Thus, the prospects before an economy that resembles Harrod's model are unattractive — it will experience either a succession of booms and slumps or a steady advance accompanied by growing unemployment, with the chances in favor of the first alternative because of the instability of the warranted growth path.

It is easy to see that there would be no problem of reconciling steady growth with full employment if the "required" capital-output ratio C_r were a variable.[22] Even with s and G_w fixed, the equality of G_w and G_n

---

will eventually become negligible relative to total income, so that the economy will ultimately return to the warranted growth path instead of moving ever further away from it.

[22] It may be noted that Harrod allows the possibility of *temporary* variations in C_r; for example, when the economy is recovering from a depression and is able to expand output by bringing idle plant back into use instead of investing in newly pro-

would be permanently assured if C_r could be relied on to assume whatever value was necessary to satisfy the equation $s/C_r = G_n$. Under certain circumstances, indeed, this may happen: if an excess supply of labor (*i.e.*, the unemployment associated with $G_w < G_n$) forces down real wages, while the cost of employing capital remains unchanged, labor will be substituted for capital in the productive process, the value of C_r will fall and that of G_w will rise. Conversely, a shortage of labor ($G_w > G_n$) will raise real wages, alter the relationship of factor prices, cause capital to be substituted for labor, and thereby increase C_r and reduce G_w.

If nevertheless, C_r remains constant, it must be either because it is physically impossible to substitute labor for capital and vice versa, or because the prices of the factors remain unchanged relative to one another in spite of imbalances of supply and demand — the latter being the explanation put forward by Harrod.[23] In either case, given certain assumptions about the technique of production,[24] both factors will be employed in fixed proportions to each other and to the level of output; the amount of labor required to increase output by one unit will be constant, just as capital requirements are. Once full employment has been attained, therefore, output cannot grow any faster than the supply of labor, except to the extent that labor's productivity is raised by technical progress as time passes. In the absence of the latter, output *per head* cannot rise, since output and population will be growing at exactly the same rate; no increase at all in output will be possible if the population is stationary.[25]

It is hard to believe that upward trends in per capita output are to be attributed entirely to improvements in technology and not at all to increases in the amount of capital per worker — yet this is what is implied by the assumption of fixed factor proportions. On the other hand, to aban-

---

duced equipment, C_r will be below its normal value until full-capacity output is regained.

[23] He concentrates attention on the possibility of changes in the interest rate rather than in real wages (which are assumed constant) and concludes that interest is not sufficiently flexible and investment demand not sufficiently interest-elastic to bring about the necessary changes in C_r. See *Towards a Dynamic Economics*, p. 96 ff., or Harrod's "Comment" (on an article by H. Pilvin, which see also) in *Quarterly Journal of Economics*, Vol. 67 (November, 1953), p. 555 ff.

[24] They are (a) that capital and labor are the only factors of production, and (b) that there are "constant returns to scale." For the significance of these assumptions, see the discussion of production functions in the next section of this chapter.

[25] It is assumed for simplicity that population and the supply of labor increase at the same rate. They may, of course, fail to do so; for example, changes in age grouping may alter the proportion of the population that is of working age.

don that assumption as too restrictive is to change the Harrod theory out of recognition and to take the first step in the so-called "neoclassical" approach to the problem of growth.

3. "Neoclassical" Growth Theory

Harrod's point of departure was the short-run theory of income determination, originally developed by Keynes as a means of analyzing the causes of mass unemployment in the 1930's. Just as Keynes stressed the role of aggregate demand in determining output and employment in the short run, so, in his turn, Harrod approached the analysis of growth in terms of the long-run evolution of demand and (as has been seen) was not optimistic about the possibilities of combining steady growth with full employment over a long period of time. But it can be argued that Keynesian principles, now generally accepted, have provided governments with an armory of weapons for tackling short-run difficulties and that it is now legitimate to proceed on the assumption that full employment will somehow or other be assured. Output may then be expected to grow at the maximum rate permitted by the increase of productive capacity. The Harrod model could be made to give this result by including in it a government whose taxes and expenditure adjust s so as to keep G_w permanently equal to G_n, or by including a monetary authority that appropriately adjusts both s and C_r. But a simpler approach is merely to relax the assumption of fixed factor proportions, so that whatever the quantities of capital and labor at the disposal of the economy, they can always be combined in such a way as to ensure that all are employed. This is the starting point of the "neoclassical" growth theory associated with R. M. Solow, T. W. Swan, and J. E. Meade.[26]

It is now assumed, therefore, that it is physically possible to substitute

---

[26] See R. M. Solow, "A Contribution to the Theory of Economic Growth," *Quarterly Journal of Economics*, Vol. 70 (February, 1956), pp. 65–94; T. W. Swan, "Economic Growth and Capital Accumulation," *Economic Record*, Vol. 32 (November, 1956), pp. 334–343; J. E. Meade, *A Neo-Classical Theory of Economic Growth*, 2d. ed. (New York: Oxford University Press, 1961). The theory has been called "neoclassical" because it makes assumptions — perfect competition, full employment, and the payment of factors according to their marginal products — that were customarily made by the so-called neoclassical economists whose work appeared between (roughly) 1870 and 1920.

the factors in the production process for one another and that such substitution is not in any way inhibited by price rigidities — in other words,
that perfect competition exists. To produce a given output, it will then be
possible to mix the factors in any number of different proportions. A full
statement of the possible mixtures at all levels of output is a *production
function.* This concept is familiar in microeconomic analysis, which uses it
to explain the individual firm's choice of inputs at a given set of factor
prices.[27] In macroanalysis, however, the problem arises that "output" is
not a single homogeneous commodity but a mass of different ones aggre-

---

[27] See R. Dorfman, *Prices and Markets* (Englewood Cliffs, N.J.: Prentice-Hall,
1967), pp. 51–68; K. E. Boulding, *Economic Analysis*, 4th ed. (New York: Harper and
Row, 1966), Vol. I, pp. 543–555; or R. G. D. Allen, *Mathematical Economics*, 2d. ed.
(New York: St. Martin's Press, 1959), pp. 332 ff.

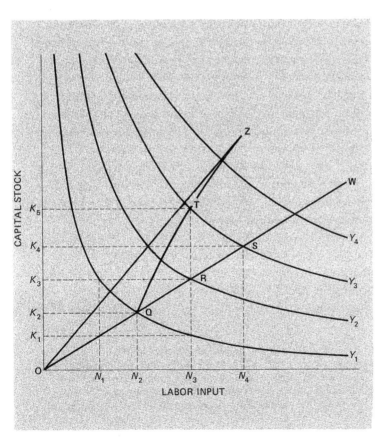

Fig. 15.3

Growth paths for an
economy characterized by
a "neoclassical" produc-
tion function

gated in terms of their money values, so that a change in the composition of output or in the relative prices of its constituent commodities can produce a change in total output even if the quantities of the factors employed remain unaltered. To avoid this difficulty, it will be assumed that the output of the whole economy consists of a single good that is equally suitable for both consumption and investment purposes. It is also assumed that the factors of production are themselves homogeneous; that capital is "malleable" in the sense that a unit of it can be used in conjunction with any quantity of labor, large or small; that labor and capital are the only factors of production; and that (for the time being, anyway) there is no technical progress.

A production function with all these characteristics is shown in Figure 15.3, whose axes measure quantities of labor and capital respectively, and whose Y curves are "isoquants," each of which refers to a given level of output and shows the various combinations of capital and labor capable of producing it. For example, output Y_1 can be produced by K_3 units of capital and N_1 of labor, or by K_2 and N_2, or by K_1 and N_3, or by any other pair of factor quantities indicated by the curve. The greater the quantities of both factors employed, the greater the amount of production, so that Y_2 represents a larger output than Y_1, Y_3 a larger one than Y_2, and so on. As growth proceeds and the economy's factor supplies increase, successively higher Y curves will be reached, and the points attained on them will form a "growth path" leading upward and to the right. If capital and labor always increase in the same proportion, the growth path will be a straight line (or "ray") through the origin, like the line OW passing through points Q, R, and S. Given "constant returns to scale," output will grow in exactly the same proportion as the factors of production, and equal distances along a ray such as OW will represent equal increases in output.[28] The Y curves of Figure 15.3 have been drawn so as to intersect OW (and any other ray through the origin) at equal intervals; with constant returns to scale, therefore, a movement from one Y curve to the next always implies the same amount of change in output.

Now suppose that the economy starts at point Q, producing output Y_1

---

[28] If "increasing returns to scale" operate, a given length along QRS will represent a greater rise in output the further away it is from the origin; the output yielded by equal successive additions to both factors will be increasing. The existence of "diminishing returns to scale" implies the contrary. In the absence of any a priori reason for assuming either increasing or diminishing returns to scale, it is reasonable to assume constant returns.

with K_2 units of capital and N_2 of labor; and that the supply of labor grows at a constant rate n which is exogenously determined. The rate of growth of capital ($\triangle K/K$) is the rate at which the initial stock K is being increased by net investment, which is assumed [29] equal to *ex ante* saving. If the community saves a constant proportion s of income, $\triangle K/K$ will be equal to sY/K, or s/v when the capital-output ratio K/Y is written v. If s/v equals n, capital and labor will be growing at the same rate, so that the growth path will be along one of the many possible rays, for example, OW. Along this line, output will be increasing at the same rate as the factors of production because returns to scale are constant, so that

$$\frac{\triangle Y}{Y} = \frac{s}{v} = n.$$

This equation defines a condition of *steady growth*, because as long as the values of s, v and n that satisfy it remain unchanged, output will continue growing indefinitely at the same rate.

At first glance, this result seems to be identical with that obtained from the Harrod model when $G_w = G_n$, since G_w equals s/C_r, C_r is equivalent to v, and G_n equals n when there is no technical progress. The difference lies in the fact that C_r is a constant, while v is not. If, in Harrod's model, the value of C_r happens not to satisfy the equation $s/C_r = n$, no pressures arise to bring it into line,[30] and G_w and G_n continue to differ. In the neoclassical model, on the other hand, v will adjust to whatever value is required to satisfy the steady-growth condition given above.

The following example illustrates such an adjustment. Suppose the economy has hitherto experienced steady growth, advancing up OW in Figure 15.3 as far as Q; at this point, however, it is assumed that there is a sudden once-for-all increase in the propensity to save. The rise in s means that s/v now exceeds n; a larger proportion of income is being saved and invested, so that the capital stock is growing faster than the supply of labor. Instead of rising from K_2 to K_3 in the next period, capital rises to K_5; the labor supply, however, rises only to N_3 (as it would have done in

---

[29] This condition may be regarded as a necessary consequence of the assumptions of perfect competition and continuous full employment. Alternatively, it can be assumed that a monetary authority behind the scenes constantly adjusts interest rates so as to ensure saving-investment equilibrium at full employment. See Meade, *op. cit.*, p. 3.

[30] Where $s/C_r > n$ (*i.e.*, $G_w > G_n$), there will of course be a fall in the *actual* growth rate G, but this does not imply any adjustment of G_w; it merely means that the system is out of equilibrium.

any case, since labor's growth rate is exogenously determined); and the system consequently moves to point T (on Y_3) instead of point R (on Y_2). At T, the capital intensity of production is greater than it was along the original growth path OW. Had Y_3 been reached at S instead of T, the amounts of capital and labor employed would have been K_4 and N_4 respectively, instead of K_5 and N_3; that is, less capital and more labor would have been used to produce the same level of output. This means that the capital-output ratio v has risen, so that s/v is now somewhat smaller than it was just after the initial increase in s occurred; capital is growing more slowly, but its rate of growth still exceeds that of labor. As long as s/v continues to be greater than n, the capital intensity of production will go on increasing, and v will continue to rise until the value of s/v once more equals n, and steady growth is resumed at the original rate. However, the growth path will now be steeper than it was at first: it is shown in Figure 15.3 as OZ, which like OW is a straight line through the origin, but which represents a higher capital-labor ratio. Because the capital stock has increased faster than n for a time, it is greater than it would have been if the economy had continued to expand along OW; consequently, the resumption of steady growth means that capital is growing by a larger *amount* per period even though its *rate* of growth is identical with that implied by OW. It may seem paradoxical that an increase in s should bring about no permanent increase in the rate of growth of capital and income — yet this is a necessary consequence of the adjustment of the proportions in which the factors are employed.

In the case just examined, the system was pushed off the original growth path by an increase in the propensity to save. If s had fallen instead of rising, the consequence would have been a reduction in the value of v, to the point where s/v regained equality with n; production would have become less capital intensive, and the system would have moved on to a new steady-growth path less steep than OW. A fall in n itself, unaccompanied by a change in s, will be accommodated by a rise in v; to offset the slower growth of the labor force, production will become more capital intensive, but because s is unchanged, the growth rate of capital will fall until it is equal to the reduced value of n. In all cases, the system will react to a disturbance by forcing a change in v sufficient to allow a resumption of steady growth at the rate n.

As long as steady growth continues at a given rate, the fact that $\triangle Y/Y$ equals n means that no change in output per head can occur; but any of the disturbances described above will raise or lower per capita output to a new level, at which it will remain when steady growth is resumed. An initial rise in *s*, causing capital to grow faster than labor, also causes output to rise faster than it would otherwise have done. In the example given earlier, the increase of capital from K_2 to K_5 in Figure 15.3 allowed the system to reach output Y_3 instead of Y_2, as it would have done had steady growth continued. As long as s/v is greater than *n*, output will be growing faster than labor, and output per head will be rising; when s/v is at last equal to *n* again, output per head will have been stabilized at a higher level than before. Conversely, a reduction in the value of *s* will bring about a fall in output per head. The effects of changes in *n* are similar to those of *opposite* changes in *s*; thus, output per head will rise when the growth rate of labor diminishes and fall when the latter increases.

Nothing has been said so far about the time likely to be needed for the system to adjust back to steady growth after a disturbance has occurred. It seems probable that the process will be a lengthy one. Suppose, for example, that *s* is 0.06, *v* is 3, and *n* is 0.02; if all rates of change are annual rates, output will be increasing steadily at 2% per year. Now let *s* suddenly rise to 0.08; to restore s/v to equality with *n*, *v* must be raised from 3 to 4. This implies a substantial increase in the capital stock, which (since $K = vY$) must now rise by an amount equal to a whole year's output. Even after the initial rise in *s*, however, only 8% of current income is being saved and invested, so that it would take 12½ years to bring capital up to the required level even if output were stationary. And since output will, in fact, be growing at annual rates higher than 2% during the adjustment process, it is easy to see that a very long time will elapse before steady growth is resumed. Indeed, R. Sato has shown that on realistic assumptions regarding the values of the parameters of a neoclassical model, the system may take more than a century to accomplish as much as nine-tenths of the adjustment back to steady growth.[31]

It is hardly likely that such a lengthy period will go by without fresh disturbances occurring, so the chances of steady growth ever being attained seem very small. Accordingly, it may be said that the system's behavior during the adjustment process is of much greater interest than its

---

[31] Ryuzo Sato, "Fiscal Policy in a Neo-Classical Growth Model," *Review of Economic Studies*, Vol. 30 (February, 1963), pp. 16–23, and "The Harrod-Domar Model *versus* the Neo-Classical Growth Model," *Economic Journal*, Vol. 74 (June, 1964), pp. 380–387. Sato's model is more complicated than that discussed in the text, since it includes technical progress, direct taxation, and public investment; but his general conclusions are still valid in the simpler case.

behavior when following a steady growth path. From this point of view, it is of less consequence that (for example) a rise in *s* will *eventually* be offset by a rise in *v* so that the growth rate is unchanged than that the rise in *s* will cause *s/v* to exceed *n* for a considerable time, in the course of which both capital and output will be increasing faster than they would have otherwise. Though their rates of increase will be gradually falling towards equality with the steady growth rate, the diminution may be so slow that for quite long periods it will be reasonable to treat them as constants. Economic policy will be realistic if it seeks to produce a continual rise in output per head by encouraging a high rate of capital accumulation, even though this will in the long run be offset by the adoption of more capital-intensive methods of production.

4. The Influence of Technical Progress

There is one way, however, in which output may continue to increase faster than the factor supplies even when steady growth has been attained, though this possibility has up to now been excluded by assumption — that is, through technical progress. The effect of new and better techniques of production[32] is to enable the existing quantities of capital and labor to produce more than they were capable of doing previously. This may be illustrated in Figure 15.3 in either of two ways. The *Y* curves can be shifted inward toward the origin, so that Y_2 replaces Y_1, Y_3 replaces Y_2, and so on; any pair of quantities of capital and labor will then reach a higher *Y* curve than before. Alternatively, the *Y* curves may be left as they are, and the points K_1, K_2, N_1, N_2, etc., moved further out along their respective axes in proportion to the increase in productivity brought about by technical progress. The effect will then be shown as precisely equivalent to that of an increase in the physical quantities of the factors.

Even if the capital stock and the labor supply remain unchanged in physical terms (*i.e.*, if *s* and *n* are both zero), continuous technical ad-

---

[32] It is important to distinguish between "changes in methods of production," in the sense of changes in the proportions in which the factors are employed (which in Figure 15.3 would be represented by a movement along one of the isoquants, *e.g.*, from S to T), and "technical progress," by which a given combination of factors is enabled to produce more than it did before (and which, as will be seen, involves a shift in the isoquants themselves).

vance will allow the system to reach successively higher Y curves, tracing a growth path similar to that which would be followed if the factor supplies were themselves increasing. If technical progress raises the productivity of both factors in the same proportion r, output will itself rise at the rate r, and the system will move along a steady growth path such as OW or OZ. When the physical quantities of the factors are already increasing in such a way as to give steady growth, the addition of technical progress will cause a more rapid advance along the same growth path, and the steady growth condition will become

$$\frac{\triangle Y}{Y} = \frac{rK + \triangle K(1+r)}{K} = \frac{rN + \triangle N(1+r)}{N}$$

or

$$\frac{\triangle Y}{Y} = r + \frac{s}{v}(1+r) = r + n(1+r),$$

where, it will be noticed, the influence of the capital-output ratio v diminishes in proportion to the rate of technical progress.

Of course, the productivity of one factor may increase more quickly than that of the other. Suppose the rate of growth of capital productivity, a, exceeds that of labor productivity,[33] b, and that factor supplies are fixed in physical quantity (*i.e.*, $s = 0$, $n = 0$). If capital and labor inputs are respectively K_2 and N_2 in Figure 15.3 (so that in the absence of technical progress, output would have been stationary at Y_1), the system will move upward along a straight line starting at Q and sloping more steeply than OW. Because a is greater than b, the scale of the capital axis will be increasing faster than that of the labor axis, and K_2 will be moving outward more rapidly than N_2. As they move, K_2 and N_2 will trace a growth path that, not being a ray through the origin, cuts the successive Y curves at continually increasing intervals, which means that output grows at a rate

---

[33] In this case, technical progress might be described as "capital biased"; this implies "labor bias" when b exceeds a, and "neutrality" when a and b are equal. But this usage conflicts with that already noted (note 11) in connection with the Harrod model, where technical progress was said to be "neutral" if it did not change the value of C_r. "Harrod neutrality" therefore requires that $a = 0$. The definition of neutrality as the condition in which $a = b$ is associated with J. R. Hicks (*The Theory of Wages*, 2d ed. [New York: St. Martin's Press, 1963], pp. 121–123). Accordingly, technical progress is said to be "Hicks neutral" when the productivity of capital is rising at the same rate as that of labor, leaving the capital-labor ratio unchanged; and "Harrod neutral" when only the productivity of labor is rising and the capital-output ratio remains unaltered.

less than a and greater than b, which gradually diminishes as time goes by. Eventually, the growth rate of output will approach the value of b, and the path along which output is rising will approximate one of steady growth.[34]

When, in addition, the physical quantities of capital and labor are increasing, the effects just described will be superimposed on those of the growth of the factor supplies themselves. If the latter by themselves would have brought about a steady growth of output, technical progress with a greater than b will push the system off the steady growth path; on the other hand, a growth rate of labor in excess of that of capital might conceivably just offset the excess of a over b, leaving the system on a steady growth path that it could not otherwise have attained. The greater the difference between a and b, the more it will complicate the adjustment process that takes place when the values of s and n change.

So far it has been assumed that technical progress raises the productivity of each unit of capital, old or new, and of the entire labor force, in exactly the same proportion; like manna from heaven, it descends on the whole of the system's factor supplies. This assumption is clearly unrealistic. When an advance in the design of machinery makes it possible to produce higher output for the same cost as before, only newly built machines benefit; technical progress must be "embodied" in new investment if it is to exert an effect on the level of output. (Similarly, the productivity of labor may be increased by improvements in the educational system, but only new recruits to the labor force will embody this sort of progress; older workers' abilities will not be affected.) Thus, the rapidity with which the economy reaps the benefits of technical advance depends on the rate of growth of the factor supplies as well as on the rate of technical progress itself.

The steady-growth condition given earlier may be amended to show this by the omission of the terms rK and rN, so that it becomes

$$\frac{\triangle Y}{Y} = \frac{\triangle K(1+r)}{K} = \frac{\triangle N(1+r)}{N},$$

where, if $\triangle K$, and $\triangle N$ are both zero, output remains stationary whatever the value of r. This formulation, however, ignores the possibility that some part of the capital stock and labor force is being retired and replaced as

---

[34] In mathematical language, the growth path is *asymptotic* to a ray, *i.e.*, the two will meet only at infinity; thus, the rate of growth of output will never fall quite far enough to be precisely equal to b.

time goes by; that is, it neglects the question of depreciation. Even if the factor supplies are not growing in total amount, technical progress may still be embodied in new units that replace those currently being withdrawn. The faster the rate of depreciation, the greater the response of output to technological advance. The steady growth condition is

$$\frac{\triangle Y}{Y} = \frac{rdK}{K} = \frac{rdN}{N},$$

where d is the proportion of K and N replaced per period of time, and where $\triangle K$ and $\triangle N$ are assumed to be zero. It is, of course, unlikely that the value of d will be the same for both capital and labor,[35] and a difference in the factors' replacement rates may be supposed to have consequences similar to those of a difference between their rates of productivity growth.

The analysis of these effects, however, runs into difficult problems of aggregation. Instead of the homogeneous, "malleable" capital stock assumed at the outset, there will now be a collection of assets of various vintages, each embodying a different technology and each differing in productivity from the others. Whatever device is adopted to aggregate them (*e.g.*, the addition of money values or the use of some physical measure such as horsepower) is bound to be more or less unsatisfactory; and when physical differences between capital goods are allowed to come into the reckoning, the original assumption of a one-product economy becomes more artificial than ever.[36] Another difficulty arises concerning the "malleability" of capital, *i.e.*, its ability to cooperate with any amount of labor, large or small. When the adoption of a newly devised technique requires the capital embodying it to differ in physical characteristics from capital of earlier vintages, it is hard to imagine it still to be malleable; yet without the assumption of malleability, the factor proportions are no longer

---

[35] It need not be supposed that labor s d is simply the rate at which high school and college graduates step into the shoes of elderly workers (in which case it would be about 0.02). Workers can be retrained at any age; those who acquire new skills may be regarded as replacing their old, unskilled selves, so that d will be higher the greater the amount of on-the-job training.

[36] But not completely untenable. Suppose (as suggested by Meade, *op. cit.*, p. 6) the single product is cows, which may be consumed as meat or used to breed more cows. Improved breeding may make the currently-produced cows more fecund than previous "models"; technical progress will be embodied in them, yet production will still consist of a single homogeneous commodity.

variable (*i.e.*, the isoquants of Figure 15.3 can no longer be drawn as smooth curves) and the model ceases to conform to neoclassical specifications.

5. Extensions of the Basic Neoclassical Model

Complications of the sort described in the previous paragraph draw attention to the extreme simplicity of the basic model, in which as many problems as possible have been avoided by making appropriate assumptions; when these are relaxed in an attempt to achieve greater realism, the model becomes much more difficult to handle. It is not feasible, within the limits of a single chapter, to explore all the possibilities that then arise, but it will be useful to note some of the more important modifications that can be made.

The first, and perhaps the most obvious, one is to abandon the assumption that output consists of a single all-purpose commodity. The simplest way of doing this is to divide the economy into two "sectors," one producing a capital good K and the other a consumption good C; the labor supply and the capital stock are divided between them, and the K sector provides new equipment both for itself and for the C sector. Each sector has its own production function. No stocks of C are accumulated, so that investment is equal to the output of the K sector; given the neoclassical assumption that investment demand equals saving at full employment, K output equals sY, where s as usual represents a constant propensity to save. But Y itself is now an aggregate of C and K. To reduce Y to a single measure it is necessary to know the relationship between the prices of the two commodities, p_k and p_c; a change in p_k/p_c can alter Y and sY, thereby causing the output of the K sector to vary.

Under perfect competition, factor prices are the same in both sectors and equal the value of the factors' marginal physical products; for example, $\mathrm{MPL}_c p_c$ equals $\mathrm{MPL}_k p_k$, where MPL is the marginal physical product of labor and the subscripts refer to sectors. To find relative prices (*i.e.*, p_k/p_c) it is necessary to evaluate $\mathrm{MPL}_c/\mathrm{MPL}_k$. The uniformity of factor prices also means that the proportion between the wage rate (W) and the rate of profit per unit of capital (π) is the same in both sectors, which implies that $\mathrm{MPL}_c/\mathrm{MPK}_c$ equals $\mathrm{MPL}_k/\mathrm{MPK}_k$ (where MPK is the marginal physical product of capital). To satisfy this equation, the capital stock and labor force must be allocated between the sectors in certain proportions.[37] The ratio $\text{MPL}_c/\text{MPL}_k$ gives the commodity-price ratio p_k/p_c, which in turn defines Y; given the value of s, the output of the K sector will then be determined, while that of the C sector will be whatever is produced by the labor and capital not in use in the K sector.

If the output of K is such as to increase the total capital stock at the same rate as the labor force, total output will grow steadily as long as the allocation of new factor supplies is such as to maintain the conditions set out above. When this is not possible (for example, because the K sector itself has a very high requirement for additional capital), the ratios W/π and p_k/p_c will change as output grows, thereby altering the valuation of Y; this will cause sY, and therefore the output of K and the rate of increase of the capital stock, to differ from their steady-growth values, and the rate of growth of output will be changed in consequence. The adjustment process is more complicated than that in the one-sector model, but the general presumption is that a stable steady-growth path exists — that is, there must be a set of values of all the variables that will permit output to grow at a constant rate, and the system will return to this steady-growth condition after a disturbance.[38]

A second way of modifying the original model is to relax the assumption that saving is a constant proportion of income. An alternative hypothesis is the *classical saving function*,[39] which makes saving depend on the distribution of income between wages and profit by assuming that the proportion of profit saved (s_π) is greater than that of wages (s_W). Total profit equals the capital stock, K, times the rate of profit π, which itself is equal to MPK;[40] the share of profit in total income is thus $K \bullet \text{MPK}/Y$.

---

[37] In either sector, the greater the amount of capital used and the less the amount of labor, the greater the value of MPL/MPK (on the usual assumption of diminishing marginal rates of substitution). If $\text{MPL}_c/\text{MPK}_c$ is higher than $\text{MPL}_k/\text{MPK}_k$, a transfer of labor from the K sector to the C sector and/or a transfer of capital in the opposite direction will equalize the two ratios. This would be consistent with a number of allocations of the factors; however, when K output is determined as above, only one of these allocations is possible. The system could be described algebraically by a set of simultaneous equations; see Meade, *op. cit.*, Appendix II.

[38] See Hahn and Matthews, *op. cit.*, pp. 820–821.

[39] So named by Hahn and Matthews, *op. cit.*, pp. 793–794; because of its affinity with the saving behavior postulated by Ricardo and other "classics."

[40] The assumption of a single homogeneous product is now restored, so that all quantities except N are measured in the same units. It is unnecessary — indeed, it would be meaningless — to specify a price in order to indicate the value of a factor's marginal physical product.

Similarly, the share of wages is $N \bullet MPL/Y$, and the overall propensity to save is

$$s = s_\pi \frac{K \bullet MPK}{Y} + s_W \frac{N \bullet MPL}{Y}.$$

Given steady growth, K, N and Y will all be increasing at the same rate; MPK and MPL will remain unchanged;[41] and s will be constant.

If, however, K is growing faster than N, the share of profit will increase unless MPK falls relative to MPL sufficiently to restore the balance. Whether it will do so depends on the shape of the production function,[42] but if it does not, the fact that s_π exceeds s_W means that s will increase as Y grows. To restore the steady-growth condition $s/v = n$, the value of v must rise by more than would have been necessary had s remained constant; the adjustment process will take longer and will bring the system onto a more capital-intensive growth path than would otherwise have been reached. There is no doubt, however, that steady growth will eventually be restored, because s cannot rise above some maximum value less than 1.0, but no similar restriction applies to v. When the shape of the production function is such[43] that MPK/MPL falls by more than is needed to keep the factor shares constant, the value of s will decline, the adjustment process will be shorter, and the new growth path will be less capital intensive than it would have been with s constant.

It may be noted that where s_W is zero (*e.g.*, because the wage rate is at subsistence level), s equals s_π times the profit share; and the condition

---

[41] Had N remained unchanged, the growth of K would have meant diminishng returns to capital, *i.e.*, a falling value of MPK; similarly, N increasing with K unchanged would have reduced MPL. But since N and K here rise at the same rate, marginal returns to the factors remain constant in the "homogeneous" production function shown in Figure 15.3.

[42] In Figure 15.3, the slope of an isoquant at a given point is the inverse of MPK/MPL (for proof, see Boulding, *op. cit.*, p. 562); the steeper the slope, the smaller this ratio. As the system moves from Q to T, diverging from the steady-growth path because K is growing faster than N, QT crosses the successive isoquants at points of increasing slope, so that MPK/MPL is reduced. Whether it falls sufficiently to offset $\triangle K/\triangle N$ depends on how much steeper the slope of Y_3 is at T than that of Y_1 is at Q; and this depends on the shape of the isoquants.

[43] That is to say, where the slope of Y_3 at T is very much greater than that of Y_1 at Q, because the isoquants have a very pronounced curvature. In this case, the isoquants may be said to have a low "elasticity of substitution" (on which see R. G. D. Allen, *Mathematical Analysis for Economists* [New York: St. Martin's Press, 1938], pp. 340–343).

$s/v = n$ becomes $s_\pi(P/Y)(Y/K) = n$, where P is total profit and Y/K replaces $1/v$. The left-hand side of this equation reduces to $s_\pi\pi$ (π being the rate of profit P/K), and in the extreme case in which $s_\pi = 1.0$ (*e.g.*, because all profits are earned and retained by companies), the steady-growth condition becomes $\pi = n$ — that is, the growth rate must equal the rate of profit.

The next variation from the basic model concerns n, the rate of growth of the labor supply, which instead of being exogenously determined might be assumed to depend in some way on the growth of output. An obvious example is Malthus' celebrated population theory, whereby the labor force expands or contracts in such a way as to maintain the real wage rate at subsistence level; n would thus depend on the rate of growth of the capital stock, s/v, instead of the other way around. This effect may be seen by considering a case in which both capital and labor have hitherto been stationary (*i.e.*, $n = 0$ and $s = 0$) with the wage rate at subsistence level, but in which s now becomes positive so that the capital stock begins to grow. If n were to remain zero, the profit rate would decline and the wage rate would rise; but as soon as the wage rate begins to exceed subsistence level, population will grow, the labor supply will increase, and the wage rate and profit rate will be maintained at their original values.

If the production function is of the type shown in Figure 15.3, then the labor force will be induced to grow at the same rate as the capital stock (so that $n = s/v$), and there will be only one possible growth path, namely, one that cuts the successive isoquants at points whose slope (*i.e.*, MPL/MPK) is consistent with a subsistence wage value of MPL. Variations in s will then be offset, not by changes in v as described earlier, but by changes in n. There will, however, be a considerable time lag involved in such adjustment. When a rise in real wages causes an increase in the birth rate, as Malthus assumes, it will be some years before this increase brings about a corresponding rise in the growth of the labor force; in the meantime, the system will have behaved as though n were exogenous — v will have risen, only to fall again when n attains its steady-growth value.

In the original model, not only n, but also r, the rate of technical progress, was assumed to be given exogenously; this assumption, too, might be dropped and the model further modified by relating r to one or more of the other variables in the system. For example, a rapid rate of capital growth may be supposed to stimulate inventiveness by providing opportunities for testing new processes, so that r varies with the value of s/v;

and r may itself influence the growth of capital by furnishing new investment opportunities. If the amount of capital (as distinct from its growth
rate) is large relative to output, technical knowledge will be greater and
more widespread than if production were less capital intensive, and this
situation will be favorable to the discovery and adoption of new techniques; in this case, r will be greater, the higher the value of v. If the neoclassical full-employment assumption is relaxed to allow the possibility of
a discrepancy between *ex ante* investment and saving, technical progress
may be stimulated by the existence of shortages of capital and labor — or,
of course, discouraged in the face of excess supplies of the factors. Yet another kind of complication arises if technical progress has the effect of
altering returns to scale, for example, causing them to increase where previously they had been constant. Finally, there is the possibility that the
value of r varies over time in some way, because new inventions tend to
be "bunched" — one invention leads to another until all possible applications of a newly discovered principle are for the time being exhausted.

Other modifications of the basic model include the employment of a
third factor of production, such as a fixed quantity of land, which would
affect returns to the other factors and make the distribution of income
more complicated (and which would, incidentally, make it impossible to
depict the production function in a two-dimensional diagram such as Figure 15.3); the replacement of Figure 15.3's smoothly curving isoquants by
"kinky"[44] ones so arranged as to offer only a limited number of possible
steady growth paths (the so-called "linear programming production function"); the dropping of the assumption of perfect competition so that factors are no longer remunerated at rates equal to the value of their marginal
physical products; and the introduction of money to serve as a means of
exchange when the system has two or more sectors. These modifications,
and those noted in the previous paragraphs, may be combined and re-
combined in a variety of ways. By making alternative sets of assumptions,
it is possible to construct a very large number of models of varying degrees of complexity and realism according to the purposes for which they
are required. The original neoclassical model, highly simplified though it
is, provides a useful point of departure for such further developments.

---

[44] Such isoquants have the same general shape as those of Figure 15.3, but are
made up of a number of straight lines coming together at obtuse-angled corners. For
an illustrative diagram and discussion, see R. G. D. Allen, *Mathematical Economics*,
2d. ed. (New York: St. Martin's Press, 1959), p. 338.

By assuming from the outset that full employment is continuously main-tained and that factor proportions are variable, neoclassical theory avoids sharing the pessimism of Harrod and Domar about the long-run prospects of advanced economies. It will be recalled that Harrod's assumption of "fixed proportions" made it highly unlikely that the natural and warranted growth rates would coincide for long, so that the economy would suffer a continuous sequence of booms and slumps. Domar thought it improbable that his steady-growth condition $\triangle I/I = s\sigma$ would be continuously satis-fied: "It is difficult enough," he wrote, "to keep investment at some reason-ably high level year after year, but the requirement that it always be rising is not likely to be met for any considerable length of time."[45] His doubts recall Keynes' discouraging picture of an economy in which capital has become so abundant that there is no further incentive to invest, yet whose saving propensity is still positive at full employment; the accumulation of capital has caused it to "suffer the fate of Midas," in the sense that severe and chronic unemployment will prevent it enjoying the standard of life that its wealth makes possible.[46]

In the depressed conditions of the 1930's such pessimism seemed justi-fied, and it was reinforced by the arguments of the *secular stagnation thesis* associated with the name of A. H. Hansen.[47] Hansen drew attention to the current decline in the rate of population increase in the United States and Europe and suggested that the rapid economic growth experi-enced during the century before 1914 had been "unique in history" be-cause of the unprecedented rise in population and the settling of new territories. He estimated that about one-half of the investment expenditure of that period was attributable directly or indirectly to these two influ-ences. By the 1930's, however, there were no important areas left for set-

---

[45] *Essays in the Theory of Economic Growth*, p. 99. It is fair to add that the article from which these words are taken was actually written in 1947, while the col-lected *Essays* were not published until 1956. In his foreword to the 1956 volume, Do-mar modified his earlier pessimism, though without completely renouncing it.

[46] *General Theory*, pp. 217–219.

[47] See A. H. Hansen, "Economic Progress and Declining Population Growth," *American Economic Review*, Vol. 29 (March, 1939); reprinted in G. Haberler, ed. for the American Economic Association, *Readings in Business Cycle Theory* (Homewood, Ill.: Irwin, 1944).

tlement, and population growth seemed within sight of complete cessation; technical progress was slowing down and assuming an increasingly "capital-saving" character and was less important than before as a stimulus to new investment. Consequently, in the absence of massive deficit spending by governments, investment demand would henceforth continue to be inadequate to absorb full-employment saving, and chronic unemployment was to be expected in the future.

As a forecast of what was to happen in the next few decades, the stagnation thesis was a failure. Instead of declining, population growth accelerated in the 1940's, output rose in most countries at unprecedented rates, and levels of employment were much higher than before the war — which by itself, of course, would have been enough to upset any prediction based on prewar trends. But even had there been no war and no "population explosion," it is not clear that stagnation must have ensued. The connection between population growth and investment is not as straightforward as Hansen made it seem; for example, in a country where incomes are very low, a rapid increase of numbers may merely turn its cities into overcrowded slums rather than stimulating new construction, whereas a rich country may still do much new building even when population is stationary, because its people can afford to improve their standards of accommodation. Similarly, the fact that no empty lands remain to be opened up does not necessarily imply a great reduction in the demand for investment in communications, public utilities, etc.; there are still plenty of "underdeveloped" countries that, though already well settled, are poorly equipped with capital of this kind and would like to have more.

A deceleration of technical progress, with a capital-saving bias, would certainly depress investment demand relative to saving if it existed; but it is impossible to say whether this condition held in the 1930's. Even if it did, there are reasons for supposing it to have been reversed since then. One of the striking features of the 1950's and 1960's has been the rapid growth of expenditure on research and development, both by governments and by private enterprise — in the United States, for example, it rose from 1.4% of GNP in 1955 to 2.8% in 1960, and in Britain from 1.7% to 2.5%.[48] This increase does not, of course, provide a measure of the rate of technical progress itself, but it certainly suggests a speeding-up rather than a slow-

---

[48] United Nations, Economic Commission for Europe, *Economic Survey of Europe in 1961*, Part 2, "Some Factors in Economic Growth in Europe During the 1950's" (1964), Chap. V, p. 5.

ing-down. The examples of post-1940 technological advance that most readily come to mind – the application of atomic power and the automation of manufacturing processes, for example – are of an eminently capital-using rather than capital-saving nature.

These considerations suggest that the pessimism of the stagnationists was unjustified and that there is no inescapable reason why aggregate demand should in the long run fall further and further below the economy's capacity to produce. This is not to say that demand and capacity can always be relied on to grow at exactly the same pace: changes in the rate of technical progress and population increase, as well as autonomous shifts in the propensity to save, may always upset the balance. But there is no presumption that advanced economies must, in the long run, either suffer increasing unemployment or else run larger and larger budget deficits in the effort to keep employment full. It is true that in the post-1940 period there has been, in most countries, a marked increase in government spending both in absolute terms and as a proportion of GNP, but this has been accompanied by corresponding increases in taxation; there has been no need to use it as a device to offset demand deficiency in the private sector. The growth of public expenditure has, in fact, been an autonomous development, arising not only from the scale of armaments maintained since 1945 but also from the rise in demand for many publicly provided services, such as the construction of highways to accommodate the growing automobile population and the expansion of educational facilities to train the increasing number of scientists and technologists required in industry. Its upward trend is another reason for supposing that the long-term growth of capacity is likely to be matched by a similar growth of demand.

7. Growth Policy and the Management of the Economy

If continuing expansion is not to be feared for stagnationist reasons, it might seem that the government ought positively to encourage it: the greater the annual increase in output, the better the living standards the community will be able to enjoy, and the more easily can social tensions be alleviated insofar as they arise from economic causes. To raise the growth rate, the tax system can be used to stimulate technical progress; for example, by the favorable treatment of research expenditures and by depreciation allowances that encourage the early replacement of machinery.

Educational programs can improve labor skills and diffuse new technology; fiscal and monetary policies can be applied so as to favor investment rather than consumption and to redistribute income toward groups with high propensities to save. The higher the growth rate aimed at, however, the stronger the measures that must be used to achieve it, and the greater the likelihood that the government's growth policy will be incompatible with its other objectives.

Suppose, for example, that it is possible to stimulate investment sufficiently to make output rise 5% a year, but that other elements of demand cannot be reduced by an amount equal to the increase in investment; aggregate demand will then exceed full-employment output, with the result that prices rise at, say, 6% per annum. To prevent prices rising at all, it is assumed that investment would have to be kept down to a level sufficient to give only a 1% annual increase in output. In this case, then, the government can aim at rapid growth or at price stability, but not both. It could, perhaps, try for an intermediate outcome, such as a 3% growth of output combined with a 2% increase in prices, if that is the highest rate thought to be tolerable; as long as it does not allow output to grow at the maximum 5% rate, it will be "trading off" some potential growth against a lower rate of price increase. The trade-off could, of course, be more complicated than this, for instance, since money wage increases are no longer offset to the same extent by rising productivity (as described on p. 342) when the growth rate is reduced, cost inflation may take over when demand inflation is eliminated — so the growth rate will have to be neither more nor less than, say, 2½% to minimize the rate at which prices are rising.

Similar trade-offs may be called for between growth and other policy objectives. As output expands, it will induce a greater demand for imports, thereby weakening the balance of payments. On the other hand, rising productivity will be cutting costs and permitting reductions in export prices, which (given a large enough demand elasticity) will cause overseas earnings to rise; this rise, plus the possibility that advancing technology may be developing entirely new products for sale abroad, will improve the balance of payments and offset the effect of rising imports. But if the expansion of imports tends to pull ahead of the rise in exports whenever output growth exceeds, say, 3%, there will be a further constraint on government policy. If the 5% growth rate is nevertheless chosen, part of it will have to be "bought" with a balance-of-payments deficit.

It might seem that no trade-off problem can arise between rapid growth and full employment as aims of policy; the higher the level of employment, the higher the level of output and the greater the margin of resources that should be available for growth-promoting investment. Yet even here the possibility of conflict cannot be ruled out. If high levels of employment are accompanied by redistribution effects in favor of groups with low saving propensities (for example, because labor unions are very powerful and use their strength to raise money wages faster than prices), consumption may increase so much in proportion to income that less is left for investment than would have been available had employment been lower. Again, the faster the growth rate, the larger may be the proportion of frictional unemployment as new technologies are rapidly introduced, and demand patterns change. If, for social reasons, the community prefers to keep employment as high as possible, it may be prepared to accept a lower growth rate in order to do so.

Because of the difficulty of reconciling growth policy with its other objectives, the government may decide to abandon it altogether and to concentrate its attention wholly on short-run measures to avoid inflation, unemployment, and balance-of-payments deficits. The growth rate will then be determined entirely by private decisions regarding saving and investment and by such technical progress as will be made independent of government encouragement. There is a good deal to be said for such a course. Full employment, price stability, and external balance are relatively simple objectives; there is not much difficulty judging the degree of success or failure in attaining them, nor is there any doubt of the unpleasant consequences following failure, so that they are clearly worthwhile policy aims. Growth is a different matter; there is no obvious way in which the government can be sure that a growth rate of, say, 5% is the correct policy objective rather than 4% or 6%, while a failure to achieve the 5% target can hardly be regarded as disastrous if the community already enjoys an ample amount of consumption per head. National pride will no doubt suffer if other countries are seen to be progressing faster, but no positive hardship will arise as long as living standards do not actually decline below their existing level. It is only in countries whose standards are intolerably low that faster growth must be taken as the overriding policy objective. Elsewhere, it can be argued that whatever growth takes place without government intervention will be in accordance with the community's preferences between current consumption and provision for the future, and that the government has no business to force the economy to behave differently.

Even so, it is possible to make out a case for a positive growth policy.

It has already been seen that in the absence of technical progress, income per head will rise only if the stock of capital is increasing faster than the labor force is growing, *i.e.*, if $s/v > n$. However, as capital per worker will then be rising, there will be diminishing returns to capital, so that the productivity of capital (Y/K) will gradually fall — that is, the value of the capital-output ratio v (or K/Y) will slowly increase. As it does so, the value of s/v will decline until the economy at last converges on a steady-growth path along which $s/v = n$; and income per head will be stabilized at the level reached at the end of the convergence process. If it is to rise further, s must be increased so that s/v once more exceeds n; when the consequent increase in v has again restored s/v to equality with n, yet another rise in s will be needed to bring about a further increase in income per head. If private preferences are such as to give a stationary value of s, income per head cannot in the long run go above the level that obtains along the growth path determined by that value of s. By taking action to increase s, therefore, the government can ensure that income per head goes on growing.

Provided that short-run stabilization policies succeed in maintaining a noninflationary full-employment equilibrium throughout (so that full-employment saving is always exactly matched by investment demand), there is no limit to the level of income per head that can eventually be reached. But income per head is not, after all, the best measure of the community's economic welfare. It is much more important to know how much income remains available for consumption after the amount of current saving has been deducted. If, in order to raise income per head from 100 to 110, the proportion saved must increase from 34% to 40%, there can be no increase in consumption per head, which will remain unchanged at 66. The rise in s will have served no good purpose unless the community for some reason derives satisfaction from the mere possession of a larger capital stock, as well as from the consumable goods and services it produces. If this possibility is ruled out, it follows that income per head should not be raised beyond the point where consumption per head is a maximum.

Along any given steady-growth path, consumption per head (c) will be equal to the amount of capital per head (k) times its average productivity (σ), minus the output that must be set aside to equip each new entrant to the labor force with the necessary capital equipment (kn); that is,

$$c = \sigma k - nk = k\,(\sigma - n)$$

where σk is income per head and nk is the saving needed to maintain the existing capital/labor ratio.[49] As long as steady growth is maintained, the capital stock and the labor force will be growing at the same rate, so that k will be constant over time; but the value of k will be larger, the steeper[50] the growth path the economy is following, *i.e.*, the more capital intensive the method of production. By causing the value of s to increase, the government is pushing the economy onto successively steeper growth paths, along each of which the value of k will be greater than it was on the last the equation shows that increases in k will in themselves have the effect of raising c. But as capital per head grows, diminishing returns will cause the average product of capital (σ) to fall, so that equal successive increases in k will give smaller and smaller increases in c. Eventually a point will be reached at which the influence of the decline in σ begins to outweigh that of the rise in k, so that c will first cease to grow and then, given further increases in k, actually diminish. When the economy is moving along the growth path on which c is at its maximum value (in other words, where the gap between σk and nk is greatest), it will be following what E. S. Phelps has called "the Golden Rule of Accumulation."[51] If private preferences do not happen to give a value of s that is exactly the right size to put the economy on the "golden rule" path (and there is no reason to suppose that they will, except by accident), maximum consumption will be reached only if the government takes appropriate action to adjust s to the required level.[52]

---

[49] The equation can be derived from the steady-growth condition, $s/v = n$, by putting $1 - c$ in place of s, multiplying both sides by v, and rearranging to give $c = 1 - nv$. Replacing v by K/Y and multiplying through by Y gives cY (or C) $= Y - nK$. Putting σK in place of Y and dividing through by the numbers of workers, N, gives $C/N = \sigma K/N - nK/N$, or $c = \sigma k - nk$ where $c = C/N$ and $k = K/N$ as in the text.

[50] "Steeper," that is, in terms of the slope it would have in Figure 15.3; see p. 383.

[51] Edmund S. Phelps, "The Golden Rule of Accumulation: A Fable for Growthmen," *American Economic Review*, Vol. 51 (September, 1961), pp. 638–643; see also his *Golden Rules of Economic Growth* (Norton, 1966).

[52] The criterion of "golden rule" growth is that $\triangle c / \triangle k = 0$, which means that it is no longer possible to increase consumption per head by moving to a steeper growth path through raising the amount of capital per head. In general, $\triangle c = \triangle k \ (\mu - n)$, where μ is the marginal productivity of capital; the condition that $\triangle c / \triangle k$ is zero thus implies that $\mu = n$. If factors of production are remunerated with their marginal products, total profit is μK; on any steady-growth path, saving is nK, *i.e.*, just enough to equip new workers with the existing amount of capital per head. Since

The preceding argument is, of course, subject to many qualifications. Technical progress can easily be fitted in if it is "Harrod neutral" (*i.e.,* such that it leaves all capital-output ratios unchanged[53]), since it will then be equivalent to an increase in the rate of growth of the labor force. Instead of n, the rate at which labor supply rises in physical units, it will now be $n + \tau$, where τ is the rate of increase in labor efficiency due to technical progress; and the problem will be to maximize $k(\sigma - [n + \tau])$ instead of $k(\sigma - n)$. Any other kind of technical progress, however, will reduce, prevent or, even reverse the decline in σ that would otherwise have resulted from diminishing returns to capital, with the result that $k(\sigma - n)$, and therefore c, may have no maximum value. *Every* increase in capital and income per head will then be accompanied by an increase in consumption per head.

Further complications (which will not be explored here) arise if factor proportions are assumed to be fixed, instead of variable as shown in Figure 15.3; if the assumption of constant returns to scale is dropped; if it is no longer supposed that only one commodity is produced, so that the economy now has two or more sectors; if an additional factor of production is introduced — and so on. The "golden rule" path then becomes much harder to discern, even if it can still be supposed to exist. Nonetheless, the mere suggestion that there may be such a path is a useful corrective to the uncritical presumptions that growth performance is always to be judged by the increase of income rather than consumption per head, and that no matter how large the capital stock has already become, a further increase can do nothing but good.

However, even though the Golden Rule may indicate the ultimate objective of growth policy, it offers no guidance as to the best way of getting there. It may seem that all the government need to do is to cause the community to save the proportion of income, s^*, that is consistent with "golden rule" growth; as income and capital per head gradually increase, the system will then converge on the steady-growth path along which consumption per head is maximized. But a community whose income per head is low, and which at present saves a proportion of it much smaller than s^*, would suffer hardship if the amount of consumption per head were suddenly and severely reduced through the immediate raising of s to the

---

$\mu K = nK$ when $\triangle c / \triangle k = 0$, it can be said that "golden rule" growth will be characterized by the equality of saving with total profit.

[53] See footnote 33, p. 389.

s^* level. It has already been seen (on p. 387 above) that the convergence process is likely to be slow, perhaps spanning several generations; the assurance that their grandchildren's consumption will be high may be small comfort to the present generation if they must pass their lives on short rations to make it possible.

If the government therefore raises s only a little at first, with the intention of gradually increasing it when the subsequent growth of income per head permits it to do so without causing hardship, it will be reducing the benefits accruing to the next few generations (compared with benefits resulting from s^*), but diminishing the burden placed on the present one. The problem is to choose the value of s that will bring about the best possible distribution of burdens and benefits between the generations — that is, one that could not be changed without causing more loss of satisfaction by those whose consumption per head was reduced than would be gained by those whose consumption was increased.

But this prescription raises enormous difficulties, even in theory. Obviously there is no way of knowing in advance how much satisfaction future generations will derive from increased consumption, even if it is thought meaningful to compare the degrees of satisfaction enjoyed by different generations; nor is it at all clear how many generations ought to be brought into the reckoning, nor whether the expected gains of the more distant ones should be discounted according to their remoteness in time. Even in a highly simplified theoretical model, it is impossible to fix on a particular value of s as being "optimal" without making some drastic assumptions, and it is clearly out of the question in the complex economy of real life. It can, perhaps, be argued that if the choice of s is left to the private decisions of the present generation, they will naturally tilt the distribution of burdens and benefits in their own favor — undervaluing their successors' gains relative to their own losses of satisfaction through forgoing consumption — and that the government should therefore try to redress the balance by making them save more. But even this general presumption is a doubtful one. It may turn out, for example, that technical progress raises future generations' gains to an extent unforeseen by the present one, more than offsetting the present generation's underevaluation — in which case, the present generation will have imposed a burden of saving on itself that, instead of being too light, will actually prove to have been too heavy.

It follows that measures to increase s and thereby raise the growth rate can be firmly recommended only when the economy seems to be settling down on a steady-growth path along which consumption is not maximized. In any other situation, it is conceivable that an overenthusiastic growth policy may diminish economic welfare rather than increase it. It must be remembered, too, that the expansion of the economy can involve certain social costs, such as the destruction of natural amenities through urban sprawl and water pollution, which are not reflected in statistical indicators of growth but which are nonetheless real. Apparent advances in personal consumption per head may be offset to a considerable extent by deterioration in the consumers' environment. In the light of current emphasis on the importance of growth as a policy objective, it is important to bear in mind that it can be too fast as well as too slow.

Keynes and the Classics

The ideas set forth in this book have been offered on their own merits, not as the views of a particular school of thought. Twenty-five years ago, they would inevitably have been labeled "Keynesian," not only because the main lines of analysis derive from Keynes' work, but also because his theories continued to be controversial for some time after *The General Theory of Employment, Interest and Money* appeared in 1936. In that book, he vigorously attacked the teachings of what he called "the classical school" — the line of economists beginning with Ricardo and descending through John Stuart Mill to Marshall and Pigou. He drew the sharpest possible distinction between his own theories and those of "the classics," denouncing the doctrines of the latter as misleading and disastrous. A long and often bitter controversy ensued, in which questions of definition and terminology were sometimes debated as hotly as issues of substance, till at length the "Keynesian Revolution" had run its course, and the Keynesian teaching, developed and refined in various ways, was absorbed into the canon of accepted theory. The present-day student may feel that this controversy should now be regarded as a past episode in the history of economic thought and that the battles of an earlier generation need not be refought within the covers of a modern textbook. He will find, however, that references to "the classics" and "classical theory" occur frequently in the literature of the subject; the object of this Appendix is to clarify the usage of the terms "Keynesian" and "classical" by means of a brief comparison of the theoretical systems to which they refer.

The economists characterized by Keynes as "the classics" were not, as the label might suggest, the exponents of a single, monolithic system of thought, in unanimous accord on every detail. Nevertheless, they did agree in emphasizing the importance of the "theory of value," the purpose of which is to explain the relative prices of commodities in terms of one another; the tradition in which Keynes was brought up visualized the economy as a set of markets in which the forces of supply and demand together determined output and relative prices. The natural approach to the problem of unemployment, therefore, was to examine the labor market and the determinants of supply and demand within it. An excess of supply over demand for any commodity implied that its current price was higher than the competitive equilibrium price. If, in the labor market, more people were seeking work than could be employed at the existing wage rate, it could be presumed that current wages were too high and that the situation would itself create pressures to bring them down. If this failed to happen, it was to be attributed to the existence of minimum-wage laws, to the bargaining power of workers' organizations, or to some other restraint on the forces of competition. The remedy for chronic unemployment, then, was to make wages "flexible" by removing such restraints. Once competition was allowed to work, it was thought, the market would move toward equilibrium and full employment would be achieved.

Whatever the input of labor at full employment, it would cooperate with other factors of production to produce given quantities of goods and services. For the economy to be in *general* equilibrium, demand and supply had to balance in each of the markets to which these goods and services were being furnished; but as long as there were no impediments to the free movement of prices, it could be assumed that each commodity's price would rise or fall sufficiently to bring about such a balance. For any economy in which prices and wages were flexible, it was thought that there must exist some pattern of relative prices (including wages, as the price of labor) that would permit equilibrium to be attained in all markets (including the labor market). This seemed so obvious to "the classics" that they could find little use for a separate concept of aggregate demand, since it was logically identical with aggregate supply.

Under the principle known as "Say's Law,"[1] the very act of production implies an equivalent demand for goods and services, since the aim of each producer must be either to satisfy his own wants directly or to exchange his output for other commodities. It is true that producers offer their wares in exchange for money in the first instance, but they want the money not as an end in itself but for the sake of what it will buy; money, indeed, is merely a device for avoiding the awkwardness of barter, a "veil" concealing the fact that "what constitutes the means of payment for commodities is simply commodities."[2] The supply of any particular commodity, then, is *ipso facto* a demand for other commodities, and it follows that the mass of goods and services produced in the whole economy is at the same time *both* aggregate supply and aggregate demand. Of course, supply might exceed demand in the market for a particular commodity, but

---

[1] Propounded by Jean-Baptiste Say in his *Traité d'Economie Politique* (1803) and adopted by Ricardo, John Stuart Mill and others. There has been much disagreement as to the interpretation of the Law: for quotations, references, and further discussion, see D. Patinkin, *Money, Interest and Prices*, 2d ed. (New York: Harper and Row, 1965), Note L, pp. 645–650; and J. A. Schumpeter, *History of Economic Analysis* (New York: Oxford University Press, 1954), pp. 615–625.

[2] J. S. Mill, *Principles of Political Economy* (New York: Augustus M. Kelley, Publishers, 1965), Bk. III, Chap. XIV, sec. 2.

this would merely imply a corresponding excess of demand over supply in some other market or markets. It is logically impossible, under Say's Law, for the sum of demands in *all* markets to be greater or less than the sum of supplies, since they are merely two ways of describing the very same thing.[3]

The fact that producers save part of their money receipts instead of spending them all on commodities was not admitted as an objection to this principle. Saving (argued "the classics") requires abstention from immediate personal consumption, but not the accumulation of idle cash: rational individuals, seeking remunerative employment for their savings, either spend them on capital goods for use in their own enterprises or lend them at interest to others who in turn use them to buy the means of production. The higher the interest rate, the more they will save; and the equilibrium rate is that which exactly balances the amount of saving against the amount that entrepreneurs wish to borrow for investment purposes. Since the borrowed funds reappear on the demand side of the market for capital goods, the identity of aggregate demand and supply is maintained — all that has happened is that savers have purchased commodities indirectly instead of directly. Thus, saving does not diminish aggregate demand, but merely determines the proportions in which the latter is allocated between consumption and investment.

So far, it has not been necessary to mention the quantity of money, for it is not essential to the main part of the classical system, in which all prices are *relative*, in the sense of being ratios in which goods and services are exchanged for one another. Such relationships can hold true at any level of *absolute* money prices; the statement that a banana is worth twice. as much as an orange is just as valid whether their money prices are respectively 10¢ and 5¢, 50¢ and 25¢, or $600 and $300. So far, then, money values are indeterminate, and something else is needed to explain them. Here "the classics" invoked the Quantity Theory of Money. They assumed that payments habits are not liable to change in the short run and that transactions will be at the full-employment level if the labor market is in equilibrium. Given constant values of V and T in the celebrated equation $MV = PT$, the level of money prices P depends entirely on the quantity of money M. On the other hand, M and P have no influence on any of

---

[3] It should be noted that Say's Law is not just another way of stating the accounting identity by which National Product $\equiv$ National Expenditure, though it has sometimes been so interpreted.

the "real" variables in the system except through the Pigou effect, whereby price level changes cause the owners of money assets to feel richer or poorer and consequently to alter their saving behavior.[4] If the Pigou effect is neglected, on the ground that it was a very late addition to the classical edifice, it can be said that a complete dichotomy existed between the real and the monetary sides of classical economics.

The essence of the classical doctrine, then, was that the economy would tend to move towards a full-employment equilibrium if the forces of competition were allowed to work without restraint; that any departure from that equilibrium would necessarily set up forces pushing the system back to it; and that these tendencies held true whatever the quantity of money might be and whether the disposition to save was great or small. Every one of these propositions was denied by Keynes. He argued that full employment was only one of the possible situations in which the economy might find itself, and that the classics had merely treated a special case that was subsumed in his own *general* theory of output and employment.

Keynes' two great innovations were the consumption function and the liquidity-preference schedule. The first of these made saving depend on income instead of the interest rate, so that the amount of saving done at the full-employment level of income might exceed planned investment even when interest was fairly low. A further reduction in interest might raise investment to equality with full-employment saving, if the demand for investment happened to be sufficiently elastic with respect to the interest rate. The liquidity-preference theory, however, showed that this change in interest might require very large increases in the supply of money and that the rate of interest could not, in any case, fall below a minimum level given by the "liquidity trap" (as shown in Figures 11.4 and 11.5, pp. 282 and 284. If, when this minimum interest rate had been reached, the amount of investment demand was still insufficient to absorb the whole amount of full-employment saving,[5] the level of income would be forced down until saving was reduced to equality with investment. At this point, aggregate demand would be in equilibrium with current

---

4 See pp. 114–116.

5 This extreme situation is the "Keynesian case" referred to on p. 288. Its opposite, the "classical case," would be one in which liquidity preference is inelastic with respect to the interest rate. See F. Modigliani, "Liquidity Preference and the Theory of Interest and Money," *Econometrica*, Vol. 12 (February, 1944), pp. 45–88.

output, but there would be an excess of supply over demand in the labor market. If money wages were flexible, they would fall and bring down the price level with them, but full employment would not be restored (in the sense of an equilibrium of demand and supply in the labor market) unless the drop brought about an appropriate rise in investment demand and/or the propensity to consume. Though this sequence might conceivably occur, there was no reason to suppose that it would *necessarily* do so, and the consequence could well be a bottomless deflation without any diminution of the amount of unemployment.[6] However, since money wages are not, as a matter of observed fact, very flexible downward, their rigidity would prevent such an outcome, and the economy would continue (for the time being, at any rate) in a situation of less than full employment.[7]

By making the level of output and employment depend on aggregate demand, Keynes put Say's Law into reverse: instead of supply creating its own demand, it was now demand that called forth an equivalent supply — which might not require the employment of the whole labor force in its production. The focus of analytical interest was thus shifted to the determinants of consumption and investment, particularly to the connections between them and the level of income; the originality of Keynes' approach lay in combining all these elements, both real and monetary, into a single system of interlocking relationships that together determined employment and output. Even those who disagreed with his conclusions were constrained to adopt his methods and to express the classical tradition in terms of systematic models that they would not otherwise have been led to construct.[8] When these were compared with the Keynesian model, it became clear that the choice between them was essentially a matter of empirical assumptions. If the speculative demand for money is not, after all, very important quantitatively nor very elastic with respect to interest rates; if wages are not, in fact, very inflexible downward; if saving does

---

[6] See the *General Theory*, pp. 262–269.

[7] Such a situation is often described as "under employment equilibrium"; but since excess supply persists in the labor market, it is clear that no *general* equilibrium exists, and the term is used in a loose sense to mean that no forces are set up to dislodge the system from the position it has reached.

[8] They were, as G. Haberler put it, "forced to think through things which they used to leave in an ambiguous twilight, and to draw from accepted premises conclusions of which they were unaware or which they left discreetly unexpressed." ("The General Theory," in S. E. Harris (ed.), *The New Economics* (New York: A. A. Knopf, 1947), p. 197.)

respond more to changes in interest rates than in income; and if the economy adjusts quickly to changes in the various parameters – then the classical presumption of a strong tendency to full-employment equilibrium is justified. If, on the other hand, one or more of these assumptions cannot be made, the Keynesian apparatus is needed to show what levels of employment and output will actually be reached in the short run, and the Keynesian policy prescriptions (for example, budget deficits and low interest rates when aggregate demand is too low to give full employment) become appropriate.

The original Keynesian model of the *General Theory* was unsatisfactory in a number of ways.[9] It was completely static, in the sense of being wholly concerned with equilibrium conditions during the short period in which changes in technology and in the capital stock could be ignored; it contained no lagged relationships, thus excluding both the dynamic Multiplier and the Accelerator; and it was drawn in terms that made it much more adaptable to demand-deficiency situations than to those of excess demand and inflation. Keynes did not distinguish clearly enough between *ex post* and *ex ante* magnitudes (so that a sharp controversy raged for some years on the exact meaning of saving and investment), and he offered no empirical evidence for some crucial assumptions (for example, those concerning the characteristic shapes of the consumption and liquidity-preference functions). But he did, nevertheless, set out his system in terms of relationships that could be statistically tested, thereby stimulating empirical investigation and giving a great impetus to the growth of econometrics; his emphasis on the importance of expectations and uncertainty about the future gave a strong impulse to the development of dynamic analysis; and his clear distinction between macro- and microanalysis[10] caused many fallacies to be discarded. By providing a base from which later economists were able to go forward – even though their work often caused his own detailed conclusions to be changed – Keynes opened a new and vital chapter in the history of economics.

---

[9] On this, see H. G. Johnson, "The General Theory After Twenty-Five Years," *American Economic Review*, Vol. 51 (May, 1961), pp. 1–25.

[10] See the *General Theory*, p. 293.

BIBLIOGRAPHICAL NOTE

A list of suggestions for further reading must, as a matter of course, be headed by J. M. Keynes' *The General Theory of Employment, Interest and Money* (New York: Harcourt, Brace & World, 1936). It was not intended by its author to serve as a textbook, however, and it contains a good many difficulties for the beginner; so it is advisable to read it along with A. H. Hansen's *A Guide to Keynes* (New York: McGraw-Hill, 1953), which elucidates and comments on the *General Theory* chapter by chapter, and with *The New Economics*, edited by S. E. Harris (New York: Knopf, 1947), in which a number of contributors discuss the whole of Keynes' work. L. R. Klein's *The Keynesian Revolution* (2d. ed.; New York: Macmillan, 1966) will also be found helpful. *Post-Keynesian Economics*, edited by K. Kurihara (New Brunswick, N.J.: Rutgers University Press, 1954), is a collection of essays extending and developing Keynes' work. Retrospective opinions from the standpoint of the 1960's, by economists who originally reviewed the *General Theory* in the 1930's, are given in *Keynes' General Theory: Reports of Three Decades*, edited by R. Lekachman (New York: Macmillan, 1964).

Among general textbooks on macroeconomics, G. Ackley's *Macroeconomic Theory* (New York: Macmillan, 1961) is to be recommended; so also is M. J. Bailey, *National Income and the Price Level* (New York: McGraw-Hill, 1962). A very useful discussion of the use of quantitative methods in this branch of economics has been provided by M. K. Evans in his *Macroeconomic Activity* (New York: Harper & Row, 1969). D. Patinkin's *Money, Interest and Prices* (2d. ed.; New York: Harper & Row, 1965) is a rigorous and scholarly analysis from the side of monetary theory.

Many articles that are essential reading on the subject have been compiled by committees of the American Economic Association (and published by Irwin). The most important volumes in this series are W. Fellner and B. F. Haley (eds.), *Readings in the Theory of Income Distribution* (1946); G. Haberler (ed.), *Readings in Business Cycle Theory* (1951); F. A. Lutz and L. W. Mints (eds.), *Readings in Monetary Theory* (1951); and R. A. Gordon and L. R. Klein (eds.), *Readings in Business Cycles* (1965). Another important collection is the *Surveys of Economic Theory* prepared by the American Economic Association and the Royal Economic Society (and published by St. Martin's Press). Volume I of the AEA-RES series (1967) contains surveys of monetary theory (by H. G. Johnson), inflation theory (Bronfenbrenner and Holtzman), and interest theory (by G. L. S. Shackle). Volume II (1965) includes the indispensable survey of growth by Hahn and Matthews. Each of the surveys is accompanied by an extensive bibliography of the literature in its special field.

In addition to these publications sponsored by the professional societies, there are many other books of collected readings. Two that deserve special mention are those compiled by W. L. Smith and R. L. Teigen, *Money, National Income and Stabilization Policy* (Homewood, Ill.: Irwin, 1965), and H. R. Williams and J. D. Huffnagle, *Macroeconomic Theory: Selected Readings* (New York: Appleton-Century-Crofts, 1969).

For a detailed treatment of the national income accounts, the reader is referred to two supplements to the *Survey of Current Business: National Income* (1954) and *U. S. Income and Output* (1958). Another source is S. Rosen, *National Income* (New York: Holt, Rinehart and Winston, 1963).

On the working of monetary institutions, see Shapiro, Soloman and White, *Money and Banking* (5th ed.: New York: Rinehart and Winston, 1968). To accompany this, a useful set of readings has been compiled by R. S. Thorn, *Monetary Theory and Policy* (New York: Random House, 1966). On inflation, a good source is R. J. Ball, *Inflation and the Theory of Money* (Chicago: Aldine, 1964).

For further reading on cycles, see A. H. Hansen, *Business Cycles and National Income* (New York: Norton, 1964); R. C. O. Matthews, *The Business Cycle* (Chicago: University of Chicago Press, 1959); and J. S. Duesenberry, *Business Cycles and Economic Growth* (New York: McGraw-Hill, 1958). On the theory of growth, refer to R. G. D. Allen, *Macro-economic Theory* (New York: St. Martin's Press, 1968); and for discussion of related policy questions see W. W. Heller (ed.), *Perspectives on Economic Growth* (New York: Random House, 1968).

Finally, for factual evidence about the behavior of the United States economy and attempts to control it, the reader should consult the annual *Economic Report of the President* (Washington: U. S. Government Printing Office). And, for an introduction to some of the urgent issues that will confront the national administration in the 1970's, see the excellent collection of essays edited by K. Gordon, *Agenda for the Nation* (Washington: Brookings, 1968).

INDEX